Acknowledgments

THE INSIDE STORY OF PEARL HARBOR, by Edwin Muller, Reader's Digest, Apr. '44. THE LAST INSTANT OF PEACE by Gordon W. Prange, from "Tora, Tora, Tora!" Reader's Digest, Oct.-Nov. '63, cond. from the book to be pub. by McGraw-Hill, Inc. FIVE CHANCES MISSED, by Walter Lord, from "Five Missed Chances at Pearl Harbor," Reader's Digest, Dec. '57, cond. from an address. THE SPY-CATCHERS, by Frederic Sondern, Jr., from "This Spy-Catching Business," Reader's Digest, Feb. '42, *The American Mercury*, Feb. '42; © 1942, The American Mercury, Inc. BRITAIN'S TREASURE GOES WEST, by Leland Stowe, from "The Secret Voyage of Britain's Treasure," Reader's Digest, Nov. '55. PARIS—ESCAPE, by Etta Shiber, from "Paris—Underground," Reader's Digest, Oct. '43, cond. from the book pub. by Charles Scribner's Sons; © 1943, Press Alliance, Inc. THE ONE THAT GOT AWAY, by Kendal Burt and James Leasor, Reader's Digest, Nov. '56, cond. from the book pub. by Random House; © 1956, Harry Kendal Burt and Thomas James Leasor. FOOLING ENEMY AIRMEN, by Don Wharton, Reader's Digest, May '42, *Air Facts*, Apr. '42; © 1942, Air Facts, Inc. THE THIEF AND THE PATRIOT, by Karin Michaëlis, from "The Reform of H.P., Burglar Extraordinary," Reader's Digest, May '46. HUMAN TORPEDOES AT GIBRALTAR, by Frank Goldsworthy, Reader's Digest, Nov. '50, *The London Sunday Express*, Dec. 25, '49, Jan. 1, 8, '50. WE ORGANIZED THE FRENCH UNDERGROUND, by André Girard as told to George Kent, from "The French Underground Fights," Reader's Digest, May '44, *Tricolor*, May '44; © 1944, Tricolor. BRITAIN'S PET SPY, as told to Al Newman, Reader's Digest, Aug. '45, *Newsweek*, May 28, '45; © 1945, Weekly Publications, Inc. THE CRUISE OF THE RAIDER ATLANTIS, by Robert Littell, Reader's Digest, Oct. '53. THE MYSTERY OF THE HESS FLIGHT, by William J. Snyder, from "Inside Story of the Hess Flight," Reader's Digest, July '43, *The American Mercury*, May '43; © 1943, The American Mercury, Inc. THE EVADERS, by Roman Turski, from "Turn About," Reader's Digest, Jan. '53. HITLER'S UNDERCOVER INVASION OF THE UNITED STATES, by Lawrence Elliott, Reader's Digest, Mar.'60. THE GREAT MANILA BAY SILVER OPERATION, by John G. Hubbell, Reader's Digest, Apr. '59. THE MICRO-DOT, by J. Edgar Hoover, from "The Enemy's Masterpiece of Espionage," Reader's Digest, Apr. '46. JOEY'S QUIET WAR, by Thomas M. Johnson, Reader's Digest, Aug. '51. THE HUNT FOR A SPY, by Carl B. Wall, Reader's Digest, Oct. '45, *The American Legion Magazine*, Oct. '45; © 1945, The American Legion, Inc. SHEPHERDS OF THE UNDERGROUND, by George Kent, Reader's Digest, Apr. '45, *Christian Herald*, Apr. '45; © 1945, Christian Herald Assn., Inc. GHOST SHIP, by Colonel Robert L. Scott, Jr., Reader's Digest, Jan. '45, cond. from the book *Damned to Glory*, pub. by Charles Scribner's Sons; © 1944, Robert L. Scott, Jr. GIRAUD'S BRILLIANT ESCAPE, by Frederick C. Painton, from "Giraud's Brilliant Escape from a Nazi Prison," Reader's Digest, Sept. '43. OPERATION NORTH POLE, by H. J. Giskes, from "Operation Nordpol: Master Hoax of the 'Secret War,' " Reader's Digest, Aug. '53, cond. from the book *London Calling North Pole*, pub. by British Book Centre; © 1953, Opéra Mundi. SECRET MISSION TO NORTH AFRICA, by Frederick C. Painton, Reader's Digest, May '43. THE GRAND SURPRISE CAMPAIGN, by Don Wharton, from "How the North African Campaign was Organized," Reader's Digest, Feb. '43. WE WERE EXPECTING YOU AT DAKAR, by Donald Q. Coster, Reader's Digest, Aug. '46, *The American Legion Magazine*, Aug. '46; © 1946, The American Legion, Inc. SURREPTITIOUS ENTRY, by Willis George, Reader's Digest, Feb. '47, cond. from the book pub. by D. Appleton-Century Co.; © 1946, Willis George. THE CORPSE THAT HOAXED THE AXIS, by Ewen E. S. Montagu, Reader's Digest Nov. '53, *Maclean's Magazine*, June 15, July 1, '53, © 1953, Maclean-Hunter Pub. Co., Ltd.; cond. from the book *The Man Who Never Was*, pub. by J. B. Lippincott Co., © 1953, Walter Louis D'Arcy Hart and Oliver Harry Frost. CENSORS AND SPIES, by Mary Knight, from "The Secret War of Censors vs. Spies," Reader's Digest, Mar. '46, *The Washington Post*, Feb. 3, '46; © 1946, The Washington Post. JUNGLE OF HIDDEN FRIENDS, by Ralph E. Henderson, from "Jump-In to Adventure," Reader's Digest, June '45. THE SECRET AT PEENEMÜNDE, by Allan A. Michie, from "Forty Minutes That Changed the War," Reader's Digest, Oct. '44, *Saturday Night*, Sept. 2, '44; © 1944, Consolidated Press, Ltd. THE MAN WHO SAVED LONDON, by George Kent, Reader's Digest, Sept. '61; based on the book by George Martelli, pub. by Doubleday & Co., © 1960, George Martelli and Michel Hollard. THE SPY WHO DOUBLE-CROSSED HITLER, by J. Edgar Hoover, Reader's Digest, June '46, *The American Magazine*, May '46; © 1946, The Crowell-Collier Pub. Co. THE BRAIN INVASION, by Frederick C. Painton, from "Fighting with 'Confetti,'" Reader's Digest, Dec. '43, *The American Legion Magazine*, Dec. '43; © 1943, The American Legion, Inc. ELEVEN AGAINST THE NAZI A-BOMB, by Frederic Sondern, Jr., Reader's Digest, Nov. '46, *The Minneapolis Tribune*, Oct. 6, '46; © 1946, The Minneapolis Star-Journal and Tribune. THE HIGHEST-PAID SPY IN HISTORY, by Robert M. W. Kempner, Reader's Digest, June '50, *The Saturday Evening Post*, Jan. 28, '50; © 1950, The Curtis Pub. Co. TRAPPING THE SCHARNHORST, by C. S. Forester, from "How the British Sank the *Scharnhorst*," Reader's Digest, May '44, *The Saturday Evening Post*, Mar. 25, '44; © 1944, The Curtis Pub. Co. CONSPIRACY OF MERCY, by George Kent, from "200,000 Persecutions Prevented," Reader's Digest, Mar. '63, *Together*, Feb. '62; © 1962, The Methodist Pub. House. TUNNEL TO FREEDOM, by Flight Lieutenant Paul Brickhill as told to Allan A. Michie, Reader's Digest, Dec. '45. I WAS MONTY'S DOUBLE, by M. E. Clifton James, Reader's Digest, May '55, cond. from the book pub. by Rider and Company; © 1954, Rider and Company. THE GOLDEN SPHINX: THE ARMY'S COUNTER-INTELLIGENCE, by Thomas M. Johnson, from "CIC: The Army's Spy-Hunters," Reader's Digest, Jan. '52, *Blue Book Magazine*, Jan. '52; © 1951, McCall Corp. THE IDOL OF SAN VITTORE, by Indro Montanelli, translated and adapted by Erwin C. Lessner, Reader's Digest, Oct. '50, *Il Borghese*, Mar. 15, '50. THE CODE BOOKS OF THE DEEP, by Rear Admiral Daniel V. Gallery, from "Away Boarders!" Reader's Digest, May '52, cond. from the book *Clear the Decks!* pub. by William Morrow & Co., © 1951, Daniel V. Gallery; portions of this article appeared in *The Saturday Evening Post*, Aug. 4, '45; © 1945, The Curtis Pub. Co. "BAGGY PANTS," by William E. Brougher, Reader's Digest, Jan. '56. THE PHANTOM ARMY, by Blake Clark, from "Spark Plugs of France's Secret Army," Reader's Digest, Apr. '45, *Tricolor*, Mar. '45; © 1945, Tri-color. FAKERY IN THE AIR, by Allan A. Michie, from "The Greatest Hoax of the War," Reader's Digest, Oct. '46. A QUESTION OF COURAGE, by Dorothy Cameron Disney, Reader's Digest, Sept. '45. THE LONGEST DAY, by Cornelius Ryan, Reader's Digest, June-July, '59, cond. from the book pub. by Simon and Schuster; © 1959, Cornelius Ryan. WHAT REALLY HAPPENED TO ROMMEL, by Countess Waldeck, Reader's Digest, Dec. '48, *Forum*, Nov. '48. DEATH ON THE WING, by Captain Rikihei Inoguchi and Commander Tadashi Nakajima, translated by Commander Masataka Chihaya and Roger Pineau, from "Eyewitness Story of the Kamikaze Suicide Missions," Reader's Digest, Dec. '53, *United States Naval Institute Proceedings*, Sept. '53, © 1953, U.S. Naval Institute. THE AMERICAN WHO DID BUSINESS WITH HIMMLER, by Edwin Muller, from "The Man Who Did Business with Himmler," Reader's Digest, Jan. '46. A PRIVATE TRUCE, by John Hereward Allix, from "A Case of Neutrality," Reader's Digest, May '58. THEY CARRIED OUR TOP SECRETS, by Frederic Sondern, Jr., from "They Carry Our Top Secrets," Reader's Digest, May '56, *The Denver Post*, Mar. 25, '56; © 1956, Post Printing & Pub. Co. THE MOST DANGEROUS MAN IN EUROPE, by Thomas M. Johnson, Reader's Digest, Mar. '49, *Argosy*, Mar. '49. THE FROGMEN, by Edwin Muller, from "Exploits of the Navy's Frogmen," Reader's Digest, Apr. '52, *The American Weekly*, Mar. 16, '52; © 1952, Hearst Pub. Co., Inc. THE HIDDEN ANNEX, by Louis de Jong, from "The Girl Who Was Anne Frank," Reader's Digest, Oct. '57. THE GREAT AMBUSH, by William L. White, from "Some Affairs of Honor," Reader's Digest, Dec. '45. THE NAZI COUNTERFEIT PLOT, by Major George J. McNally with Frederic Sondern, Jr., from "The Great Nazi Counterfeit Plot," Reader's Digest, July '52. ADOLF HITLER'S LAST DAYS, by Frederic Sondern, Jr., Reader's Digest, June '51. MYSTERY MAN OF THE A-BOMB, by John Gunther, Reader's Digest, Dec. '53. THE SILENCE OF 600,000, by Thomas M. Johnson, from "How the War's Best-Kept Secret was Kept," Reader's Digest, Nov. '47, *Foreign Service*, Oct. '47; © 1947, Veterans of Foreign Wars of the United States. THE SECRET THAT WON THE WAR, by Fletcher Knebel and Charles W. Bailey II, from "No High Ground," Reader's Digest, Nov. '60, cond. from the book pub. by Harper & Brothers; © 1960, Fletcher Knebel and Charles W. Bailey II. HIROHITO'S STRUGGLE TO SURRENDER, by Colonel Bonner Fellers, Reader's Digest, July '47, *Foreign Service*, July '47; © 1947, Veterans of Foreign Wars of the United States. NOW IT CAN BE TOLD, by Thomas M. Johnson, from "America Has to Know," Reader's Digest, May '46, *The Washington Post*, Mar. 10, '46; © 1946, The Washington Post.

CONTENTS

Part Three—AGAINST THE ENEMY TIDE: 1942

Part Four—CUNNING VS. CUNNING: 1943

CBS-TV: page 331 top. Navy Department in the National Archives: pages 331 bottom, 343 top, 348 top. Wide World Photos: pages 332 top, 333 top, 336 top, 347 top. Birnback Publishing Service: pages 332 bottom, 333 bottom, 341 bottom, 342 bottom, 343 bottom, 344 top. United Press International: page 334 top left and right. FBI: pages 178, 334 bottom, 335, 338 bottom left and right, 339. Publifoto/Black Star: page 336 bottom. Robert Doisneau/ Rapho Guillumette Pictures: page 337 top. Institute for War Documentation at Amsterdam: page 337 bottom. Harris & Ewing: pages 338 top, 346 top left. From the collection of Flight Lieutenant Ley Kenyon: page 340. London *Mirror* from Gilloon Agency: page 346 top right. Gilloon Photo Agency: page 342 top left. Courtesy of General Mark W. Clark: page 344 bottom. Imperial War Museum, London: pages 345 bottom, 349 top. Stern: page 346 bottom. Official U.S. Air Force Photo: page 348 bottom. Owen from Black Star: page 349 bottom. Page 341 top left and right: photographs © 1952 by Otto H. Frank, from *Anne Frank: The Diary of a Young Girl* and reprinted by permission of Doubleday & Company, Inc.

PART ONE

DECEMBER 1941

THE INTRIGUE OF INFAMY

MANY stories have been written about the great campaigns, the incidents of battle, the scenes of heroism and daring of World War II. The most gripping of all are the stories of the secret plans of both friend and foe — stories of surprise attacks, spy networks and acts of espionage.

Ever since man made war there has been espionage. The ancient Egyptians had a finely organized corps of spies. Moses sent Joshua into Canaan to "spy out the land." Queen Elizabeth I had informants planted at the Spanish Royal Court and was told well in advance of the grand schemes of the Armada. Napoleon declared that one good spy was worth 20,000 soldiers in the field.

From the days of George Washington, the United States has always made good use of intelligence and counter-intelligence when the nation was at war. At such times the gathering of military information abroad was handled mainly by the Army and Navy, operating separately, while the FBI concerned itself only with domestic problems. During peacetime there was no unified United States intelligence system collecting information in foreign countries, no highly developed bank of information about our potential enemies.

This was changed by the events of one day—the quiet Sunday of December 7, 1941, when the Japanese launched their secret attack on Pearl Harbor. The Pacific Fleet was destroyed, the country shaken. All Americans agreed that the United States must never again be caught so completely off guard.

As a prologue, three stories of the conspiracy of Pearl Harbor are presented here. Together they reveal the drama of secret battle plans and espionage that pitched the United States into the greatest conflict in the history of mankind.

The Inside Story of Pearl Harbor

By Edwin Muller

The Japanese attack on Pearl Harbor, as everyone knows, followed a craftily conceived and elaborately detailed plan. But, as few people outside the Navy know, *that plan was not conceived in Tokyo*. It was created in Washington, D.C., by the U.S. Naval Planning Board.

The story goes back to January 1932, when our fleet of nearly 200 warships, perhaps the most tremendous concentration of naval power ever assembled up to that time, gathered in California waters for maneuvers which were to test the defenses of

Pearl Harbor. One part of the fleet would "attack"; the other, with the Army garrison, would defend.

The attacking fleet revolutionized naval strategy when, leaving all the proud battleships and cruisers behind, two aircraft carriers—the *Saratoga* and the *Lexington*—streaked across the eastern Pacific with four destroyer escorts. Admiral H. E. Yarnell himself was on the *Saratoga* (instead of a battleship), in command of a brand-new naval group called a "task force." The Admiral was an air-minded officer who had made many flights with his squadrons—unusual in the Navy of that day. Now he was applying the new carrier attack strategy on an objective already familiar to him from the air.

The defense of Pearl Harbor, planned primarily to meet a naval attack, was entrusted to a fleet that protected the approaches to the islands, a flotilla of submarines in the harbor, a full division of troops ashore and an immense concentration of heavy coast artillery which could be rapidly shifted on a well-planned system of railways and roads. An air defense had also been superimposed—batteries of anti-aircraft guns and 100 fighter planes and bombers.

As he had hoped, Admiral Yarnell ran into thick weather 24 hours off Oahu. This made it less likely that the defending fleet would spot him. Two carriers and four destroyers are a rather small group on the ocean—especially when the defenders are expecting a great invasion fleet. Nobody did see them.

By dusk on Saturday, February 6, they were in position to reach Oahu by dawn in a forced run. Early on a Sunday morning, the Admiral figured, the defending forces might be a little less alert than usual.

When darkness fell, the task force, running without lights and in radio silence, drove ahead full speed through rain squalls, low clouds and a rising wind. It was excellent weather in which to escape observation, but could they get the planes off in it? The destroyers were dipping their rails and even the big flat-tops were rolling heavily.

Admiral Yarnell held his planes until less than half an hour before dawn, when he was 60 miles off Oahu. Then, in complete darkness, 152 of them took off miraculously from the carriers pitching in the heavy seas.

This first aerial attack on Pearl Harbor came in from the northeast, exactly as the second and lethal Japanese attack was to do nine years later. Most of the winter the trade wind blows steadily from the northeast against the 2800-foot Koolau Range, where it discharges its moisture. This condition is made-to-order for attack, because planes can approach hidden in the towering wall of rain clouds and then emerge suddenly into clear weather over Pearl Harbor before defenders can rise to intercept.

And so it happened on Sunday, February 7, 1932, when the bombers, fighters, dive bombers and torpedo planes from the *Saratoga* and *Lexington* emerged from the clouds to find the greatest naval base in the world spread helpless beneath them. Each group had its appointed task. The fighters "knocked out" the planes on the ground by simulated machine-gun strafing. No defending plane went up during the attack. Other groups, meanwhile, dropped their theoretical bombs on the military installations or "sank" all the hypothetical vessels in the harbor.

Complete domination of the air had been attained by the attackers. If our entire fleet had been lying in the harbor, and if Admiral Yarnell's fliers had carried real bombs, they could have sunk or damaged every ship.

The commanding officers of the Navy held a "critique" right there in the theoretical ruins. The discussion there begun was continued in naval circles everywhere. It was evident to many strategists that something had happened which was to upset all existing naval concepts.

Of course there were some who discounted what had occurred, saying it had been due largely to the element of surprise. It is true that, as had been foreseen, the defenders were less alert on that Sunday morning; yet it seemed likely that even if they had been alert they would not have been able to meet the attack effectively.

Some high-ranking officers wanted to revise the entire basis on which the Navy was organized. They advanced the revolutionary idea that the Navy, instead of being organized around the battleship with air power as one of its supports, should be based on air power with the battleship and other surface craft as supports. Unfortunately their views were not heeded.

Not heeded, that is, *in Washington.* For the critique at Pearl Harbor wasn't the only one held on the maneuvers. The Navy now knows that another took place soon after in Tokyo.

When our planes flew in for the mock attack, the highly efficient Japanese spy organization in Oahu had observers on all the high points of the island, each with a plausible reason for being there. There were watchers in the thick brush that borders the harbor. Little sampans "fished" offshore. And there were listeners later in Honolulu wherever Navy men gathered.

After intensive study in Tokyo, the information thus obtained formed the basis for a series of secret maneuvers. We know now that the Japanese naval experts concluded—as had some of our admirals—that the primary weapon of the modern navy is air power and that the striking force of a fleet should be built around its air arm rather than around its surface craft. And so, learning from our maneuvers what our battleship admirals unfortunately refused to learn from them, the Japanese Navy was basically reorganized.

The Japanese further realized that they had been presented with a brilliant and workable plan for putting the greater part of the United States Fleet out of commission. They carried out that plan on December 7, 1941.

On December 8 some of our officers who had flown the planes from the *Saratoga* and *Lexington* in 1932 read the details of the Japanese attack with bitter understanding. Yes—this, and this, and this—yes, that was exactly how we did it in maneuvers nine years ago.

In some ways the problem of the Japanese on December 7 was more difficult than that of the maneuvers. Theoretically the defense was stronger. Great progress had been made in the development of devices for the detection of approaching aircraft. But, because of our lack of alertness, the Japanese planes were a complete surprise when they burst through the cloud wall over the Koolau Range.

In other ways the problem had been made easier. Planes were bunched conveniently on the airfields and were easily strafed. And practically all the battleships in the Pacific Fleet were lying in the harbor. (See photograph on page 331.)

The tragedy of Pearl Harbor tore up the old plans. For it happened that none of our carriers was in Pearl Harbor on December 7. *Of necessity*, then, the carrier task force became our chief naval weapon. Almost at once we began to use the carriers with greater skill than the Japanese—at Coral Sea, Midway, Rabaul, the Marshalls and Truk.

The Last Instant of Peace

Condensed from the book Tora, Tora, Tora!

By Gordon W. Prange

It was one of the most desperate gambles in history, played against almost impossible odds. Until December 7, 1941, Pearl Harbor, America's "Gibraltar of the Pacific," was considered by many to be the best-defended naval base in the world. For her daring assault on it Japan assembled an armada of 31 warships—including six great aircraft carriers and 353 planes—and sent it undetected across thousands of miles of ocean. The treacherous mission, planned in deepest secrecy, was carried out with complete and stunning surprise, and without a scratch to any task-force vessel. Until the publication of this book, the full account of the planning and execution of this fantastic action has been among the great untold dramas of World War II.

Three submarines sped through the black ocean swells 100 miles ahead of the main body of ships. Prowling low to the surface, they kept alert for the slightest hint of interception. Behind them churned the destroyers, cruisers, battleships and aircraft carriers of the attack fleet itself—a massive formation spread out across the sea for a distance as great as that between

Washington, D.C., and Harrisburg, Pa. Yet this sprawling armada was lost in the endless reaches of the Pacific. It had sailed almost 3500 miles from its home port undetected.

On the flight decks of the carriers, bombers and fighters were lined up in launching position, their noses pointed toward the bows as if eager for take-off. The plane mechanics, looking like shadowy gnomes in the eerie gloom, scurried to and fro making a final check on engines, radios, landing gear and fuel tanks. Machine-gun ammo boxes were full; bombs and torpedoes were in their racks. One of the mechanics smiled to himself as he came upon a message chalked on the side of a bomb. The scrawled ideographs read: "This one will open the war with America."

For this was the First Air Fleet of the Imperial Japanese Navy, assigned to launch the surprise attack on Pearl Harbor— an act of utter treachery from which the Japanese did not shrink. This perfidy was a fantastic military gamble upon which a desperate nation had elected to stake its future.

In the pre-dawn hours of that morning of December 7, 1941, the atmosphere aboard the Japanese warships was grim. The veteran pilots, those with hundreds of flying hours behind them, felt more tense anticipation than fright. But, for the young officers who had barely completed their training, cold fear mingled with excitement. The untested fliers of the spanking new flat-tops *Shokaku* and *Zuikaku* were particularly nervous, and as they gulped down their pre-combat meal of green tea and rice balls they felt the food coagulate in their stomachs. After their final briefing many of the pilots paused before a miniature Shinto shrine to bow in silent prayer. Others said good-bye to their friends and comrades among the ships' crews.

Uneasiness was by no means confined to the junior officers. The commander of the entire expedition, Admiral Chuichi Nagumo himself, had paced his cabin in sleepless anxiety throughout the voyage, convinced from the beginning that the mission was doomed. The officer in charge of air operations, Commander Minoru Genda, felt overcome with awe at the responsibility that had been entrusted to him. Ordinarily immune to worry, in the last hours before the launch he brooded on the danger of unforeseeable pitfalls. The day might bring a glorious victory or—the ancestral gods forbid!—a stupendous failure. On his decisions, Genda reflected, rested the future of 100 million of his countrymen.

The plan to strike Pearl Harbor had been conceived and pushed through against all opposition by the commander in chief of the Japanese Combined Fleet, Admiral Isoroku Yamamoto. The circumstance was ironical, for Yamamoto was a brilliant strategist who was flatly opposed to war with the United States. He had seen America's industrial might at first hand when he had studied at Harvard University, and later when he served as a naval attaché in Washington. But Yamamoto was a robust nationalist and a Japanese to the very marrow of his bones. His love of Emperor and homeland was of volcanic ardor, and his warrior heart followed the traditions of the true samurai: duty first. Yamamoto believed, as did most people of Japan at the time, that the Japanese were a chosen race, selected by a far-seeing Providence to fulfill an ineluctable destiny. So, in his pattern of thinking, it was only logical for Japan to play the dominant role in the Asian community of nations.

The Japanese had long dreamed of bolstering their empire by exploiting the resources of the rich lands to the south—the Philippines, Malaya and the Netherlands East Indies. But if the operation was to succeed, the U.S. Navy would have to be barred from southern waters, at least during the first critical months. How could this be done? Yamamoto's approach to the problem was conditioned by both training and temperament. He was an aviation expert, a bold, original thinker and a gambler. He liked to quote maxims to drive home points in his speech, and one of his favorites was, "If you want the tiger's cubs, you must go into the tiger's lair." Inevitably his eyes were drawn to the tiger's lair at Pearl Harbor, Hawaii—where the U.S. Pacific Fleet was based. Would it be possible to destroy this fleet before the strike at the southern regions began?

One day in January of 1941, Yamamoto repaired to his cabin on the flagship *Nagato* and wrote to his close friend Admiral

Takijiro Onishi, who was one of the few genuinely air-minded admirals in the Japanese Navy. Cautioning Onishi that the subject was to be kept top-secret, he swiftly brushed out a three-page letter outlining a plan for a surprise air attack on Pearl Harbor. Did Onishi think such an attack feasible? "Please study the problems involved carefully," Yamamoto requested.

One of Admiral Onishi's first moves was to summon Commander Minoru Genda, 36-year-old air officer on the carrier *Kaga*. He could scarcely have taken a more dynamic step. Genda was the most brilliant airman in the Imperial Navy. His hawklike, aristocratic face, with its thick eyebrows, straight nose and firm chin, was dominated by piercing black eyes of almost frightening intensity. His ideas were bold and imaginative, and he had already considerably influenced the Navy's aviation tactics and design.

When Onishi showed him Yamamoto's letter, Genda read it thoughtfully. The daring and originality of Yamamoto's idea immediately appealed to him. "The plan is difficult, but not impossible," he said. The prime target would have to be the U.S. carriers, he believed, since these offered the most danger to the Japanese Navy.

Genda returned to the *Kaga* bursting with ideas. In the quiet of his cabin, he went to work at once. Two weeks later he gave Onishi a complete draft of the projected attack. Every available aircraft carrier should participate, he thought, and the attack should be made around dawn so that most of the approach would be under cover of darkness. The aircraft should include dive bombers, high-level bombers, torpedo planes and fighters.

Onishi approved nearly all of Genda's ideas and added a few of his own; the draft he forwarded to Yamamoto early in March was essentially the plan finally used. Within a month it was being implemented, when a strategic concept long advocated by the Navy flyboys was put into effect. Five carriers, then assigned to separate forces, were assembled with 10 destroyers, two to each flat-top, to form the First Air Fleet. The move met strong opposition from the "battleship admirals," who knew nothing of the Pearl Harbor plan (and would not have approved of it if they had). But Yamamoto plowed ahead, and from now on Genda worked on the operation like one possessed, living it each day with the religious intensity of a monk.

Yamamoto would have dearly loved to lead the new fleet himself, but since he was indispensable where he was, the post went to Vice-Admiral Chuichi Nagumo, largely on the basis of seniority. Nagumo was an unimaginative old-line sailor, an acknowledged authority on navigation and ship maneuvers. During none of his long and honorable career had he had the slightest connection with aviation, however, and when he was informed of the Pearl Harbor plan he was aghast.

But, for the moment, the phlegmatic Nagumo took comfort in believing that the reckless plan was unlikely ever to come about. Negotiations with Washington were still going forward. (In an act of calculated duplicity, Japan continued these talks to the very moment the first bombs fell.) Nagumo felt that war with the United States was by no means certain. Also, Yamamoto had exceeded his authority in initiating such a plan; the planning function belonged to the Naval General Staff. Unless that body approved Yamamoto's project—which Nagumo thought unlikely—it was doomed to collect dust in the secret files.

Despite Nagumo's hopes, the inexorable march toward war continued. On July 25, Japan established a "protectorate" over French Indochina, and elements of her "New Order," already occupying the northern part of the country, moved swiftly to take over the whole. The next day President Franklin D. Roosevelt froze all Japanese assets in the United States; prohibited Japanese vessels from loading or unloading cargo in any U.S. port; and, having already stopped shipments of iron and scrap the autumn before, now also barred sales of U.S. petroleum to Japan. England and Holland took similar measures.

"Economic war is already declared," said a Japanese newspaper. "It is not difficult to imagine what will come next."

On September 6, Emperor Hirohito convened Japan's leaders for a grim stocktaking. They gathered round a long, rectangular table in No. 1 East Room of the Imperial Palace, with the Emperor on a dais at the head. His Majesty sat motionless and

seemingly impassive as Premier Fumimaro Konoye opened the
conference by reading an "Outline Plan for National Policy,"
which disclosed that:

1. The empire was determined to risk war with the United
States, Britain and the Netherlands to achieve its economic ends
in the South Pacific. War preparations were to be completed by
late October.

2. Until that provisional cut-off date, the empire would try to
realize its demands through negotiations.

The nation's minimum demands, however, doomed the ne-
gotiations to failure, since their fulfillment would secure for
Japan a powerful empire while virtually tying the hands of the
United States and Britain in the Far East.

One by one the various leaders now stood up and discussed
the situation. All emphasized the need for haste. The clutch of
economic circumstances was causing Japan to become weaker
rather than stronger. She had to act while she still had stock-
piles of essential materials, since British hostility and the U.S.
embargo made it impossible to replenish them. General Teiichi
Suzuki, for example, pointed out that scarcely more than a year's
supply of oil remained. If Japan did not move soon, she would
not be able to move at all.

Last to talk was the Emperor's spokesman, Baron Yoshi-
michi Hara. The outline of national policy bothered him, he said
(speaking for the Emperor). "The proposal left the impression
that war was stressed and diplomacy given secondary consideration. Am I right in believing that everything possible is being
done to save the situation by diplomatic means?" There was a
brief silence. Then Admiral Koshiro Oikawa, the Navy Minister, hastily gave his assurance that this was so. But apparently
he was not convincing.

Presently, to everyone's astonishment, the Emperor himself
rose to address the conference. Never before had Hirohito addressed an Imperial Conference personally. Yet there he stood,
the living symbol of empire, Japan's 124th Emperor, shedding
his "divine radiance."

He took from his pocket a poem entitled "The Four Sides of

the Sea," written by his grandfather, Emperor Meiji. With all members of the conference hardly daring to breathe, Hirohito in a mood of high seriousness read the poem aloud:

> I think all the people of the world are brethren.
> Then why are the waves and winds so unsettled today?

The Emperor told his listeners that he had read the poem over and over again. Why wasn't it possible to introduce into the present his grandfather's ideal of international peace? A taut stillness ensued, until finally the chief of the Naval General Staff answered that certainly the Supreme Command recognized the importance of diplomacy; they advocated armed force only as a last resort. The chief of the Army General Staff echoed this opinion, but the Emperor was far from satisfied. The conference adjourned, Premier Konoye wrote, "in an atmosphere of unprecedented tenseness."

Those Americans who believe that the Emperor could have vetoed the Pearl Harbor plan had he wished, or had he been a stronger character, do not understand the Emperor's subtle and complex position in the Japanese way of life. He could only counsel, advise—and ratify. For the Emperor must be at one with his government to preserve the monolithic unity of the nation. He was lashed to the mast of his own boundless prestige. At this juncture, however, Emperor Hirohito did not even know of the projected Pearl Harbor attack.

It should not be supposed that there was unanimous support for Yamamoto's bold scheme. In fact, almost none of the higher-ranking Navy men approved of it. Some critics thought the whole scheme unwarrantedly reckless. Others, with their eyes fixed on the Southern Operation, felt that this alone would strain Japan's naval resources to the limit. Lastly, the battleship admirals were honestly convinced that it was a mistake to rely on ships as thinly armored as carriers. But in Yamamoto these conservatives were up against an opponent of formidable strength.

A photograph of Yamamoto taken at the height of his powers reveals a man short even by Japanese standards—five feet three inches. His broad shoulders are accentuated by massive epaulettes, and a barrel chest is crowded with medals and orders. The effect would be comic except for the face. Full-lipped, straight-nosed and large-eyed, with gray hair worn in an uncompromising crew cut, it is the face of a man of action, of immense willpower.

As a youth, his devotion to his studies had been fanatical. To concentrate more intensely, he would peel off successive layers of clothing with the hope that the cold might chase away fatigue. Many a freezing night his parents found him almost naked in his small room, poring over algebra or a book of geometry.

Now, when he heard about the "babbling" against Pearl Harbor, Yamamoto on October 11 summoned about 50 of his fleet commanders to the flagship *Nagato*. One by one, various admirals voiced their misgivings. Time was running perilously short for operations in the northern Pacific. High seas and bad weather would make refueling impossible. Moreover, Soviet Russia had to be watched. Even Admiral Onishi, in whom Yamamoto had confided in January, now believed the plan unwise with the available carrier-plane forces.

The last flush of sunset had almost died on the horizon when Yamamoto arose. He began slowly, but with unmistakable determination. He had noted the points made, he said, and they would be considered. But he had been studying the entire strategic situation a long time. The operation against Hawaii was essential to Japan's grand strategy. Without it the southern thrust would fail. Therefore, he wanted one thing understood: "So long as I am commander in chief of the Combined Fleet, Pearl Harbor will be attacked." The statement cleared the atmosphere once and for all. Every fleet commander knew that from now on there would be no more bickering, no more complaints. If Japan fought, the fleet would go to war with the exhilarating unity of a great crusade.

But the Naval General Staff was still adamantly opposed to Pearl Harbor, and here the problem was more knotty. For here Yamamoto was dealing with the pinnacle of naval hierarchy. The Admiral was not a good poker player for nothing, however.

Late in October he decided to send an emissary to the Naval General Staff for a showdown. He picked his senior staff officer, Captain Kameto Kuroshima, for the task, and armed him with a final, bold weapon for use if nothing else availed.

Kuroshima went straight to Captain Sadatoshi Tomioka, capable chief of the Operations Section of the Naval General Staff. He did not dally with niceties.

"Admiral Yamamoto insists that his plan be adopted," he said. "He has authorized me to state that if it is not, then he can no longer be held responsible for the security of the empire. He and his entire staff will have no alternative but to resign."

Tomioka's eyes went wide, his mouth fell open. The hugeness of the threat impressed him deeply. Yet still he agreed to the attack only as far as he personally was concerned—and so Kuroshima was bucked to the next man in line. Once more Kuroshima was forced to hurl Yamamoto's thunderbolt, and finally the Naval General Staff, acting as a body, sanctioned the Pearl Harbor attack. It was a great victory, but Yamamoto's position and influence in the Japanese Navy were unique. Not once did any member of the Naval General Staff consider going to war without Yamamoto at the helm of the Combined Fleet. "It was inconceivable," one of the admirals said later.

From this time on, Japanese espionage in Hawaii was urgently stepped up. Pearl Harbor was divided into five areas, designated A,B,C,D,E, and the regular reports noting merely which U.S. warships were in port were no longer enough. Instead, Tokyo now had to know exactly where each ship was berthed, and innumerable questions were asked about air patrols and the disposition of planes. Most of this information was to be had by perfectly legal means, simply for the looking. Certain members of the Japanese Consulate in Honolulu made an efficient team for this task, the star performer being a young clerk who called himself Tadashi Morimura. His actual name, however, was Takeo Yoshikawa, and he was a former ensign in the Imperial Navy. (See photograph on page 331.)

When Yoshikawa arrived in Hawaii on March 28, 1941, he

reported to Consul General Nagao Kita, a career diplomat recently transferred to Honolulu to work with him. Examining his new junior with interest, Kita saw a slender, handsome lad of medium height who seemed much younger than his 29 years and wildly unlike a master spy. Indeed, he appeared touchingly naïve, the type older men call "son," old ladies fuss over and young girls flutter around. He had no previous experience as an agent, and moreover he had lost the first joint of his left index finger—a disfigurement that could be a dead giveaway. Kita wondered seriously whether Yoshikawa was the man for the job.

But Tokyo did not make mistakes in such matters. Yoshikawa's very lack of experience was an advantage, as he had never appeared on a list of attachés to arouse the curiosity of U.S. intelligence agencies. And his preparation was exemplary. Coming from a modest background (his father was a policeman), he attended the naval academy and had served as an ensign for about a year when illness forced him to retire from the Navy.

His taste of salt water had spoiled him for civilian life, and for months he moped unhappily. Then a naval personnel officer visited him and suggested that the Navy could still find a place for him if he was willing to serve as an intelligence agent. He would have to forgo all hope of further advancement; but this seemed a small price to pay for a return to his beloved Navy.

Instructions to Yoshikawa were simple. He was to become an expert on the U.S. Pacific Fleet and its Guam, Manila and Pearl Harbor bases; and he was to improve his English. For the next four years he remained on the American Desk, studying *Jane's Fighting Ships* and *Aircraft*, and scouring U.S. newspapers, magazines and technical books. In time he knew every U.S. fighting ship and aircraft by name, hull number, configuration and technical characteristics.

In late 1940 he was instructed to take the Foreign Ministry's English-language examinations so he could be appointed a junior diplomat to "cover" his true mission. According to Admiral Kanji Ogawa, who was assistant chief of Naval Intelligence at the time, this arrangement was not unusual. A Navy officer would be cashiered and deliberately made a civilian. He would then get a job in the Japanese Foreign Office and be sent where he could do the Navy the most good. In general, this procedure fits Yoshikawa's case: a discreet hint to the Navy's medical corps that Ensign Yoshikawa would be more valuable out of uniform than in, a suitable period of idleness to put him in a receptive mood, and then . . .

In Honolulu, after being assigned a nominal job—he was officially registered with the U.S. State Department as chancellor of the Consulate—Yoshikawa plunged into work. He read the Honolulu papers from beginning to end each day, paying particular attention to shipping news and to social items about U.S. naval personnel. A daily stroll through Pearl City gave him a perfect view of Ford Island and its air strip. And two or three times a week he stopped in for a snack at a lunchroom and soda fountain run by an elderly Japanese alien on the pier at the end of the Pearl City peninsula. This was just opposite Ford Island, and the nearest he could get to Pearl Harbor.

Here he could learn many things—Was the fleet going out soon? Was it taking on new supplies?—by direct observation. At night he also frequented bars popular with U.S. servicemen, standing them drinks and listening to service gossip, but seldom posing a direct question lest he attract attention to himself. Fear of detection always kept him edgy, for the shadow of the FBI hovered over him unceasingly. Kita had warned him of that formidable organization, and he was constantly afraid it would install recording mechanisms in the Consulate or in one of the restaurants he frequented. Yoshikawa often reported to Kita late at night, after the rest of the staff members were in bed; and he and Kita would carry on their top-secret discussions by writing notes to each other, then burning them.

Yoshikawa became a boon to Honolulu's taxi drivers, taking many drives and sometimes changing cars several times on the way. Kita vetoed his having a car of his own. The license tag would make him too easy to identify and trail, and the slightest accident would mean an embarrassing police report.

Hawaiian tourist traffic offered Yoshikawa many opportunities. Until the United States embargoed all trade with Japan, he would meet each incoming Japanese ship, round up a group of disembarking Japanese nationals and take these unsuspecting and pleasantly surprised travelers on sight-seeing tours. This gave him cover for the large number of trips he made, which might otherwise have become suspicious. Once he donned his brightest Aloha shirt and took one of his geisha friends for a tourist flight over Oahu, a jaunt that gave him a clear air view of both Wheeler and Hickam fields. He also scouted the airfields from the water, sometimes on fishing trips, sometimes as a swimmer.

The cane fields at Aiea gave the best possible view of Pearl Harbor. Several times Yoshikawa dressed in laborer's garb and studied the fleet from there, using a different cane field each time and never staying longer than 30 minutes.

One of Yoshikawa's favorite haunts was Shuncho-ro (Spring Tide Restaurant), a Japanese-style teahouse on Alewa Heights that commanded an excellent view of Pearl Harbor and Hickam Field. Sometimes he would feign getting too drunk to be moved, and the friendly Shuncho-ro management would discreetly tuck him away for the night in a room overlooking the harbor.

On one such occasion Yoshikawa saw the fleet steam out of the harbor in the early morning—a majestic sight to thrill the heart of any sailor. He watched with keen professional interest, checking the length of time necessary to get the fleet out, the type of maneuver used and the position each ship assumed. This was important information for Tokyo, for if the U.S. fleet attempted to sortie when the attack commenced, the Japanese could adjust their schedule accordingly.

On August 7, when Wheeler Field held a "galaday" to which the public was cordially invited, Yoshikawa was among those who eagerly accepted the invitation. Cameras were strictly forbidden, but this prohibition bothered him not at all. He saw everything, missed nothing, and wrote up his impressions the moment he returned to the Consulate.

Yoshikawa's schedule was killing. Holidays did not exist for him, and Sunday was just another day. Although Japan had other espionage networks in Hawaii, Yoshikawa considered them, with some reason, the work of amateurs.

Were American leaders aware that Pearl Harbor was a potential target? Certainly! "If war eventuates with Japan," Secretary of the Navy Frank Knox wrote to Secretary of War Henry L. Stimson on January 24, 1941, "it is believed easily possible that hostilities would be initiated by a surprise attack upon the fleet or the naval base at Pearl Harbor."

Three days later (scarcely two weeks after Yamamoto had confided his scheme to Onishi) the U.S. Ambassador to Japan, Joseph C. Grew, sent a coded message to the U.S. State Department:

> My Peruvian colleague has heard from many quarters, including a Japanese one, that a surprise attack on Pearl Harbor is being planned in case of trouble between Japan and the United States. He said he was passing this on because it had come to him from many sources, although the plan seemed fantastic.

State passed this tip-off—one of the greatest in history—to the Navy, which forwarded it to Admiral Husband E. Kimmel, commander in chief of the U.S. Pacific Fleet, with this comment:

> The Division of Naval Intelligence places no credence in these rumors. Based on known data regarding the present disposition and employment of Japanese naval and army forces, no move against Pearl Harbor appears imminent or planned for in the foreseeable future.

Nevertheless, in a Pacific Fleet confidential letter on February 15, Kimmel assumed that "a declaration of war might be preceded by a surprise attack on ships in Pearl Harbor." This assumption was also included in three brilliant and startlingly accurate staff reports made in 1941. The last, a study of "the air situation in Hawaii," was prepared by Colonel William E. Farthing, commander of the Fifth Bombardment Group of the Hawaiian Air Force. This prophetic document, which was sent to the War Department on August 20, suggested that Japan might stage a surprise attack on Pearl Harbor in which she would probably use six carriers; that the most advantageous time to launch such an air strike would be at dawn; and that the most likely approach would be from the north.

To forestall such an attack, the report recommended, among other defense measures, that air patrols "maintain a complete and thorough 360-degree search of the Hawaiian area during daylight." To do so, the Hawaiian Air Force would need "180 B-17D type airplanes or other four-engine bombers with equal operating range."

If planning could have killed, the Japanese would have been dead ducks. But the U.S. Army Air Force did not have 180 Flying Fortresses. And what were available were heavily committed to the Philippines, to Britain and in the Atlantic area, where national policy was focused on the defeat of Nazi Germany. Thus, when the Japanese struck on December 7, the Air Force had only 12 B-17's in Hawaii.

By the summer of 1940, U.S. cryptologists had broken the Japanese diplomatic code, one of the most brilliant coups in intelligence annals. Yoshikawa's espionage reports and Tokyo's replies, the entire flow of messages to and from the Japanese Embassy in Washington—all were now open to the United States. But this vast treasure trove might as well have remained buried. Vital intercepts piled up untranslated, sometimes for more than a week. Dissemination, that most crucial of intelligence requirements, was faulty, partly from sheer ineptness, partly from a zealous anxiety to protect sources. Since dissemination might lead the Japanese to suspect that their code had been broken, information was often withheld from those who needed it most. Admiral Kimmel asserts that none of the so-called "magic" intercepts ever reached him at all.

Autumn saw the Americans turn their backs on Pearl Harbor to face the steadily mounting crisis in the Atlantic. The battle of the shipping lanes reached a climax on September 4, when a German submarine torpedoed a U.S. destroyer near Iceland. In the excitement Japan was relegated to the back pages, never quite to regain the headlines until December 7. "The Pacific is still very

much a part of the world situation," Kimmel wrote wistfully to
Admiral Harold E. Stark, Chief of Naval Operations, on September 12. But Stark replied comfortingly, "Personally, I do not
believe the Japs are going to sail into us."

The mood was general. As Americans fixed their eyes on the
Atlantic, they tended to forget that the back door was open.

Late in September, Commander Genda began training the
First Air Fleet fliers specifically for the strike at Pearl Harbor.
The task was formidable, the more so since the need for absolute
secrecy made it impossible to tell the airmen what they were being trained *for*. Different types of aircraft—high-level bombers,
torpedo planes, dive bombers, fighters—had to be welded into a
coherent striking force capable of flying in perfect mass formation, not with just 40 or 50 planes but with several hundred. There
was little time to accomplish this; time was running out with
every tick of the clock.

The leader of such a force would need absolute mastery of his
craft, endless patience and unusual qualities of leadership. There
could be no question of assigning him "by the numbers" from
the personnel bureau's grab bag. But Genda knew exactly the
right man for the job: his naval-academy classmate Lieutenant
Commander Mitsuo Fuchida. At 39, Fuchida was still an active
pilot (as Genda was not). He was a veteran of the war in China,
had logged over 3000 air hours, flew his plane as though he were
part of it and had the reputation of being the hardest-working
officer in the Japanese Navy. When Genda told him of the Pearl
Harbor plan, Fuchida took to it as a hawk to the wind.

Meanwhile, Japan brought off another intelligence mission of
great importance. In September the Tokyo government opened
negotiations aimed at getting the U.S. embargo on Japanese shipping relaxed. After weeks of discussion between Ambassador
Kichisaburo Nomura and Secretary of State Cordell Hull, it was
agreed that three passenger vessels could sail from Japan to
Hawaii and the United States, provided they did not carry commercial cargo. The U.S. government made this concession in
good faith, believing that it would help ease existing tensions.

Japan hastened to betray this trust. Wrote Sun Tzu, a classic Chinese military authority much admired in Japan: "If the enemy leaves a door open, you must rush in."

The *Tatuta Maru*, first of the three Japanese ships to sail, put into Honolulu on October 23. Shortly after the vessel docked, Consul General Kita stepped aboard and the captain handed him a sealed envelope. It was from the Naval General Staff asking, along with other requests, for a detailed map providing the location, size and strength of every military establishment on Oahu. A special mission would soon arrive to pick this up and to confer on other urgently important matters. The mission consisted of Lieutenant Commander Suguru Suzuki, who was an authority on U.S. air power in the Pacific, and Commander Toshihide Maejima, a submarine expert. They were to make their own estimate of the situation at Pearl Harbor, then report back to the Naval General Staff in person.

The *Tatuta Maru*, after stopping in Hawaii, proceeded to the United States. The second U.S.-approved Japanese ship, the *Taiyo Maru*, which carried Suzuki and Maejima, was slated to go to Hawaii only. In Tokyo a government spokesman explained to curious foreign correspondents that this was simply a matter of "convenience in scheduling."

The *Taiyo Maru* sailed from Yokohama on October 22. The name of neither Suzuki nor Maejima appeared on the passenger roster; Suzuki was listed as assistant bursar, Maejima as the ship's doctor. Once beyond sight of land, the vessel turned northward and followed the northern route that the Pearl Harbor attack fleet planned to take. Throughout the voyage the two officers, spelling each other day and night, carefully scanned the horizon. The results were beyond expectations. Not a single vessel of any kind was sighted during the entire passage to Hawaii. The weather was uniformly good—mostly leaden skies with just enough fog to provide a thin curtain of concealment. Not until the ship was about 80 miles off Oahu did the first U.S. patrol plane poke its nose through the clouds.

The *Taiyo Maru* nudged into Honolulu harbor at 8:30 a.m. on Saturday, November 1. The timing was carefully planned. It was a weekend, and the approximate hour of the projected attack. The liner anchored at Pier 8 near Aloha Tower, and from the stern the two officers could, with binoculars, keep a steady watch on Pearl Harbor and the surrounding area. The *Taiyo Maru* was in port five days. During the entire time both Suzuki and Maejima remained aboard ship. This was according to orders. The Naval General Staff wanted neither agent to be seen or questioned by U.S. officials; they wanted to arouse no suspicion of any kind. Consul General Kita visited them three times in all, bringing two members of the Consulate with him to carry materials on or off the ship. Thus, if a body search were made by U.S. counter-intelligence, nothing would be found on him. If a minor official were caught violating regulations, it might be explained away.

Kita did not allow the master spy Yoshikawa near the vessel, lest the FBI be trailing him, but Suzuki handed Kita a long questionnaire for Yoshikawa. Among other things, the Naval General Staff asked whether Oahu was on the *qui vive*. Would the Americans spring to war on a moment's notice? Or could they be caught napping? Yoshikawa's answers were favorable.

Yoshikawa gave the detailed map, the long questionnaire and all his other findings to Kita, and one of Kita's assistants walked blithely up the gangplank with this precious cargo hidden under a local newspaper. There was a general sigh of relief when the task was safely accomplished. The *Taiyo Maru* sailed back to Japan on November 5. The passengers who embarked on her were subject to "one of the most extensive customs inspections to be held on Honolulu's waterfront." No contraband was found in the baggage or on the person of any of them.

The pace of preparation was now in crescendo. On November 6, Fuchida staged a final dress rehearsal which duplicated the Pearl Harbor attack in every possible way, using a task force of six carriers and more than 350 planes, and with the target ships 200 miles from the launching point, as they would be at Oahu.

When the time arrived for the departure of the attack fleet, elaborate security measures were taken to conceal the fact from the Japanese people. To minimize the exodus of so many carrier planes, nearby air units were instructed to send extra flights over the air bases and towns so no sudden absence of planes would be noticed. All shore units were encouraged to grant leaves to as many men as possible, so that plenty of bluejackets would be visible on the streets. The fleet itself was to travel in total radio silence. The volume of messages and instructions from Japan would necessarily increase once the fleet was under way, but the Navy had been building up dummy traffic for several weeks so that there would be no noticeable upsurge of radio activity. Everything was to give the impression of "business as usual."

In the late afternoon of November 17, Yamamoto and his staff boarded Nagumo's flagship, the *Akagi*, then anchored in Saeki Bay, to wish key members of the fleet good fortune. Yamamoto's speech was not the usual stereotyped pep talk. He told the men bluntly that although the Japanese hoped to achieve surprise, everyone should be prepared for "terrific American resistance." A farewell party was then held in the wardroom. The atmosphere was serious and full of dignity, even a little heavy. But during this interlude Yamamoto bared his true feeling. "I expect this operation to be a success," he said. By ritualistic custom, the commanding admiral usually merely expressed *hope* for the success of a coming mission. The positive confidence of Yamamoto's phrasing immensely heartened his hearers as they ate the symbolic *surume* for happiness and *kachiguri* for victory, then drank a toast to the coming battle in the name of the Emperor. *"Banzai! Banzai! Banzai!"*

As night settled, the *Akagi* blacked out, weighed anchor and slipped out to sea in the silent company of two destroyers. Similar groups left harbors up and down the coast, some to sail close to shore, others as far out as 100 miles. There were 31 ships in all—six carriers, two battleships, two heavy cruisers, one light cruiser, three submarines, nine destroyers, eight lumbering tankers. Last to leave her base was the carrier *Kaga*, which had remained at Sasebo for repairs.

The spot picked for rendezvous was Hitokappu Bay, a bleak, craggy bight on Etorufu, one of the Kuriles, or "smoking" islands—so named for their eternal mists. It lay almost 1000 miles north of Tokyo in sparsely traveled seas, an ideal hideout such as pirates might have used in buccaneering days. From here the fateful voyage began in the gray pre-dawn of Wednesday, November 26. Wreathed in the morning mists like ghost ships, the vessels of the great task force glided from their anchorage.

A brilliant, deceptive maneuver was the departure of the *Tatuta Maru* from Yokohama on December 2. This was one of the three passenger ships Japan had been permitted to send to the United States, and her purported mission of "exchanging American evacuees from the Orient for Japanese nationals in the United States" was plausible and was widely publicized in the U.S. press. The *Tatuta Maru* was scheduled to reach the United States on December 14, and on December 3 a New York *Times* dispatch from Tokyo took this "as a token that so far as Japan was concerned nothing was likely to happen for some time." After December 7 the *Tatuta Maru* reversed her course and returned to Japan.

On the task force's seventh day at sea, radio instructions from Japan resolved at least one of Nagumo's many anxieties. The date was December 1 east of the international date line (December 2 in Japan, the same day on which the *Tatuta Maru* began her deceptive voyage), and the message said, "Climb Mount Niitaka." This was the code phrase announcing that negotiations had failed, that war was now certain. For the first time the date of attack was given: December 7.

The fleet had just passed through the dangerous waters north of the U.S. base at Midway. Tension had run high, for in this area the possibility of being discovered by a stray U.S. ship or plane was considered great. Miraculously, the fleet had escaped detection, and it was with relief and subdued elation that all hands now prepared for combat. Ambassador Nomura and special envoy Saburo Kurusu were instructed to keep peace conversations alive in Washington.

On December 6 every ship in the task force was fueled to capacity, and the tankers (except for three already sent home) were dispatched to a post-attack rendezvous. Shortly after midday all crews were summoned on deck. There the Emperor's war rescript was read, followed by this message from Yamamoto: "The fate of the empire hangs on this one battle. Let every man-jack do his best."

In Japan all eyes of the naval hierarchy were now riveted on Pearl Harbor. "Hawaii, you will be caught like a rat in a trap," Admiral Matome Ugaki, Yamamoto's chief of staff, confided to his diary. "Enjoy your dream of peace just one more day." Then, unable to repress his emotion, he added, "What a tremendous thing it is to gamble thus the fate of a nation!"

At 5:30 a.m., December 7, the two long-range seaplanes first sent ahead as scouts were catapulted from the decks of the heavy cruisers *Chikuma* and *Tone*. These sinister doves were to fly over Oahu and Lahaina Anchorage off the island of Maui for a last-minute check on the U.S. fleet. If they were discovered, it would certainly alert the enemy. But this was a calculated risk, balanced against the urgent need for sure information.

Soon afterward, in the half-light of approaching dawn, emotion-swept deck crews readied the runways to signal off the first attack wave of Nippon's "wild eagles." As the plane crews prepared to enter their craft, each man tied a *hachimaki* around his leather helmet. This is a long, narrow kerchief which the samurai of old traditionally bound about their heads before entering battle. On each *hachimaki* the airmen now wore was written the word *Hissho*—Certain Victory.

When Fuchida, on the carrier *Akagi*, started to climb into his bomber with its yellow-and-red-striped tail rudder, the senior officer of the *Akagi's* maintenance units proffered him a specially made white *hachimaki*. "This is from the *Akagi's* crew," he said. "We would like you to carry it to Pearl Harbor on our behalf." Fuchida bowed deeply, and affixed the white scarf to his helmet.

The entire launching operation was executed smoothly and swiftly. The first wave included 43 fighters, 49 high-level bombers, 51 dive bombers and 40 torpedo planes. Within 15 minutes from the moment the first aircraft left its mother ship, all 183 planes were in the air. It was the fastest launching on record. Adding the aircraft of the second wave, there would be 353 airplanes in the attack, the largest concentration of naval air power in the history of warfare to that time.

The rising sun of Imperial Japan had never vaulted so high into the heavens, and all were aware of it. The cheering crewmen, some with tears running down their faces, waved their caps till the planes shrank to pinpoints. Genda, too, felt a tremendous surge of pride. With hoarse "*Banzais*" still echoing in his ears, he went to the *Akagi's* control room to await the message that would be sent when Fuchida reached the target.

Spread across the Pacific, the Second, Third, Fourth and Fifth Fleets also awaited this message, which would send them crashing into battle on a dozen fronts. In the distant homeland Yamamoto waited, too, while in Tokyo key members of the Naval General Staff had gathered in grim apprehension in the Navy Club. Would the attackers achieve surprise? Or would they be prematurely discovered and decimated?

The earliest information came when one of the two scout

planes reported its findings to the attackers: the U.S. ships were still in Pearl Harbor, and there was no evidence of an alert.

At exactly 7:49 the air waves crackled with Fuchida's electric message, sent from Hawaiian skies. *"To-To-To!"* It was the first syllable of the Japanese word for "Charge," and it meant that the first wave was now attacking. But it told nothing about the circumstances of that attack.

A few minutes later there was another message. To his anxious superiors on the *Akagi* and in Tokyo, Fuchida radioed a reassuring *"Tora, Tora, Tora!"* (Tiger, Tiger, Tiger!) It was the prearranged code word for conveying the news that complete surprise had been achieved.

Five Chances Missed

By Walter Lord, author of A Night to Remember

Ever since December 7, 1941, we've been arguing about who was to blame for Pearl Harbor—and with reason. For the surprise attack by some 353 Japanese planes was surely one of the cheapest military victories in history. By the time it was over, a matter of two hours, all eight of our battleships in the harbor were sunk or damaged. Many of our cruisers and destroyers were hit. All six of our major air bases on Oahu were wrecked. Nearly all of our planes were gone. More than 2400 American lives were lost. As the Japanese planes winged back to their carriers they could count a loss of only 29 planes and 55 men.

Many learned men have spent a great deal of time on the military aspect of the subject. But far more fascinating to the layman is the role played by human nature in our failure to avoid calamity on December 7. For entirely apart from the question of whether Washington sent enough information, or whether the Hawaiian command made adequate use of the information and equipment it did have, there were five golden opportunities in the last few hours to avoid disaster. But because human beings are only human beings, all five opportunities were lost.

The first came at 6:30 the evening before the blow fell, with the Japanese fleet still 500 miles away. As Honolulu basked in its last peacetime sunset, Lieutenant Colonel George Bicknell, Intelligence Officer, hustled up to Lieutenant General Walter Short, the Commanding General, with a most interesting message. A telephone conversation had been monitored by the FBI— a call from Tokyo to a Japanese in Honolulu. Tokyo asked about planes, searchlights, ships, the weather . . . and flowers. "Presently," the Japanese in Honolulu offered, "the flowers in bloom are fewest out of the whole year; however, the hibiscus and poinsettia are in bloom now."

The two officers thought about it. Why on earth would anyone spend the money for a transpacific phone call to talk about flowers? Yet if this were espionage, why would anybody use anything as easily monitored as a telephone?

Even today we're not sure of the significance of that Tokyo phone call, although with the advantage of hindsight it looks most suspicious. But at the time General Short, after debating with his staff about an hour, reached a very human conclusion: he decided to sleep on it and take it up again the following day. And so the evening wore on. A quiet evening, not a night of revelry and debauchery as has often been thought._

At 3:42 the next morning, with the Japanese fleet now only 275 miles away, the small minesweeper *Condor* sighted a periscope outside the mouth of Pearl Harbor. She flashed a warning to the destroyer *Ward* on patrol. The *Ward* dashed over and searched for an hour but could find nothing.

The *Condor* never reported this sighting to headquarters because the skipper, humanly enough, thought he must be mistaken if they couldn't find anything in an hour. The *Ward* never reported it because the *Condor* didn't, and, after all, she was the ship that said she saw something. The naval radio station, which was listening in all the time, never reported it because the *Ward* and the *Condor* didn't. So well-meaning, decent men who later proved themselves brave, resourceful and intelligent let another opportunity slip by, for the periscope was indeed Japanese. It was one of the midget subs that were to coöperate with the air attack. (See photograph on page 348.) And as the last messages flashed between the *Condor* and the *Ward*, the first Japanese planes were taking off from their carriers 230 miles away.

Now it was 6:45 in the morning, with the Japanese air armada only 180 miles off. Just outside Pearl Harbor the *Ward*—still on patrol—saw the conning tower of a strange submarine. She raced over, fired at it, dropped depth bombs on it, sank it. A Navy patrol plane joined in the fight, dropped some bombs of its own. Both the *Ward* and the plane radioed the shore that a submarine had been sunk in forbidden waters. The shore reacted in a very human way: telephone calls back and forth between high officers. What did this mean? Was it true? Was it not? They decided that perhaps it was a spar or a buoy the *Ward* had seen. They decided that, Heaven forbid, it might be an American submarine that had been sunk by mistake. They ordered the ready-duty destroyer to the *Ward's* assistance and decided—so humanly—to await further developments.

At seven o'clock the Japanese planes were only 137 miles away and a couple of Army privates at the Opana radar station picked up more blips than they had ever seen before—so many they thought the machine was broken. But they quickly found this wasn't the case—it was an enormous fleet of planes sweeping down on the islands. They telephoned the information center. There, a young lieutenant was on duty. He had handled this assignment only once before in his life and he knew nothing of radar. The officers who were normally above him didn't have duty this day. The men below him had all gone to breakfast.

So everything hung on a young officer who was about as helpless as a soldier could be—no one above him, no one below him, no knowledge of the problem. But he did remember that coming to work for the four-to-eight-a.m. shift he had heard, on his car radio, Station KGMB playing Hawaiian records, and he also remembered that when planes were coming in from California the station played all night to beam them in. So he decided that these were American planes. A very human decision, and he gave a very human answer to the men at the radar station: don't worry about it. The two privates continued watching the planes come in: 7:15, 92 miles away; 7:25, 62 miles away. Finally at 7:39 they lost contact on the radarscope because the planes were too close to be picked up any more.

Just about that time a young messenger boy, Tadao Fuchikami, was walking out of the RCA cable office in Honolulu with a message addressed to the Commanding General. It had been drafted an hour and a half before by General George Marshall in Washington. He had just learned that the Japanese were finally breaking off all diplomatic negotiations with the United States and that one o'clock was the time their emissaries were ordered to advise Secretary of State Cordell Hull in Washington. Obviously something was going to happen somewhere at one o'clock Washington time, and it very quickly was apparent that this was 7:30 in the morning at Pearl Harbor—the ideal time for a surprise air attack.

The General had one thought in mind: send out a warning. He wrote a message at once, but he didn't pick up a telephone that was right beside him. The phone had a direct scramble line to Honolulu. It was a human decision that he didn't, because he was afraid he would endanger the security of his communication system. And so the message was to be sent by radio, which was—well, almost as fast. But this morning there was atmospheric disturbance which might ruin reception. The message was too important to risk that. So some well-meaning communications officer decided to send it by commercial cable instead.

The message got to Honolulu an hour and a half after General Marshall drafted it, and it was now 7:33. Even then the envelope had nothing that indicated urgency, and when Tadao Fuchikami came out with it in his hand, he whiled away a few minutes with the boys in the parking lot across the street. Then he got on his two-cylinder Indian motorcycle and started off. But as he did, he saw angry clouds of black smoke boil up over Pearl Harbor and anti-aircraft fire pock the morning sky. So it was too late; the attack was on.

And today the arguments still ramble on. But in the midst of the name-calling let's not forget that, whatever the high command in both Washington and Pearl Harbor did or did not do, there were these chances to avoid disaster. Chances missed, not because of wickedness or incompetence, but because human beings are, after all, human beings.

And so it has always been. At the Sepoy Mutiny against the British in India, blazing arrows seared the night sky in warning before disaster broke. At Johnstown wise men foretold that the dam would collapse. On the Titanic six wireless messages were received warning of icebergs ahead.

The student of human nature, after studying the strange ways that people behave, comes away thinking not of policy and strategy but that man's best chance to avoid disaster is very simple indeed: we have only to learn to recognize danger signals when we see them.

PART TWO

1939-1941

BACKS TO THE WALL

WORLD WAR II exploded in the West when Hitler invaded Poland in 1939. Britain and France, unprepared, realized the perfidy of Hitler at Munich and saw that "peace in our time," which they thought they had achieved, was a mirage. Japan, at the same time, widened its already vast conquests.

Within two years, 1939-1941, most of Europe fell before one enemy and most of the Orient before the other. Only Britain withstood in the West, and Nationalist China—bottled up in the interior—remained defiant in the East.

The peace in the United States was unquiet. Highly

trained saboteurs and spies operated on the mainland and in Hawaii. Military information was stolen, defense plants were sabotaged, disunity was sown wherever hatred could be stirred up. The Federal Bureau of Investigation infiltrated and ensnared whole enemy spy rings within American borders, but the United States had no organization abroad to detect enemy plots before they could strike her shores.

In the captured European countries, many patriots who refused to surrender soon formed the Underground. Stealth and guile and boldness were their only weapons until British intelligence forces parachuted in agents, arms and supplies. Their wits about them, their backs to the wall, the men, women and children of the subjugated lands carried the war to the vital spots of the foe.

The nature of modern conflict changed greatly. Surprise attacks on a massive scale, the use of secret weapons — from frogmen to radar — created incidents which could never have been imagined by warriors of other times.

The Spy-Catchers

By Frederic Sondern, Jr.

In the pre-Pearl Harbor days of World War II, the United States was regarded as a spy's paradise. The Gestapo agent, the Comintern agitator and the cameraman of the Japanese intelligence service roamed the country at will. With the approach of war, it was a paradise no longer. The FBI and our military and naval intelligence services built organizations whose scientific methods, personnel and efficiency were more than a match for the dictators' emissaries. And they did their jobs without the brutality and witch-hunting which scourged the authoritarian countries.

In 1941 the counter-espionage branch of the Federal Bureau of Investigation pulled off one of the most ingenious coups in the history of the spy business. Early in 1940 the Gestapo had picked up one William Sebold, a naturalized American who was on a visit to his family in Germany. He had been a German machine-gunner in the last war. The Nazis stole his passport and made it clear he would not be allowed to leave the Reich unless he entered their service. Sebold finally agreed, and was sent to Hamburg for the rigorous training with which the Gestapo equipped its agents. Only then did he learn what plans the Nazis had made for him. He was to return to the United States and set up a short-wave radio station. This was intended to be the main clearing point for information on the movement of British ships, on American rearmament and other matters of interest to the German High Command.

Sebold was a better American than Nazi, however. He went on the FBI payroll. He set up a radio transmitter, as directed, in a quiet house in Centerport, Long Island, but it was run by G-men. For over a year they were in daily touch with a Gestapo station near Hamburg, using the elaborate code which Sebold had been given.

The G-men fed the High Command with credible but misleading nonsense, and they obtained a clear picture of the Nazi espionage organization over here. Nazis who came to Sebold's office were photographed from a neighboring room by a concealed movie camera; their conversations were recorded by dictaphone. (See photographs on pages 334-5.) Finally, in June 1941, in a single dramatic sweep, 33 men and women—the backbone of the Nazi espionage system—were arrested.

Spy-catching requires not only experience, courage and infinite patience—which any good detective must have—but also a broad knowledge of foreign peoples, their languages, mentality and peculiarities. Above all, the counter-espionage agent must have a peculiar knack which lets him weed out witch-hunters from among the earnest citizens who are his informants. As the tension of feeling against Nazis and Italian Fascists mounted, floods of mail, telephone calls and visitors deluged the offices of the FBI and the other agencies.

Mr. Jones telephoned that there was a tavern opposite his house, operated by an Italian. Although no Italians lived in the neighborhood, there was always a group of them in the rear of the establishment. They used the telephone a lot, they acted furtively and disappeared by way of private stairs to the second floor. Once or twice he had heard a phonograph play the Fascist anthem.

Mrs. O'Brien cleaned in a big office building. She worked from nine p.m. to five a.m. In a loft across the street was a printing shop. It often worked late at night, behind drawn blinds. One night the draft from an open window had repeatedly blown the shade sideways and she had seen in. The men looked like Germans. And before they closed the shop they emptied the trash baskets into a pile which they put into a big stove and burned. She had seen spies do that in the movies. So she had decided to tell the FBI about it.

Mrs. Smith wrote that there was a German, Mr. Schultz, in her neighborhood who carried a camera and took walks in the country. Near her home were a city aqueduct and two important bridges. Mr. Schultz had been seen taking pictures of them.

The field office had received many other tips, inevitably including one or more from agitated ladies who had seen mysterious flashlight signals from rooftops to German U-boats in the harbor. But the first three mentioned seemed likeliest for investigation.

Mr. Schultz, the photographer, was processed through a tremendous collection of information on all alien and domestic suspects in the country, which was one of the FBI's most important counter-espionage weapons. Ehrich Schultz was a refugee from Vienna. There was nothing against him. But there had been fake refugees, complete with records and proof of internment by the Gestapo, and even equipped with scars of whippings. An agent consulted the local police, the mail carrier, the owner of the shop where Schultz had his films developed, and finally Schultz himself. The agent established that Schultz was a harmless elderly man who photographed flowers.

Signor Benito Ricco, the tavern proprietor, proved to be less harmless. He once had been arrested for felonious assault and set free by a political judge of questionable honesty. He had joined the New York Fascists. He had made trips to Italy and been given a Fascist decoration. His recent movements had escaped the FBI record. The agent who went to Signor Ricco's tavern every night for a drink and a bite found that the neighbor's report was substantially correct: there were suspicious-looking Italians hanging around, and the place reeked of conspiracy. The agent-in-charge ordered a surveillance.

On the telephone line to Ricco's tavern the telephone company—on a court order—spliced a wire which led to an FBI listening post. Whenever Ricco's telephone was used, a light flashed at this listening post and an agent recorded the conversation on a dictaphone. Recorded conversations would not be admitted as evidence in court, but might so horrify a guilty man that he would confess.

Meanwhile, somewhere near Ricco's tavern there was always a car with two men in it. If Ricco or one of his friends left by car, the FBI men rolled after it. If he went on foot, one of the G-men took up the "tail" on foot. And here the shadowing got tricky. "Tailing" was the toughest job in the business, the most boring and most difficult. It was strictly not for amateurs. The trained spy was taught to find out whether he was being followed. He got on a car in the subway, for example. Just as the door was closing he stepped back onto the platform. If anyone else did the same, he could be fairly sure that someone was after him.

In an office building the suspecting suspect took an elevator to any floor he chose. Then he stood in front of the directory of that floor, apparently trying to figure out what room he was supposed to go to. While the suspect pondered, the shadower managed to disappear. The suspect pushed both "up" and "down" buttons and dived into the first car that arrived. If someone bowled around the corner and dived in after him, he would try the final trick, a public lavatory with several exits.

After months of work on Ricco, the agent-in-charge concluded that there was nothing sinister in the Italian's design. His telephone conversations, his friends and their friends showed no contact with Italian espionage and indicated that Ricco was fed up with Il Duce. He held meetings to encourage his companions to spend money at Ricco's tavern. That was about all there was to it. He might be approached by the Italian intelligence service and would then become dangerous. So Signor Ricco would be reinvestigated from time to time.

Meanwhile Mrs. O'Brien's printing shop had developed into a case of the first order. Inquiries by the police, who did much of the FBI's spade work, revealed that it belonged to an old Norwegian who made greeting cards and commercial folders. His employes were German-born, but they were all naturalized American citizens with clean records, according to the files. He had a sound business and paid his taxes. The telephone tap had brought nothing but legitimate conversations. The employes shadowed had been guilty of nothing more than visits to German beer halls with innocuous friends. But the agent-in-charge couldn't get it out of his mind that Mrs. O'Brien had seen them burning the contents of their trash baskets. Military Intelligence had informed him that somewhere in his area a printing plant was turning out seditious pamphlets which were being distributed to Army camps. Naval Intelligence had found forged passes which had admitted saboteurs to dockyards and arsenals, printed with the same type as the pamphlets. The agent-in-charge had a hunch.

The superintendent of the loft building was checked and watched until the FBI was sure he was reliable. An agent plied him with beer. Yes, there were some funny things about that printing shop, he confided. One man always slept there at night. Nobody they didn't know was allowed beyond the front office. And they had elaborate photographic equipment. The agent was not much impressed, but finally the superintendent said, "They do a big business with Army camps." Once he had been cleaning near the door of the shipping room and had heard them talking: "This one is for Camp Dix, that one's for Mc-Clellan," and so on.

That report clinched the suspicion of the agent-in-charge. He was onto a big case. The chief of such a plant would be an important Nazi and would lead the FBI to other important Nazis. The agent knew also that one false step would set off an alarm which would make the Nazi organization fade into the night, only to spring up somewhere else. So the FBI became really scientific.

In the print shop a "telephone inspector" installed a microphone in a telephone bell box. Every word spoken went to the earphones of an agent stationed a few floors above. Postal inspectors checked incoming and outgoing letters. (See "Censors and Spies," page 258.) In the building across the street was a well-hidden agent with a telescopic camera. On the street, as soon as one pair of "tailers" moved off after a suspect, a second rolled up to cover the next. By this time 20 or more agents were involved in the job.

Mistakes, disappointments were inevitable and harrowing. Just as the print-shop owner was about to meet his Nazi higher-up, he pulled the subway trick and the agents had to "drop the tail." It might take months to make contact again, but they could not jeopardize the whole case by a move which would excite suspicion.

Finally the associates of the man who ran the shop had been found. The microphones had revealed that the printers were indeed members of a secret Nazi organization which was sending subversive literature into Army camps. The German-owned trucking line that transported it and the method of distribution in the camps had been uncovered by coöperation with Military Intelligence. Evidence for an open-and-shut case had been gathered. And early one morning a fleet of cars fanned out from the FBI field office. The homes of all those to be arrested had been studied in case of resistance or an attempt at flight, and at the same time Military Intelligence struck in the camps. The print-shop case was over—except for a quick trial.

Up to 1939 the counter-subversive branch of the FBI had been the laughingstock of foreign agents. Trained to deal with the American underworld, it had little knowledge of the technique and skill of the Axis, which became an increasing threat as the war spread over country after country, from Canada to the middle of Asia. Officers of the intelligence services had been frowned on as "snoopers" by many private citizens and many in control in the government, who had restricted their personnel to a minimum. The intelligence system of the State Department had consisted of one man. The spread of war and the appearance of spy rings changed all that.

Britain's Treasure Goes West

By Leland Stowe

This amazing exploit was one of the best-kept secrets of World War II—perhaps because, of the many people who took part in it, few ever knew the whole story. It remained for three determined investigators to collect the scattered pieces and weave them together. Sidney J. Perkins, formerly of the Bank of Canada, provided the initial information based on his own part in the event. Writer A. J. Stump correlated the leads to long-hidden facts and figures. Then Leland Stowe, Pulitzer Prize-winning foreign correspondent, after spending weeks in Canada and England ferreting out the strange details, wrote his report of what he called "one of the most exciting stories I have been involved in."

At five p.m. on July 2, 1940, 17 days after Paris fell to the Nazi blitz, a special train pulled into Bonaventure station, Montreal. Waiting to meet the train were David Mansur, Acting Secretary of the Bank of Canada, and Sidney J. Perkins of the Foreign Exchange Control Board. Both men knew that the train carried secret cargo under the code name of "fish," and that their assignment was important. But only Mansur knew that they were about to walk into the middle of the biggest financial gamble ever made by any nation in peace or war.

As soon as the train stopped, armed guards stepped down and surrounded it. Mansur and Perkins were led into one of the coaches. There they met Alexander S. Craig of the Bank of England; with him were three aides.

"Hope you won't mind our dropping in unexpectedly like this," said Craig with a smile. "The fact is, we brought along quite a large shipment of 'fish.' " The slight, spectacled Englishman paused and then, in the best undramatic British manner, added, "Actually, the 'fish' are a very large portion of the liquid assets of Great Britain. We're cleaning out our vaults—in case of invasion, you know. Rest of the stuff will be coming over shortly."

Sidney Perkins' startled mind began translating "liquid assets" and "rest of the stuff." It could mean only that the Bank of Canada was about to take over virtually everything Britain possessed which could be turned into dollars. Quite a tidy bundle of "fish"! Just how tidy a bundle he was soon to learn.

Two weeks earlier, when the fall of France threatened Great Britain with imminent invasion, Winston Churchill had called his Cabinet into secret session and had decided on the desperate gamble of transporting over seven billion dollars' worth of securities and gold to Canada.

The decision meant that, if necessary, Churchill's government was secretly determined to do far more than "fight on the beaches." If a German invasion should succeed, the British would carry on the war from Canada. The transfer of the treasure was thus part of a two-stage, last-ditch survival plan.

A farsighted move at the war's outset made the whole gamble possible: all British citizens in the United Kingdom had been required to register with the Treasury all the foreign securities they owned. This was part of the treasure which Churchill and his Cabinet now decided to commandeer. Never before had the investments of a nation's private citizens been pre-empted for national defense without first securing consent from the owners. But early in June 1940, when Paris was threatened, the Churchill government made its move.

"In 10 days," said a participant, "all selected securities in the banks in the United Kingdom were scooped up, packed in thousands of boxes, orange-crate size, and delivered to regional collection centers." Here were all the vast profits brought to England by generations of British world-tradesmen and investors. Together with tons of Britain's empire-accumulated gold, they would now be sent across the sea.

And what a sea! In that month of June, 57 Allied and neutral ships totaling 349,117 tons had been sunk in the North Atlantic alone.

The British cruiser H.M.S. *Emerald*, commanded by Captain Francis Cyril Flynn, was selected to carry the first secret shipment. She would sail from Greenock, Scotland, on June 24. On Sunday, June 23, four of the Bank of England's "gilt-edged" specialists, with Alexander Craig as chief, entrained for Glasgow with only a suitcase apiece. Meanwhile, heavily guarded secret trains rushed final deliveries of gold and securities to the cruiser at Greenock, on the Clyde. Late that night the destroyer *Cossack*—at 30 knots and heavy risk—sped through thick fog to join the treasure ship's escort.

By six p.m. on the 24th the *Emerald* was crammed with a load of treasure such as no one ship had ever carried before. Her magazines were heaped high with 2229 heavy bullion boxes, each containing four bars of gold. (The tons of gold were so heavy that before the voyage was over they bent the angle irons beneath the magazine's floors.) Elsewhere were stored 488 boxes of securities whose value, conservatively estimated, was more than 400 million dollars. More than half a billion dollars in one shipment was about to be committed to the hazards of war on the North Atlantic.

"We left the Clyde that night with reports of bad weather ahead," recalled Captain Flynn, a sturdy, ruddy-faced man. "The reports were correct. The seas whipped up as we rounded the north coast of Ireland next morning. When we turned out into the Atlantic we were punching into a rising gale."

The ship's paymaster, encountering Alexander Craig on deck, remarked: "The skipper's just had a flash from the Admiralty. There's a couple of German subs waiting for us." Then the paymaster sauntered nonchalantly away, leaving the Bank of England's mathematical expert to compute the odds against his precious cargo arriving in Canada.

The odds grew longer as the weather grew worse. The gale cut down the speed of the escorting destroyers. Finally Captain Vian, in command of the escort, signaled to Captain Flynn that he would hold a straight course while the *Emerald* zigzagged behind the destroyers. That way the *Emerald* could maintain a higher, and safer, speed.

But the ocean got rougher and rougher. It cut the destroyers' pace so much that Captain Flynn decided to travel alone. "We found it wiser," he said, "for the escorts to turn back. I put my ship up to 22 knots. Those first three days the going was such that many of our crew became seasick." But on the fourth day the weather cleared, and shortly after five a.m. on July 1 the Nova Scotia coast showed dimly ahead. Now, in a calm sea, the *Emerald* churned straight for Halifax at 28 knots. By 7:35 a.m. the treasure ship was safely at her dock.

On a railroad spur beside the dock a special train was waiting. On hand were officials of the Bank of Canada and the Canadian National Express. The quays were blocked off under extreme precautionary measures; every box was checked off the *Emerald* and rechecked into the cars in double-quick time. At seven p.m. the gold train rolled away. At Montreal the security-bearing cars were cut off; the gold cargo sped on to Ottawa.

This was the train which David Mansur and Sidney Perkins met in Montreal. Now the treasure was tossed in their laps. Where could the hundreds of crates of securities be temporarily hidden? David Mansur had found the answer.

The Sun Life Assurance Company's 24-story granite building, occupying an entire block on Montreal's Dominion Square, was the largest commercial building in the British dominions. It had three subterranean levels; the lowest of these had been selected for the wartime home of what was now christened "The United Kingdom Security Deposit."

The big move started that night as soon as Montreal's streets grew quiet and free of traffic. Shortly after one a.m. city police isolated the few blocks between the railway yards and the Sun Life building and the trucks began to roll. Accompanied by armed, civilian-clad Canadian National Express guards, they shuttled steadily through the streets and down Sun Life's rear ramp. Royal Canadian Mounted Police hovered hawklike as the boxes were lowered to the "Buttress Room" in the third basement. With the last box shunted into place—and checked— Deposit Manager Craig, for the Bank of England, handed David Mansur a receipt to sign for the Bank of Canada.

Construction of a permanent burglarproof vault was now rushed. But a vault 60 feet square and 11 feet high required a lot of steel. Where to get it in wartime? Fortunately, someone thought of an unused, forgotten railroad. Two miles of its tracks provided 870 rails which went into the vault's three-foot-thick cement walls and ceiling. Also into the ceiling went dozens of microphonic sound-detection devices, so supersensitive that they would record even the sliding click of a filing-cabinet drawer. To open the vault door, two different combinations were required. Two bank officials were given one combination; two more were given the other. "I never knew what the other combination was from first to last," said one. "To open the vault, we had to pair up every day."

Three dozen similar trainloads of securities arrived during the next three months. To accommodate all the certificates, nearly 900 four-door filing cabinets were needed. Twenty-four Canadian Mounties guarded the hidden treasure round the clock, eating and sleeping in the building.

The *Emerald's* epic voyage was merely the first dash in the historic transatlantic race. On July 8 five ships left British ports with the greatest combined load of treasure ever transported by land or sea. Out of the Clyde at midnight slipped the battleship *Revenge* and the cruiser *Bonaventure*. At daybreak they made a rendezvous in the north channel off Scotland with three former liners: the *Monarch of Bermuda*, the *Sobieski* and the *Batory* (the latter two being Free Poland ships). Four destroyers served as escorts. Under command of Admiral Sir Ernest Russell Archer, this convoy carried approximately 773 million dollars' worth of gold bullion, plus 299 boxes of securities—a total value of about $1,750,000,000.

"We had the usual Admiralty reports of submarines active in the vicinity," Admiral Archer recalled. (In the two previous weeks 28 Allied ships totaling 139,000 tons had been destroyed by the enemy.) "We managed to dodge their U-boats. Enemy raiders were also active, but none showed up. Were we nervous? We knew what we had on board. You took the ships and did what you could."

Three fourths of the way across, an engine defect slowed down the *Batory*. To avoid risking the rest of his ships, the Admiral diverted her for St. John's, with the *Bonaventure* to see her in. As the others dashed for Halifax these two ships ran into grave trouble. "We hit a most frightful fog, with floating ice at the same time," said the *Bonaventure's* commander, Vice-Admiral Jack Egerton. "For nearly 12 hours it stopped us dead. I had to stick close to the *Batory* in the fog. Between us we carried some 60 million sterling in bullion [about a quarter-billion dollars]— and you couldn't see an iceberg until it was practically on top of you." Somehow Vice-Admiral Egerton kept contact with the *Batory* and chaperoned her into St. John's—then lit out full speed for Halifax.

All across the Atlantic the *Revenge's* eight 15-inch and 12 six-inch guns, plus her 4-inch anti-aircraft batteries, were ready for instant action. "The gun crews were always at their stations," said Commander Jenkins. "At night they slept beside their guns. Damage-control parties constantly inspected all parts of the ship for possible leaks or fire."

On July 13 the first three ships slipped safely into Halifax harbor, shortly followed by the *Bonaventure*, then the *Batory*. Five special trains were needed to carry the convoy's bullion from Halifax to Ottawa. The gold was so heavy that only 150 to 200 boxes could be laid on each car's floor. Each train had 10 to 14 loaded baggage cars. Two guards, on four-hour shifts, were locked with the bullion inside each car.

All these gold shipments traveled without insurance. Who could or would insure hundreds of millions of dollars in bullion, especially in wartime? But the *Revenge* convoy set a cost record of another kind. Transportation charges of the Canadian National Express were the largest in its history—"something over one million dollars."

In Ottawa the CNR juggled the arrivals of the specials so that the gold could be trucked from the station at night to the Bank of Canada on Wellington Street. Who could imagine that this five-story structure, with scarcely a 140-foot frontage, was soon to be Fort Knox's only important rival anywhere in the world?

For three days the *Revenge* convoy's golden flood poured into
the bank's 60-by-100-foot vault. Unpacking was pushed feverishly. At last tens of thousands of 27-pound ingots were neatly
piled like huge cakes of yellow soap inside the wired cages: shelf
after shelf, row after row, tier above tier, all solid gold, up to the
ceiling.

Meanwhile, in Montreal, just outside the crammed securities
vault a huge, high-ceilinged room had been equipped as the
Deposit's office. Now, deep in that subcellar the strangest, most
secret stock-and-bond business in the world, a "Little Wall
Street," mushroomed. Mansur had recruited some 120 Canadians—retired bankers, brokerage-house technicians and invest-
ment-firm stenographers—as a staff. Taking oaths of secrecy,
they began to unravel what some called "our bundles from
Britain."

It was an incredibly exclusive office. Only one elevator operated down to the third basement. Every employe had to present a
pass (changed each month) first at the elevator entrance and
then to Mountie guards below, signing in and out daily. Beneath
the guards' tables concealed triphammer alarms connected directly with RCMP and Montreal police headquarters and with
the Dominion Electric Protection's service. Once a Mountie
accidentally tripped his alarm. Within three minutes the place
swarmed with trigger-ready police.

All summer, as other arrivals pushed the total of boxes of
securities up to nearly 2000, Craig's staff worked 10-hour days,
six days a week. The securities were a gigantic hodgepodge of
thousands of separately owned issues; all had to be unpacked,
checked and classified. In the end, some 2000 different stocks
and bonds were identified, including virtually every "blue chip"
listed. Each individually owned parcel was tied (more than 70
miles of tape were required) and its contents double-checked. To
correct discrepancies in cross-checked lists, more than 6000
"query slips" were dispatched to London. All business was urgent, because none of these negotiables could be marketed until
the lists, amounts and ownership were verified.

"Craig had a whole squad of secretaries doing nothing but

cutting coupons," recalled one Canadian. "I never saw so many coupons in my life. Quantities of owners hadn't touched their bonds for a long time."

By September, Deposit Manager Craig, who knew all along what he was *supposed* to have, knew at last that he *had* it: every certificate was accounted for and filed. "I believe we didn't lose a single coupon," he said. "Not a certificate was missing. In view of the pressures under which they were assembled and shipped, it was quite extraordinary."

The gold, as well as securities, kept on arriving. In the three months of June, July and August the Admiralty's records show that British ships (with a few Canadian and Polish) carried to Canada and the United States gold worth more than $2,556,-000,000. Most amazing fact of all: in those three months 134 Allied and neutral ships were sunk in the North Atlantic—but not one gold-carrying vessel went down.

Winston Churchill and his war Cabinet won their gigantic gamble. Not only did Britain's means-to-fight arrive safely in Canada—a treasure worth more than seven billion dollars—but the whole vast operation was successfully kept tightly veiled in secrecy. At one time or another well over 600 persons were involved in the Security Deposit's clandestine services. The gold deliveries involved thousands of ships' personnel, hundreds of dock workers on both sides of the ocean. Perhaps never before had so many kept so great a secret so incredibly well.

Paris—Escape

Condensed from the book Paris—Underground

By Etta Shiber

Dorothy Canfield wrote of this book: "This absorbing record of the experiences of two women vs. the Gestapo, and of the moving heroism of millions of little people in France, is not only literally, factually true, it sounds true. The author just sets down what happened, with a singularly honest absence of any effort to dramatize the facts or to make herself out a heroine. But she is a heroine—of hair-raising adventures. No American should miss this astonishing story of bravery, daring and self-sacrifice."

I said no good-bye to Europe. In the evening haze the coast of Portugal was already out of sight, and the great ship moved alone in a blaze of brilliance, the black letters on her white hull lit up by powerful reflectors: "Diplomat—*Drottningholm*—Diplomat."

I was on my way home after serving more than a year in a Nazi prison. Somewhere in the United States a cell door had swung open for a German prisoner, for whom I had been exchanged.

At Lisbon, United States Consul Wiley had told me the exchanged prisoner was Johanna Hoffmann, the hairdresser of the German liner *Bremen*, convicted in 1938 of being a member of a dangerous German spy ring operating in the United States. Was my release really worth such a price?

An official of the American Consulate of Lisbon answered that question for me. "My dear Mrs. Shiber," he said, "the State Department knows very well what you did in Paris. Suppose the British in the last war had had a chance to exchange Edith Cavell. You, after all, are the Edith Cavell of this war."

I couldn't let that pass unchallenged. "No," I said. "I'm not, but perhaps my dear friend Kitty was. Whatever merit there was in what we did belongs to her. I only followed where she led.

And she alone has paid the price. She is still in the hands of the Gestapo, if she is alive; or dead, if the sentence passed on her has been carried out. Yes, Kitty Beaurepos may well have been the Edith Cavell of this war."

I met Kitty in 1925 on one of my annual trips to Paris. The daughter of a London banker, she had married a French wine merchant, Henri Beaurepos, from whom she was separated—though on a thoroughly friendly basis. Kitty was financially independent, but to keep herself occupied she ran a small dress shop in the rue Rodier. It was there I met her, and a deep friendship developed between us.

In 1933, when my brother Irving died suddenly in Paris, Kitty saw me through the terrible emergency and even made the arrangements for his burial. Three years later, at the death of my husband, she cabled me to come to live with her in Paris. I was lost without my menfolk to look after me, and cabled, gratefully, "Coming."

We settled down together in her comfortable modern apartment, sharing a pleasant existence for which our moderate means sufficed. The end of our ivory-tower existence came one day before the Nazis entered Paris—June 13, 1940. Secure in the belief that the French would, as Premier Paul Reynaud had said, defend Paris building by building, we had ignored persistent rumors and growing panic. But on that day, when repeated phone calls to our friends brought no response, we woke up to the realization that all had fled.

"I'll call the American Embassy," I said, still disbelieving. "They'll tell me what's happening, and whether the Germans are going to besiege Paris."

A startled voice answered me: "Are you still in town? Don't you know that the government has moved to Tours? The Germans will be in Paris in a matter of hours!"

In a blind frenzy we packed a few things and started off. But Route Nationale No. 20, which connects Paris with the south of France, was crowded with a stream of frightened humanity which tried to flow along it to safety. In autos, on foot, on bicycles, thousands of refugees jammed the road ahead of us for 200 miles. It was dark when we heard a faint hum which rose to a fierce crescendo over our heads. With a jerk, Kitty stopped the car. We could see the black hulk of the airplane against the dark sky, and the flame spitting from the nozzles of its machine guns as it poured death into the trapped ranks below. In seconds the highway was emptied. Terror-stricken drivers turned their cars off the road into trees, into ditches. Some overturned and their occupants squirmed out and ran. Only a few cars remained in the road, the figures in them motionless. They had not joined the mad rush to get off the road, because they were dead.

In the darkness the noise of many motors was heard, and with a rush the German army was upon us. First came motorcycle troops, speeding through the dark with complete assurance that the planes ahead of them would have swept the road clear. Light armored cars followed, then tanks. They seemed to be everywhere, to possess the whole earth. Every 200 yards, unfolding in a regular pattern behind the moving army, a motorcyclist stopped and took charge of the civilians. The one nearest us came up and said, in excellent French, "You will go back to Paris."

"But," Kitty pleaded, "we want to go to Nice."

The German's words were polite, but there was a sneer on his lips. "That, Madame, is the way *we* are going. *You* will go back to Paris."

Hours later we stopped at a roadside inn, exhausted, ready to drop; but the innkeeper motioned us away. "I have nothing to give you. A million people have been through here in the last two days."

"A cup of tea will do," Kitty said, turning her most winsome smile on him. And she marched in and sat down. It worked. The innkeeper locked the door and produced not only tea, but also a small piece of salami and a little cheese.

"You are English?" he asked. "Then you can do something for me. I have someone here who speaks only English. Please tell him I shall get into trouble if he stays. . . . I am very sorry." And from an inner room he led in a tall young man wearing a leather coat over his gray-blue RAF uniform.

The boy's name was William Gray, he told us. A pilot caught at Dunkirk, he had been unable to get to the evacuating ships. "If you will please ask this chap to get me some civilian clothes, I'll be able to take care of myself," he explained.

Kitty translated.

"*Quelle folie!*" the innkeeper exclaimed. "If he is in civilian clothes, the Germans will shoot him as a spy. In uniform he'd be treated as a prisoner of war."

Gray sat still for a moment. Then, with an embarrassed smile, he rose. "I'd better get out of here and not involve anyone," he said. "Will you please ask the innkeeper how much I owe?"

I pressed Kitty's arm. "Don't let him go," I whispered. "Have you noticed—he looks exactly like poor Irving when he was 20." Kitty had known my brother well. "Our car is just outside," I begged. "We could put him in the luggage compartment."

The luggage compartment of Kitty's car didn't open from the outside, but into the interior, behind the back seats. Even if we were stopped by the Germans they'd hardly look for anyone there. Kitty beamed on me. "I say, Mr. Gray," she said. "We want to talk to you."

And there we were, two middle-aged respectable ladies in enemy territory, with an English pilot on our hands, embarked on an adventure which even a few hours ago would have seemed fantastic.

It took us all night to reach Paris. With a constriction of the heart I saw the Eiffel Tower again, for at its top the Nazi swastika now flew. We circled the Arc and stopped in front of number 2, rue Balny d'Avricourt—home!

"Do—I get out first?" I gulped. I sensed imaginary Nazis everywhere, waiting to pounce.

"Wait!" Kitty whispered tensely. A German military guard came marching down the street, surrounding a French soldier. When they had disappeared around the corner, Kitty turned toward the luggage compartment. "Mr. Gray!"

"Yes," came his muffled voice.

"We're going to get out now. Wait a few moments, then follow us." We hurried into the apartment. I threw myself against the door and pushed the safety bolt. For a moment my legs seemed too weak to support my weight.

"I shouldn't have let you take so much risk on my account," William Gray said. "I didn't realize . . ."

"Now, listen to me, young man," Kitty said firmly. "We're all in this together. What we have to do is figure how to get out of it."

It was easy enough for Kitty to say that we must find a way out of our predicament, but where could we turn for help? The only one who shared our secret was our Breton maid, Margot, who we knew would not betray us. The Gestapo was conducting its search for hidden soldiers, shutting off the exits to whole city blocks at a time and then methodically going through them, house by house. We expected daily that they would get around to us. We lived for a week in an atmosphere of constant terror.

Kitty was late for supper one night, and I knew when she breezed in that she had good news. "Etta!" she burst out, "do you remember Chancel?" I remembered him well. We had worked with him at the Foyer du Soldat—the French equivalent of the USO—before our attempt to get out of Paris.

"I ran into him on the subway," Kitty said. "I trust him, and think he can help us. We're seeing him tomorrow afternoon."

We sat together in the living room after supper, drinking the last of our treasured coffee, talking of that interview next day which we hoped would end our troubles. For the first time, I saw a smile on William's face.

And then the doorbell rang. I can still see the frightened face of Margot as she slipped into the room and closed the door. "The Germans are here."

Kitty was the first to recover. "Soldiers?"

"No, civilians."

"The Gestapo!" Kitty gasped. In the silence, I could hear her breathing. Then she swung to me. "Take Bill to your room. Try to hide him." She cast a swift glance around the room. "Take the third cup with you. Hurry!" As we went out, she

lifted her voice in a tone indicating impatience with a frightened servant: "Don't be silly, Margot. Don't keep the gentlemen waiting."

William sat on the edge of the sofa in my room, his head bent forward, his hands clenched. In my terrified confusion, two familiar objects suddenly took on clarity—the photographs on my dresser of my husband and my brother. And suddenly I understood how my brother could help. I darted to the sofa, grasped William by the arm. "Quick! Take your clothes off and get into bed. Pretend you're ill." He was in bed in a matter of seconds. I tied a towel around his head—just in time. For at that moment I heard Kitty calling: "Etta, where are you? This gentleman wants to see your room."

It seemed to me that the piercing glance of the Gestapo agent bored right through me. Behind him were two other plain-clothesmen and Mme. Beugler, our concierge. From her belligerent mien it was easy to see they would get no help from her. "This is my dear American friend, Mrs. Shiber," Kitty said. "She finds herself an unwitting victim of the war—far from home, like yourself."

I steeled myself to be natural. "You'll have to excuse the appearance of my room. My brother is in bed with intestinal flu—there's so much of it in town now. I hope you won't have to disturb him."

"His papers, please," the Gestapo man said curtly. I opened the drawer in my bureau and took out Irving's red wallet, with his American passport and identity card. I blessed myself now that I had kept them. The Gestapo official flipped through the pages of the passport, came to the picture of my brother and flashed a swift glance at the man in the bed. William made a realistic invalid with the towel about his head, and his unshaven face added years to his appearance. The policeman examined the identity card more closely. "Why hasn't this card been renewed?" he asked.

"We had intended to return to America long ago, if his health had been better. Under the circumstances it seemed hardly worth while." I knew that unrenewed identity cards were not unusual, and so, apparently, did the German. He asked for my papers, checked them and left the bedroom.

But back in the living room the Gestapo officer asked Mme. Beugler for the list of tenants. He looked through it carefully. "I do not find the name of Madame's brother," he said.

Kitty said calmly, "Irving isn't a regular tenant, of course. He has only been here since he needed someone to take care of him."

Mme. Beugler rose nobly to the occasion. "I'm sorry, sir," she said. "I forgot about the gentleman. He never asked me for a certificate of domicile, so he isn't on my list."

The Nazi sat down at the table slowly, took out his fountain pen. What did he intend to write? A warrant for our arrest? But he took the list of tenants and added to it in his own writing the name of my brother Irving!

The next afternoon we went to see Chancel. Kitty opened the conversation cautiously. He sensed the general trend of her talk, and interrupted her with a smile. "*Ma chère madame*," he said, "I didn't change my politics when the Germans came in. Exactly what sort of a scrape have you got into?"

Kitty gulped. "We're hiding an English pilot in our apartment." And she told him the whole story, including last night's visit from the Gestapo.

M. Chancel whistled. "Well! That's quite an exploit for two ladies who certainly wouldn't be taken by anyone for adventuresses. It's a pity you didn't come to me at once. You would have saved yourselves a great deal of worry." Chancel belonged to an Underground group which helped soldiers escape into unoccupied territory. The organization had a house on the Left Bank where refugees could stay until traveling passes could be secured for them. Then they were sent by train to other friends who owned an estate on the frontier. From there they crossed over into unoccupied France.

"But if your boy doesn't speak French," Chancel said, "he can't travel safely by train."

"I'll take him to the frontier estate in the car," Kitty said.

"That's not so easy now. You can't buy gasoline, you know." Chancel slapped his hand down on the table. "I have it! The

Foyer du Soldat is still operating, under the Germans. Offer
your services again, and you can put the Red Cross emblem on
your car and be allowed 10 gallons of gasoline a week. Besides,
you'll have an excuse for moving about the country, visiting
hospitals and prison camps."

The actual escape of William Gray was so uneventful as to be
almost disappointing. We secured our identification papers from
the Foyer du Soldat and began visiting hospitals in the Paris
region. Chancel procured a travel permit for William, and when
everything was ready we stowed him once more in the baggage
compartment. We had parcels and gifts from the Foyer du
Soldat for a number of military hospitals, but our first stop was
at the small town on the demarcation line, where we found
Chancel's friends without trouble.

A week later Margot rushed into the living room waving a
postcard. William had sent a cautious message telling us that
he had been promised he might soon "visit his parents." I knew
that meant England, and I was so happy that I would almost
have been willing to start a similar process all over again.

Yet when Kitty suggested something of the sort, I was terrified. She had come across what seemed to her a very interesting
advertisement in *Paris-Soir*. The "Missing Persons" column was
now the most widely read part of the paper in France—hardly
anyone was without a friend or relative who had disappeared in
the war. *Paris-Soir* published several hundred such advertisements daily. This one seemed different.

Jonathan Burke is looking for his friends and acquaintances.
Address Military Hospital, Doullens (Somme).

"That's an English name," Kitty said thoughtfully. "Who ever
heard of a Frenchman named Jonathan? I'm going to write to
him."

"Kitty!" I said, alarmed. "You aren't trying to hunt up more
English soldiers, are you?"

"No-o. But if I run across any, the least I can do is get them to
Chancel."

A few days later she brought me a note, written in English and signed with Jonathan Burke's name: "It will be wonderful to have someone to talk to . . . I shall look forward to your visit."

"The Foyer du Soldat expects us to take packages to soldiers," Kitty said, eyeing me eagerly.

"All right," I said. "I'm going—to keep you out of trouble."

We set out for Doullens early the next morning, with packages of food and cigarettes for the soldiers. Kitty also carried a box wrapped in brown paper, about which she was noncommittal. "Just something I want to leave at the Foyer on the way back."

The military hospital at Doullens was still operated by its French staff, though under the control of the Germans. Two German guards, standing stiffly at either side of the gate, appeared not to notice us. Inside, the place was dark, filthy and infested with vermin. We wandered through the hospital, talking with the soldiers, keeping an eye out for Jonathan Burke. In the garden we noticed an English officer sitting by himself on a bench. His RAF uniform was crumpled and faded, and he wore a bandage over his right eye. As we approached, he seemed suddenly to come to life.

"I hoped you would come," he said. "But I didn't dare count on it."

"You're a countryman of mine," Kitty answered. "It's disgusting that you must stay in this filthy place."

"Maybe it seems so to you," he replied in a low voice, "but I'm stalling for time. I'm perfectly fit to leave, and when they discover that, they'll send me to prison. There's hardly any guard here, and I might be able to escape. But there's little chance of escaping from prison."

Kitty paced a few steps from the bench, then turned back. "Would you like me to take you to Paris?" she whispered.

Burke clutched at her hand. "How, Mrs. Beaurepos?"

Kitty produced the mysterious brown paper parcel. "Here's a pair of overalls," she said. "Our car is parked on the other side of that low wall, where all those bushes are. Behind the back seat is the opening to the luggage compartment. Get in—it's roomy enough—close it behind you, and wait."

The hardest thing I ever did in my life was to walk back
through the wards, talking with patients as if nothing had happened. In the corridor a blond young man limped toward us.
"I'm Lawrence Meehan—I saw you with Burke. Please—get me
out, too." He was trembling all over and looked very ill.

"You have a fever," I said.

"No—it's only my leg wound. It's nearly healed. I'll be all
right if I can get out of here."

"Look," Kitty said. "We can take only one at a time in our
car. If the Germans don't catch us, we'll come back for you." She
strode off and I scurried after her. At the gate, Kitty said loudly,
"Wait here. I'll drive the car around." I stood riveted with terror,
watching her stop the car in front of the two German sentries.
"What time do you open the gates for visitors in the morning?"
she asked in German. One of them told her.

"We may have to make several trips here," she said. "Have a
cigarette?" He accepted one, and struck a light for hers.

"*Danke schön*," she said, and started the car. I was about to
upbraid her, when she spoke quietly. "I wanted him to see there
was no one in the car but us."

"But suppose he had asked us to open the luggage compartment."

"I locked it. And I would have told him I'd left the key in
Paris."

With Burke safely in our apartment, Kitty and I felt like tried
and triumphant conspirators.

"You're both wonderful," he said. "I wish other English soldiers could have my luck. There are supposed to be about 10,000
of them, trapped after Dunkirk, hiding like beasts in the woods
and caves of northern France. They are without food and arms.
The Germans have organized a special armed motorcycle unit to
track them down. There's no way of saving them."

For a while we sat in gloomy silence. After dinner, when Burke
had gone to bed, Kitty turned to me with a look of determination.
"Etta, you will have to go back to America. I can't simply sit
here while this cruel manhunt is going on—I've got to help my
countrymen escape. But I have no right to involve you."

"I won't leave you, Kitty," I said. "If you have to save soldiers, I have to help you."

Our main problem was to get in touch with the soldiers. We finally decided to use the "Missing Persons" column, just as Burke had done. Kitty went out early next morning to insert an advertisement in *Paris-Soir:*

> William Gray is looking for his friends and relatives. Address
> Café Moderne, rue Rodier, Paris.

We didn't dare use either of our names or our address. But William Gray was safely out of German territory. And Kitty knew the proprietor of the Café Moderne, M. Durand, a loyal Frenchman who promised to deliver secretly to us any mail which arrived for William Gray.

Just as we were starting for the Left Bank house with Burke, Chancel arrived with bad news. One of the group had turned traitor, and the Left Bank house had been raided by the Gestapo. The Nazis also knew about the frontier estate.

"Then they'll be here any minute!" I gasped.

"Oh, no!" Chancel answered. "You're all right. The traitor knew only a few of us. Our friend at the Préfecture—the one who fixes up the exit visas for us—is trusted completely by the Germans, and he knows everything they know. They've never heard of you."

Our accomplice in the Préfecture had warned our friends, and fortunately everybody had got away from the two houses in time, but the escape route was no good any more. Chancel himself was headed for the unoccupied zone. "I shall stay there long enough to grow a beard," he said, "and organize a group to take care of the men we smuggle across the line. I'll get in touch with you when I come back."

He took his leave, and with him went the slight courage his presence had given us. We could hear Lieutenant Burke pacing back and forth in the bedroom. His safety was our chief immediate problem.

"There's only one thing to do, Etta," Kitty said. "Tomorrow

we must find some French peasant living on the border who'll
agree to smuggle Burke across." Then she interrupted herself.
"We can't do it tomorrow! We have to get Lawrence Meehan."

"Kitty! You aren't going to bring him here now!"

She looked at me in surprise. "Not bring him here? But we
promised."

Our second trip to Doullens was a quick one. Meehan was in
bed, looking very ill. His eyes lighted up, but he was clever
enough to make no sign of recognition. Kitty stopped at the bed
next to his, then steered me out into the corridor. As we passed
the hospital office, the door swung open and a French major
barred our way.

"I am Major Thibaud, in charge here. I believe you ladies have
honored us with a previous visit," he said slowly. Then, abruptly,
"Will you kindly tell me where Lieutenant Burke is?"

My heart leaped into my throat, but Kitty said calmly, "You
must be a mind reader. We have just been through the wards
looking for him."

Major Thibaud scrutinized Kitty carefully. Then he stepped
back through the door, saying, "Kindly come into my office."
Inside, he motioned us to be seated. "I have made a careful investigation. You, Mme. Beaurepos, are British-born. It therefore
does not surprise me that after your visit one of the very few English prisoners here should escape. I am not a fool, Mme. Beaurepos. That you helped Lieutenant Burke to escape is obvious. It
is my duty to hand you over to the German authorities. I am a
soldier. It is my habit to obey orders." He paused for another instant. My heart was beating madly. "But I am not only a soldier,
ladies," he said slowly. "I am a Frenchman. That is why I have
not yet reported the disappearance of Lieutenant Burke. You
ladies must leave this hospital at once, and not return. I must ask
your formal promise that you will not repeat your act."

I sat bolt upright in my chair, thunderstruck at the unexpected-
ness of this development. Kitty rose. "Thank you, Major," she
said, holding out her hand. "I am very happy to meet a real
Frenchman."

Major Thibaud took her hand. "You will pardon me," he said

dryly, "if I take the precaution of escorting you to your car."

We were several kilometers outside Doullens before I could find my voice. "We'll just have to forget about poor Meehan," I remarked. "We surely can't go back." Kitty smiled. "I slipped Meehan a note when we were standing at the bed next to his," she said. "He's in the luggage compartment."

At the apartment, Meehan had great difficulty in getting out of the car. He hobbled into the building, leaning heavily on us.

"Everything all right?" Burke called out, coming from the bedroom. Meehan dropped heavily to the floor and lay there, unmoving. Burke bent over him with an exclamation. "His wound has reopened!" Sure enough, one leg of Meehan's trousers was soaked with blood.

"Phone for a doctor!" Kitty ordered. Then: "No! We can't tell a doctor. Get some towels—" The doorbell pealed, loudly and insistently. We stood as though turned into statues. The bell rang again. "It's no use," said Kitty hopelessly. "We can't hide this. Etta, answer the door."

Never in my life have I performed any task with such reluctance—but our fears were unfounded. Henri Beaurepos, Kitty's husband, entered. He invariably called on Kitty when he was in Paris. This time his visit was providential, for after his first astonishment had passed, he took complete charge. He phoned a doctor who he knew could be trusted completely. The doctor arrived in five minutes. In 15, Meehan was bandaged and in bed, but the doctor shook his head dubiously over his condition. "He has a serious infection," he said. "But I'll do what I can for him."

When the doctor had gone, Henri solved the rest of our problem for us. "My friend Tissier at Libourne has vineyards which stretch across the line. He can pass your boys across. There's a slight charge, though—50 francs a head—tips to German sergeants." He grinned. "It seems that the *Herrenvolk* like to make a little small change now and then. I know a man at the Préfecture, too, who'll give us passes in French names for your English friends. You needn't worry—they'll be all right."

Next morning Emile, Durand's boy, brought us letters addressed to William Gray, Café Moderne. Kitty tore one open. It contained no message, only an address:

B. W. Stowe
12, rue de la Gare, Reims

"That looks suspicious to me," I said.

"Oh dear," Kitty said to Burke. "Etta is going to see the fine hand of the Gestapo behind every one of these letters."

The next letter was in French:

Dear Sir:

I am the parish priest of Conchy-sur-Conche, and I am writing you at the request of a few of my parishioners who seem to recognize an old friend in you. According to them, I can approach you with confidence on a matter very important to my congregation.

Our church building is in need of urgent repairs, otherwise this beautiful product of the art of the Middle Ages will undoubtedly collapse—a catastrophe which may be expected any day—and irreparable, irreplaceable values would be lost. I have already secured the permission of the Church and the local authorities for this restoration project.

I beg you, my dear sir, to inform me immediately when and where we can meet to discuss the broadening of our collection campaign.

Asking God's blessing upon you, I am

Yours very faithfully,
Father Christian Ravier

"Just an appeal for funds," I said.

"Etta!" Kitty almost screamed. "It was addressed to William Gray, in answer to our advertisement! It's written so we'll understand, and no one else. Listen: 'A few of my parishioners seem to recognize an old friend in you.' He must be in touch with some of the men in William Gray's unit. 'According to them, I can approach you with confidence.' 'A catastrophe may be expected any day'—in other words, his 'congregation' may be discovered and arrested."

We all agreed that the letter seemed genuine, and we set out immediately to see Father Christian. He turned out to be young, bright-eyed and energetic—I judged no more than 28. He suggested that we talk in the rectory behind the church and led us through the garden into a small, low-ceilinged room. He told us there were at least 1000 English soldiers hiding in the Conchy-sur-Conche forests, and that he maintained regular contact with them. "They are so starved, so exhausted. My congregation gives food and clothing, but we are so closely rationed that even if they gave all, it would not be enough. I can get identity cards and escort them to Paris a few at a time, if you can take care of them from then on. Can you do that?"

"We certainly can," said Kitty. And she told him of our escape route from Paris, which could start operating in about a week.

The young priest closed his eyes for a moment. "You are like an answer to my prayers."

Lawrence Meehan had responded amazingly to the doctor's treatment and would soon be strong enough to travel. We anticipated sending him off with Burke. Henri's friend at the Préfecture had secured for us a large number of blank permits on which we could fill in names and details. But one morning the newspapers announced that the death penalty would be imposed on any persons found aiding English soldiers to escape.

"I must go to Libourne and see Tissier at once," Kitty said. "I'm afraid this order will frighten him out of helping us."

Since we already had passes for our two refugees, however, she decided to take them with her. She returned full of praise for M. Tissier. "Burke and Meehan are safely over the border," she said. "M. Tissier is a wonderful old chap. When I mentioned the death decree to him, he just spat."

Kitty wrote at once to Father Christian, telling him that everything was ready for his collection campaign, and in a few days he arrived at the apartment with four boys. Provided with traveling permits, they took the evening train for Libourne. Tissier was to notify us of their safe arrival, but two days passed without word from him, and we had begun to fear that something had happened to them, when Tissier himself turned up.

"You ladies made a bad mistake," he informed us bluntly. "In the future you must not let those boys travel without a quick-witted escort who can answer questions for them—in French." The English boys, it developed, had escaped arrest only by a miracle. French gendarmes, checking the passengers on the train, had discovered that they all had official permits but were unable to speak French. If the French passengers in the compartment had not protested indignantly, the gendarmes would have taken the boys off the train.

"What on earth can we do?" sighed Kitty. "I've no idea where to find escorts for them."

M. Tissier hadn't been gone half an hour before Margot announced another visitor—a M. Corbier.

"I don't know him," Kitty said distrustfully. "What does he want?" Margot didn't answer, for M. Corbier simply opened the door and walked in. He looked like a French doctor—black, uneven beard, thick-rimmed spectacles. We stared at him.

"My dear ladies," he said, "I'm happy to see you don't recognize me." Kitty and I shouted almost in unison: "Chancel!"

Chancel was now working for a new organization whose object was to smuggle to England any Frenchmen who wanted to fight with De Gaulle. He had come to ask us to work with him, and when Kitty explained our problem, he saw at once how he could fit his plans to ours. "Nothing is easier," he said. "Whenever you have Englishmen to send, I'll provide the same number of French boys on their way to join De Gaulle."

"God must have sent you to us once again," Kitty said to him. We now had a route of escape not simply to the unoccupied zone, but all the way to England! By November we had sent out over 100 Englishmen, accompanied by an equal number of Frenchmen. The process operated with clockwork precision. We hardly ever thought of the danger any more.

By October our wholesale traffic in escapes had run us into financial difficulties. Traveling expenses, including the 50 francs per head for getting the men across the border, amounted to a substantial sum; but even more expensive was feeding them while they were in Paris. We had only three food cards in the household, and we often had to resort to the Black Market, paying from 10 to 20 times the legal rate fixed by the authorities. Kitty knew some well-to-do families in the Free Zone who would be glad to help, but she couldn't, of course, write to them; she would have to go to see them.

"How long must you be gone?" I asked. I tried to mask with a smile the fear I felt at being left alone.

"Two weeks—possibly three. Don't worry, Etta . . . if anything happens, you can always go to Chancel."

Father Christian sent me three parties during the first week of Kitty's absence, and three times I handed them over to Chancel's escorts. Hardly half an hour after the third group had been started on their way, Emile, the boy from Durand's café, came to the door and asked for Kitty. "M. Durand says there is a Mr. Stowe in the café who wants to talk to her, Madame."

"Mr. Stowe" was the name which had been signed to one of the letters we had received from the advertisement in *Paris-Soir*. For a moment I sat paralyzed. How did this man know Kitty's name? Our advertisement had mentioned only William Gray.

I must escape! Perhaps I could still get to the unoccupied zone, out of danger. But then Kitty would return and find me gone. I began to grow calmer. After all, we had avoided dangers before. I went to a small restaurant a block away from the Café Moderne and told Emile to tell M. Durand to slip out to meet me. M. Durand came at once.

"Did you give our address to this Mr. Stowe?" I asked.

"Of course not," he answered. "Mme. Kitty told me not to give the address to anyone. The man asked for William Gray. I sent Emile around to you." I breathed again. "You may be sure, Madame, I am not so stupid as I look. I told him I didn't know any William Gray. I suggested that he wait, and if William Gray came in to ask for mail, I would introduce them."

"What do you think of him, M. Durand?"

"Well . . . his French wasn't bad—not, perhaps, quite like an Englishman's French. He said he was afraid to speak English, though his voice was so low no one could possibly—" He stopped suddenly, his mouth ajar. "*Diable! Que je suis stupide!* He lit a cigarette while he was talking. It was the kind they issue to German soldiers."

I grasped his hand across the table. "Sit tight, M. Durand. Your Mr. Stowe is a Gestapo man."

His face turned white. "What shall I do? What will happen to me?"

"I have traveling permits," I said. "You could go to the station now and take a train to the unoccupied zone."

"No," he moaned. "My wife—my children—all I have is here." His face clouded as though he were grappling with a difficult idea; then it spread into a broad smile. "There is a way out—a beautiful way. I am going to phone Gestapo headquarters that there is a suspicious Englishman in my café. Then they cannot possibly suspect me."

Hardly had he left the table when I was seized with fear that we had made a mistake. Suppose Mr. Stowe really were an English soldier. I walked to the café and sat down on the terrace. I had to see what happened, to reassure myself if I could.

A German official car drove up and three men jumped out. They went into the café and in a moment came out with another man, whom two of them were holding by the arms. My heart sank. Apparently we had been wrong. But as they stepped into the dusk of the street, they all broke out into boisterous laughter. Before they climbed into the car, "Mr. Stowe," still laughing, courteously offered the others cigarettes from a package which I was now quite sure was German military issue.

It was a few days later that Durand burst into the apartment, a newpaper in his hand and rage in his face. "Have you gone crazy?" he shouted. I read the advertisement on which he was holding a trembling finger.

William Gray (formerly of Dunkirk) is looking for his friends.
Address: Café Moderne, rue Rodier, Paris.

"M. Durand," I said, "we did not place this advertisement. We gave no orders that ours should be repeated."

He looked at me uncertainly. "Then who did, Madame?"

"The Gestapo," I said. I was sure of it. "They wanted to see whom you would come to when you saw it."

"*Mon Dieu!*" Durand was stricken. "What have I done? What can I do now?"

"Nothing," I said. "If they have followed you, the damage is done."

That night I went through the apartment, closet by closet, drawer by drawer, leaving nothing unburned that might be incriminating. I was eating my breakfast the next morning when the doorbell rang.

Two men stood in the hall.

"Where is Mme. Beaurepos?"

"At Tours," I said. I knew I mustn't admit she had left the occupied zone.

"When will she be back?"

"Why are you asking me these questions?"

He produced a badge. "German Secret Police."

Somehow the scene was anti-climax. For five months I had lived in dread of this moment. And now that it had come, I was calm and cool. The event was so much less spectacular than I

had expected—simply two men in civilian clothes, with brief-cases, standing politely at my door, like salesmen.

The Gestapo men assumed I did not understand German. "The Englishwoman's gotten out," one of them said. "Don't leave the place, and be sure to answer the phone." He turned to me, switching back to French. "You're coming with me. Pack a bag, and be sure to put some warm clothing in."

I went into my room and began to put things in a suitcase. I was trying desperately, as I dawdled with my packing, to think of some way of leaving a warning behind me. Father Christian was due to arrive at noon. Chancel was likely to drop in at any time. As we started slowly downward in the elevator, I hoped that we might meet the concierge in the hall, but she was no-where in sight.

At Gestapo headquarters I was escorted into a room where two Germans sat at desks. One was in uniform. The other, Dr. Hager, was a mousy little man in civilian clothes.

"Mrs. Shiber," he said persuasively, "we do not want to be obliged to imprison a citizen of your great country. If you are a sensible woman, you will simply tell us everything that hap-pened. We know most of it anyway. We know that Mme. Beaurepos was carrying on her activities under cover of her work for the Foyer du Soldat, smuggling English soldiers across the frontier. All we want from you is some of the details of the case, for the record."

The panic which had on many occasions gripped me merely at the thought of being arrested was surprisingly absent now, and I found I was thinking rapidly and easily. The raid on our apartment and my questioning were not necessarily evidence that the Germans had information, but that they wanted to get it. "I'm sorry," I said firmly, "but I know nothing whatsoever about any such activity on the part of Mme. Beaurepos."

On the opposite wall was an electric clock. Father Christian would soon be at the apartment. He would ring the bell and shout joyfully, as was his custom: "I have a few hungry boys with me. May I bring them in to lunch?" And, too late, he would notice that an unknown man had opened the door.

Dr. Hager alternately wheedled and threatened me. It was just after 12 o'clock when the phone rang. Dr. Hager picked it up, listened for an instant, gazed triumphantly at me. "Bring him here at once," he said, and then hastily corrected himself: "No, you may have other visitors. I'll send someone over." Turning toward me with a smile, he said: "Have you ever noticed, Mrs. Shiber, that when a string of pearls breaks and one of them drops off, the others invariably follow?"

When Father Christian was led into the room, he said, "How do you do, Mrs. Shiber?"

"Then you recognize her, do you?" Hager said.

"Of course," Father Christian said. "I was trying to call on Mme. Beaurepos, who is helping with the restoration of my church, and was arrested. I have no idea what this is all about."

That was all I needed to know. He had denied everything also. In the hours that followed, we were plied with question after question, but we both stuck to the simplest version of our relationship, indicated by Father Christian's opening remark. They gave up at six o'clock. Dr. Hager summoned the policeman and said: "The woman will remain under investigation."

For two weeks I was inmate No. 1876 in the German military prison of the rue du Cherche-Midi. The cell I shared with three other women prisoners contained four filthy cots, jammed so closely together that it was impossible to walk around. Twice I was summoned to Dr. Hager's office and bombarded with hundreds of questions. Then, to my amazement, on December 14 Dr. Hager told me affably that I was to be released. Dazed and suspicious, I received my stamped release papers and walked out of the prison into the free air of the rue du Cherche-Midi.

Mme. Beugler, when I knocked at the door of her *loge*, appeared not to recognize me. Then the tears came into her eyes. "*Mon Dieu*, what have they done to you, Mrs. Shiber?"

Neither Kitty nor Chancel, Mme. Beugler said, had come back to the apartment. She had not seen Henri Beaurepos. He must be safely back in unoccupied territory. From behind the door of her *loge* she had watched the Gestapo arrest Father Christian. He had had no boys with him. Margot had been arrested, but the police had released her, and she had gone back to her family in Brittany.

Everywhere I went, during the next few days, I was aware of a shadow behind me, dogging my footsteps, turning the corners that I turned. And then one day Chancel came out of a subway entrance and moved toward me. My first reaction was joy. "So he is still free!" And then: "I mustn't show I know him." My shadow from the Gestapo was only a short distance behind. Chancel saw me and smiled. I looked at him coldly, with no sign of recognition. As I passed, I whispered sharply, "Don't recognize me. I am being followed."

I hurried on to the corner and then glanced back over my shoulder. My shadow was nowhere to be seen, but a little crowd had gathered by the subway exit and I heard a police whistle blowing.

That night the Gestapo came to my apartment and arrested me, "for questioning." Once again at Gestapo headquarters I faced the ironic Dr. Hager. "Well, the comedy is over," he said. "We got M. Corbier this afternoon, thanks to you, Frau Shiber. And Mme. Beaurepos was arrested in Bordeaux two hours ago."

He had not mentioned Chancel's real name—I noted that with relief—but when he said that Kitty had been arrested, the thought of Chancel was driven from my head. So they had her at last!

My examination this time was very different from the others. A clerk was called in to take down everything I said. This was to be my official deposition for the court records. I continued to deny everything. When the typed deposition was finally brought in for me to sign, I read it carefully—10 long single-spaced pages—fearing a trick, but everything in it was exactly what I had said. I signed my name to the bottom of each sheet.

A guard was called in to take me back to prison. As I left, Dr. Hager addressed me cruelly: "It will be two or three months before your case comes up for trial, Mrs. Shiber. That isn't very long. Therefore I advise you to start preparing yourself. For the crime which you have committed, it is mandatory for the court to impose the death sentence. Good-bye, Mrs. Shiber."

My first tidings about Kitty were provided by the prison authorities during the second month of my imprisonment. I was called to the warden's office, where I found Dr. Hager waiting for me. He handed me a document 15 pages long. "Would you like to see Mme. Beaurepos' confession?"

I leafed through it. Each paragraph began with the words "I confess . . ." and it seemed to contain a fairly complete account of our activities. I was thunderstruck. How could Kitty have done such a thing?

"Well, you see," said Dr. Hager triumphantly. "Now how about your confession?" I remained silent. "Come, come, Mrs. Shiber, this is ridiculous! You will provoke the anger of the court. I am acting only in your own interest."

I said simply: "I have nothing to add to my original deposition." I was led back to my cell.

At eight o'clock on the morning of March 7 the guard ordered me to accompany him for trial. At the head of the staircase he jerked open a cell door and called: "Number 2017—for trial!" Kitty appeared in the door. Her face was pale, and there were deep shadows under her eyes; but she did not seem broken either in body or in spirit. She looked at me with the shadow of a smile and said softly, "Hello, Etta."

"Silence!" the guard roared. "Prisoners must not talk."

A green-painted convict-transport van stood at the curb. The guard opened the door and we got in. The door was locked behind us, and with a lurch the van started. The moment we were alone Kitty looked at me reproachfully. "How could you, Etta? How could you have had the weakness to tell everything to those people?"

"I . . . ?" I stammered, taken aback.

"They must have terrorized you, Etta. But you should have been firm. I ought to be angry, God knows. . . ."

"Kitty," I exclaimed, "I swear to you that I have always denied everything."

"But I saw your confession with my own eyes. It was a 10-page deposition, signed by you. I recognized your handwriting."

"I made a 10-page deposition," I said, "and I signed it, but it was a denial, not a confession. If you saw anything else, it was a forgery."

"My God!" said Kitty. "I believed in it—and I *did* confess!"

I put my arm around her shoulder. "It wasn't your fault, Kitty."

Kitty shook her head slowly. "We're lost, Etta, lost. . . ."

The van jolted to a stop. Kitty threw her head up proudly and smoothed her dress. "Heads up, Etta!" she said. "Don't let these Germans see we're afraid of them!"

In the center of the courtroom was a long table covered with thick bundles of documents. There were high-backed chairs for the judges and, facing them, a long bench for the defendants. Kitty and I were seated there, and a moment later Tissier and Father Christian joined us. Chancel was the last to arrive. He greeted us with a slight nod, as though we were strangers. I watched the door anxiously, expecting to see Durand enter at any moment. But no one else appeared.

"Frau Kitty Beaurepos," the presiding justice called. Kitty stepped before the long table.

The first questions put to her were the usual formal ones: name, address, age, place of birth, nationality, religion and so forth. Then the judge stated: "You are charged with having conspired with Mme. Shiber, M. Christian Ravier, M. Tissier and M. Corbier for the purpose of smuggling English soldiers out of the country."

"That is inexact," said Kitty in a clear voice.

"Indeed!" said the judge sarcastically. "That is very curious, since I have your signed confession before me."

"I am not retracting my confession," Kitty said steadily, "but these others were not involved in my activities."

"Frau Shiber, who occupied the same apartment with you, must have been singularly obtuse."

"Nevertheless," Kitty insisted, "she knew nothing."

"And M. Tissier? I note that you used his estate to cross the boundary line."

"We did not ask his permission," Kitty said. "We picked his estate because of its position. Then we simply crossed it."

"Better and better," said the judge sarcastically. "Now, M. Ravier. What interesting excuse have you prepared for him?"

"I used him as a cloak for my travels," Kitty said. "He thought I was helping him collect funds for the restoration of his church." I listened to Kitty with mingled admiration and pity. It was splendid of her to try to save the rest of us, but her story was pitifully thin.

"Well, we have one left," the judge said. "What about M. Corbier?"

"I do not know M. Corbier," Kitty answered quietly. She, too, had noticed their failure to identify Chancel.

"You are very noble," the judge said, "but, of course, childish and clumsy. You made a confession, and you have just stated that you do not retract it. That is all we need hear from you." He made a gesture of dismissal.

"Frau Etta Shiber!"

I took my place before the table, and went through the preliminary questions.

"You know the charges against you," the judge said. "Are you guilty?"

"I am innocent," I said.

The judge turned his cold, steely eyes on me. "Nonsense!" he roared. "How dare you claim to be innocent! The apartment where you lived was constantly filled with escaping soldiers. You were second in command of this band of criminals! You are guilty, Frau Shiber! The court will take note of your attitude! If that is all you came to tell us today, you might as well take your seat." I stumbled back to the bench.

Tissier moved up to the long table. He admitted that he had allowed anyone who wanted to do so to cross his estate because, he said, he did not admit the right of foreigners to make regulations binding Frenchmen in France.

Father Christian followed Tissier. I wish I had a stenographic record of his testimony. As nearly as I can remember, he said: "I am a priest, but in this war I have been a soldier, and a soldier who has not surrendered. I was fighting for justice. I do not expect to find that justice in this court. But I know that, in the end,

divine justice will prevail; and the verdict of God will be pronounced against you, who presume to judge us."

Last to be called was Chancel, and once more he was addressed as Corbier. He was accused of being one of us, although
the only evidence against him was a picture postcard found in
his apartment, a caricature of the Führer, with "*Vive la France!...
A bas les Boches!*" written on it.

Then the prosecutor, mingling correct details with pure
imagination, asked that we be sentenced in the name of Hitler.
The lawyers for the defense were allowed to speak, and the judge
announced that he and his associates would retire to discuss the
verdict. Just as they rose to leave the room, Dr. Hager rushed in,
out of breath and excited. He conferred with the judge, pulling
out papers from a folder. The judge rapped with his gavel. "The
trial is reopened," he said. "New evidence has been discovered.
M. Chancel, stand up!"

I had to admire Chancel's presence of mind. He remained
motionless at this unexpected pronouncing of his name. But the
rest of us were trapped. Involuntarily, our heads swung toward
him.

"Dear me, Herr Chancel," the judge said. "I see that if you
have forgotten your name, your friends have not. You might as
well abandon the comedy, Herr Chancel—or Herr Corbier, if
you prefer. Would you like to modify your statement that you
don't know the defendants and had nothing to do with their
activities?"

"If you are so well informed already," said Chancel, "it seems
unnecessary that I should add anything."

The judge scowled. "It is a matter of indifference to this court
whether you admit or continue to deny your obvious connection
with this criminal conspiracy."

The prosecutor rose. "I should like to include the name of
Herr Chancel among those for whom the death penalty is
demanded."

"The alteration is noted," said the judge.

It was two o'clock when the doors opened and the judges filed
back into the courtroom. The presiding judge pronounced sen-

tence: for Kitty, death; for Father Christian, death; for Chancel, five years at hard labor; for Tissier, four years at hard labor; for myself, three years at hard labor.

The horror I felt must have been apparent in my face. Although my sentence was lightest of all, I couldn't face the thought of three more years of that terrible prison. Then I remembered the judgment just passed on Kitty and Father Christian—death—from which, so far as I have ever learned, neither was able to escape. Kitty caught me by the arm. "Don't cry, Etta. Don't let these Germans see us lose our dignity." I squeezed her hand hard and choked down my sobs. Kitty, condemned to die, was consoling me!

Once more we were locked into the prison van together. Both of us realized that this would probably be the last time we would ever see each other. I broke down and, laying my head on Kitty's chest, wept bitterly. Kitty smoothed my hair.

"I should have made you go home when there was still time," she said. "Don't worry about me. There was a time when I was terrified at the thought of death; but I have become accustomed to that thought now. Millions will have died before this war is over, and one more death will make little difference—especially when you remember that I was not the one who failed, but who succeeded, who won a 150-to-1 victory against the Germans. Promise me that you will never think of me sadly, Etta. Remember only the strong young boys with the brave hearts whom we sent home again. I have given England back 150 lives for the one she is losing now."

The van came to a clanking stop. We had reached the prison.

And so I come to the end of my story. You know the rest—how, after serving a year in prison, I was exchanged for Johanna Hoffmann, how I boarded the *Drottningholm* for the return to the free soil of my own country.

My only desire now was to forget all that had happened to me. Yet I knew that I could never forget the faces of those I had left behind me—Kitty, Father Christian, Tissier, Chancel and all the others.

The One That Got Away

Condensed from the book

By Kendal Burt and James Leasor

Oberleutnant Franz von Werra was one of the most flamboyant and reckless German fighter pilots of World War II. When he decided to break out of a British prisoner-of-war camp, circumstances and his own quick wits had made him an exceptionally dangerous man to British security. The British knew this, yet he eluded them—by means which were to make his feat an escape classic. The British authors Kendal Burt and James Leasor carefully researched this all-but-incredible story from both British and German sources.

Oberleutnant Franz von Werra, marching between impassive guards, traversed the long corridors of the British Air Interrogation Center at Cockfosters and was ushered into a pleasant, richly paneled room. It was completely dark save for a powerful reading lamp which cast a circle of light on a massive mahogany desk. Behind this sat an RAF officer with a thin, lined face, bushy eyebrows and an upcurling mustache.

He spoke in facile but slightly accented German. "I am Squadron Leader Hawkes. Sit down, Oberleutnant."

As the prisoner clicked his heels and bowed stiffly, he noted a silver-knobbed walking stick propped against the desk. It reminded him of the foppish British officer of German newspaper cartoons.

"Oberleutnant, 13 English aircraft shot down and half a dozen destroyed on the ground is quite a respectable score." There was cold mockery in the interrogator's voice. "As a minor ace of the first war, I am especially thrilled to meet one of the major aces of the second."

Von Werra mimicked the other's casual drawl. "I have not read of your exploits in studying the Royal Flying Corps' fascinating history," he said, "and, intrigued as I am to meet you, I am not going to reveal any military information." He paused for a moment, then added with sneering insolence, "But how stupid of me, Herr Major! No doubt it was you who shot me down!"

The Squadron Leader said nothing. The long silence which ensued was finally broken by the wail of an air-raid siren. Another siren began, and then another, until the screaming cacophony covered the whole London area. Von Werra smirked. More German bombers overhead. It was September 7, 1940, and the all-out Battle of Britain was well under way.

Presently the wailing died down siren by siren.

"Tell me, Oberleutnant," Squadron Leader Hawkes said casually, "which of your friends in the Headquarters *Staffel* of the Second *Gruppe* of Number Three Fighter *Geschwader* will look after Simba, your pet lion cub? 'Sanni,' perhaps?"

Von Werra gasped. Since his capture two days before, he had divulged only his name, rank and serial number. Yet a British interrogator knew not only his unit but the name of his pet lion and the nickname of his best friend. Nor was Hawkes bluffing; he seemed to know everything. He even commented on how slender was Von Werra's claim to being a baron, a title which the young flier often used.

For the next two hours Squadron Leader Hawkes continued his attack, his sarcastic voice cutting deeply into the German's arrogance. "I must congratulate you, Oberleutnant," he said, "on your flair for publicity." He brought out a transcript of a German radio program on which Von Werra had told of shooting down five Hurricanes and destroying four more on the ground, all in one solo raid. Although there had been no witnesses, the feat had been lauded in Germany as "the greatest fighter exploit of the war."

Hawkes' voice was icy. "You know as well as I do, Oberleutnant 'Baron' von Werra, 'The Red Devil,' 'The Terror of the RAF,' that there was no incident even remotely resembling your alleged exploit."

The RAF could hardly have suffered the loss of nine Hurricanes without being aware of it, Hawkes said. And item by item he pointed out the absurdities and holes in the fabrication, including the discrepancies between what Von Werra had said over the radio and what he had told the press. In the end the spuriousness of the story was manifest, and Von Werra sat silent and abashed.

And now the Squadron Leader struck. "Suppose your fellow prisoners get to know what you and I know about your famous exploit—what sort of life would you lead in prison camp? You'd be the laughingstock of the place."

Von Werra smiled weakly. "Herr Major, I know what price you are likely to ask for keeping quiet—military information." His voice gathered firmness. "I will tell you nothing, Herr Major! You may make it impossible for me to live with my comrades, but the alternative would be worse. I couldn't live with myself."

The interview was over. Von Werra had not broken under the grilling. And as Hawkes rang for the guard, the prisoner showed a flash of his irrepressible spirit. "Herr Major, I'll wager a magnum of champagne against 10 cigarettes that I escape in six months." It was as well that Hawkes did not accept the wager.

Then 26 years old, willful, exuberant, intensely ambitious, Franz von Werra had been in the Luftwaffe since its inception more than five years earlier. He had quickly got the measure of that service: the only way to get ahead was to get oneself talked about. What impressed was dash, aggressiveness, a touch of daredeviltry. Von Werra tried to outfly all the others in mock combats, indulged in such prohibited stunting as diving under bridges and low aerobatics over his girl's house. Whereas other pilots had pet dogs, falcons, even pigs, Von Werra must keep a lion cub. To add to his glamour, he adopted the title of Baron, which, despite its dubious legitimacy, had a certain snob value even in Hitler's forces.

When war came the important thing, of course, was to become an ace, and Von Werra actually downed eight verified planes, which was not a bad record. But the Polish, Norwegian, Dutch and Belgian air forces had been demolished in a matter of days, and the French Air Force was hard hit. In a few weeks the RAF too would be knocked out, and all the Nazi fliers were scrambling for honors before it was too late. Von Werra's boast of destroying nine Hurricanes in his famous unwitnessed raid put his score near the top. The authorities, after reducing his claim from nine planes to five, awarded him the Knight's Cross. (See photograph on page 342.) But before he could receive it, on his 10th mission over England he was shot down.

However vainglorious his boasting, Von Werra had an acute sense of security. At a time when the supremely confident Nazis expected few losses and scarcely bothered to give their airmen security briefings, the carelessness of captured fliers was a boon to British Intelligence. They often carried secret documents, maps, strength reports, technical data, diaries—or tattered bus tickets, movie ticket stubs and crumpled sales slips from which it was possible to deduce the location of various units. But Von Werra burned all the papers on his person immediately after his plane crashed.

His first interrogation convinced him that the German leaders were right: the British *were* stupid. A courteous, informal Army captain offered him a cigarette and, ignoring their roles as captor and captive, seemed bent only on talking about German politics, Nazi ideals, Germany's claim to colonies and the like. Vastly relieved not to be questioned on military matters, Von Werra had relaxed, become expansive and talked freely. Only later did he realize how astutely the interview had been managed: the interrogator had simply been sizing him up to decide which techniques would yield the best results in future interrogations.

Although Von Werra had now successfully withstood the hammering of Squadron Leader Hawkes, who was his second interrogator, RAF Intelligence was by no means finished with him. In the ensuing days he was questioned repeatedly at all hours of the day and night by half a dozen different German-speaking officers working separately and in collaboration. Between them they tried every trick in the business to get him to talk.

Before they had finally finished with him, the interrogators had worked on Von Werra for a total of three weeks. During that time he had not knowingly given away any military information whatsoever. But in the process of questioning him the British had unavoidably provided him with an almost complete picture of their methods and techniques. As it turned out, this information was of far greater importance than anything he could have told them. For Oberleutnant von Werra was profoundly impressed by the subtlety and insidiousness of British interrogation methods, and he now knew more about them than did any other German—a fact that later had far-reaching consequences for both the Royal Air Force and the Luftwaffe.

Von Werra was sent to Grizedale Hall, a prisoner-of-war camp situated in the wild moorland country, 20 miles from the Irish Sea. The building was a gaunt stone mansion of 40 rooms and was very closely guarded. Within 10 days of his arrival Von Werra had devised a scheme for escaping.

Every other day 24 prisoners were taken out on the road for exercise. They turned either north or south—apparently at the whim of the mounted sergeant who accompanied them—and were marched at a smart pace for three kilometers, then rested at a bend in the road for 10 minutes and were marched back. Discipline was strict and surveillance heavy; in addition to the mounted sergeant there were an officer on foot in charge, four guards in front and four in the rear.

The rest area on the northern route, where a wire fence gave onto an open meadow, offered no possible cover. On the southern route, however, the rest area was beside a stone fence. If some of his fellow prisoners distracted the guards, and others massed to shield his movements—and Von Werra had worked out the details of how this could be done—he might vault the fence and run crouched behind it until he reached a blind spot in the road, then escape into thick woods. Once free, he would make his way to the coast and try to stow away on a neutral vessel.

Two days later the plan was put into action. At the camp gates, since there was danger that the northern route might be taken, one of the prisoners gave the orders to turn south. This was not challenged. The officer in charge thought the mounted sergeant had given the order; the sergeant assumed it had been given by the officer.

When the usual rest was called, the guards took their positions on one side of the road while the prisoners went to the opposite side and stood or milled around in front of the stone wall. The appearance of a greengrocer's cart on the usually deserted road was at first dismaying. But it proved the perfect distraction, for the guards bought apples from it and the sergeant fed one to his horse. When the cart had gone, Von Werra moved in behind the tallest of his comrades, who by prearranged plan were carefully grouped together. He hoisted himself onto the wall. An elbow nudged him as a signal that no guards had been alerted, and he rolled over, dropping noiselessly into the field behind.

The prisoners re-formed in column and the sergeant gave the order to march. When they had gone 300 yards the Germans broke into a song—one of two alternative songs they had agreed to sing at this point. It was the favorable one, and it let Von Werra know that he had not yet been missed. Now safely out of sight of his captors, who had disappeared around the bend, he dashed across the road and disappeared into a thick pine wood on the other side.

Singing on the walks was strictly forbidden, and when the prisoners suddenly burst into full-voiced song the guards had been taken by surprise. Suspecting something amiss, the sergeant rode up and down the column trying to count the prisoners. But they kept moving from one rank to another and back again—a ruse suggested by Von Werra—so that it was difficult to tell how many there were. After a word with the officer, the sergeant finally rode ahead of the column, drew his revolver and ordered a halt.

When the POW's shuffled to a stop, the officer went down the length of the column, counting. The count was 23 instead of 24. There could be no doubt about it: one prisoner was missing.

Local residents still recall the furor that ensued. By 5:30 the whole anti-escape machinery of the area had been set in motion.

Lorries, staff cars, Bren-gun carriers and motorcycles dashed about the countryside frenziedly. The Home Guards and police were brought into the hunt.

Von Werra disappeared completely for three days and nights. As the days went by, more and more police and troops were called in. The German had simply vanished.

Even in the wildest parts of the Lake District there were many small stone huts, used for storing sheep fodder. About 11 p.m. of the fourth day two Home Guards patrolling the Broughton Mills area, only four or five miles from the coast, found a hut on which the padlocked door had been forced open. Shining a bicycle lamp within, they discovered the fugitive. His face was thin and drawn, his clothes bedraggled, his boots worn down.

While one of the Home Guards held a gun on him, the other tied a cord tightly around Von Werra's wrist, then tied it to his own wrist. But before they could lead him away, Von Werra in a perfectly timed maneuver sent the man he was tied to sprawling, and at the same time knocked out the light. Then, leaping out of reach of the second man and jerking with all his might, he snatched the cord free and disappeared into the night.

He was not found again until after two more days of intensive search. At 2:30 p.m. on the sixth day of Von Werra's freedom a shepherd spotted him sneaking through the bracken on a 1200-foot hill overlooking the Duddon Valley. The Cumberland and Westmorland Constabulary quickly threw a tight cordon around the base of the hill. When they had closed in on Von Werra, they at once put handcuffs on the captive. This time he did not get away.

After serving 21 days of solitary confinement as punishment for his escape, Von Werra was removed from Grizedale Hall and sent to Swanwick, a POW camp in the Midlands. But having got away once, he was confident that he could do it again and was determined to try.

Swanwick was surrounded by two heavy barbed-wire fences, and the narrow land between them was patrolled constantly. Watchtowers, set at intervals of 50 yards along the outside fence, were equipped with machine guns and searchlights, and the fences were floodlit at night except during air-raid alerts, at which time the guard was reinforced. The only possible means of escape, he decided, was by tunneling.

The building he was assigned to was only a yard or so from the inner boundary fence, and Von Werra figured that a tunnel only 14 yards long, starting from a small unused room on the ground floor, would emerge beyond the outer fence. The exit would be uncomfortably close to one of the watchtowers, but a few shrubs and trees offered a little cover. The project seemed possible, and within a few days five other officers enthusiastically joined with him to organize the *Swanwick Tiefbau A.G.* (Swanwick Mining Co.).

From the first the undertaking went well. All the prisoners coöperated, standing lookout at strategic spots and shouting

coded warnings when the noise of digging or prying out large stones threatened to reach the sentries' ears. When noise was unavoidable it was drowned out by group singing, harmonica playing, loudly boisterous card games, even a staged free-for-all fight. One month after it was started, the tunnel, a "rabbit hole" just big enough to crawl through, was completed.

Meanwhile the five tunnelers (one of the original six pessimistically gave up midway) had made their plans for getting out of England. The sale of a diamond ring to a guard for a pound had given them each four shillings. With this scant fund for bus fare, two of the men hoped to reach Liverpool and stow away on a neutral ship for Ireland. Two others would make for Glasgow, where they would also try to board a neutral ship. Only Von Werra decided to go it alone.

His experience while on the run in the Lake District had convinced him that a German escaper in Britain stood very little chance unless he could somehow get out of the country before the search for him got under way. The only means of doing this was by air. Von Werra therefore decided on the boldest possible course: he would make his way to the nearest RAF field and try to get his hands on a plane.

Casting about for a simple but convincing masquerade, he decided to pass himself off as a Dutch pilot who had crashed in returning from a bombing mission. This was plausible, for there were now a great many Czech, Dutch, Norwegian and Polish refugees serving in the RAF, speaking broken English (his own English was fair) and wearing relatively unfamiliar uniforms. Since few airmen in the Midlands were likely to know much about the workings of the Coastal Command, he would be from the "Mixed Special Bomber Squadron, Coastal Command," based at Aberdeen. Aberdeen would be a long way away, and the vague and ambiguous designation "Mixed Special Bomber Squadron" would allow him a certain latitude for explanations.

For a uniform, one prisoner donated a flying suit which he had somehow managed to retain, a second supplied fur-lined flying boots and a third leather gloves. To complete his wardrobe, he bought a woolen tartan scarf from the camp shop. He could forgo identification papers, but would certainly need a British service identity disk, which was made of vulcanized fiber. This was impossible to obtain, but the camp's "Forgery Department" provided him with an exact replica made of cardboard.

At nine p.m. on December 20, wearing black pajamas over his flying suit to protect it, Von Werra cautiously broke through the last layer of earth above the tunnel exit. Conditions were ideal. The night was dark, and an air-raid alert had caused the floodlights to be turned off. Silently Von Werra made his way through the darkness and a few minutes later his companions emerged one by one from the tunnel. At a barn some 200 yards distant they whispered their good-byes to Von Werra, shook his hand and then went their separate ways.

Since the raid was still on, Von Werra decided to wait for the all-clear before venturing farther, lest he be picked up as a survivor of a crashed German aircraft. There was no hurry. With any luck, the escape would not be discovered until roll call next morning, which gave him at least 10 hours' start. He crouched down near the barn and waited.

At three o'clock the all-clear had still not sounded. Von Werra dared not wait any longer. He emerged from his hiding place, tucked the camp's copy of *The Times* under his arm as a prop and set off across the fields.

Von Werra walked for miles along country roads without encountering a soul. At 4:30 he heard a locomotive hissing on a nearby siding. He stepped over to it and climbed into the cab.

The engineer's jaw dropped. "What d'you think you're up to?" he demanded.

"I am Captain van Lott, formerly of the Royal Dutch Air Force, now with the RAF," Von Werra explained matter-of-factly. "I've just made a forced landing in a Wellington after being hit by flak in a raid over Denmark. I must get to the nearest RAF field quickly. Where is the nearest telephone, please?"

The engineer was helpful. "My mate Harold here's just going off duty. He'll walk you along to the station."

Walking along the track with the engineer's mate, Von Werra reached the Codnor Park station at 5:30. But the telephone was in the office, which was locked, and the clerk, Sam Eaton, did not arrive till almost six. Nervously, Von Werra waited.

When Eaton appeared, he was out of sorts and listened impatiently to Von Werra's story of crashing a bomber nearby and of leaving the uninjured crew at a farmhouse which had no telephone. "Will you please ring up the nearest RAF field and ask them to send a car to fetch me? My base at Aberdeen will send a plane for me and my crew there."

Manifestly skeptical, the booking clerk asked several questions about the crash, then picked up the telephone. "Put me through to the police, please!"

Von Werra sat rigid while the other spoke at length into the telephone. But apparently Eaton merely wanted to rid himself of the problem. For when he hung up he said, "Don't worry. Somebody will be right along. They're in a better position to help you than I am."

A porter now brewed tea. Eaton offered Von Werra a cup and took one himself, and as the three sat waiting for the police, Von Werra's magnetism and genial plausibility began to have their effect. For half an hour he answered questions about the crash and the bombing raid and talked expansively about the RAF. Finally he confided—"I really should not tell you this"— that he belonged to a special squadron, and that the night's raid had been a test for a new bombsight. "Now you see why it is urgent that I get back quickly?"

Eaton was visibly impressed. "Really! I'm very sorry. If you'd said so before . . . Should I ring up the base?"

"Please do."

The clerk lifted the receiver and asked for Hucknall aerodrome. When he finally got through to the duty officer, he explained about Von Werra briefly, then motioned Von Werra himself to the phone. The Hucknall duty officer was hard to convince. He asked a great many questions about the crash and remarked that it was curious that he had not heard about it. But at last he said, "I suppose I'll have to do something about you. I'll send a vehicle to pick you up."

At one minute past seven the police arrived. There were two

plain-clothes men and a uniformed sergeant. For a time they eyed Von Werra in silence, their looks neither friendly nor hostile. Then one of the detectives suddenly rapped out: "*Sprechen Sie Deutsch?*"

Von Werra answered in English, "Yes, I speak a little German. Most Dutch people do."

Instantly the tension relaxed. "*Sprechen Sie Deutsch?*" was evidently the only German they knew. The second plain-clothes man said, "So you're one of the Coastal Command boys, eh?"

Von Werra now knew that they had not come to arrest him. They were simply checking on his story. He had read enough accounts of RAF bombing raids in the British papers to be convincing. "Yes," he said, giving his most disarming smile. "Last night it was a wizard show, but we nearly bought it."

At this knowing RAF slang, the three policemen looked significantly from one to the other and grinned. "Where are your papers?" the sergeant asked.

Von Werra was commendably patient. "Do you not know that it is forbidden to take personal papers into the air? With us, the special squadron, that rule is strictest."

After that they did not even ask to see his identity disk. And although they asked a great many more questions, Von Werra's answers, together with the fact that Hucknall was sending a car for him, seemed to satisfy them. Five minutes after the police had left, an aircraftman came in and saluted smartly. "Transport for Hucknall, sir," he announced. Von Werra's spirits soared again. As he settled himself comfortably for the 10-mile ride to the RAF base, he felt that he might yet steal that airplane.

Contrary to Von Werra's supposition, the Hucknall duty officer had not sent the car because he was convinced Captain van Lott was genuine but because he strongly suspected he was bogus. He had not heard of the escape from Swanwick; but Van Lott had talked too much. And it seemed incredible that a bomber could crash in the dark without injuring any of the crew. The officer decided he'd better check Captain van Lott's story on the spot.

As a precaution the duty officer gave the driver of the car a

gun and warned him that Van Lott might be a saboteur or escaped prisoner. The windows of the station headquarters were
barred, and he locked all the doors except the main entrance. In
the adjutant's office he made a roaring fire so Van Lott would be
forced to take off his flying suit and disclose his uniform.

It had just turned daylight when the driver drew up at HQ
and ushered Von Werra into the adjutant's office. The duty
officer, who wanted to be occupied so that he could study his
visitor covertly, was taking down the blackout shutters.

He saw a man of five feet seven inches with curly hair, a frank
boyish face and a pleasant smile. He looked neither villainous
nor Teutonic. But his flying suit was non-regulation and of a
strange type—pale gray-green with a long diagonal zip.

Still fumbling with the blackout shutters, the officer casually
inquired, "Van Lott?—I won't keep you a moment. You may
find it a bit fuggy in here. Take your flying suit off. Sit down,
make yourself at home!" The room was in fact as stifling as the
stokehold of a ship. But Von Werra replied, "It is not worth the
trouble. My plane shall arrive any minute from Aberdeen."
And, unobtrusively, he moved as far as possible from the fire.

The duty officer finished with the shutters and returned to his
desk. Von Werra shook hands with him. "I am sorry to bother
you," he said. "I wish not to make you trouble. I shall go and
wait by the control tower for my plane, yes?"

"That's not necessary. Stay in here in the warm! Control will
ring me as soon as contact is made with your aircraft." Since his
visitor betrayed no signs of discomfort at the heat and seemed
to find it perfectly normal, the duty officer tried a new tack.
"You certainly had the most amazing luck with that crash," he
said. "The details sounded very confusing over the phone.
You'd better tell me the whole story again—you understand I
have to make a report."

While Von Werra hurriedly described the raid and the crash,
the officer made notes and asked probing questions. When Von
Werra told of being interviewed by the police, it gave him pause.
If true, this put a rather different complexion on the problem. If
the police had been satisfied with his story . . .

Nevertheless he now picked up the phone and asked to have a call put through to the base at Aberdeen. A talk with the commanding officer there would settle the matter.

"Is that really necessary?" Von Werra asked. "My plane must arrive soon."

"Sorry. You know how it is—red tape and all that. And you realize," the duty officer added, "that you must identify yourself properly. Suppose you show me your identity disk."

Von Werra laughed tolerantly at this insistence on formality. He had worn his carefully forged cardboard disk suspended around his neck. Confidently he unzipped the top of his flying suit and reached for it. As his fingers touched it, he gasped. Perspiration and the heat of his body had reduced the cardboard to a clammy pulp. He dare not produce it.

As he continued to fumble uncertainly and the other waited patiently, the telephone rang. He was saved. The duty officer picked up the receiver. "Right!" he said to the operator. "About time! Put me through. . . . Hallo, Aberdeen?" The connection was evidently a bad one, for he soon began shouting in exasperation.

But Von Werra had no desire to hear the conversation. Backing to the door, he caught the officer's eye, raised his eyebrows interrogatively and went through the motions of washing his hands. "Won't be long!" he said and stomped down the corridor to the door marked "Gentlemen." This he opened and slammed—from the outside. Then he tiptoed on to the main door. As he opened it he could hear the duty officer shouting:

"Captain van Lott . . . two words. . . . A Dutchman . . ."

Once outside, he crouched low until he had passed under the adjutant's windows, then sprinted toward the hangars. Time was now the vital factor. Fractions of seconds mattered.

Near the first hangar he slowed to a brisk, purposeful walk. Construction was under way here, and carpenters looked down curiously at him from scaffolding. Dodging around a cement mixer and almost bumping into a laborer who was cutting open a cement bag, he came to a row of twin-engine bombers. These were no good to him, so he strode on.

Ahead, at the second hangar, was a group of Hurricanes. One part of Hucknall was an RAF training base for pilots, another part a highly secret Rolls Royce experimental station. It was this secret, heavily guarded section that Von Werra had now penetrated. The confusion of the construction area had provided a loophole in its normally faultless security.

He approached the only mechanic in sight. "Good morning," he said authoritatively. "I am Captain van Lott, a Dutch pilot. I have just been posted here. But Hurricanes I have not yet flown. The adjutant sent me to you to learn the controls and make a practice flight. Which one is ready to take off?"

The mechanic, a civilian employe of Rolls Royce, looked puzzled. "Haven't you come to the wrong place?" he asked. "This is a private firm."

"I know. But the adjutant said it was to you I should come. I haven't much time."

The mechanic pondered. Then the probable explanation dawned on him. The airman must be a civilian ferry pilot from the Air Transport Command, come to take delivery of a Hurricane. Such civilian pilots were known by the courtesy title of "Captain," and many of them were foreigners who spoke little English. "I can't do anything for you until you've signed the Visitors' Book," he said. "Hang on a minute, Captain. I'll go fetch the manager."

When the mechanic went into the hangar, Von Werra leaned against the fuselage of a Hurricane. A brand-new beautiful Hurricane with not a scratch on it! (It was a Mark II, a still-secret type not yet used in combat.) He was tempted to climb in and try to start the engine on his own. But this might wreck his chances altogether. There were certain controls he must be sure about before he attempted to take off.

The mechanic reappeared with a man in a khaki smock, presumably the manager. The official smiled and greeted him pleasantly. "I hear you've come to collect a Hurricane. If you'll come with me, we'll get your paper work fixed up."

"It shall take long? I have little time," Von Werra replied. "I just want to learn controls of the Hurricane."

"I'm afraid nothing can be done until you sign the Visitors' Book. We'll soon fix you up, though."

Reluctantly Von Werra followed him into the hangar. The manager led him to a small office where a man in a blue uniform, evidently a works policeman, presided over a large ledger. The policeman now took over. "If you'll sign here, sir . . ."

Using printed characters, lest his German-style script betray him, Von Werra completed the form. The manager now pronounced everything in order save for the receipt of the written orders covering the collection of the Hurricane. Von Werra said these were with his kit, which should arrive any moment by plane. Meanwhile, could he have instruction on the Hurricane controls?

"Righto," said the manager. "We can do that all right now you've signed the book."

As he emerged from the hangar with the mechanic, Von Werra glanced apprehensively about. No RAF uniforms were yet in sight. If the duty officer would only give him five more minutes!

The mechanic walked over to one of the new Hurricanes and slid back the hood, and Von Werra climbed in. The mechanic began to explain the unfamiliar instrument panel and controls. Von Werra hung on every word. Much of it was confusing, but he tried to concentrate on essentials so that he would not stand the Hurricane on its nose in the take-off. Before the mechanic could anticipate his move, he jabbed the starter button.

"Don't do that!" cried the mechanic in alarm. "Can't start without the trolley accumulator."

"Fetch it, then!" Von Werra ordered.

"Somebody else is using it."

Von Werra smiled warmly. "Please get it, yes? I really am in a hurry." Obligingly, the mechanic went to get it, and presently returned driving the electric starter across the tarmac. He halted it under the engine, jumped off and raised the cable over his shoulder to plug it in. As Von Werra operated the fuel-injection pump, the aircraft swayed slightly and a voice above him ordered quietly: "Get out!"

Von Werra looked up and found himself facing the muzzle of

an automatic pistol and the cold blue eyes of the duty officer.

"I spoke to Aberdeen," the officer said flatly. The connection to Aberdeen had been very bad, and only by constant shouting and repetition had the duty officer been able to make himself understood or to understand the man at the other end. But at long last he had learned that Van Lott was bogus.

In retrospect, the gaping holes in Von Werra's story were evident—one glaring implausibility, for example, being that there is no such rank as captain in the RAF. But the fact remains that it *did* succeed in getting him onto a British airfield, where he all but took off in a Hurricane. The British, always taken by audacity, enterprise and an engaging personality, were inclined to admire the exploit. As one of the Rolls Royce officials remarked, "A lot of us were rather sorry he didn't make it!"

The five escapers, all of whom were caught within 24 hours, were given 14 days of solitary confinement at Swanwick. Perhaps the mildness of the punishment was due to the fact that the commandant knew he would soon be rid of the lot. On the last morning of their sentence he announced that they would be sent to Canada the next day with a batch of other prisoners.

To Von Werra this simply meant another opportunity to escape, and Canada had the great advantage of being adjacent to the then *neutral* United States. From one of the other prisoners who knew something of the country he at once began to learn all he could about Canadian geography and customs.

When the *Duchess of York* sailed from Greenock, Scotland, in January 1941 with 1050 prisoners aboard, Von Werra was kept under special guard until the moment of departure, an attention he found rather flattering. During the voyage he spent long periods immersed in a tub filled from a tap which ran ice-cold water. He wanted to harden himself, in case he got a chance to leap overboard when the ship landed.

No such opportunity occurred when the vessel docked at Halifax, and he now looked hopefully at the train into which the prisoners were shepherded. In Von Werra's coach there were 35 prisoners and 12 guards. Three guards were on duty at a time, and they stood in the center aisle: one at each end of the car and one in the middle. Prisoners were escorted to the toilet one at a time, and the lavatory door was always kept open. There was ice between the coach's double windows.

When Von Werra learned that the train was bound for a camp in Ontario on the shore of Lake Superior, he knew that it would pass near the border. If he escaped in a reasonably settled section he might be able to hitchhike to the United States in a day. The only feasible way to get away was to dive out the window into the snow. This would be suicidal while the train was at full speed; yet it couldn't be done during a halt, for the guards were then particularly alert. While his seatmates watched the guards, Von Werra knelt down and managed to raise the inside window a quarter of an inch. The opening was hardly noticeable, but it allowed the car heat to reach the ice on the outer window.

Once the window was melted free, how was he to evade the scrutiny of the three guards to open it? And how was he to put on his overcoat? He would need it in the freezing Canadian winter, but if he donned it in the heated car he would certainly arouse suspicion. An escaper must have luck, and luck now solved these problems for Von Werra.

At the evening meal that day the prisoners were given a whole case of apples. They were starved for fruit and ate the lot. But the apples proved too much for their systems. From midnight onward long lines waited to go to the toilet, and some prisoners had to be escorted to the guards' toilet. Frequently there was only one guard left in the coach.

Despite the heat in the car, some of the sicker prisoners, white-faced and shivering, wrapped their coats or blankets about them and sat hugging their stomachs. Thus it seemed natural for Von Werra to put on his overcoat. Afterward he sat with his head in his hands.

As the train slowed for the next station, he waited for a signal that the guards were occupied, then stood up, unfolded his blanket and shook it out. Concealed behind this, one of his companions knelt down and slid the inner window open wide. During the station stop the remaining ice on the outside window melted quickly. The conspicuously clear glass now constituted a danger, but fortunately none of the guards noticed the window. When the train started up, several prisoners raised their hands to go to the toilet. While one of his companions repeated the blanket maneuver, Von Werra stood up, caught hold of the outside window and jerked upward. It did not move. He tried again. The window opened smoothly.

The next moment Von Werra dived through it head first and landed dazed but exhilarated in the snow. The others were able to close both windows unobserved, and his escape was not discovered until the train was several hundred miles away.

According to the Canadian authorities, Von Werra escaped from the train near Smith Falls, Ontario, when he was only 30 miles from the border. Characteristically, Von Werra later told the New York reporters that he left the train 100 miles north of Ottawa—a location that gave him a lot more elbow room for recounting extravagant Canadian adventures. In view of his talent for lying, how he actually got to the border is hard to say.

Indisputably, however, at seven p.m. on January 24 he did arrive at Johnstown, on the north bank of the St. Lawrence, and saw the twinkling lights of Ogdensburg, N. Y., beckoning from the other side. The river was frozen, and he hoped at first to cross it on the ice. But a quarter of a mile from the American shore he came on a channel of black, open water. He returned to the Canadian bank and walked along it until he came to a deserted summer camp. Here he eventually found what he was looking for, a long cigar-shaped mound in the snow. It was an overturned rowboat.

Using heavy wooden fence palings as levers, he laboriously pried it free from the ice and righted it. Then, exerting all his strength to push it, he inched the heavy boat across the ice to the open channel. He had no oars, but again luck was with him; the boat drifted smoothly to the American shore.

The instant it scraped the shore ice, Von Werra leaped out. On a road close to the riverbank he saw a parked car bearing New York license plates. The driver, a nurse from a nearby hospital, was just preparing to start it.

"Excuse me," he asked anxiously. "Is this America?" He

wanted to make sure, for he knew that in places the Canadian border extended well below the St. Lawrence.

"You are in Ogdensburg," the nurse replied.

He smiled wearily. "I am an officer of the German Air Force. I am—" he corrected himself—"I *was* a prisoner of war."

He was by no means safe yet. A German prisoner who had recently escaped into Minnesota had been jailed there for three months, then returned to Canada. Von Werra was saved from a similar fate by his flair for publicity.

When U.S. Immigration authorities charged him with illegal entry and turned him over to the Ogdensburg police, the reporters and feature writers quickly besieged Von Werra's cell. His boasting, exaggerations and colorful inventions gave them plenty to write about. Much of the newspaper comment was caustic. As the Ogdensburg *Journal* wrote: "At his mass press conference he spun stories that would have amazed Horatio Alger, Joseph Conrad or the author of the *Arabian Nights*." But the publicity given to him by the press, newsreels and radio made his case an international issue.

The German Consul, anxious to muzzle his embarrassing indiscretions, posted a $5000 bond, spirited him away to New York City and for a time saw that he was entertained royally at theaters, night clubs and social functions. In Germany the publicity given to his escape quickly elevated him to a national figure. Meanwhile Canada had tried to have him arrested for the theft of the $35 rowboat. And Britain was also making every effort to extradite Von Werra. On March 24 German consular officials told him certain new moves in Washington made it likely that he would soon be handed back to Canada. He was to forfeit his bond, which had now been raised to $15,000, and leave the country illegally at once.

FBI men had been detailed to follow Von Werra's movements, but he eluded them by a series of taxicab changes, took a train for El Paso and crossed the international bridge disguised as a Mexican laborer. The German Embassy in Mexico arranged a passport for him under an assumed name and secured air passage to Germany via Rio de Janeiro and Rome. He reached

Berlin on April 18, 1941. Goering promoted him to Hauptmann (Captain), and Hitler personally congratulated him on his escape and awarded him the long-delayed Knight's Cross for his supposed earlier exploit. There were many parties and receptions.

Von Werra's escape had consequences out of all proportion to its significance as an individual feat of daring. His report on British interrogation methods, subsequently expanded into a 12-page booklet which became standard issue for all German aircrews, had an immediate effect. Thereafter the British found the German airmen they captured extremely security-conscious.

A fortnight after Germany attacked Russia, Von Werra maneuvered to be sent to the front there. As commanding officer of the First *Gruppe* of No. 53 Fighter *Geschwader*—famous as the "Ace of Spades" *Geschwader*—he was credited with eight more air victories, bringing his supposed total to 21.

In September his *Gruppe* was moved to Holland and assigned to coastal-defense patrol. During a routine patrol late in October, Von Werra's plane developed an engine fault and dropped into the sea. German newspapers announced that he had been killed in action. But the court of inquiry which investigated the loss of the aircraft reported the accident due to "engine failure and the pilot's carelessness."

Fooling Enemy Airmen

By Don Wharton

By the end of 1941, World War II developed a bagful of new military ruses—especially in the air.

When the Germans began using radio beams to guide their aircraft to targets in England, British scientists found a neat answer. Two German beams, originating at widely separated points on the Continent, were aimed at the target so that Nazi night bombers, following one beam, could unload at the intersection. British wireless experts created a false intersection with a beam of their own—and the German bombers wasted their bombs on country fields. As a refinement, the British, using beams of the same wave length as the Germans, deflected the enemy beams. After that, Nazi pilots not only dropped their bombs in the wrong places but sometimes, homeward-bound, followed a British beam and ended up in the open sea when their gas ran out. (See "Fakery in the Air," page 390.)

A favorite ruse of a pilot in a tight fix was to pretend his plane had been hit and was falling out of control. The Germans equipped some planes with chemicals which created clouds of smoke, giving the impression the plane was on fire. This trick had a parallel in submarine warfare. A fake oil slick—and even phony debris—could be released, to make it appear that the craft had been shattered.

In the summer of 1941, before Pearl Harbor, an American walking along a road near Berlin stumbled upon one of the most elaborate ruses of the war. What caught his eye was a network of wires over an open field. He looked around cautiously. The wires started from a dugout and spread fanlike to small buildings a quarter of a mile apart. The buildings had no roofs or windowpanes, and the floors were piled with brush and wood shavings. The flick of a switch in the dugout could ignite the shavings, and at night the flames would flare through the windows and roofless tops like serious fires, hoodwinking Britain's night bombers.

My informant had discovered part of the dummy city of Berlin. Other cautious trips led to the discovery of miles of false streets, factories and railways. The phony streets were lined with large packing crates, each crate containing an electric light. From the air they looked like a section of Berlin incompletely blacked out. For extra realism the dummy city was given lots of anti-aircraft protection. Experts said that it was difficult for bomber crews not to be taken in, even when forewarned.

The Germans built other decoy cities and constructed an imitation of Ploesti, the Rumanian oil center, copying the big refineries and putting up canvas "oil tanks" which sent up clouds of black chemical smoke if they were bombed.

In England, where a single factory might be the objective of German raiders, an inexpensive building was erected some distance away. The real factory was perfectly blacked out, while blackout regulations seemed to be slightly violated by the decoy building. The result was a prodigious waste of expensive bombs.

Tricks of camouflage were amazingly refined. English factory areas were painted to resemble apartment houses, and military installations disguised as innocuous filling stations. Fake runways made of lime or white dust crisscrossed dummy airfields, while fake highways bisected real fields. An American observer back from Britain estimated that in certain sections a third of the "airfields" were dummies. One real airfield, bounded by a housing development, concealed the hangars by painting them to look like more housing, with doors, windows and flower boxes to match those of the real development.

The Germans transformed the airface of Berlin. Roofs blossomed with foliage, the outlines of ponds were altered by rafts covered with sod, and small lakes completely concealed by nets stretched from shore to shore. The broad Unter-den-Linden, normally an unmistakable landmark, was reduced to half its true width by means of scaffolding and netting.

At Hamburg the Germans were cursed with the Alster Basin, a bull's-eye in the heart of the city. With rafts and scaffolding they made the basin appear crisscrossed with streets and buildings; they built a fake bridge, created a false basin farther out in the bay, camouflaged nearby railroad tracks and painted streets across the station. British cameras finally uncovered the ruse. (See photograph on page 347.)

A ruse was expected to be detected eventually and was considered successful if it caused delay, waste and uncertainty. The Germans outwitted the British for several nights by putting a few "landing lights" on a dummy airfield—and lighting up the real field like a Christmas tree. The British got their revenge in Egypt when 18 Axis bombers escorted by 30 fighters bombed an array of imitation tanks camouflaged just badly enough to be detected by the enemy. In 1942, General Montgomery used decoys and other devices with superb success to confuse German reconnaissance before the surprise attack at El Alamein.

In many cases camouflage was successful if it simply blurred the target from the bomber's oblique view. Traveling five miles a minute at 20,000 feet, he had to see the target 10 miles away, get set at five, drop his bombs at three. If the camouflaged target was recognizable only from directly above, it was difficult to hit.

Nature often betrayed the camoufleur. One German airfield adjoined a farm clearly marked by irrigation ditches; the Nazis carried these across the airfield with paint which looked genuine in British photographs—until the real water in the ditches froze. Then the painted water on the field stood out like a neon sign. In foliage screens, artificial leaves had to be changed as the season advanced, for the deterioration of chlorophyll is so rapid that the difference soon showed in photos.

The camera was the main reliance of the air observer in uncovering the deceptions of the camoufleur. Paint might look genuine in a single photograph. But if pictures of the same spot were taken both morning and afternoon, the very similarity would often be a giveaway: the sun had changed, but the painted shadows had not; therefore they were fakes. British stereoscopic cameras pierced many German ruses. They took two parallel aerial photos at the same time; examined together through a stereoscope, these had a third-dimensional quality which showed the painted object's lack of depth.

The notion that the Germans and Japanese had a corner on military ingenuity is poppycock. Allied air corps had infrared photographs which detected paint and the difference between natural and artificial leaves. They were pioneers in night photography and in the use of color films that produced the picture as seen by the human eye.

Even before Pearl Harbor, Yankee ingenuity sprang into action. Bases were built to resemble farm communities. Coastal industrial areas were being equipped with the means of making artificial fog. American brains and inventiveness played a big part in military events that were to come.

The Thief and the Patriot

By Karin Michaëlis

Karin Michaëlis, who contributed this true story from her personal experiences, was a native of Denmark. One of the foremost literary figures of her country, she died in 1950.

In prewar Denmark we had many petty thieves but few real criminals, so there was great excitement when Hans Petersen became known as Denmark's "most dangerous burglar." But, although he had spent half of his 40 years in prison, he was not so frightening as he sounded, for pride in his craft would not allow him to dabble in vulgar forms of crime or harm anyone.

Petersen specialized in antiques. He would loot a house and the next day send a detailed report to the newspapers and to the police, telling them exactly what he had taken and what it was worth. If he had entered the home of a person with bad taste, he described this too, and often exposed prized "antiques" as fakes.

His most uproarious exploit was spending a weekend in the home of the chief of police, who was in the country with his family. Petersen reported that it was a very nice house but that the bedsprings sagged and the china was chipped.

The Danes will forgive almost anything if it makes them laugh, so the entire country keenly enjoyed this burglar's exploits. Nobody wanted the police to catch "H.P." But finally he was caught.

Acting as his own defense counsel, he told the court that during an earlier imprisonment someone had promised to help him if he would go straight, but when he left the penitentiary the only help he got was a pair of old trousers. There was no doubting the man's sincerity, and that in his bitter disappointment he had reacted violently against society.

H.P. confessed that he had taken his loot to London and had opened an antique shop there, engaging a reliable man to manage it without letting him know how the stock was acquired.

I decided to offer H.P. the moral support he obviously needed so badly, and wrote him that I would help him build up a new life when he was released. From his letters it was evident that he dreamed of leading a settled life. I went to the King and requested him to pardon the man. His Majesty asked if I realized the risk involved. "Your Majesty," I answered, "I am not at all afraid. I will take this man into my own home until he has shown us how he will behave."

His Majesty promised nothing, but when the King's next birthday came my friend the burglar received a pardon. Petersen wrote me that he would not arrive at my home on the island of Turö for a week because he had some errands to attend to in the nearby town of Svendborg. When he finally arrived and my mother saw him get out of the car, well dressed, very slender, slightly stooped, she could not believe her eyes. "That man a burglar?" she exclaimed. "He looks like a professor!"

After lunch I took our guest to one of the bungalows in my large garden. It was a tiny place, but sunny and attractive. He looked around and smiled. "Why, it looks quite homelike!" he said. He began to unpack several elegant suitcases, explaining that his trunks would come later. They did—several iron-bound affairs that disgorged fine Oriental rugs, vases and books.

One day I remembered that the kerosene in H.P.'s lamps must be low, and took a container over. When I knocked he answered, but let me wait; meantime there was great thumping and dragging of furniture. Finally he opened the door. The room was transformed with tastefully arranged objets d'art.

"I had barricaded the door," he said in a matter-of-fact voice. "But why?"

"Really, you are too naïve," he said. "You don't know those men—in the prison. The reason I went to Svendborg was to take out burglary insurance. As soon as the insurance papers come I won't have to be so careful. But now any one of them might sneak in and steal my first editions!"

H.P. had a way with people, and soon he was invited everywhere on the island—even for Sunday afternoon coffee at the parsonage. He was godfather at the christening of children. At parties he told marvelous stories of his more daring burglaries. He showed how to open locks with a hairpin, and how he could wriggle through an opening big enough for his head only.

On weekdays H.P. usually stayed in his cottage and worked at his memoirs. Unfortunately his writing was so pompous and his vocabulary so limited that the manuscript was dull reading.

After some months H.P. realized a long-cherished ambition—he opened an attractive shop for old and rare books in Copenhagen. The money he had earned in prison was not enough capital, but lawyers, police officials, judges and others who were interested in him had taken up a collection.

One day H.P. met and fell in love with a pretty young woman who was employed in a prominent Copenhagen law firm. His doubtful past proved no handicap to his courtship, and their wedding was an event. It was held in the home of a Supreme Court attorney who invited many of his colleagues. The marriage turned out well. Every year, on the anniversary of his pardon, H.P. sent me a small gift and a note. Sometimes in the summer he and his wife came to my little island and spent a month in the bungalow. I noticed that H.P. had become not only a diligent shopkeeper but a thoughtful husband and a quiet and modest man. Our ex-burglar had really changed.

Then the Germans came to Denmark. The Germans knew all about H.P. He was on their list of people who might prove useful. Soon he was seen everywhere with German officers, even eating and drinking with them. He wore a beautifully tailored German uniform and bore himself with his old arrogant pride. All his former friends were disgusted. They had gone into the Underground, maintaining close contact with England and receiving directives and supplies for sabotage work.

On the island of Refshaleö the Germans seized and operated an important airplane-parts factory. The Underground decided to blow it up. Hundreds of people worked on the plan. Many of them got jobs in the factory; others arranged for automobile "accidents," street brawls and false fire alarms that would distract the German police in Copenhagen on the night chosen for the job. The time was set for midnight on a night when there would be no moon. Picked members were assigned to take care of the German sentries guarding the factory. Dynamite had been smuggled in and was ready for use. The time drew near.

Then the plan, so near perfection, seemed about to fail. Try as they might, the saboteurs could not find out how to open the special locks of the huge steel doors at the factory entrance.

Two days before the date set, one of the Underground chiefs received a note. He had had others in the same handwriting, giving information of German plans, but no one knew the sender. This one, however, was signed. "I shall be at the factory entrance at midnight two days from now," it said. "I shall be in German uniform. I will open the locks." The note was signed "H.P."

Did they dare to trust him? In desperation they decided to take the chance. At the appointed time he arrived, clad in his Nazi uniform. The nearest German sentries had been efficiently silenced; the group of dynamiters gathered in darkness at the gates had freedom of action for a few moments.

"I am here to keep my promise," H.P. said quietly. "I ask only one thing of you. If anything should happen to me, see that my name is cleared. My wife—"

He broke off and, stooping to the lock, went to work. In three minutes the door swung open.

Now he could have left quite safely, but he refused. "I want to set one of the fuses myself." Everything was ready. At the signal the men dispersed quickly to their places. There was a tense wait. Then one by one the dynamiters came running out of the building. From a safe distance they watched a mighty explosion rend the earth and light the sky for miles around. Nothing was left of the factory but twisted machinery and rubble.

But, quick as Hans Petersen had been with the lock, he was too slow in his dynamiting. He was the only man who did not come out. It was a grandiose ending. Somehow I feel that it was the one H.P. would have chosen. Who knows? Perhaps he *did*.

Human Torpedoes at Gibraltar

By Frank Goldsworthy

On a moonless night in September 1941 a submarine with decks awash crept into Cadiz Bay on the southwest coast of Spain and moored alongside the Italian tanker *Fulgor*. The submarine was the *Scirè* of the Italian Navy; its commander was Prince Junio Valerio Borghese; its mission was to collect human-torpedo crews for an attack on British ships at Gibraltar, only 80 miles away. That night began a two-year war within a war, fought in silence below the surface of Gibraltar Bay.

When Italy entered the war in 1940, the 6500-ton *Fulgor* took refuge in Cadiz Bay. Within a few months she was transformed into a secret depot ship for Italian submarines. Now, aboard her, as the *Scirè* moored, were six human-torpedo operators who had passed through Spain on false passports.

Within minutes the *Scirè* had them and was on her way. The submarine moved at periscope depth into the southwest corner of Gibraltar Bay, in Spanish waters four miles from the British harbor. While it was still below the surface, six men—wearing rubber suits with breathing equipment—passed out through the escape hatch onto her deck. There, clamped in cradles, lay three two-man, 22-foot torpedoes with detachable war heads. The crews—an officer and a petty officer for each—set themselves astride their torpedoes, pulled the release levers and floated to the surface. The attack was on.

The Italians called the torpedo a *maiale* (pig) because it looked like a swimming pig and was about as easy to maneuver. In its body the torpedo carried compressed-air tanks to regulate its depth and batteries to drive its double propellers. The maximum speed of those used in 1941 was three knots: a higher speed would have dragged the operators from their perch. The maximum range was 10 miles. (See photograph on page 336.)

The officer sitting in the forward position had controls for speed, steering and diving, a luminous depth gauge and luminous compass for use below the surface. The crews normally traveled with their chins just above the surface, but if patrol vessels were about they steered a course below the water.

One of the crew members has told the story of an attack: "You see your target ship outlined against the sky. At 50 yards you take a compass bearing, flood the diving tank, and the water closes over your head. It is cold and dark and silent.

"Now you are deep enough. Close the flooding valve, start up the motor and creep forward. Darkness turns to deeper darkness and you know you are below the ship. Stop the motor now and turn the valve which will push the water out of the diving tanks. As you rise you put your hand above your head. You wonder if it will meet smooth plates or knife-edge barnacles that will cut your fingers or—worst of all horrors—tear your rubber suit and let the sea seep through.

"Ah, there is the ship's bottom. Now push the torpedo back until your No. 2 man can grasp the foot-wide bilge keel which runs along each side of every big ship's hull. There is a tap on your shoulder. No. 2 has found the bilge and is fixing a clamp to it. Two taps. The clamp is fixed. Now forward to the other bilge keel.

"No. 2 is paying out a line. He fixes his second clamp, then back again to the center of the ship. No. 2 clambers around you to the war head in front and fastens it to the line. The torpedo bucks gently as the war head is detached. The clock which will fire its 500-pound charge in two and a half hours is ticking away the seconds. No. 2 climbs back to his seat. Three taps. The job is done. You start the motor, move forward from under the ship, rise gently. Now you may think of escape."

Licio Visintini, the most daring man in the group and one of the brains behind the human-torpedo offensive, took his torpedo into the actual harbor of Gibraltar that night in September 1941.

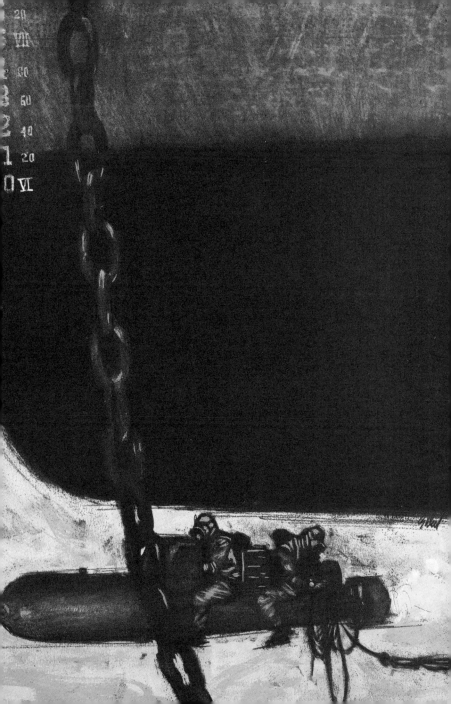

He had a device with which to cut the steel net that screened the harbor, but he did not have to use it; when the net was lowered to let a destroyer through, he slipped in, too. He left his war head fastened under a tanker, forced his way out beneath the net and got away.

The two other crews left their war heads dangling below ships in the bay, sank their torpedo craft and swam to the Spanish shore. Waiting on the beach was Commander Pierleoni, an Italian naval officer sent to Spain to direct sabotage activities under the cover of a consular appointment in Barcelona. As he was leading the men away, a roar and a cloud of smoke announced that a charge had broken the back of the naval tanker *Denbydale*. Soon after, there were similar explosions below the cargo ship *Durham* and the storage tanker *Fiona Shell*.

Pierleoni spent the winter of 1941–42 building up a sabotage organization in Spain. In July he was ready for his first land-based operation against Allied shipping at Gibraltar—a mass attack by 12 members of the "Gamma," a swimming assault group. The swimmers assembled in a villa near La Linea, which is Spanish territory just north of British Gibraltar. In the kitchen they put on long thick woolen combinations, toe-to-neck rubber suits, breathing equipment and camouflage-net helmets. At 11 p.m. on July 13 they set off to the beach.

On back and chest each man carried "bed-ring bombs"— small charges suspended in the center of inflatable rubber rings which would hold the charges against a ship's bottom until the firing clock had run its course. The five-pound charges were tiny compared with the human-torpedo war heads, but big enough to blow a hole in steel plates. Out in the bay were the dark shapes of 30 Allied ships. Each man was told to choose his own target.

Among the swimmers was Vago Giari, a tough, broad-shouldered peasant lad with the underwater dexterity of a seal. In the darkness below the ship he had selected, Giari bumped into another swimmer. They argued about whose target it was. "He was mad, quite mad," said Giari afterward. Giari went down and placed his bombs. When he came up, the other man had removed his mouthpiece and was shouting at him. "Why the ship's crew didn't hear him, I never understood," said Giari. This time he didn't argue, he pushed the other man's head under water and held it there till he had no more breath for yelling.

Six swimmers reached safety; the other six fell into the hands of a Spanish patrol and were sent to "internment" in a Seville hotel.

The attack was only a qualified success. Some operators never reached their targets, and some of the bombs were swept out by the current and exploded on the surface. Four ships were damaged. A couple of months later Giari and a companion badly damaged another ship.

Just inside the Spanish harbor of Algeciras, within sight of Gibraltar, lay the Italian tanker *Olterra*. Scuttled in shallow water by her captain when Italy declared war, in 1942 she was under a "neutrality" guard. But the young Spanish soldiers were more interested in scrounging cigarettes than in reporting suspicious activities.

Here a human-torpedo crew was organized by Licio Visintini. Inside the *Olterra* Visintini began to build a secret base. First the Italians cut a 25-foot-long section in the steel bulkhead separating the bow compartment from a small cargo hold, and hinged it. Telling the Spaniards they must clean the trimming tanks, they then pumped out the forward tanks till the bow rose high out of the water.

Early one morning, with the brandy-filled guard sound asleep, a door was cut in the side of the ship, opening into the bow compartment below the normal water line. It was hinged to open inward, and so neatly done that only a diver could have detected it. When the ship resumed her normal trim, the bow compartment was flooded but the hold was dry.

The plan was to sling human torpedoes on pulleys in the bow compartment. When the night came for an attack, they could be lowered into the water and pass out of the ship through the door in the side.

But first the torpedoes had to be brought from Italy. So the Spaniards were told, "We must overhaul the ship's engines to be ready for victory." If the Spaniards had been inquisitive about the cases of "boiler tubes" that were brought from Italy by lorry, they would have found that each case contained a 22-foot torpedo.

Several attacks were made from the *Olterra*. The first, on the night of December 7, 1942, cost the life of Visintini and his companion. The British Navy dropped explosive charges into Gibraltar Harbor at frequent intervals every night. One such charge killed the two torpedo men. Their bodies were found inside Gibraltar Harbor two weeks later. But the secret of the *Olterra* was still safe.

It was May 1943 before the Italians could bring enough new "machinery" to the *Olterra* to resume the attacks. This time they abandoned all hope of penetrating Gibraltar Harbor and selected targets from ships in the open anchorage. On the night of May 7 three human torpedoes left through the *Olterra's* open door, made an attack and returned safely. Two Allied cargo ships were heavily damaged, a third was a total loss.

Another attack from the *Olterra* was made on the night of August 3, 1943, with Lieutenant Commander Ernesto Notari in charge. Beneath his target, the 7000-ton U.S. Liberty ship *Harrison Grey Otis*, Notari encountered a new defense device—barbed wire hanging in the darkness. His No. 2 was Petty Officer Giannoli, a last-minute substitute. Comparatively inexperienced, Giannoli dropped the line between bilge-keel clamps, and the war head had to be clamped direct to the port bilge keel. While this was being done the torpedo began to rise. Notari opened the diving valves too wide and suddenly the torpedo plunged down out of control. Lungs bursting, head splitting, Notari fumbled with the controls as the luminous depth-gauge needle crept past its 34-meter (112 feet) limit—three times the normal training depth.

As suddenly as it had gone down, the torpedo began a rush to the surface. Notari expected to break his neck against the ship's bottom or rip his rubber suit to shreds on the barbed wire; but with a resounding splash he broke surface a yard from the ship's side. Half conscious, unable to think or act, he lay over the controls, expecting shouts or rifle shots. Nothing happened.

Slowly Notari gathered his wits. The motor would run only at top speed, and at that speed diving was impossible.

Notari took his only slender chance—a full-speed retreat on the surface for nearly four miles, expecting any moment that the fiery sparkle of his phosphorescent wake would bring a patrol boat in pursuit. Then a miracle happened. A school of porpoises joined him and frolicked around him all the way to Algeciras, providing the perfect cover for his wake and a safe return to the *Olterra*.

Meanwhile Giannoli, torn from his seat by the plunge of the torpedo, surfaced on the other side of the ship, and thought Notari drowned. He swam to the stern, stripped off his breathing gear and rubber suit and for two hours shivered in his woolen combinations on the rudder of the ship. When he judged the other crews would be back in the *Olterra* and the time was approaching for the explosion of the war head he himself had fixed, he swam along the side of the ship and shouted for help.

He was hauled on board. News of his capture was flashed to naval headquarters. A launch patrolling with a diver hurried to the *Harrison Grey Otis* to collect the prisoner and search the ship. The launch tied up alongside. Giannoli had been taken onto that launch and Petty Officer Bell, the diver, was putting his foot into the water when the 500-pound charge exploded on the other side of the ship. It blew a terrific hole in the engine room.

Within minutes of that explosion, the war head of a second torpedo crew broke the 10,000-ton Norwegian tanker *Thorshovdi* in two and sent great masses of thick oil drifting across the bay. The charge placed by a third crew heavily damaged the British 6000-ton *Stanridge*. All three ships sank in shallow water. With the exception of Giannoli, all the Italians reached the *Olterra* safely and left the next day for Italy.

The Italian assault groups did not confine their activities to the Gibraltar area. In 1941 three Italian human torpedoes penetrated Alexandria Harbor, and by the work of the six men who operated them the balance of naval power in the eastern Mediterranean was turned overnight against the Allies.

About three o'clock in the morning of December 19 two

Italians—Lieutenant de la Penne and Petty Officer Bianchi—
were seen swimming alongside the British battleship *Valiant*,
which with her sister ship, the *Queen Elizabeth*, was in the harbor.
The two men were hauled on board, but neither would answer
questions. Captain Morgan (later Vice-Admiral Sir Charles
Morgan) ordered their detention in the bottom of the ship at the
point where he thought their war head had been attached. For
two and a half hours the Italians sat tight-lipped and silent.

At 5:45 Lieutenant de la Penne asked to speak to the Captain.
He said: "I wish to warn you that your ship will blow up soon."

He would say no more. Captain Morgan ordered his men on
deck and closed the watertight doors. At 6:04 a.m. a heavy explosion put the *Valiant* out of action. There were no casualties.
Almost simultaneously the *Queen Elizabeth's* boiler room was
wrecked and flooded. A naval tanker nearby lost her stern and
propellers.

In 1944, after the Italian Armistice, Lieutenant de la Penne
joined the Allied side and took part, with conspicuous gallantry,
in a combined British and Italian attack on German-controlled
shipping at La Spezia. A cruiser and a submarine were sunk.
Admiral Morgan tried to get him a British decoration for this
feat, but Italy was still technically at war with Britain, and the
decoration was refused.

In March 1945 the Crown Prince of Italy went to Taranto
to inspect Italian naval units serving the Allies, and to present
decorations. Lieutenant de la Penne stepped forward to receive
the Gold Medal for his courage in attacking the *Valiant*. Prince
Umberto turned to Admiral Morgan.

"Come here, Morgan," he said. "This is your show."

Admiral Morgan took the medal and pinned it on the breast
of the man who had knocked out his own ship three years before.

We Organized the French Underground

By André Girard as told to George Kent

This article was written in 1944, while France was still occupied. No postwar historical account could recapture the courage of those hours and days of the secret soldiers of France as do these words by one of their leaders.

I know the French Underground from grim personal experience, for I became one of its organizers and officers immediately after the Armistice of 1940. Contrary to general opinion, it is not made up of isolated saboteurs, gunmen and pamphleteers operating haphazardly. The Underground is a real army, made up of the toughest and smartest of the old French *poilus* and their officers, as well as civilians organized into commando, sabotage, signal-corps, intelligence and engineering units. They cover the country; they include men of all classes and political beliefs.

Organization began while thousands of civilians and former soldiers stumbled south along the roads ahead of the invading Germans. Families often became separated. The newspapers ran columns of ads imploring information of lost ones: "Urgent. If you have seen my brother, Charles Pettigny, last heard from on the road to Chartres, please write Box —."

The Underground organizers answered the ads, saying in effect: "You are grief-stricken and homeless. But the war goes on. Lift your hand for France! Copy this and send it to three friends. Be a link in the chain that will break our chains!"

The idea grew and spread. The organizers rounded up their friends, telling them of the plan, warning them of the danger. And to each they put the question: Have you a friend you can trust? Then tell him, instruct him.

Aid came from high military men. Theoretically, all French war matériel was turned over to the German Army; actually, tons of munitions were secretly trucked away into hiding. A hoard of several million francs was seized and concealed. Also seized was a record of exultant telephone conversations between German officers and their French Quislings. This was filed away for use in the days of reckoning.

In the mountains of France the Underground constructed fastnesses which are called *places d'armes*. The passes and defiles are guarded by pillboxes, machine guns and artillery, and the terrain is such that one man could hold off a formidable enemy. Here is the France that has never been conquered.

The major effort at first was to control and direct acts of vengeance against the Germans. There was too much aimless murder of unimportant Nazis. For example, one girl of excellent family, whose fiancé had been shot by the invaders, lured six German soldiers in succession to her room and stabbed each one to death. A man made a practice of going out each night to kill a Nazi to avenge his eight-year-old daughter who had died in the flight before the enemy; he slew 15 before he was captured and executed. A farmer buried in his strawberry patch eight Germans whom he had strangled because his daughter had been murdered. Hundreds of Germans were killed—but hundreds of French people were slain in retaliation.

The Underground frowned upon this personal vengeance, because it hampered the development of more effective blows directed toward military objectives. "It's a matter of simple bookkeeping," said a colonel attached to the general staff. "If the Germans kill one or more Frenchmen for every German we do away with, we lose. We cannot afford it. We must make every act count."

In the early days the Underground's organizers made the Paris subway their headquarters. They did their work in the cars as the trains went around and around. Then the Germans discovered the ruse and they had to abandon it. The conspirators moved frequently. Records were kept on tiny strips of paper. Each record gave the name of a recruit, his job, his connections, whether he owned a bicycle, how many persons he could lodge and feed, and what he enlisted for: sabotage, transport or commando duty. The cataloguing was done by bank accountants working at night.

Files were made for every community in France. A record was compiled listing every railroad tunnel, every place where trains were obliged to slow down, every factory, garage and shipyard. The secret newspapers, appearing first in mimeograph form, later in printed four-page tabloids turned out on small presses concealed in attics and cellars, helped to crystallize opinion and inform the people. By the beginning of 1944 some 40 of these papers were being published, with a combined circulation of about 500,000.

The Underground sent agents through the country to listen to what people said, to refute German propaganda, to enlist new workers. The thousands who registered with the Underground had to be trained. Instructors were sent to visit them. These men—former lawyers, schoolteachers, soldiers—traveled at night and across country, to avoid German road patrols.

The instructors held classes for only two persons at a time. They taught their pupils how to plant incendiary bombs; how to place a charge on a railroad track in order to derail a train; how to sabotage production in factories turning out goods for the Germans. They also taught the use of the garrotte (a way to strangle a man before he can make a sound); how to attach silencers to pistols; how to assemble and use automatic rifles.

To test the courage of a recruit, the instructors often have him deliver a machine gun—wrapped in an innocent-appearing package—to a town some miles away. This means going to a railroad station, checking the parcel into the baggage car, then checking it out and delivering it, all under the eyes of the police. Recruits are also asked to cut a long-distance military telephone line or lay a charge of explosives on a railroad bridge. The instructors judge a man fit for service only after he has passed these primary tests for courage.

Authority goes with ability; former generals take orders from ex-lieutenants. Under the staff are 20 regional units, each led by officers in charge of command posts which move every eight to 10 days. An advance agent, called a forager, finds in a village some 10 houses in which the command may reside safely. Though the Germans have decreed that anyone who shelters an Underground member will be put to death, house-owners rarely refuse aid.

The shock troops of the Underground army are the Corps Francs, the equivalent of the American Rangers or British Commandos. They are called *gorilles* (gorillas) because when they hole up after an operation they let their beards grow, to save soap and razor blades. They are hard, reckless men, most of them under 40. Their jobs require nerve, strength and indifference to death. The saboteurs, on the other hand, are often old men, women and youngsters. Their task is equally important, and they face death if caught. But in this work stealth and cunning are more important than muscles.

Each operation is planned with scrupulous attention to detail. Here, for example, is a warehouse containing small arms which the Underground army wants. A careful study is made of the number of guards, their habits, the inhabitants of nearby buildings, and means of access to the warehouse. Say there are eight Germans on guard. To take care of them, the officer in command chooses 16 men of the Corps Francs. To haul away the munitions he provides two trucks and 50 men. To destroy the warehouse, four demolition men are selected and told exactly what to do. The time schedule is closely calculated: 10 minutes for the gorillas; 40 minutes for the truckers; 10 minutes for the demolition squad.

One moonless night the men of the Corps Francs arrive at the warehouse. There is a hiss of guns equipped with silencers, then thuds, gasps. The first part of the job is completed. The gorillas depart. Their identity is unknown to the transport men, who now back the trucks against the warehouse door. When they have finished loading, four figures dart into the empty building. A few minutes later flames are leaping from the rafters. The sound of the trucks fades in the distance as the last of the Underground slips swiftly away.

Often three months are spent in planning an operation such as the destruction of Radio Paris, France's most powerful broadcasting station. London was asked to determine exactly what amount of explosive would be needed. To find out, the British built a full-sized model of the station and blew it up. Four men of the Corps Francs were chosen to do the job. They rehearsed their parts a hundred times under the eye of an Underground instructor. On the day set, the four men slipped over the wall, set the charges and escaped. Twenty minutes later—boom! The men were never caught.

Another instance of careful planning and successful execution took place after the American invasion of Africa. It was thought at the time that southern France itself was going to be invaded, so it became important to shut off the Axis troops in Italy from access to France by blocking the railroads that connected the two countries. One Underground group set charges in a curving tunnel, causing a train to crash and buckle, effectively jamming the passage for days. Another group dynamited a mountain cliff, creating an avalanche which demolished an important railroad bridge. A third group killed the guards at another bridge, then blew it up.

When the Nazis began moving trainloads of French food to Germany, Underground chemists worked out methods for poisoning the shipments. Then agents slipped into the cars in the marshaling yards at Paris and carried out the plan. Hundreds of Germans died as a result. The Nazis then tried using marshaling yards in other parts of France. But in each yard the Underground had watchers, usually railroadmen on normal duty in those places; and food continued to be poisoned.

The Underground laboratory that prepared the poison also developed an abrasive for use in factories. The Germans, for purposes of safety, had spread out production. One factory made the chassis of a truck, another the engine, and so on. In all but one of these factories, production would be right up to the mark. But in that one a member of the invisible army would smear some vital part, say the bearings, with the abrasive. The truck would roll off the assembly line—in fact, it might roll along smoothly for 100 kilometers; then it would break down mysteriously. For a period of 10 months 90 percent of the trucks put out by one big assembly plant developed these strange ailments. The same grim gremlins pursued airplane production, shipbuilding and every other kind of machine manufacture in France. One shipyard has yet to produce a sound vessel.

The Germans have fought the Underground directly by arrests, murders and torture, and indirectly by trickery. A favorite trick of the Germans, when they catch one of the army, is to torture him until he is half dead, then leave him bleeding on the sidewalk in the hope that other members of the organization will be moved to aid him. It's hard to ignore a comrade in such a plight, but it must be done.

The Germans often used to employ women spies, on the theory that love is a Frenchman's chief interest in life. Handsome German girls who spoke French fluently sat around in cafés and night clubs and strolled on the boulevards, hoping to pick up men who might let slip information as to plots against the Nazis. However, these women didn't discover much, because the Underground soon spotted them. Furthermore, in a surprising number of cases Frenchmen succeeded in making the girls fall in love with them—a condition which destroyed their usefulness as spies. Also, municipal authorities required many of the women to conform to all the unpleasant regulations governing prostitutes. After a while the Germans abandoned the method.

One of the greatest problems of the Underground is how to keep contact with its various units and with England. Much of it is done by secret radios.

Sometimes the Germans, using cars with radio direction finders, have been able to make an approximate location of a house containing an Underground transmitter. Then they send a man, equipped with a tiny set and earphones, to walk the street until he finds the exact spot. A cordon of troops is thrown about the place, the radio operators are killed and their apparatus is smashed. The Underground has countered by ambushing the Nazi radio cars and slaying their operators.

Word-of-mouth communication is effectively used to pass

along a message. Communications agents always learn their messages by heart instead of carrying documents, except in cases involving the transfer of munitions, when a signature is required. Such messages are put on rice paper, so that they can be chewed and swallowed if the agent is arrested.

For a time the baggage compartment of a high Vichy official's automobile was used regularly to carry messages between command posts in two towns. The matter to be transported was introduced as the car stood at the curb and retrieved at the other end by a friendly mechanic. The regular German express service is employed with satisfying regularity by the Underground, thanks to loyal mechanics in the terminal stations. German Army. trucks have also been used.

Lack of food is causing a physical deterioration of the French people. When a man breaks a bone, it knits badly and with painful slowness. A cut finger will not heal for months. Teeth grow black and crooked and fall out. A trick of the Germans upon arresting a man is to yank his mouth open. If the teeth are sound and white, they know the man is someone who has recently come to the country from abroad, probably a spy. Not long ago a man from the Underground who visited London instructed his dentist to fix his teeth in such a way as to leave them looking unhealthy, in order not to jeopardize his safety when he went back.

Underground workers' travel has been skillfully organized. People on bicycles are for some reason less suspect than those on foot, and a good-looking girl can usually get through where a man fails. One man succeeded in traveling over a great deal of France in the automobile of some friendly gendarmes. The ruse was simple: the policemen put handcuffs on him. The German patrols, thinking him a prisoner, paid no heed.

Every patriot who uses the travel route between France and Germany brings some bit of information: a German railroad station where a man can sleep in safety, a house where the Germans are friendly, a farm where food can be obtained. Underground agents have actually crossed Germany into Russia by following tips of this kind. British and American prisoners in the

Reich who escape and reach France by such routes are then whisked into Spain or sent by boat to England.

One member of the Underground deliberately joined a shipment of slave labor rounded up in France by the Nazis, in order to discover the location of a secret submarine plant. Once in Germany, he escaped from his captors and wandered over the countryside for a month, half starved, until he found the place. This plant built its submarines entirely underground. The agent fixed its location in his mind, then rode back into France "on the rods." Later, well-directed bombs crippled the plant for a long time.

The French Underground is ready for the Allied invasion. German communications will be cut, centers of operation destroyed, the arrival of reinforcements held up.

Many men and women have been instructed in *one* simple job, such as scissoring a telephone line, or attaching a few sticks of dynamite to a railroad track, or squeezing a detonator which sets off a charge—already laid—that will wipe out a German pillbox. Around airports and garages, humble employes will shed their meek demeanor and fiercely carry out their one job, thereby helping to cripple the operations of the enemy's air command. The delicate jobs that need timing—for instance, the blocking of railway lines that can bring reinforcements—will be performed by the Corps Francs and the saboteurs.

The hidden soldiers of France await impatiently the day when they can take an active part in the final annihilation of the German enemy. (See "The Phantom Army," page 384, and "The Longest Day," page 400.)

Britain's Pet Spy

As told to Al Newman by a former British undercover agent

In October 1940 Franco's government requested admission to the British Isles for a Falangist who had something to do with the youth movement in Spain and wanted to study the British Boy Scouts during wartime. The Foreign Office said, "Righto, come ahead." They knew all about the man and were positive that everything he saw or heard would go straight to Berlin.

He was our own pet spy and we loved him dearly. A few of us, acting as Scout officials, met him at an airfield and tucked him into a suite at the Athenaeum Court Hotel. That suite was probably the greatest job of concealed microphones and tapped wires ever accomplished. We furnished him with liquor and everything else he wanted.

At that time there were only about three heavy ack-ack batteries in the London area. One of them we moved into the park across the street from the hotel. They had orders to fire continuously, as fast as possible, all through every raid, whether there was anything within miles or not.

What a row they made! Since there was at least one raid every night, our pet spy spent most of his time in the air-raid shelter, convinced by the noise that London was thickly studded with ack-ack protection. We let him inspect the battery—a crack three-incher outfit—and even furnished a few Boy Scouts for the occasion.

Next we took him out toward Windsor to look at more Boy Scouts. By what might have been the sheerest coincidence, but wasn't, just about the only fully equipped regiment in all the British Isles and all the tanks we possessed were assembled there. We said that this outfit of fine, tough-looking guardsmen was merely a small force which could be spared from the defense of the island and had been detailed as a ceremonial bodyguard for the royal family. We could see how surprised he was, but he swallowed it whole.

Then we took him to a seaport where every available fleet unit had been mustered. We hinted delicately that secret additions to the Home Fleet enabled us to keep these ships as the defense of one port. His eyes popped a little at that, but there it was before him and he had to believe what he saw. We also showed him more Boy Scouts. He was beginning to get awfully sick of them by this time and so were we, but it was part of the game.

Our greatest triumph of stage management was his trip to Scotland by plane. You remember how thin our air power was at that time—a few Hurricanes, fewer Spitfires. Well, all the way up we ran into squadron after squadron of Spits. The sky seemed full of them. How could he know that it was the same squadron ducking in and out of the clouds and coming at us from all angles and altitudes?

On maneuvers in Scotland we showed him the same regiment of guards and the same tanks that he had seen near Windsor. I was afraid he might recognize a few of the guardsmen, but he didn't. We explained that this was just a small, poorly equipped force reoutfitting to join others training over a wide area, and that the whole maneuver army was merely what could be spared from the main defense forces. Oh, yes, there were a few more Boy Scouts about the premises.

On the way back to London we ran into more Spitfires— hundreds of them. If I hadn't known what was going on, I'd have been taken in myself. Shortly after this he left, thanking us effusively for our splendid coöperation.

Later I saw portions of his report—we arranged to have it copied. The document was appalling. Britain was an armed camp. Any rumors of her weakness were merely attempts of a crafty foe to inveigle Germany into an inevitably disastrous invasion. All this was eyewitness stuff, and apparently great weight was given to it in Berlin.

I often wonder what happened to our pet spy. He was quite a presentable chap. We loved him dearly and cared for him tenderly. But I'll bet 10 pounds he still dreams of Boy Scouts. I know I do.

The Cruise of
the Raider *Atlantis*

By Robert Littell

When the lookout of the British liner *City of Exeter* reported a strange mast on the South Atlantic horizon, the captain was suspicious. It was May 1940, and Nazi Germany was on the march. But half an hour later, with relief, the skipper put the approaching stranger down as the 8400-ton *Kashii Maru*—Japanese, and therefore neutral.

On her deck a woman was pushing a baby carriage. Nearby lolled several of the crew—their shirttails fluttering in the breeze, after the fashion of Japanese seamen. The two ships passed without pause or signal.

Actually, the baby carriage was empty, the "woman" was not a woman at all. The deck hands had names like Fritz, Klaus and Karl. The rest of the crew of 350 technicians and fighting men were hidden below. The ship herself, behind a camouflage of plywood ventilators, canvas funnels and paint, was the German raider *Atlantis*, one of the deadliest birds of prey ever let loose.

The Germans armed nine such raiders during World War II. Together they sank 136 ships. But the *Atlantis* had the biggest haul, the longest voyage, the most remarkable commander. She had begun life as the *Goldenfels*, a 7800-ton express cargo ship. When war broke out she was fitted with six concealed 5.9-inch guns, many smaller guns, torpedo tubes, a scout seaplane and a cargo of mines. She carried enough disguise props to impersonate any of a dozen innocent-looking merchantmen.

In March 1940, commanded by Bernhard Rogge, a big-featured, imposing officer of 40, the *Atlantis* sneaked up the

Norwegian coast dressed as a Soviet steamer and broke free into the North Atlantic. Her orders: to strike with all possible surprise at ships rounding Africa's Cape of Good Hope. After crossing the equator on April 25 the *Atlantis* lowered her Soviet flag and with a flick of her counterfeit funnel became the "Japanese" motorship met by the *City of Exeter*—which Captain Rogge refrained from attacking because of the large number of passengers aboard.

First victim of the *Atlantis* was the British ship *Scientist*. The order to heave to and not use her wireless came as a complete surprise to the *Scientist*. But her wireless officer had the presence of mind to send out a frantic "QQQ"—meaning "Armed enemy merchantman wants to stop me." The *Atlantis* opened fire, hitting the *Scientist* amidships and destroying her wireless. The 77 members of the stricken ship's company took to the boats, two of them wounded, one fatally. All were taken aboard the *Atlantis* as prisoners, and the *Scientist* was sunk. The *Atlantis* sped around the Cape of Good Hope.

Two weeks later Captain Rogge intercepted a British warning that a German auxiliary cruiser, disguised as a Japanese ship, might be roaming the Indian Ocean. Immediately the *Atlantis* took off her kimono and became the Netherlands motorship *Abbekerk*.

The second victim was the Norwegian motorship *Tirranna*, laden with supplies for Australian troops in Palestine. Captain Rogge sent a prize crew aboard and had her trail along for some weeks as a prison ship. A month after the *Tirranna*, three victims turned up in rapid succession. And then in the next month, five more. Messages found in the wastebaskets of one vessel made it possible for the Germans to break the British merchant naval code.

By now the British Admiralty had ordered all ships to report suspicious vessels by radio, regardless of consequences. As a result, the *Atlantis* was under orders to shoot on sight and ask questions afterward. About half of the raider's victims managed to send a message before they were subdued. Most of them were shelled, sometimes with heavy casualties. But Captain Rogge's solitary maritime war was as nearly "civilized" as war can be. He had room for prisoners and took aboard all that he could rescue. In 20 months at sea he sheltered—at one time or another—more than 1000 prisoners, of all ages, both sexes and 20 nationalities. He gave them the same rations as the ship's company. They were allowed on deck in the daytime unless the *Atlantis'* crew were at battle stations. They swam in the canvas swimming pool. The captured captains had quarters to themselves. When prisoners were transferred to other ships Captain Rogge gave farewell parties for the skippers.

Through the autumn of 1940 it was fisherman's luck for the *Atlantis:* only one ship in 40 days. Then suddenly, in mid-November, three ships within 48 hours. The Norwegian *Ole Jacob*, bursting with high-octane gasoline, was seized without resistance when two officers in the *Atlantis'* motorboat masqueraded as British officers. The Norwegian tanker *Teddy* burned for hours, a sky-high torch visible to every ship in the area. And the British *Automedon*, whose papers included a top-secret War Cabinet report and the mail for the British Far-Eastern High Command, surrendered when a shell killed everyone on her bridge.

Captain Rogge had a genius for managing men. Everyone got exactly the same share of the small luxuries—beer, candy, food parcels—found on captured ships. As a substitute for shore leave he gave a week's leave on board ship. Twelve vacationers at a time took over the isolation ward. Unless there was a call to battle stations, they were free to do as they pleased, whether it was sleeping, mending clothes, writing poetry or playing the guitar. This official loafing in the midst of other men's hard work had a wonderfully relaxing effect. Captain Rogge, whose grandfather had been a clergyman at the court of Kaiser Wilhelm II, insisted that all his officers attend church service on Sundays. But after the service he always gave them a drink, which they called the "church cocktail."

The year 1941 began badly for the *Atlantis*—only four ships in as many months. One of them was the Egyptian liner *Zam Zam* with 140 American missionaries on board. The *Zam Zam's* passengers and crew, 309 persons, were all safely transferred to the *Atlantis*. Next day another German ship, the *Dresden*, relieved the *Atlantis* of all these captives and eventually brought them safely to Bordeaux.

The terror the raider spread probably hurt the Allies as much as the sinkings. British warships, badly needed elsewhere, had to be sent south to hunt for her. Merchantmen had to zigzag on lengthened routes, wasting time and fuel. Crews were harder to find and had to be paid danger-zone allowances. Official mail was delayed or lost. War insurance rates went up, harbor lights went out.

Through most of the summer the *Atlantis* crisscrossed the southern reaches of the Indian Ocean without meeting anything larger than a sea gull. Then on September 10, 1941, she captured her 22nd—and last—victim, the Norwegian *Silvaplana*.

On November 21, while touching down after an early morning flight, the *Atlantis*' scout plane was disabled—just when its eyes were needed most. For next day U-boat 126 was to meet the raider to take on fuel—a delicate operation during which the *Atlantis* would be defenseless. At a rendezvous midway between Brazil and Africa the two ships met, and by breakfast time fuel oil was being pumped between them. In the motor launch alongside the submarine were several members of the *Atlantis*' crew; the submarine's captain was on board the *Atlantis*. At the same time the raider's port engine was dismantled for repairs.

Suddenly the lookout, scanning a sunlit sea, caught sight of the pencil point of a mast. Minutes later the British heavy cruiser *Devonshire*, Captain R. D. Oliver commanding, was bearing down on the two Germans.

At first glimpse of the *Devonshire* the Germans' securing lines were cast off and the U-boat dived, stranding its captain on board the raider. Had the U-boat been seen? From the disconnected fuel hose a telltale patch of iridescent oil spread upon the water. There was only one hope for the *Atlantis:* bluff, talk, gain time, so as to lure the *Devonshire* within range of the U-boat's torpedo tubes.

Captain Oliver was highly suspicious. Except for such parts as ventilators, the ship he had found spreading oil on a calm sea fitted the Admiralty's description of the mysterious raider. He therefore steamed to and fro, well out of torpedo range, and bracketed the *Atlantis* with two salvos.

Captain Rogge radioed that he was the vessel *Polyphemus*. Captain Oliver signaled a query to the Commander in Chief, South Atlantic, asking if this stranger could be the genuine *Polyphemus*.

For almost an hour the *Atlantis*, hove-to and gently rolling in the swell, dragged out the conversation. There was still a faint chance that the U-126 might get close enough to the British cruiser to fire a torpedo. But the submarine's senior officer stayed near the *Atlantis* instead of going for the cruiser.

At 9:34 Captain Oliver got his answer from the South Atlantic Commander in Chief: "No—repeat—No!" A minute later the *Devonshire* opened fire. When the third salvo of eight-inch shells crashed down upon the *Atlantis*, Captain Rogge gave orders to set time charges and abandon ship.

Just before 10 a.m. the forward magazine blew up. A few minutes later the *Atlantis* sank by the stern. As she went down, the men whose home she had been for 20 months cheered her, and Captain Rogge, with his little Scotch terrier Ferry beside him, stood up in one of the boats and saluted.

Because Captain Oliver, in the words of the Admiralty's report, could not have stopped to pick up survivors "without running grave risk of being torpedoed," the *Devonshire* soon disappeared over the horizon. By whistle and by voice the *Atlantis'* crew were called together. Only seven had been killed by the shelling. At least 100 were swimming about or clinging to wreckage. The submarine took on board the wounded and the irreplaceable specialists. Six lifeboats packed in 200 more. Fifty-two men, provided with life belts and blankets, had to huddle on the submarine's deck. In case of a dive they were to swim to a lifeboat. The nearest land was Brazil, 950 miles away.

The strange flotilla—six lifeboats towed by a submarine—got under way on the afternoon of the sinking. Twice a day a rubber dinghy put out from the sub to make the tour of the boats with a hot meal.

Three days after the sinking the U-126 was met by the German submarine supply ship *Python*, and the survivors were picked up—only to be cast upon the waters again. For the *Python* was intercepted and sunk by another British cruiser, the *Dorsetshire*, famous for having given the *Bismarck* her *coup de grâce* a few months earlier.

Eventually, in German and Italian submarines, the *Atlantis'* crew members reached St. Nazaire and made their way to Berlin, arriving just after New Year's Day 1942.

Captain Rogge was promoted to Rear Admiral and put in charge of training naval cadets. But his anti-Nazi feelings were discovered, and he was later relegated to an unimportant post.

What was rare after so long and bitter a war, not a few of the *Atlantis'* victims felt kindly toward Rogge. Captain White of the *City of Bagdad* wrote his thanks for the treatment he had received as a prisoner. Captain Woodcock of the *Tottenham* invited Admiral Rogge to come aboard when his present ship docked in Hamburg. During the lean years after the collapse of Nazi Germany former prisoners sent their ex-captors many CARE packages.

"He made the *Atlantis'* crew into a real family," explained Lieutenant Dehnel. "If Rogge called me, I would follow him like a shot—no matter what navy it was."

The Mystery
of the Hess Flight

By William J. Snyder

One of the most fascinating tales of World War II is the story of Rudolf Hess and his secret flight to Scotland. No. 3 in the Nazi hierarchy and Hitler's deputy, Hess was a fanatical follower of the Führer. When the British continued to stand and fight after all of continental Europe had fallen, Hess conceived the wild idea of going secretly to Britain and making peace, thus leaving Hitler free to launch his "holy war" against Russia. Hess had grown up in the English quarter of Alexandria, Egypt. He spoke English and believed he "understood the British mind." He decided to fly to the estate of the Duke of Hamilton, an Englishman he had met at the Olympic Games in Berlin in 1936. So it was that shortly before six o'clock on Saturday, May 10, 1941, Reich Minister Walter Richard Rudolf Hess climbed into a Messerschmidt-110 fighter plane and, telling no one his destination, took off into the twilight.

According to some reports, Hess had tried to contact the Duke of Hamilton through an intermediary and did not know his message had been intercepted by British Intelligence.

On the night of Hess's flight one of the heaviest Nazi bomber forces ever sent to Britain was attacking London. Suddenly a radio location station on the Scottish coast announced the approach of a lone plane that failed to identify itself properly. Its speed indicated that it was a fighter plane. In the plotting room it was pinpointed far up on the eastern coast of Scotland, with an arrow to indicate that it was moving west.

Two RAF interceptors were quickly dispatched to trail the mystery plane. While the small red arrows on the plotting table crept across Scotland, officers at Fighter Command watched. Near the city of Paisley the arrows stopped. It was later reported that an enemy aircraft had crashed in flames after its pilot had bailed out. (See photograph on page 344.)

In Lanarkshire, Scotland, David McLean, a farmer, saw a man parachute into his field and ran up to him. "Are ye a Nazi enemy, or are ye one o' ours?" he asked. "Not Nazi enemy; British friend," the man replied. He spoke with difficulty because he had wrenched his ankle and was in extreme pain. Helped into the farmer's kitchen, he admitted to Home Guards and police who had arrived on the double that he had come from

Germany and was hunting the Duke of Hamilton's estate, 10 miles away. "Please tell the Duke that Alfred Horn has arrived," he said.

Hess was taken to Maryhill Barracks near Glasgow. There he changed his story. "I have come to save humanity," he said. "I am Rudolf Hess."

The Duke of Hamilton, a wing commander in the RAF, was sent for. He had no memory of ever having met Hess before. Hess talked excitedly to the Duke of his mission. The next day Ivone Kirkpatrick, a super-spy in World War I and secretary of the British Embassy in Berlin for five years, flew to Scotland to see Hess. To Kirkpatrick the Nazi poured out the details of the armistice and peace proposals. He was enthusiastic and voluble. The stenographic report of what he said filled many notebooks. Since he was convinced that Britain was licked and knew it, Hess's tone was that of a munificent enemy offering a reprieve to a doomed foe.

In outline the basic points were as follows: Hitler offered total cessation of the war in the West. Germany would evacuate all of France except Alsace and Lorraine. It would retain Luxembourg, but would evacuate Holland, Belgium, Norway and Denmark. In addition, the Führer was ready to withdraw from Yugoslavia, Greece and the Mediterranean area generally, and Hitler would help arrange a settlement between Britain and Italy. In return for these concessions, Great Britain would agree to assume an attitude of benevolent neutrality toward Germany in eastern Europe.

Hess explained the importance of Hitler's eastern mission "to save humanity," and indicated how England and France would become the arsenals of free capitalism against Asiatic communism. Germany, he pointed out, would take the full production of Allied war industries until they could be converted to a peacetime basis, thus preventing economic depression. He gave no information on Hitler's military plans for eastern Europe. That, he said, was a problem for Germany alone.

For two days Hess unfolded his proposals. He emphasized that the Führer would not quibble over details—Britain could practically write her own peace terms. Hitler was eager, as a humanitarian, to stop the "senseless war" with a brother nation—and, incidentally, safeguard his rear while fighting in the East.

The German public was told of Hess's flight in a terse press release: "It seems that Party Comrade Hess lived in a state of hallucination, as a result of which he felt he could bring about an understanding between England and Germany. . . . This, however, will have no effect on the continuance of the war. . . ." Hitler was beside himself with rage when he heard the news. He gave orders that Hess was to be executed if he ever returned to the Reich.

With Hess's proposal in his notebooks, Kirkpatrick went to 10 Downing Street. The plan was communicated to Washington. Both London and Washington made repeated efforts to warn Russia of the coming German blows. The Russian leaders would not believe—or pretended not to believe. (Hess landed by parachute on May 10, 1941. Germany invaded Russia on June 22, 1941.)

Only after he had talked himself out and could provide no further useful information was Hess informed that his plan had been rejected and that Britain was already Russia's ally. His shock and dismay resulted in a minor nervous breakdown, and for a while the Nazi story about Hess's insanity came near being true. When he heard of the sinking of the *Bismarck* he wept an entire day.

Hess demanded that he be sent back to Germany because, having come as an emissary, he was entitled to safe return. The British government reasoned differently—and he became a special prisoner for the duration of the war. He was kept in the manor house of a large English estate, with considerable freedom of movement on the well-guarded grounds. In October 1945, after the war had ended, Hess was taken to Nuremberg to stand trial as a war criminal. Mentally unbalanced, he escaped a sentence of death and was imprisoned for life by the International Tribunal. He is confined at Spandau War Crimes Prison in West Berlin.

The Evaders

By Roman Turski

I was born in Poland, where before the last war religious intolerance was not uncommon. In spite of my father's objection to my participation in anti-Semitic demonstrations in Warsaw, I often heaved stones at windows of stores owned by Jews. I had no qualms about my actions, and later it took months of hardship and persecution—and a Jew—to show me how to abide by the Biblical injunction: "Love thy neighbor as thyself."

When Hitler annexed Austria and war seemed imminent, I quit my job as instructor of a flying club in Lyons, France, and started for home. My plane developed engine trouble and I had to land at Vienna and stay there overnight to have it repaired.

The following morning, just as I stepped out of my hotel to buy a few souvenirs before checking out, a man who came running past the door bumped into me and sent me reeling. Outraged, I grabbed him and was about to give him a piece of my mind when I saw that his face was white with fear. Panting heavily, he tried to wrench himself from my grip and said, "Gestapo—Gestapo!" I knew only a little German but understood he was running from the dreaded German secret police.

I rushed him into the lobby and upstairs to my room, pointed to the foot of my bed and motioned to him to lie down. I covered his slender, jackknifed body with artfully draped blankets so that the tousled bed looked empty. Then I pulled off my jacket, tie and collar so I could pretend I'd just got up if the Gestapo men came. In a few minutes they did. They examined my passport, returned it and shouted questions, to which I replied: "*Ich verstehe es nicht*—I don't understand it," a phrase I knew by heart. They left without searching the room.

As soon as they had gone I locked the door and lifted the blankets. The poor man let out a stream of rapid German. It was not necessary to understand a word to comprehend his gratitude.

I got out my flight chart and, by gesturing and drawing pictures on the margin of the map, explained that I had a plane and could take him out of Austria. He pointed to Warsaw, and his expressive hands asked: "Would you take me there?" I shook my head and made him understand that I had to land for fuel in Cracow. I drew pictures of police and prison bars to illustrate that he would be arrested upon arrival at any airport, and made it clear that we would land in some meadow just over the Polish border and he could get off. He nodded with satisfaction, and his narrow face and dark-brown eyes again conveyed deep thanks.

The customs and immigration men at the airport waved us through when I told them my friend wanted to see me off. My plane was warmed up and ready for flight. We quickly climbed into it and took off. We crossed Czechoslovakia and soon saw the thin ribbon of the Vistula River and the city of Cracow. Landing in a large field by a wood near a country railroad station, I showed my companion where we were on the map, gave him most of my money and wished him luck. He took my hand and looked at me wordlessly, then walked rapidly into the woods.

When I arrived at the Cracow airport there was a detachment of police waiting beside the immigration inspector. One of the police said, "We have a warrant to search your plane—you have helped a man escape from Vienna."

"Go ahead and search it. Incidentally, what was the man wanted for?"

"He was a Jew!"

They searched my plane, and of course had to let me go for lack of evidence.

The war came, and after Poland's short and bloody struggle against the Germans, in which I served as a fighter pilot in the Polish Air Force, I joined the thousands of my countrymen who wanted to carry on the fight for freedom. We crossed the border into Rumania and were promptly caught and sent to concentration camps. I finally managed to escape and joined the French

Air Force. After France collapsed I went to England and fought in the Battle of Britain. The following June I was wounded while on a fighter sweep across the English Channel, when the Luftwaffe hit us over Boulogne. In those early offensive missions we were always outnumbered and outperformed by the Luftwaffe, and our only superiority was our morale.

As we started for home I rammed an Me-109 and was hit by a piece of its sheared-off tail. I was half blinded with blood. My squadron covered my withdrawal across the Channel, but I was unconscious when my Spitfire crash-landed in England. (I learned later that my skull had been fractured, and that I was so near death that the head surgeon of the hospital to which I was taken believed it would be almost useless to operate on me.)

When I returned to consciousness, I gradually realized that a narrow face with large brown eyes was looking down at me. "Remember me?" their owner said. "You saved my life in Vienna." He spoke with only a trace of German accent.

His words ended my confusion. I recalled this sensitive face and managed to say, "How did you find me?" I noticed his white smock. "Do you work here?"

"It's a long story," he replied. "After you dropped me off I made my way to Warsaw, where an old friend aided me. Just before the war I escaped and reached safety in Scotland. When one of your Polish squadrons distinguished itself in the Battle of Britain, I thought you might be in it, so I wrote to the Air Ministry and found you were."

"How did you know my name?"

"It was written on the margin of your map. I remembered it." His long fingers felt cool on my wrist. "Yesterday I read the story in the newspapers about a Polish hero shooting down five enemy planes in one day and then crash-landing near this hospital. It said your condition was considered hopeless. I immediately asked the Royal Air Force at Edinburgh to fly me here."

"Why?"

"I thought that at last I could do something to show my gratitude. You see, I am a brain surgeon—I operated on you this morning."

PART THREE

1 9 4 2

AGAINST THE ENEMY TIDE

AMERICA awoke from her dream of peace to find herself involved in a new era of warfare where psychology, high adventure and deceptions great and small were among the necessities of survival.

Staggered by the disaster of Pearl Harbor, America almost overnight formed a system of world intelligence to warn her of when and where future enemy attacks might come. The FBI, the Office of Naval Intelligence, the Army's Counter Intelligence Corps and the Air

Force's Office of Special Investigation all moved into high gear. Under the command of Colonel (later Major General) "Wild Bill" Donovan, the Office of Strategic Services sprang from blueprint to global reality.

With the expansion came confusion, competition and a scramble of activity. Scientists, professors and other specialists from almost every walk of life flooded Washington, forming a multitude of intelligence units and special organizations, some of which were completely new to warfare. Using the experience and information of Britain and other allies, America made up for lost time.

The blackness of retreat and defeat began to lift. The explosive Japanese conquest reached its limits. By the end of the year a British army had stopped the famed Afrika Korps and an Anglo-American invasion force had landed in North Africa to challenge the enemy.

It was a year of surprises, mysterious maneuvers and bewildering ruses; secrecy and espionage played no small part in the Allied effort to halt the rampant enemy.

Hitler's Undercover Invasion of the United States

By Lawrence Elliott

A little past midnight on Saturday, June 13, 1942, Coast Guardsman John Cullen set out from the Amagansett, Long Island, N.Y., Coast Guard station to make a routine beach patrol. He carried a flashlight and, from time to time, flicked the beam out in front of him. Still, he could see no more than five or six yards ahead in the swirling fog.

The 21-year-old Coast Guardsman was about a half-mile east of the station when suddenly he came upon four men clustered ankle-deep in the surf around a small boat. "What's going on here?" he snapped.

One man, long-faced and speaking with a slight foreign accent, explained that he and his friends were fishermen and that they had become lost in the fog.

Cullen was unsatisfied. "You'd better come to the station with me," he said.

The long-faced "fisherman" grabbed at Cullen's arm. "Listen, boy!" he said. "Have you got a mother and father? Would you like to see them again? Here, take this money and have yourself a good time. Forget what you saw here. Understand?"

Stunned, young Cullen clutched the sheaf of bills thrust into his hand. He was unarmed, and he sensed that he had stumbled onto something far beyond his ability to cope with singly. He backed off, then ran for the Coast Guard station.

The long-faced man and his three confederates quickly fell to unloading the rubber boat which had carried them ashore from the submarine U-202. In a hastily dug trench they buried four waterproof cases, each packed tight with explosives, timing devices and detonators—enough for a massive assault on the core of America's industrial might. (See photographs on pages 338-9.) And then, even as Cullen pounded toward the old wooden Coast Guard station for help, they moved swiftly up the beach road toward the Amagansett railroad station. By the time Cullen and two mates armed themselves and raced back, they found only the deserted beach and the silent gray haze.

Thus began the first phase of the landing of a German sabotage team on the shores of the United States.

The broad outline of the plot to bring production in key industrial plants to a halt was the work of the Abwehr—the intelligence division of the German High Command. The mechanics of the plot were entrusted to a brilliant and choleric intelligence officer, Lieutenant Walter Kappe, who for 12 years had propagandized for Nazi-front organizations in Chicago and New York. Kappe's plan was to recruit Germans who had lived and worked in the United States—men so at home with American habits and language that they could lose themselves anywhere in this country.

Small teams of these men, intensively trained and lavishly equipped, would be landed by submarine. Their targets would be pinpointed in advance. Kappe had convinced himself that they would be abetted by countless German-Americans loyal to the Fatherland. They would maintain contact with Kappe and with each other by coded advertisements in the Chicago *Tribune*. Once the sabotage network was established, Kappe himself would slip into the United States and take charge from a secret headquarters in Chicago.

Walter Kappe began his recruiting in the winter of 1941. It was a tedious chore. He consulted Gestapo lists of recent repatriates. He addressed rallies of the Ausland Institute, organized to recruit Germans abroad into the Nazi Party. He combed the files of the Wehrmacht. He interviewed every likely prospect. And finally, on April 10, 1942, there gathered on a heavily wooded estate just outside Berlin the little band of volunteers soon to be charged with leading the German "invasion." Among them were:

George John Dasch, the long-faced man, 39, oldest of the group, who had entered the United States illegally in 1922, worked as a waiter in New York and even served for a brief period with the Army Air Corps before returning to Germany in 1941. (See photograph on page 339.)

Werner Thiel, who had come to the United States in 1927, stayed 14 years, filed first citizenship papers.

Edward Kerling, a dedicated Nazi who had worked as a chauffeur and domestic in the United States for 11 years.

Hermann Neubauer, a cook.

Herbert Hans Haupt, youngest of the candidates, who had spent 16 of his 22 years in the United States and was an American citizen by right of his parents' naturalization.

Ernest Peter Burger, a Nazi Party member who had worked in the United States as a machinist and served in the National Guard. (See photograph on page 339.)

Heinrich Heinck, a toolmaker who had lived in America for 13 years.

Richard Quirin, who had come to the United States in 1927, then some years later taken advantage of the Reich's offer to finance the return of any German national qualified as a skilled mechanic.

On the afternoon of April 10, Lieutenant Kappe took his charges on a tour of the estate. Besides a dormitory, there were a gymnasium, a classroom, an extravagantly equipped laboratory, a tower for experiments with explosives, and two rifle ranges. Kappe told the group that from that moment they would be lost to the world. No one was to know where they were.

At dawn next morning the rigid routine began: calisthenics; classroom lectures on incendiaries, explosives, fuses, timing devices and secret writing; grenade throwing, riflery and wrestling; and practice missions of actual sabotage.

The instructors concentrated on materials which anyone could buy at a drugstore without exciting suspicion. An effective incendiary, for instance, could be ignited with the help of sulphuric acid and powdered sugar. A concealed-writing process required only an aspirin tablet dissolved in alcohol: dry, the writing disappeared; rubbed with alcohol-dipped cotton, it showed plainly.

Ingenious, and deadly, were the methods for triggering an explosive charge. One required only a wire-tipped cork floating in a slowly leaking can. When all the water had seeped out and the agent had had time to put miles between himself and the target, the cork reached bottom, metal touched metal and an electrical circuit was completed. This activated the explosion.

In the final week of training the class was taken to the Berlin freight yards. Experts showed how a handful of sand thrown into a bearing box would decommission an engine, how a small explosive charge, judiciously placed, could block a vital section of track for days. From the freight yards the saboteurs went on a three-day tour of the aluminum and magnesium plants of I. G. Farbenindustrie. Kappe demonstrated how easy it would be. A high-tension wire cut, a transformer shattered by a rifle shot, and the plant's counterpart in America would be powerless for at least eight hours—long enough for the liquid aluminum to congeal and destroy the intricate network of stoves and baths. Result: stagnant weeks while new equipment was being installed.

Final examinations began on April 29. Sealed instructions directed each team to the site of a mock-up factory, railroad terminal or oil tank. After appraising the situation secretly, they were to prepare the proper explosives and, within 36 hours, destroy the target. Two men were summarily dismissed when they bungled their job and were trapped in a surprise raid by school guards.

Examinations over, the remaining candidates were promised a monthly income and a soft government berth after the war, then divided into two teams and handed their sabotage assignments. Team No. 1, under the leadership of Dasch and including Burger, Heinck and Quirin, was to attack several aluminum plants (in Alcoa, Tenn.; East St. Louis, Ill.; Massena, N.Y.) and the cryolite works at Philadelphia; and they were to blow up the locks in the Ohio River between Pittsburgh and Louisville. Team No. 2—Kerling, in command of Neubauer, Thiel and Haupt—would concentrate on railroad bridges and tunnels, blow New York's Hell Gate Bridge into the East River, destroy New York's water-supply system. At every opportunity both groups were to plant bombs in public places to promote panic.

Kappe ordered each of his charges to kill, without compunction, any of the others who weakened or endangered the mission. He also made a big mistake.

On the morning of May 26, two days before the two teams embarked on the U-201 and U-202 from the submarine base at Lorient, he doled out the money that was to finance the venture: 50,000 American dollars to each of the two leaders, and money

belts stuffed with $4400 to each of the others. Dasch was pack-
ing his money into a false-bottomed suitcase when he suddenly
realized that a substantial part of it was in gold notes, which
had been withdrawn from circulation some nine years before.
Though the incriminating bills were quickly replaced, a subtle
change began taking place in the hearts of the saboteurs. As
Dasch later put it, "I kept thinking about that money. If they
could be that stupid, how much did they really care about any
of us? What chance did we have?"

Hurrying up the beach road toward Amagansett on the morning of June 13, Dasch had fresh reason to worry. Their first
mishap—that damned Coast Guardsman—had hit them even
before they could get their landing boat out of the water.

Dasch was still worrying at 6:30 a.m. when the station agent
at Amagansett opened his ticket window. The four Germans
were waiting to buy tickets. "You fellows are up early," the
agent said pleasantly.

"We've been fishing," Dasch said.

Dasch bought some newspapers and handed them to his confederates. He cautioned them to bury their heads in the papers
like the commuters and to say nothing. They boarded the 6:57
New York train.

When they reached New York, Dasch and Burger checked
into the Governor Clinton Hotel on West 31st Street, while
Heinck and Quirin registered at the Martinique.

They should have been pleased with themselves. They had
landed safely. No one had so much as looked askance at them
on the train. They had successfully lost themselves in the city.
Later, when they got hold of a car, they would dig up their
equipment and carry it to a permanent hiding place in the Cats-
kill Mountains, as they had planned. There was no hurry;
Kappe had emphasized that there were to be no overt acts of
sabotage until the two teams were firmly established.

Now, however, came the turning point. Precisely why it came
about so suddenly may never be determined. As soon as Dasch
and Burger were alone in their room, Dasch began to ramble
nervously. "Listen," he said. "I'm worried. I want you to tell me

how you feel about this thing. I have a plan that will keep us out of trouble here."

"I know what you intend to do," Burger said.

"All right, but if you don't agree, I'll have to kill you—right here and now."

Burger's answer was, "Don't worry about me."

Shortly before eight o'clock on Sunday evening FBI agent Dean F. McWhorter answered his office telephone at the New York Federal Courthouse. A man with a slight foreign accent said that he had just been landed from a German submarine and that he had important information for J. Edgar Hoover. "I will be in Washington within the week to deliver it in person," he said. Then he hung up.

It was the seventh month of the war. The FBI had been besieged with calls from cranks and crackpots. Agent Mc-Whorter made a memorandum of the mysterious call and went on to other things. But the call took on significance when the Coast Guard reported to the FBI the happenings on the beach at Amagansett and delivered the cache of explosives which they had subsequently found.

Meanwhile, some 1000 miles to the south, the U-201, carrying Sabotage Team No. 2, cruised toward the Florida coast. It surfaced off Ponte Vedra Beach, 25 miles southeast of Jacksonville, in the early hours of June 17. A rubber boat was put over the side, and Kerling, Neubauer, Thiel and Haupt rowed ashore. Quickly they buried their equipment. Changing their clothing, they walked to U.S. Highway 1 and waited for the bus to Jacksonville. By next morning Kerling and Thiel were on a train bound for Cincinnati, and Haupt and Neubauer were en route to Chicago.

George Dasch dallied in New York until the following Thursday, killing time by playing pinochle with his waiter cronies from the old days, before he took the train to Washington and telephoned FBI headquarters. "I'm the man who called your New York office," he said. "I am in Room 351 at the Mayflower Hotel." He was soon pouring out his fantastic story to special agents Duane Traynor and Thomas J. Donegan.

He talked for two days. Agents Frank Johnstone and Norval Wills spelled Traynor and Donegan. A fresh stenographer reported to Room 351 every two hours. Dasch's testimony, rambling and full of irrelevancies, covered 254 single-spaced typewritten pages. Among other significant pieces of information, he told about Kappe and the sabotage training school. He listed the objectives of teams No. 1 and 2, described each man and gave the names and addresses of their most likely American contacts. He described the German food, rationing, housing and military situations. He revealed that Nazi submarines were operating at an unsuspected depth, well beneath the killing range of Allied depth charges. Finally, he voiced the hope that, in return for his coöperation, he would be given an opportunity to make propaganda broadcasts to the German people.

Just about the time that Dasch finished his statement in Washington, FBI agents in New York opened the unlocked door of Ernest Peter Burger's room at the Governor Clinton Hotel and took him into custody. He seemed more relieved than surprised. An hour or so later Heinck and Quirin, returning to the Martinique from an afternoon at the movies, found the FBI waiting for them, too.

Edward Kerling, leader of Team No. 2, had a wife in New York. He came east from Cincinnati to see her on June 22. The next evening he and Thiel, who had accompanied him, were placed under arrest.

In Chicago, meanwhile, Haupt had moved back into his old room at his parents' house. Airily confident, he walked into an FBI office one day and inquired about his draft status. He was told, "There is no problem." There wasn't. The FBI had had him under surveillance for a week, biding its time. Finally, on the night of June 27 he was arrested—after he had led the FBI to Hermann Neubauer, the last of the eight saboteurs.

Five days later, on July 2, President Roosevelt appointed a military commission to hear the case. It was the first such tribunal to be convened in the United States since the assassination of Abraham Lincoln in 1865, and it was conducted in strictest secrecy.

The trial opened with the evidence of Attorney General Francis Biddle, who, with the Army's Judge Advocate General Myron Cramer, personally headed the case for the prosecution. In addition to the amazingly detailed confession of each defendant, he introduced the explosives they had brought with them. He conceded the Germans' queasiness once they had set foot on U.S. shores. But he underlined the fact that only the FBI's sure-handed work in rounding them up had kept at least some of the group from carrying out their destructive missions. Were all the defendants to be freed because one or two had lacked the will to proceed?

The defense hinged on a single issue, and a remarkable one it was: that the Germans had not committed a single act of sabotage—*nor had they ever intended to!* They were, at most, tepid Nazis who had volunteered for the operation only because they hoped thereby to get safely out of Germany and back to friends and relatives in the United States.

One after another, Lieutenant Kappe's pupils trooped to the witness stand to affirm their secret distaste for the Hitler regime. Burger elaborated on difficulties he had had with the Gestapo. He reminded the commission that his confession had included information of great value to the United States: detailed descriptions of his confederates; the workings of the saboteurs' hidden equipment; the construction and layout of the U-202.

In reaching a verdict, it is not unlikely that the members of the commission asked themselves questions such as these: Was it logical—or even reasonable—to assume that in a first-class military power like Nazi Germany the best men the Abwehr could come up with for so delicate a mission were the likes of Dasch, a neurotic malcontent, and others equally unstable? Or was this all part of the false façade, the carefully rehearsed attitudes the plotters would take if they were captured?

Summing up for the prosecution, the Judge Advocate General addressed the eight officers of the commission thus: "To accept the version of the defense, gentlemen, is to conclude that the defendants came here not as invaders but as refugees."

On August 8 the defendants heard the findings of the commission as approved by the President: each was guilty of violating the laws of war. Dasch was sentenced to 30 years in prison, Burger to life. For the others: death in the electric chair. They were executed at noon that day and buried in unmarked graves on a government reservation in Washington.

The news was promptly proclaimed in newspapers around the world. Within less than two months after being dropped on U.S. shores, the would-be saboteurs had been sternly dealt with. When the capture of the saboteurs was announced, Admiral Doenitz was so furious that his submarines had been risked in this scheme that he refused for months to coöperate with the Abwehr on ventures requiring U-boat transportation.

The Great Manila Bay Silver Operation

By John G. Hubbell

In the late summer of 1942, when the Japanese had been in control of the Philippines for several months, their occupation currency suddenly began to collapse. Japanese soldiers found that a month's pay wouldn't buy so much as a glass of beer. The cause was a mysterious flood of silver Philippine pesos that began turning up in the markets of Manila.

Somehow the silver was reaching even the prisoner-of-war camps. American prisoners were bribing demoralized Japanese guards for food, clothing, medicine. Next they would start buying freedom! If the source of the silver wasn't found soon, it could corrupt the whole structure of Japanese control.

Where did the silver come from? The Japanese knew the Mac-Arthur forces had dumped millions of silver pesos into the deep water south of Corregidor before they surrendered. There was

$8,500,000 of it down there, lying at a depth of 120 feet. A diving crew of seven American prisoners of war had been put to work salvaging that fortune—it would be a gift from the Army to the Emperor. Japanese security police were watching the American divers, guarding every peso recovered. It seemed inconceivable that any of this silver could be smuggled into Manila. Nevertheless, the Japanese decided to tighten the guard over the Americans.

It had all started in the early months of 1942, when defeat in the Philippines had become inevitable. Quickly Philippine government officials and U.S. Army officers decided to save the Philippine national treasury. In February some two million dollars in gold bullion and $360,000 in silver were shipped to San Francisco in the ballast tanks of the submarine U.S.S. *Trout*. But now time and the enemy were moving fast. There was no way to get out the rest of the treasury: 17 million silver pesos (each worth 50 cents) still lay packed in wooden boxes in a steel vault on Corregidor.

On April 20, U.S. Army officers drew two straight lines connecting well-known landmarks of Manila Bay on a map. The lines intersected at a point in the water on Caballo Bay, formed by the thin crescent of Corregidor's curled tail. There the water was deep and rough enough to discourage enemy salvage. There the treasure would be dumped.

Lieutenant Commander George G. Harrison, commander of harbor craft in nearby Mariveles Bay, gathered up a working party—a dozen Navy enlisted men, orphans from the submarine tender *Canopus* and submarine rescue ship *Pigeon*, sunk in Manila Bay. Most of them were divers. Harrison told them Corregidor's days were numbered; the job had to be done quickly and at night.

The heavy boxes, each of them holding 6000 pesos, were wrestled aboard two flat-topped barges, which were then towed to the dump site in the bay. There the weary sailors began pushing the precious cargo into the sea. It took 10 nights to move the 425 tons of silver to the floor of Caballo Bay. When the job was finished Harrison turned the men loose with a warning: "If you are captured, don't let them find out you are divers."

On May 6, Corregidor surrendered. The divers were among those captured. Six weeks later the Japanese commandant of the prison camp at Cabanatuan, 90 miles north of Manila, sent for Bosun's Mate First Class Morris "Moe" Solomon. "We know you are a diver," he said. "Manila harbor is choked with sunken vessels. It must be cleared for traffic."

The Japanese had excellent intelligence. Besides Solomon, they had singled out Bosun's Mates Virgil L. "Jughead" Sauers, Wallace A. "Punchy" Barton, P. L. "Slim" Mann and two other experienced divers. Before leaving Cabanatuan, the group sought out Lieutenant Commander Frank Davis, who had been their skipper on the *Pigeon*. "You know what they are really after," Davis said. "Don't let them get it!"

The men knew that if the Japanese sent them down for the silver, they would have to bring some up or be shot. But they agreed they would deliver only enough to stall the enemy. They would steal as much as they could and smuggle it to other American prisoners to bribe guards for food and medicine. One thing seemed certain: sooner or later they would be caught and executed for sabotage. But this was war, and here was a chance to do the enemy expensive damage.

On the train to Manila the enemy's stern attitude changed. Smiling guards gave each man pork sandwiches and cigarettes. In Manila they were ushered to a clean room in a building near the docks. There were a locker and a cot for each. They were Very Important Prisoners indeed!

A Japanese civilian in a seedy-looking suit entered. He wore a horseshoe of grayish hair around his bald head, thick glasses and a huge smile. He looked like an actor in a bad spy movie, but his voice, soft and high-pitched, was friendly. "I am Mr. Yosobe," he said. "We will be working together. I am a little too old for diving, but I have had 20 years' experience in salvage work. Come meet our officer-in-charge."

Captain Takiuti greeted them on the dock. A pleasant, youngish man, he came from a wealthy Japanese family and spoke perfect English. He told the men they would be given a roomy boat to live on at Corregidor.

Yosobe and two Japanese guards showed the men the U.S. Navy diving gear the Japanese had found: several shallow-water helmets and two dozen suits of long, heavy diving underwear. It would be dangerous work. Should the weighted helmet tilt more than 45 degrees, it would fill with water and drown the diver. Shallow-water equipment was not designed to withstand the python-like pressures below 36 feet. Moreover, the air hoses to these helmets were at least 10 years old and might collapse with a man on the bottom.

The 60-foot boat they were to live on—an old bucket tied at Corregidor's North Pier—was serving as a dormitory for six Filipinos, hired to tend the Filipino divers who had been salvaging boxes of silver for the Japanese since the end of May. Eighteen boxes—$54,000 in silver—had been recovered. The Filipino divers, the Americans learned, had never worked in deep water before. They had stayed down too long, come up too fast. Two had died in the agony of the "bends." When a third lost his helmet and failed to come up, the survivors refused to dive, and the Japanese sent them to prison.

That night the Americans discussed the situation. Those first 18 boxes of silver proved the rest could be recovered; this sharpened the enemy's greed. Obviously, the Japanese Army wanted full credit for salvaging the silver. Otherwise, Imperial Navy divers would have been used. This explained why they were so anxious for the coöperation of the Americans. Perhaps they would make more concessions.

When Takiuti showed up, the divers told him the boat they lived on was a pigsty. It needed cleaning, paint and repair. Men who worked at such hazardous duty, they said, deserved pleasant, relaxing quarters. "Help yourself to whatever you can find on the island," Takiuti told the startled prisoners. "Only hurry, please."

From Corregidor's rubble the sailors scrounged a lush harvest. In a few days the barge, scrubbed and painted, began to look like a pleasant yacht. They fitted her with electric-light fixtures, tapping into a line from a diesel power plant near the pier; they installed plumbing, a wood stove, a first-aid cabinet, bookcases. They walled off staterooms and put down a carpet. (The carpeting wasn't too bad by prisoner-of-war standards. It had last seen duty in General MacArthur's office.)

They were just beginning to enjoy domestic life when Yosobe showed up with two Japanese soldiers and hustled the Americans and the Filipino tenders aboard a small fishing boat. They chugged slowly around the east end of Corregidor, then pointed toward Caballo Bay. In the distance the Americans saw a flat diving barge. It was anchored directly over the place where they had dumped the treasure!

In a few minutes a motor launch approached and put a big, tough-looking, impassive Japanese aboard the diving barge. His uniform showed that he was a Kempe—a member of an elite, Gestapo-like army organization. An ordinary soldier might be bribed, but a Kempe, they knew, was incorruptible, intelligent and answerable to no one for his actions. He could shoot them on the spot, no questions asked.

The Kempe's first act was to end the sham that they would be salvaging sunken ships. He spoke to Yosobe in Japanese. "Your orders are to salvage the silver dumped here before the surrender," Yosobe said to the Americans, smiling. The divers had planned to tell Yosobe they knew nothing of such silver. But a look at the Kempe changed their minds.

A small, flat vessel stood alongside the barge. A thick cable from a hand winch ran over its deck and hung down toward the water. There was a beltlike strap at the end. When a diver found a box of silver, he was to loop this strap around it and two Filipinos would winch it up.

Sauers was to make the first dive. He got into the helmet, ran the air hose and life line beneath his right arm and grabbed the cable strap. Then he let himself into the water. It was warm and calm. Slowly, carefully, Sauers inched his way down the descending line, a thick Manila rope anchored to the bottom. Soon he stood motionless on the firm, sandy bottom. Then the ocean floor came into focus, and he saw it!

A towering mountain of boxes lay some yards from him. If the enemy had the slightest hint that the silver was so concen-

trated, he would permit no delay. Competent divers could bring
the entire fortune to the surface in a few weeks.

Sauers thought hard: since the Filipinos had already brought
up 18 boxes, the Japanese knew they were in the right spot. It
would be best to send up a few boxes at once to prove the
divers' reliability and give them more time to plan. He looped
the lifting cable around a box and gave three tugs—the signal to
the Filipinos to haul it up. Fifteen minutes later he climbed
aboard the barge. When he got his helmet off, Sauers began to
grin. Yosobe and the Kempe were paying no attention to him.
Both were on the smaller vessel, standing over the sweating
Filipinos, ordering them to move the box of silver to the rear of
the boat. The Kempe stationed himself next to it and indicated
that he would guard it with his life.

Solomon made the next dive and sent up a box. Punchy
Barton made a third dive, but sent nothing up. "Couldn't find a
damn thing down there," he told Yosobe. "The others must've
got all there was around here."

"We will try again," Yosobe said.

When diving ceased for the day, Captain Takiuti met them at
the North Pier with a ham and a bottle of whiskey. Only 12,000
pesos had been recovered, but it was a promising start.

On their living barge the Americans cooked dinner and made
plans. The two boxes they had sent up were waterlogged and
beginning to rot. On future dives they would loosen the ends so
the heavy bags of silver would break out and spill as the box was
being lifted. Then they would steal the loose silver.

Moe Solomon cut up several pairs of dungaree trousers and
sewed the pants legs into bags fitted with draw strings and a cord
to tie around the diver's waist. The bag would hang under his
diving underwear. On the bottom, the diver would fill his bag
with pesos, and as he came aboard, his tenders would remove it
and stash it beneath raincoats on deck.

Slim Mann dived first. Secreted beneath his diving underwear
he had a marlinespike for breaking open the boxes. On the bottom, he stripped the metal bands from one box and pried at both
ends until they were loose. Then he signaled and watched it

rise. About halfway to the surface the box collapsed and bags of silver came drifting down. The Filipinos felt the weight slip away and lowered the cable again. Mann attached another ruined box and it too burst. Then he stabbed the marlinespike into the ocean bed and went up.

There was consternation on the barge. Yosobe was frantic. What had happened to the silver? The Kempe stood close by, silent, staring angrily. "This is going to be a helluva job!" Mann shouted with feigned disgust. "Those boxes are rotted. Fall apart when you touch 'em."

"But two boxes arrived yesterday all right," Yosobe said.

"We were lucky yesterday," Mann replied. "Look at the boxes we got. They were full of water rot."

Yosobe was pacing the deck, wringing his hands, muttering, "We must do better! We must do better!"

Barton dived next. He stuffed as many of the loose pesos as he could carry into the sack beneath his diving underwear, then sent up an undamaged box to appease Yosobe. He reached the surface as the box was being lifted aboard the smaller vessel. While the Japanese were inspecting it, Solomon untied his money bag and slipped it into a bucket beneath a raincoat. Moe Solomon went down next.

That night the Americans counted their loot: $750. To buy off any suspicious Japanese and set up a distribution system to get the silver to American prisoners on Corregidor and in Manila, they would need much more. "Gentlemen, we must do better!" Punchy Barton said.

In the next two weeks the Americans stuffed $10,000 in silver into the bilges of the living barge. The enemy's take was $55,000. On some days the water was too rough to dive. The recovery wasn't enough to satisfy Yosobe. He decided the job was going too slowly. The only answer was to find more divers.

At Cabanatuan prison camp the Japanese picked out three more veteran divers: Torpedoman Robert C. Sheats, Bosun's Mate George Chopchick and Carpenter's Mate H. S. Anderson. All were old shipmates of the divers in Caballo Bay.

When they came on board, the old hands explained the setup,

then showed off their quarters. The newcomers were flabbergasted. Nooks and crevices were filled with tobacco, candy, peanuts, salt, sugar, pepper, eggs, coffee, rum.

Sheats, Anderson and Chopchick gleefully counted the take—$1215 that day. Afterward they helped carry it through a trapdoor down to a dark lower deck. The divers hauled at long lines through the bilge hatches. Bucketfuls of silver arrived at the hatch openings.

"The interest, of course, is lousy," Jughead Sauers said. "But we don't trust the local banks." The new silver was added, and the buckets were lowered again.

Then the old hands told how the system worked. The Filipinos who manned the air pumps were allowed to visit their families in Manila. The Americans had studied them carefully, tested them with snide remarks about the Emperor of Japan. Finally, convinced of their loyalty, they told them they were stealing silver. Would the Filipinos help distribute it? They would.

The pump hands found some Chinese money-changers in Manila who were glad to exchange Japan's paper occupation currency for Philippine silver—at a black-market rate that undermined the yen. Ultimately they got so much silver into circulation in Manila that the rate of exchange fell to 30 to 1 and nobody would have anything to do with the Japanese occupation currency. The money was used to buy supplies, or smuggled to American prisoners of war. The Filipinos helped themselves to large commissions. The Americans felt the commissions were deserved. The Filipinos were risking their lives.

The day after Sheats and Chopchick arrived, Yosobe had the living boat towed to the South Pier, closer to the treasure site, to speed up the work. The Americans didn't like it, for there would be no privacy here. A tug and an enemy barge were tied on either side of them. The Japanese sailors were likely to inspect the living barge on a moment's whim. But that day, at least, they would be too busy. Skies were darkening and seas were running high. The sailors were making ready for a storm.

By next morning the area was in the shrieking, maniacal grip

of a full-fledged typhoon. The whole South China Sea seemed to
be marching into Manila Bay in endless processions of gigantic
waves. The Japanese sailors abandoned the tug for shelter in
Corregidor's tunnels. But the Americans had to save their boat.
It was old and wooden; if it smashed against the rocky shore, it
would surely spill its forbidden cargo onto the beaches.

By some miracle of effort they held on. When the typhoon
was finally past, Corregidor was a shambles. Not a tree was left
standing. The Japanese barge had been carried away. Dozens of
boxes of silver had been lifted from the watery vault far out in
the bay and smashed open on the island's south shore, where
Filipino workers were eagerly helping themselves. But the living
barge was still tied to the pier.

For two weeks the Japanese had to repair the damage, and
this gave the divers a better chance to deliver their silver to the
other American prisoners on Corregidor. After the storm, working parties of prisoners were brought out to clean up the mess.
The working parties weren't heavily guarded, and the enemy soldiers couldn't tell a diver from any other prisoner. Two or three
at a time, the divers moved into a group and started working.
When the guards weren't looking, they passed the silver to the
startled POW's. Soon the divers had delivered thousands of
pesos. They decided not to press their luck further, and it was
well they didn't, for the next morning Captain Takiuti came
aboard.

With Takiuti was a smaller, mean-looking officer. Neither of
them said a word. They moved slowly through the cabin, poked
at mattresses, looked beneath piles of diving underwear, into the
medicine cabinet, the stove, the bookcases. So the enemy suspected them! Finally Takiuti stood on the piece of carpet that
covered the trapdoor to the lower level. Takiuti knew of the
hold. There were still thousands of pesos in the bilges. The divers
thought the game was over.

But Takiuti surprised them. "You men must make better
progress in recovering the silver," he said severely. Then, un-
accountably, he turned and left.

"He must have forgotten the hold!" someone breathed.

"He didn't forget," Sauers said. "It was wet and filthy the last time he saw it. He probably didn't want to get dirty. They'll be back! Let's get that stuff out of here!"

There was only one thing they could do. They would have to return their horde of silver to the sea. Ten buckets of silver were laid on the bottom that day.

The next day Takiuti and three armed soldiers probed every inch of the living barge. The divers followed them, expressions of outraged hurt on their faces.

"We've worked hard for you, Captain," Moe Solomon said earnestly. "Now you act like we're *thieves* or something!"

"I think it is highly possible," Takiuti snapped, "that you *are* thieves—or something!" Takiuti was burning when he led his inspection party off the barge. He hadn't found a single peso. When he did, the divers would all be shot.

The next morning their fears were confirmed. As they prepared to dive, the Kempe suddenly appeared on the diving barge. He spoke in Japanese to Yosobe and began stripping. "He is going to dive," Yosobe said. "He wants to see what you have been doing on the bottom."

The divers glanced at each other. This was the finish for them all. The Kempe could not be allowed to return from the sea alive. But they too were doomed. The enemy would accept no excuse for a Kempe's death.

The Kempe was fitted with a helmet and started to descend into the water. Sheats tended the life line, Barton the air hose. When the Kempe reached bottom, Sheats planned to rip off the helmet.

The Kempe grabbed the descending line and started down. But after moving only a few feet he started up again! Out of the helmet, he got into a huddle with Yosobe.

"Kempe has claustrophobia," Yosobe explained to the divers. "He can't stand the helmet. And he has decided you have not been doing wrong on the bottom or you would not have co-operated in sending him down."

The diving continued until late autumn. By then it was obvious to the Japanese that the silver was coming from Caballo

Bay. But they would never admit even to themselves that it had been stolen by the American divers. The Americans could never have gotten it past their Kempes!

The security police now reported officially that all the silver in circulation had been taken from the boxes washed ashore in the typhoon. The case was closed. To keep it closed, they canceled the silver-recovery program, and everyone was happy, especially the Americans.

The divers were sent to Manila to work as stevedores in a group commanded by Lieutenant Commander George G. Harrison, the man who had worked with them during the dumping of the silver. They spent the next two years with "G.G.'s 400 Thieves," sabotaging every enemy cargo of food and war matériel they could reach. Many outgoing ships—overloaded in a way calculated to make them capsize in foul weather, and with holes pounded through their hulls—were never heard from again.

All of the men survived the war except George Chopchick, who died in 1944 aboard a prison ship en route to Japan.

As for the silver: the U.S. Navy raised about $2,500,000 worth after the war, then quit trying. The boxes kept crumbling from water rot and the damage the American prisoners had inflicted on them. The effort became more expensive than the silver was worth.

In 1947 two Americans got a contract from the Philippine government, but were able to raise only about $250,000 more.

More than four million dollars in silver still lies on the floor of Caballo Bay. Scattered and buried by the currents and storms of years, it will probably remain there forever—a watery monument to the men of the U.S. Navy who did their best to keep it there.

The Micro-Dot

By J. Edgar Hoover

One morning early in January 1940 a traveler stood at the rail of a ship as it entered New York Harbor. The pilot had just come aboard with the usual officials. No one else was near as one of the boarding party whispered to the man at the rail: "You are to be S. T. Jenkins. As soon as we land, go to the Belvoir Hotel. Wait in your room!"

That evening, after hours of waiting, Jenkins heard a key turn in a lock; the door to the next suite quietly opened and two special agents of the Federal Bureau of Investigation marched in. Jenkins, who was on the FBI payroll, shook hands with the agents and plunged into a disturbing report:

"I have been a student at the Nazi Espionage School, Klopstock Pension, Hamburg. My class was graduated two weeks ago. In a farewell speech the principal, Dr. Hugo Sebold, said: 'The greatest problem of the Führer's agents in North and South America is keeping in touch with us. The Americans have given us a great deal of trouble. But before long we shall be communicating back and forth throughout the world with impunity. I cannot explain the method now, but watch out for the dots—*lots and lots of little dots!*' I have been sent to America with my orders—and was told nothing more," our secret agent said.

Until this time we had kept German and Japanese espionage backed into a corner by constantly uncovering every new enemy communication technique. We had identified their couriers, traced their mail drops, broken their codes and solved their secret inks; we had tracked down their hidden radio transmitters, sometimes operating them for the enemy. Once we took from a spy's pocket a box of safety matches. Four of them, looking just like the others, were actually little pencils that wrote invisibly, the writing later to be developed by a solution made from a rare drug. This story-book contraption we exposed, along with microfilm letters rolled around a spool and covered with silk thread and others stitched into the backbones of magazines; one film was tucked inside the barrel of a fountain pen that had to be broken to extract the note.

All these devices, and more, we had detected—but what was this matter of "lots of little dots"?

Our first move was to call in from our laboratories a young physicist who had done extraordinary work in color microphotography. He was assigned to certain experiments, based on guesses in our office about the meaning of Sebold's boast. Meanwhile every agent was looking feverishly for some telltale evidence of the as yet undetected dots.

One day in August 1941 we met a youngish traveler from the Balkans on his arrival in the United States. We knew he was the playboy son of a millionaire. There was reason to believe he was a German agent. With meticulous care we examined his possessions, from toothbrush to shoes. While a laboratory agent was holding an envelope so that the light slanted obliquely across its surface, he saw a sudden tiny gleam. A dot had reflected the light. A dot—a punctuation period on the front of the envelope, a black particle no bigger than a fly speck.

With infinite care the agent touched the point of a needle under the rim of the black circle and pried the thing loose. It was a bit of alien matter that had been driven into the fiber of the paper, where it looked like a typewritten period. Under the microscope it was magnified 200 times. And then we could see that it was an image on a film of a full-sized typewritten letter— a spy letter with blood-chilling text:

> There is reason to believe that the scientific works for the utilization of atomic-kernel energy are being driven forward into a certain direction in the United States partly by use of helium. Continuous information about the tests made on this subject are required and particularly:

    1. What process is practiced in the United States for transporting heavy uranium?
    2. Where are being made tests with uranium? (Universities, industrial laboratories, etc.)
    3. Which other raw materials are being used in these tests? Entrust only best experts with this.

Now we had it! The German espionage service had found a way to photograph a full-sized letter down to the size of a midge. It was incredibly ingenious and effective, this micro-dot gadget. It perfectly counterfeited a typewritten or printed dot. The young Balkan agent, for example, had four telegraph blanks in his pocket, carrying Lilliputian spy orders that looked like periods: 11 micro-dots on the four papers. We found one tiny strip of the film, pasted under a postage stamp, that carried the images of 25 full-sized typewritten sheets!

Under questioning the Balkan playboy was bland and affable. Seeing that we knew about the dots, he began to talk freely.

He had studied under the famous Professor Zapp, inventor of the micro-dot process, at the Technical High School in Dresden. Espionage messages were first typed on square sheets of paper and then photographed with a high-precision miniature camera. This first reduction was to about the size of a postage stamp. Again it was photographed, this time through a reversed microscope, the infinitesimally small image being retained and developed on a glass slab heavily coated with the secret emulsion. The developed negative was painted over with collodion, so the emulsion could be slipped bodily off the glass. The technician then used a curious adaptation of the hypodermic needle, the point of which was clipped off and the round edge sharpened. This was placed over the micro-dot as a baker's cutting cup pinches out a piece of dough—and the micro-dot lifted out.

Next, at a point on the letter where the dot was to be placed the paper was scratched ever so slightly with a needle. The syringe plunger pressed the dot into the texture. Another very small needle scratched the fiber back over the dot, and finally it received a dab of collodion to tie down the fibers of the paper. To

read the missives, Nazi agents carried a collapsible microscope.

We were able to spot and intercept hundreds of micro-dot messages. Through the constant scrutiny of micro-dots we got a daily insight into the doings of various gangs. They were viciously active, acquiring information on ship movements through the Panama Canal, the deficient condition of one of the locks, the extent of destruction of our oil stores in the attack on Pearl Harbor. Urgent demands came from Berlin for more and more. On one spy we found what seemed an innocent telephone message on a crumpled memo form from a hotel switchboard. But the printing of that blank contained two periods which, when enlarged, contained several messages, including the following:

> Here are special orders. It is reported that a cartridge powder is being manufactured in the U.S.A. which is practically smokeless and has a weak muzzle fire. More details desired: color of the muzzle fire, color of the smoke. If possible, the composition of the powder. [Part of the message is reproduced on this page from FBI files.]

The Japanese, too, were playing the dot game. On February 12, 1942, micro-dot message No. 90 of a series being watched, imbedded in the envelope of a letter mailed to a drop in Brazil, relayed a message from Tokyo to a Japanese naval attaché in South America.

Many spies were arrested, many gang nests cleaned out, because we had the secret of the micro-dot. One day a message mentioned casually the name of a woman resident of Madrid. A search of our voluminous cross file revealed that some years before she had cabled money to a man in America. We found that this young man was idling in Washington, and that he had once been very attentive to an American girl. Later she had joined the Wacs and was now on the Pacific coast. As always, the Army coöperated; the young Wac was ordered to Washington, and 15 minutes after her arrival she was in the FBI office.

How well did she know this man? Once he had been very attentive to her, but his brooding and secretive manner had repelled her; finally she had dropped all correspondence with him. We put the problem to her frankly. What we needed was a pipeline into his innermost thoughts. As a soldier in the Army of the United States, would she be willing to try to discover if he were an enemy?

It was contrived that she would run into her admirer accidentally on the street. Taken in by the ruse, he was delighted to see her again, and for the next month the Wac played Delilah magnificently. Soon the spy was behind bars because he blabbed to her of his espionage work, believing in his vanity that she loved him enough to be his accomplice.

The most important case broken through the micro-dot was in a South American country, where we were finding letters written by all sorts of people—every one loaded with micro-dots for Berlin. Love letters, family missives, business communications, all seemed harmless, but their imbedded micro-dot messages had to do with the blowing up of seized Axis ships in southern harbors and details of war production. The letters were in different handwritings or typed on various typewriters, but the micro-dots they secretly carried were all produced by the same machines, the signatures in the same handwriting. Hence all were prepared by a single organization. The day came when in one city after another in South America, from shop and office and home, South American authorities aided by our agents were able to seize a great interlocking ring of Nazi agents—all enemies of the United States.

These are but samples of the plans we blocked because we got that tip-off on the micro-dot from an agent planted right under Dr. Sebold's enormous nose.

Joey's Quiet War

By Thomas M. Johnson

Across the battlefields north of Manila trudged a little Filipino woman bearing a knapsack on her bent shoulders. Several Japanese soldiers started to question her. Some of them, seeing her bloated, scarred brown face, understood and shrank back. To others she bared her chest and showed her sores. When she uttered the one word "Leprosy," no sentry persisted, none examined the knapsack, none found out that—taped on her back—she carried a map of the Japanese defenses north of Manila.

The map accurately indicated minefields which the advancing U.S. troops desperately needed to know about. Sick and suffering, Joey Guerrero got the map through and thereby saved hundreds of American lives. It was but one of her great contributions to our victory in the Philippines.

Among the cleverest and bravest women spies of the war, Joey was decorated by our government with the Medal of Freedom with Silver Palm—the highest award for war service by a civilian. It was made possible for her to go to Carville, La., where astounding progress was being made in treating Hansen's disease (leprosy). (See photograph on page 333.)

As a little girl, Josefina Guerrero had wanted to become a nun, but she contracted tuberculosis and the sisters said she was not strong enough for their life. Both her parents died, and a grandmother took the child to the coconut plantation she managed and brought her back to health.

Then Joey went to live with an uncle in Manila. There a young physician, Dr. Renato María Guerrero, fell in love with the lively girl and they were married. The future shone bright. But in the winter of 1941, when her daughter, Cynthia, was two years old, Joey began to lose strength and appetite. Swellings appeared. Her anxious husband called in an American-trained specialist. As gently as he could, he told Joey the truth. "It is in an early stage," he said. "You are only 23, and there are promising treatments. But children are susceptible, so you must leave your child." For hours she sat in the doctor's office praying for the surpassing self-control she would need for so many years. She went home. The child was playing in the nursery. It was like dying, but Joey dared not even take the risk of kissing Cynthia good-bye when she sent the child to her grandmother.

Husband and wife then began to plan their fight against the disease and against ostracism. It had not been long since lepers had to ring a bell as they walked the streets of Manila. Specialists told them that Hansen's disease was now recognized as only feebly contagious among adults, and that Joey was no menace to others. But she did need good medical care and rest.

There was to be neither. Three weeks later came Pearl Harbor. Soon Japanese soldiers swaggered on Manila's streets. One day five of them stopped Joey and four other young Filipinas and made clear their intent. Joey, five feet and 100 pounds of outraged womanhood, whacked the largest soldier with her umbrella until he and his companions made off. That night one of the other women telephoned Joey. "Come to our house," she said, and hung up.

Her friend's husband awaited Joey. "A woman of your spirit should join the guerrillas," he said. "You're the kind for our secret service." He told her the Filipino Underground was sending information about the Japanese to MacArthur in Australia to help plan the islands' liberation. Would she join them? "I can't do big things," said Joey, "but every little helps. O.K.!"

Joey was given a trial assignment: "Since you live opposite a Japanese barracks, for the next 24 hours count how many Japs go in and out, when, and in what direction. The same for passing vehicles."

Behind drawn blinds, Joey noted everything that passed, and the time. She not only counted a truckload of Japanese soldiers, but observed that they looked dirty, as if coming from active service. She took a full notebook to the address given her. There she signed an oath of secrecy and loyalty. She had enlisted for what she called "my quiet war." Her tour of duty was to last for three nerve-racking years.

Joey was assigned to watch the waterfront. There her keen eyes spotted hidden Japanese anti-aircraft guns. She made a sketch and concealed it in a hollowed-out fruit in a basket she carried. A Japanese soldier stopped her, pawed the fruit, greedily chose a large one and walked on. Luckily she had put the sketch in a small fruit. After that she made only mental notes, did her drawing at home.

Joey was among the group of girls permitted to bring food to the starving Filipino and American prisoners. She radiated courage and faith to hollow-eyed GI's, some of whom gave her information they had gleaned from talkative Japanese guards. Once a suspicious guard threatened her with a bayonet, finally gestured her on, giving her braided black hair a parting tug. Her hair ribbon concealed a prisoner's report, but it was tied too tightly to come off.

By September 1944 the approaching Americans were bombing Manila, smashing gun emplacements Joey had mapped for them. The Japanese counter-intelligence police had stool pigeons everywhere and many guerrillas were being caught and tortured or shot. Underground operations were now directed by the Allied Intelligence Bureau. After another cryptic telephone call, Joey met Manuel Colayco, formerly a professor at Santo Tomás University, now a captain in Intelligence. Would Joey join the AIB? It might mean her life, but—

"What can I do?" she asked.

He told her to meet a truck at a rendezvous in the outskirts of the city. She wore wooden shoes, in the hollow soles of which she had hidden thin packets of tissue paper containing guerrilla information about Japanese preparations to defend Manila. The truck took her 50 miles by rough back roads to Nagcarlán mountain. There a guide led them up a narrow path. A large boulder barred the route, and a voice from nowhere challenged them. Joey gave the password. A light flashed in her eyes from a tree above and then winked out. The guide turned the boulder as if it were on a hinge. Pushing through, they found themselves in a clearing where perhaps 100 Filipino guerrillas were living in nipa-palm barracks. Joey watched them set up a wireless apparatus and send off her message.

She became "just a little errand boy." By various routes to the guerrilla hideout she brought reports, maps and photographs. And it was at the camp that she heard the glorious news radioed through: "The Americans are landing on Luzon!"

The guerrillas made handbills on a smuggled mimeograph machine—LIBERATION IS NEAR!—and added a ringing appeal for help. Joey took the bills to Manila. She and other volunteers flitted through the blackout, slipping them under doors or into the hands of passers-by.

Next she was assigned to spotting Japanese ammunition dumps. One night she heard a signal at her door. She admitted a man in Japanese uniform who handed her what seemed to be a bag of vegetables. "Here's something for Dr. Guerrero," he whispered quickly and then slipped from the house. Her husband, who was also in the Underground, took the bag of "vegetables," but said nothing. Many nights thereafter were thunderous with exploding ammunition dumps. In the daytime Joey looked for dumps that needed more "vegetable treatment."

But soon Colayco sent word that she was needed as a messenger again, so Joey returned to Nagcarlán. She hoped the mountain air would renew her ebbing strength. With the scarcity of food and medicine, she was increasingly feverish and exhausted. She suffered excruciating headaches, her feet were swelling and more sores appeared on her body. Surely, she prayed, God and the returning Americans would bring help.

Early in 1945, when the Americans were approaching Manila, Colayco summoned her for the most dangerous mission of all. The guerrillas had sent the American Army a map of the Japanese defenses which showed a wide section free of mines. The Americans planned to attack there, but now the Japanese had mined the area heavily. A corrected map must be taken to 37th Division Headquarters at Calumpit, 40 miles north of Manila. There was fighting all the way. The Japanese guarded every road and path, searched all passers-by. Vehicles could not get through. A woman afoot might, if she was small, shabby and courageous. Would Joey try? "Just tell me where to go," Joey said.

At first she walked under cover of night, but loss of sleep

weakened her still more, and the headaches grew worse. She determined to try it by daylight. The first day a Japanese officer halted her, approached as if to search her. The map taped between her shoulder blades seemed to burn. As the officer came close, he peered at her face. It was bloated and spotted with red. He stared in fear, then quickly waved her on. Joey knew that she had a terrible passport that would get her through.

After two days and nights on the road she reached American headquarters and delivered the map. Weak from sickness and reaction, she could not eat the pancakes and coffee which the Americans offered, though she had not tasted them for years.

Her road back took her through heavy fighting. When she reached Manila, she learned that Manuel Colayco had been terribly wounded during the last days of the fighting. She went to see him in the hospital where he lay dying. He tried to raise his torn body. "Fine job!" he whispered, in a last salute.

Joey turned to nursing patients in an evacuation hospital; but her illness, aggravated by overwork, became so serious that the hospital authorities told her she must go to Tala, the Philippine government leprosarium. She found it a cluster of leaking shacks in a wilderness. There was little food and almost no medical care.

Soon after the war ended, Tala was suddenly flooded by 600 more patients. It was too much for Joey. She had been trying to bring some sort of order and sanitation to the place. Now she appealed to Aurora Quezón, the ex-President's daughter. An exposé in Manila newspapers brought results: new buildings, a laboratory, an operating room; more doctors and nurses; above all, supplies of the new sulfone drugs.

Through the intercession of friends who knew of Joey's work, Attorney General Clark granted her plea to be allowed treatment at Carville. There patients greeted her with bouquets and a birthday cake. They saw a tiny woman whose brown face was scarred and pale, but whose lively eyes still smiled. Dr. Frederick A. Johansen—kindly, famous "Dr. Jo"—started daily sulfone injections and other treatments, and her health began to improve. Her sores healed, her face glowing, she became a tribute to Carville's care and skill. She greeted her many visitors with a firm handclasp and a torrent of eager words. "By heart, I am happy," she told them.

Discharged from Carville, she made her home in California. She says, "My whole life has been a great adventure."

The Hunt for a Spy

By Carl B. Wall

This is a spy story minus false whiskers, cloak and dagger. There is no beautiful Mata Hari. No desperate cliff-edge struggle. Not a shot is fired. And yet this case is one of the most intriguing in the annals of the Federal Bureau of Investigation. It is the hunt for an unknown man lost in the swirling tides of New York City's 8,000,000 people.

On the night of February 20, 1942, an alert postal censor, scanning mail destined for Portugal, plucked a typewritten sheet from an airmail envelope. It was apparently harmless—the sort of letter one old friend writes another. But the address was one of those listed by counter-espionage agents abroad as a "mail drop" for German agents. (See "Censors and Spies," page 258.)

Hours later, in the Washington laboratories of the FBI, an expert in secret ink stroked the blank side of the paper with a chemically saturated sponge. From the empty whiteness slowly the secret writing appeared, twisting in the curious hieroglyphics of German handprinting. The message conveyed information on troop ships and freighters making up for convoy in the Port of New York. In the hands of the enemy it would be a deadly threat to the lives of soldiers and seamen and tons of valuable shipping.

The spy must be captured. But the laboratory yielded only one thin clue. The fake letter had been typed on an Underwood three-bank portable machine. Agents began an almost hopeless check on typewriter sales and rentals in the New York area.

Within the next 10 days there was a second letter and then a third, all mailed from New York post offices. Did this mean that the spy lived in New York? And what did he look like? Usually when police are hunting a criminal they have some description to go by. Here the FBI had nothing.

One night a special agent, mulling over photostatic copies of the original letters, was struck by the fact that certain passages of the typed section had a curious aura of truth. Most of it, he knew, was sheer invention; but about the inconsequential trivia of everyday life the spy might well be truthful. With surging excitement, the special agent jotted down these things which seemed to be true:

X was married. He owned his home. He had a dog which had been ill with distemper. He had a job. He left his home between seven and eight o'clock every weekday morning. He had recently had his eyeglasses changed. He was an air-raid warden.

There were 98,338 air-raid wardens in Greater New York. The agent-in-charge grinned when he heard about the idea. "That's a lot of air-raid wardens, but it's better than 8,000,000 John Does. We've at least got a toenail hold."

With grim tenacity, the FBI began the heroic task of checking every one of those wardens. How many were married? How many owned homes? How many owned dogs? Which wore spectacles? As more letters were intercepted, the image of X began to take shape. These items were added to the list: He had a victory garden. His home was threatened by mortgage foreclosure. He wanted to own a chicken farm.

The shadow of the invisible spy was still indefinite but it could no longer be cast by millions. Hardworking FBI agents, day by day, night by night, cut the figure. 98,000 . . . 88,000 . . . 81,000. But even 81,000 is a lot of people.

On the night of April 14 the 12th letter was intercepted. From it the investigators plucked this apparently innocent, nostalgic passage: "It is very warm here and the trees are beginning to bud. The spring always reminds me of that wonderful week we spent on the beach at Estoril. . . ." Estoril! The FBI knew

Estoril. A resort a few miles outside Lisbon, it was a clearing-house for German espionage agents.

There was a hurried conference. What was the best way to check every citizen and alien entering the United States from Lisbon since the spring of 1941? There was no photograph to compare with passport photographs. No fingerprints. No name. Then one of the agents clicked: "We have a fairly good specimen of X's handwriting—the signature on the letters—Fred Lewis. The name is phony, but it's almost as hard to disguise your handwriting as it is to change your fingerprints.

"Every person entering the United States," he went on, "must fill out a baggage declaration for customs. Why couldn't our boys go through the file at the U.S. Customs Office in New York and compare the handwriting on the declarations with the signature of Fred Lewis?" Next morning, FBI handwriting experts, armed with photographic copies of the hunted spy's handwriting, began working their way through thousands upon thousands of customs declarations. The spring of 1941 had been the high tide of the refugee flood out of Lisbon. The handwriting on baggage declarations was a weird assortment—in Polish, German, French, Dutch, Russian, Lithuanian. . . .

The work of the handwriting expert is an exact science. Clues hang on the slightest twist of an *e* or the looping of an *l*. Each form had to be examined with meticulous care. For days, for months, the experts burrowed through the mountainous stacks.

At nine o'clock on the night of June 9, 1943, a special agent picked one more form from the stacks in the New York Customs Office, the 4881st that had been examined. Suddenly, as his eyes focused on the signature at the bottom of the sheet, his weariness vanished. He reached for his magnifying glass. Yes, there was the same looping *e*. The same slanting *f*. The identical sloping *s*. The expert startled his colleagues with a bellow.

That night in the Washington laboratory the signature was photographed, the prints enlarged and compared with the spy letters. The experts were sure now. At 1:45 a.m. the telephone rang in the FBI's New York field office: "Check the name Ernest F. Lehmitz." The list of air-raid wardens was consulted. On it

was the name Lehmitz—123 Oxford Place, Tompkinsville, Staten Island, N. Y.

Less than an hour later special agents strode down the gangplank of the ferry from Manhattan to Staten Island. Throughout the night, FBI agents watched the house in Oxford Place. At *7:15* a tall, spare man wearing *spectacles* walked out of the door. One of the FBI men casually followed him along the street. Not far from the house the suspect turned into a restaurant.

Despite the early morning hour, the restaurant was filled with waterfront workers, soldiers, sailors. The agent went inside. His man had donned a soiled apron and was mopping the floor. He seemed to be about 55, with mild blue eyes and wispy brown hair. You wouldn't look at him twice—he was just a sparrow among thousands of sparrows. (See photograph on page 334.)

In the restaurant, men were talking: cargos, ship movements, sailing dates. The agent drank a cup of coffee and went out.

For the next 16 days and nights the spy was shadowed. Special agents, posing as salesmen and talkative bar-flies, unearthed one damning fact after another—damning because they jibed so perfectly with the chit-chat of the spy letters. Neighbors like to talk:

"Ernie? Sure, I know Ernie. He's *air-raid warden* for the block and you should have heard how he bawled people out for not dimming lights. Ernie takes the war seriously."

"Ernie? A kindhearted guy. *He had a dog that died of distemper* last summer and you'd have thought he'd lost his best friend."

"Ernie Lehmitz? Got one of the best *victory gardens* on the island."

"Too bad the bank foreclosed on that *mortgage*."

"Sure I know him. He usually stops in here for a glass of beer on the way home. He's a quiet kind of guy. All he talks about is the *chicken farm* he's going to buy one of these days."

Slowly the noose tightened. At eight o'clock on the morning of June 27, 1943, one year, four months and seven days after the first letter had been intercepted, Lehmitz was brought into the FBI offices. He was shown the letters, the great mass of evidence so painfully accumulated. The avalanche of facts was too much. He signed a complete confession.

He had first arrived in the United States in 1908 as clerk in the German Consulate in New York. There were several trips to Germany. During the last, in 1938, he was recruited by the Nazi espionage system, trained in the use of secret inks and in the labyrinthine ways of the spy. He was ordered to return to the United States in the spring of 1941, find steady employment, pose as a good citizen, lose himself among millions.

In his confession Lehmitz implicated another spy, Erwin Harry DeSpretter. (See photograph on page 334.) The second and third agents to be tried under the wartime espionage statute in World War II, both were sentenced to 30 years' imprisonment.

How well Lehmitz had played his role of John Doe was indicated a few weeks after his arrest when many of his Staten Island neighbors dropped in to offer Mrs. Lehmitz their sympathy. One of the women, who had a son in the service, said: "It can't be anything very bad. Why, that Ernie Lehmitz wouldn't hurt a flea." But to the FBI the trapping of this stoop-shouldered, mild-mannered spy had been one of the most tedious jobs of World War II. A dramatic, cloak-and-dagger spy is duck soup. A spy who rides the subways and wears rubbers may not be glamorous—but he's a thousand times harder to catch.

Shepherds of
the Underground

By George Kent

From a freight train on a siding in eastern France, a woman worker of the French Red Cross heard a strange, muffled wailing, like the sound of a radio heard through a wall. She walked along the train, listening, and discovered to her horror that inside one of the cars children were screaming. She called the station agent and they managed to get the door open.

There were 80 Jewish children packed tight in that freight car, clinging to each other in terror. They had been put aboard by the Nazis at Paris with two loaves of bread, a flagon of water and some cheese. They had been locked in for 18 hours while the train made its halting progress toward the Reich. Four had already died. The presence of these dead companions, the darkness, the fear of the unknown future had made the children hysterical. Several of them were temporarily deranged.

These youngsters probably never saw their parents again—even assuming that their parents escaped death. The Nazis had cut off their identification bracelets, and most of them were too

young to know their names. One little girl remembered brightly
that she lived at number 16 but could not remember the street.
Yet these children were lucky; they were smuggled into hiding.
Most of the 15,000 Jewish children the Nazis seized in France
and packed off to Germany were not so fortunate. Many were
put to death in the gas chambers.

My story is concerned with the children the Nazis didn't get.
There were 12,000 or more, from babies to gawky kids of 15 and
16. Four thousand were smuggled across the Swiss and Spanish
borders; 8000 were kept alive and safe right under the Nazi nose.
(See "Conspiracy of Mercy," page 311.)

The leaders in the work were two Catholic priests and a
Protestant minister—Fathers Chaillet and Duvaux and the
Reverend Paul Vergara. Father Chaillet was a nervous man with
the pallor and tired eyes of a scholar who worked 14 to 16 hours
daily. (See photograph on page 342.) Father Duvaux was a figure out of the *Canterbury Tales*, an enormous rosy tub of a man
with a full fan beard. Pastor Vergara, whose denomination
resembled the Presbyterian, was small and gnomelike, with
disheveled gray hair and high cheekbones.

These three men perfected an interlocking organization
throughout France the sole purpose of which was to save Jewish
children from the Nazis. Father Chaillet alone managed to find
safety for more than 4000. Duvaux tucked away a thousand.
Vergara with the help of other Protestant ministers accounted
for a sixth thousand. The rest were taken care of by ordinary
people inspired by love of children and hatred of Nazis.

A celebrated physician helped by taking Jewish children to his
hospital and fitting them out with fake disease and fever charts.
He also developed a chemical formula which washed the word
Jew from the children's food cards—the red ink of the stamp had
resisted all previous eradicators. One committee of 10 middle-
aged women, five Protestant and five Catholic, managed to save
358 children at the risk of their own lives. Scores of men and
women who aided the youngsters were imprisoned; some were
killed.

Father Chaillet, a Jesuit, was the outstanding figure in this labor of love. After the 1940 armistice he started a militantly liberal weekly called *Témoignage Chrétien* (*The Christian Witness*), which attained considerable Underground influence, especially among young men and women. They haunted Father Chaillet's office.

Early in 1942, Vichy rounded up and shipped to Germany several thousand Jews. In Lyons, where the priest lived, the deported men and women were forced to leave their children behind—120 in all. Father Chaillet started gathering up the youngsters. Four he found, half starved and terror-stricken, living in a cellar. A dozen more were picked up on the street. Thirty he took from a barracks where the police had put them. Methodically he set out to put the children beyond the reach of the Nazis in such a way that they might be united with their families after the war. A former detective fingerprinted each child. Records of names, addresses and identification marks were drawn up in triplicate and secreted. Then Father Chaillet sent his young aides, usually girls of 18 to 20, into the country on their bicycles to talk to peasants. They discovered if the peasants were patriots, if they could be trusted with the care of orphans—and if they had a cow or a milk goat. In a radius of 100 miles around Lyons the girls secured havens for most of the children. Arrangements for the others were made with Catholic orphanages and schools. False papers had to be prepared for each child.

Older, matronly-looking women ran the greater risk of taking the children to the new homes. It was difficult rehearsing the little ones. One small girl, given a new name, wept, "How will Mama know me when she comes back?" A six-year-old boy of Dutch parents, who spoke French with a thick accent, was warned to keep utterly silent on the journey. The ride lasted four hours and the child did not open his mouth. But on arrival his pants were wet. "You told me not to speak," he explained pathetically.

Incorporated into the peasant families, the children mingled freely with the other youngsters of the locality, in school and at play. In these small communities the status of the new arrivals was no secret. But only a half-dozen in all were betrayed.

A few months after Father Chaillet had hidden the children, the Nazis set a quota of 200 Jews to be surrendered by Lyons, and the Vichy police proposed to send the children as part of it. Father Chaillet defied the authorities to find them and was sent to a concentration camp. In prison he wrote an open letter to Catholics and Protestants which was smuggled out and sent to 10,000 priests and ministers. It appealed to all churches to join the fight against Hitler by helping the Jews.

Released at the end of three months, Father Chaillet doffed his clerical dress and took his organization underground. *Témoignage Chrétien* as an organ of the resistance achieved a circulation of more than 200,000. Father Chaillet was recognized as the spiritual leader of the resistance, and General de Gaulle appointed him chief of all the social services of the Underground.

His center of operation was a humble room in a slum street of Grenoble. Here he planned many successful coups of the resistance and worked out the complicated mechanism of hiding Jewish children. As time went on he extended his activities until he was operating in every corner of France. His staff of several hundred workers ranged from small boys who served as messengers to five countesses who acted as escorts.

In July 1942 the Nazis rounded up 13,000 Jews in Paris and herded them into the Vélodrome d'Hiver, the big sports arena. The screaming of the women, torn from their children, could be heard for blocks. Thousands witnessed the incident; it horrified the French and shocked them into activity. Neighbors picked up the children and tried to comfort them.

Father Duvaux, a Dominican, sent out nuns who brought back 30 of the children. At night he distributed them, in groups of three, among the homes of friends in Paris. There they stayed until places could be found for them outside the city. Then the nuns went back for more. This was the beginning of the work of Father Duvaux. For him, it was particularly dangerous. He had been famous in Europe before the war as an opponent of anti-Semitism. The Nazis ransacked his house and carried off his books and papers. Gestapo men kept watch on his quarters 24 hours a day.

Not all the children left behind after the July raid fell into friendly hands. The Gestapo found many of them and put them in camps, where they stayed in a sort of cold storage to await the next draft. Children who had lived in good homes were now living in filth, unwashed, uncared for, vermin-ridden.

One day a Red Cross worker who visited such a place described what she had seen to Pastor Paul Vergara. The little man went into a black rage. At the settlement house he had been running in a Paris slum, he brought together a dozen women, including his wife. They prepared an order in German, purporting to come from Gestapo headquarters, requiring the release of the children. It was a dangerous trick, but it succeeded.

Over the door of the settlement house Pastor Vergara had painted the words of Louis Pasteur: "We do not ask of an unfortunate: What country do you come from or what is your religion? We say to him: You suffer, that is enough. You belong to us; we shall make you well." That night 70 ragged, frightened Jewish children shuffled across the threshold beneath the noble inscription. On the following day the pastor embarked on the enterprise of finding permanent homes for the children, coöperating with Fathers Chaillet and Duvaux.

Twice, later on, the Gestapo raided the settlement house. They killed Vergara's brother-in-law the first time. Warned of the second raid, the office staff escaped through a window and across adjoining roofs. But the Nazis imprisoned and tortured Vergara's wife and son, and later deported the boy.

Most of the 8000 children hidden in France were still in their foster homes at the time of the liberation. About a thousand were claimed by relatives who had escaped from the Nazi net and had come out of hiding. The rest had to wait until the war was over before being restored to their relatives or placed in adoption.

These were not happy children. They had been through experiences that had aged them beyond their years. They had seen their parents beaten and dragged away. They themselves had been brutally treated. For all these happenings there was no explanation that made sense to the mind of a child. But the people who opened their homes to the youngsters had come to love them. "If Jeannot's parents come, yes, we shall give him up," one woman said. "But if they don't, Jeannot is ours, our own."

Children who have known love once are never lost. They respond to love when it comes to them again.

Ghost Ship

By Colonel Robert L. Scott, Jr.

Over the tiny airfield of Kienow, at an hour before dark, rain was falling. The eight P-40's on the runways showed their shark-noses through the haze.

Flight Leader Johnny Hampshire peered out from the operations cave, looking for a break in the weather. His squadron of the China Air Task Force had come from Kunming to this field in eastern China ready for quick action—and now they had lived through a week of stinking weather with nothing to do but gripe. At that instant the alert came. Then telephones began to ring. "What the hell is this, Captain Chow?"

The Chinese officer stuck a red flag on the map. "Don't know. R-15 reports one unidentified plane, coming this way, flying very low." The Japanese never came this far inland in this kind of weather. And a single ship! They didn't send them singly, either, because they had learned long ago that one would never return.

Still, it might be a trick. So Johnny said, "Get the alert shack. Tell Costello to get on my wing and stay close. Keep the other six planes on the ground unless I call."

Two planes nosed down the runway, red mud splashing back into the slip stream; then wet gray clouds seemed to engulf them. In the radio cave they could hear Johnny asking for the position of the unknown plane. Now it was only 20 miles to the east.

Johnny explained later what happened. He was about 10 miles from the field, he said, when he saw the plane 200 feet below. He maneuvered to attack. This was an unidentified aircraft, coming from enemy territory. Orders were to shoot it down.

Johnny and Costello both fired at once. The attack brought them so close that they could see the plane's marking. Costello screamed over the radio, "That's the American insignia—it's a P-40!" But they still suspected a trick. It was the *old* American insignia—blue background with white star and red center. The United States hadn't used it for nearly a year, because the red center looked too much like the Rising Sun.

Johnny said he and Costello must have put 100 rounds into the ship before they realized there was no use firing. The P-40 had been literally shot to pieces before they ever saw it; the cockpit had been nearly shot away, the fuselage was a sieve. Then as he moved closer he saw that the deep wells into which the wheels fitted when retracted were empty. Bullets couldn't have done that. *It had no wheels.*

Now Johnny and Costello, flying close beside the P-40, could make out the pilot behind the jagged glass of the windshield, his head slumped forward on his chest. They could see the long, dark hair and the bloody face. Costello said later he was sure the man had been dead for some time. Seconds afterward they saw the ghost plane hit the ground and explode.

Later, taking along the doctor, they navigated a truck around the rice paddies to the wrecked plane. The P-40 had been really shot to hell. It was riddled with bullets which had come from below and above, from behind and in front, proving that enemy planes as well as ground fire had destroyed the ship. None of the men could understand how the pilot had lived to fly the plane as far as it must have come. There wasn't much left to identify him. But in his leather jacket were letters, parts of which were legible, and a notebook diary partially destroyed. . . .

People who knew him called him "Corn" Sherrill. They said it was because he liked corn likker so much back in South Carolina. He went to Manila in 1937—first assigned to a pursuit squadron, later becoming officer in charge of constructing a chain of auxiliary airfields.

Corn could really fly. He could navigate to any point in the Philippine Islands; he could tell by the color of the water whether he had let down through the clouds to the Sulu Sea or the Sea of Visayan. He built airfields up and down the islands, and he knew where they were. In time his fields were completed, and Corn became a deputy squadron commander.

After the fateful December 8, 1941 (December 7 in Hawaii and the U.S.), Corn flew reconnaissance and strafing missions with the dwindling air forces, retreating step by embattled step to the little emergency fields that he himself had built in the jungles.

On May 5 he found himself part of an outfit at Miramag on Mindanao, isolated from the rest of the world. Bataan had surrendered. So far as he knew, the entire American might in the islands consisted of 11 mechanics who had escaped to the southern island by devious routes and one cracked-up P-40.

They figured that their one plane, rebuilt with odds and ends from wrecks in the vicinity, would keep them in the war for a while. Except for a bent prop and a buckled fuselage, it was in pretty fair shape. For the next two weeks they scouted every wreck in the neighborhood. Finally, four miles from the base, they found a P-40 with a salvageable fuselage. Forty Moros helped them carry it, using ropes and poles, inch by inch, yard by yard, to Miramag—a ton or more of hull. Whenever an enemy plane appeared overhead, they hastily covered their load with palm leaves.

By August they had the good wing from the old ship attached to the fuselage. Then they rigged a tripod and swung the engine into place. One wing tank was leaking, so they replaced it. They removed the radio and dynamotor, and mounted a 50-gallon tank in the baggage compartment. In the tanks of a smashed B-17 nearby they found some gasoline. They straightened the prop by hammering it with a heavy mallet on the stump of a hardwood tree.

The problem of a retractable landing gear stumped them. One

of the sergeants said jokingly, "If it would only snow, we could use skis," and everybody laughed. But suddenly Sherrill remembered that once he had taken off and landed a P-6 with skis, *on wet grass*.

The more they thought of it, the more they wanted to try it. They figured out how to attach the skis, made of bamboo, and also how to "retract" them—which was simply to drop the skis by jerking a control wire after the plane had taken off. Once that ship got off the ground there would be no return. And only one of them could go.

So they got out the maps to see where their plane could do the Japanese the most damage. They decided on Formosa. It was 1000 miles to the great Japanese naval station at Taihoku. On the China coast, 250 miles farther, was the airfield of Kienow. With careful nursing of his gas the pilot might be able to reach it. By December 6 the 5000-foot grass runway had been cut with knives and everything was ready for the take-off. The P-40 looked weird on skis. But she was complete, with four 300-pound bombs and six .50-caliber machine guns.

Sherrill said, "How about making it an anniversary party of the day those bastards struck us? I'll leave here on the morning of December 8."

At nine o'clock on December 8 the men hustled the fighter out of her cover to the top of the runway. Her nose pointed downhill to the place where the cut swathe in the grass ended at the edge of a cliff. Corn shook hands with each of the men. As he climbed into the cockpit he saw tears in their eyes. He knew he was looking at them for the last time.

The men saw the fighter bounce along the runway, teetering like a sandpiper on the unstable bamboo skids. But with every bounce she gathered speed. Then with a higher whine and a bigger bounce the queer-looking ship was in the air and out over the cliff. At 1000 feet Corn leveled the plane and dropped the guy wires of the landing gear. He brought her back once over the field, so that the cheering men could see the success of their months of labor. Then he headed for Formosa.

Corn Sherrill reached the Japanese island five hours after his take-off—the enemy affirmed that later. The Japanese had boasted that no Occidental had looked upon Formosa for 40 years. Well, one was looking down this day—and the airfield he saw must have made Lieutenant Sherrill lick his lips—with its neat rows of parked fighters and bombers.

He strafed them row on row, and he cut the Japanese flag from the headquarters building with his wingtip. He laid his first wingbomb right in the enemy offices. Enemy ships began to smoke, burn and explode.

Now the P-40 was rocking with ack-ack bursts. All Corn could do was keep low, where the gunners could not spot him too long at a time. He continued strafing every plane he could force his sights on.

Then the Zeros caught him. Dropping his last bomb into a hangar, he fired into the attacking fighters in a desperate effort to blast his way out. And between them, in some unknown way, Corn Sherrill's heart and the P-40's sturdy body pulled away into the clouds on the correct course for China—without benefit of instruments. Straight as a die from Taihoku, to Foochow, to Kienow—the warning net of the Chinese showed that.

Out of the mist there came a plane, and then two others. A sharp clatter of machine guns, and a ship and a pilot already mortally wounded were hit again. Sherrill's bloody face turned to peer through the shattered canopy at the shark-nosed American fighter, flying so close to him in formation. This was the life, all right. Coming home! Mission complete. . . . Corn Sherrill's work was done.

Giraud's Brilliant Escape

By Frederick C. Painton

On May 19, 1940, German infantry flowed out of the woods near Le Catelet, France, and surrounded a French machine-gun nest. After the emplacement had been pulverized by mortar fire, the German officer called on the survivors to surrender. To his amazement, among them appeared a six-foot, gray-mustached man with the five stars of a general on his kepi. For the second time in 25 years Henri Honoré Giraud was a German prisoner of war. (See photograph on page 343.)

It was a bitter humiliation for a man whose career had just reached its peak. Giraud had been an outstanding officer ever since 1898, when he made a brilliant record at St. Cyr military school. But ill luck followed him into battle. In the First World War, Giraud, then a captain, was wounded while leading a Zouave bayonet charge at Charleroi and left for dead on the field. The Germans captured him and placed him in a prison camp in Belgium. Even before his wounds healed he managed to escape. He pretended to be a Belgian and got a job with a traveling carnival. When the show reached Brussels he enlisted the aid of Nurse Edith Cavell, who got him into Holland. From there he made his way to England. Although permanently lamed by his wounds, he finally rejoined his regiment in France before the war ended.

During the peace years he served with distinction in Africa and as governor of Metz. He also taught at the École de Guerre, where one of his students was a Captain Charles de Gaulle. Then came the second war and he was made commander in chief of the Allied forces before Laon. When the Germans broke out of the Ardennes forest, he rushed to the front to see how the tide might be stemmed. Thus, while on reconnaissance, he had been caught in a forward machine-gun nest.

Giraud had escaped before, yes. But now he was 61. It needed youth to escape. Nevertheless he refused to give his word not to make the attempt. He was taken to the frowning fortress of Königstein, perched on a sheer cliff 130 feet high, with every entrance double-guarded and a sentry walk where guards passed every 10 minutes.

Immediately Giraud began to scheme for escape. He practiced his German until he could speak it without an accent. He obtained a map of the surrounding country and memorized every contour. With the twine from packages sent to him he patiently wove a rope that would support his 200 pounds. When it proved not strong enough, his wife sent him 150 feet of copper wire adroitly concealed in a parcel of food. He was allowed, of course, to write letters; his jailers did not know that an invalid prisoner, who had been repatriated, had conveyed a code to the General's wife. Using this, in the form of seemingly innocent letters, he sent out details of his plan bit by bit. This took the rest of 1940 and all of 1941. His raincoat could pass for a civilian garment, and in prison he had obtained a pair of civilian trousers. Presently, more food packages arrived for him. If the Germans had looked inside one of them, they would have found a gay Tyrolean hat.

On the morning of April 17, 1942, Henri Giraud stood on the balcony looking out over the sentry walk. He strapped on a package containing bread, cheese, sugar, brandy and his clothes of disguise. When the guard had passed, the General knotted his homemade rope to the balustrade. Then a fellow prisoner lowered him to the ground 130 feet below.

He limped to the cover of some trees, shaved off his mustache and put on the Tyrolean hat and the raincoat. Two hours later he reached a bridge at Schandau, five miles away. Calmly he leaned against the parapet and ate the lunch from his pack. There at one o'clock, exactly according to plan, a lean young

man carrying a suitcase and a hat in the same hand strolled toward Giraud. This was the prearranged signal. The young man had been sent by friends.

Giraud and the young man went to the railroad station, boarded the first train that came along, and went into a lavatory. There Giraud opened the suitcase and found his own Paris clothes. There were also identity papers bearing the name of an industrialist and a photograph that looked like him—without his mustache—and money. When the lavatory door opened a few minutes later, it was a grave, distinguished-looking business-man who emerged.

Now Giraud put into operation part two of his escape plan. The alarm was out and the frontier guards were alerted. He could hope to avoid arrest only by traveling continuously on trains until the uproar died away. So now began a week-long hegira by railroad through Germany.

Once, near Stuttgart, Gestapo agents began working through the train, verifying heights against the passengers' identity cards. Giraud's six feet could not be disguised. Seeing a young *Oberleutnant* of the Afrika Korps, Giraud sat down opposite him. He smiled at the lieutenant and remarked that he, too, had spent much time in Africa. The German dropped his magazine, delighted to find someone who knew the desert. They conversed animatedly. By the time the Gestapo man reached them, Giraud was illustrating graphically with his hands his idea of how Rommel could beat the British. The German lieutenant watched, his own eyes eager, his hands poised.

The Gestapo man touched Giraud's shoulder. "Your papers, please, gentlemen."

The lieutenant, boiling to present his own point, looked up angrily. "Go away! How dare you interrupt us?" He went into a tirade.

The man did exactly as Giraud had guessed he would: he apologized and backed off.

On another occasion, as the General was about to board a train, he saw Gestapo agents searching every passenger. He dallied outside until the train began to move. Then Giraud, with a supreme effort of the will, ran—without limping. His glasses jiggled. His cheeks puffed out. He had all the appearance of a flustered German businessman trying to make a train. He yelled something about how vital it was for him to catch this train, and his very boldness carried the affair off. One of the Gestapo agents actually helped the panting old gentleman aboard.

Finally he crossed the border into occupied France. He hoped to slip over the line into the unoccupied area, but found that German guards were stopping every man over 5 feet 11 inches tall. Back he went by train across southeastern Germany to the Swiss frontier. That, too, seemed tightly closed. But there were mountain trails that could not all be watched. One night he struck out over an unfrequented trail. Climbing and twisting among craggy peaks, he came suddenly upon three soldiers. Bayoneted rifles swung to cover him. Then a soldier spoke—in a Swiss dialect. He was safe. The guards took him into Basle, where he made his identity known. The Germans were furious, but the Swiss refused to surrender him.

Giraud finally made the dash for unoccupied France. He resorted to an old trick—that of changing cars several times on the lonely roads. The cars entered unoccupied France by different routes. The Gestapo stopped some of the cars, but not the one in which Giraud crossed the border.

In 1914 when he had first escaped from the Germans, Giraud had sent his wife a telegram when he reached Holland safely. It had read:

BUSINESS CONCLUDED EXCELLENT HEALTH AFFECTIONATELY HENRI

Now he sent her another:

BUSINESS CONCLUDED EXCELLENT HEALTH AFFECTIONATELY HENRI

Yet General Henri Giraud was not a free man. His spectacular escape had caught the imagination of a saddened French people and he had become a public idol. The Germans had lost face.

When Marshal Pétain refused the German demand to return Giraud under arrest, the Nazis tried to assassinate him. He was forced to go into hiding. Giraud found that he had merely escaped from one prison into a bigger one.

History, however, was to summon Henri Giraud from obscurity. On October 22, 1942, in an Arab farmhouse in Algeria, Lieutenant General Mark W. Clark conferred secretly with pro-Ally French officers about the possible Allied occupation of French North Africa. (See "Secret Mission to North Africa," page 216.)

During the conference the French officers raised the point of choosing a leader around whom the many French factions could rally. General Mast said, "I can suggest but one man—General Giraud."

General Clark objected, "But he's practically a prisoner in France."

"He must be got out—by submarine."

Such was the daring plan, put into effect a few nights later when a submarine reached the southern coast of France. Giraud arrived in North Africa in time to play an important part in the Anglo-American invasion. General Henri Honoré Giraud died in 1949 after being decorated with the Croix de Guerre and the Médaille Militaire. He was laid to rest at Les Invalides in Paris, where Napoleon and other great French military heroes are buried.

Operation North Pole

By H. J. Giskes,
former Chief of German Counter-Espionage in the Netherlands

In December 1943 the Allies had an elaborate espionage network and an Underground organization of some 1500 saboteurs operating in German-occupied Holland—or so they believed. In actual fact the "Underground" radios reporting back to London had been worked by German operators for almost two years. The men and the huge quantities of weapons and explosives which the Anglo-Dutch Secret Service parachuted into Holland in nearly 200 drops had all been met on arrival by German reception committees. Fifty-four London-trained secret agents sat in jail, while German counter-spies manufactured fairy tales about these agents' activities to report to England. This was one of the most gigantic hoaxes perpetrated on the Allies in the entire "secret war."

As a major in the Abwehr (German secret military intelligence) I was ordered to The Hague in the autumn of 1941 to take command of military counter-espionage in the Netherlands. There had been rumors of clandestine radio traffic with London. It was our business to discover the enemy agents and to thwart their plans for carrying the war behind German lines.

Our first real break came in late November. One of our own undercover agents who had wormed his way into the Dutch Underground reported that a new espionage ring was being organized in The Hague by two British agents. This report was confirmed in January 1942, when Lieutenant Heinrichs of our radio-interception unit heard a new transmitter, using the call sign RLS, operating from The Hague.

We monitored RLS constantly, noting every detail of transmission technique. Our goal was not to eliminate the radio set but to "play it back"—that is, operate it ourselves, posing as Allied agents. This would give us an inside view of the enemy's secret-service operations.

By March 6 our direction-finding apparatus had pinpointed the location of RLS, and that evening we seized its operator, an Englishman, H. M. G. Lauwers. In the next couple of hours we rounded up all collaborators in the espionage group, so as to leave no loose ends that might endanger a "playback."

With cipher material captured at the time of the seizure, and information supplied by our own undercover man in the espionage group, we quickly broke Lauwers' secret code. But Lauwers refused to send false messages to London for us over his radio, and we were reluctant to do it ourselves—yet.

The third Sunday in March I went to Lauwers and told him that he alone could assist me in my plan to save him and his fellow agent Thijs from the death sentence by a German military court. I said he would merely have to transmit the three messages he had been unable to send the day he was arrested.

Lauwers showed interest, but sat silent.

"As a soldier I respect your courage and devotion to duty," I said, "but I deplore the job London has given you, since it involves arming civilians to shoot us in the back. Any army of occupation must crush schemes of this sort by seizing hostages. I shall therefore use all the means at my disposal to prevent the delivery of arms to fanatics in this country, for their use can only mean a blood bath for the Dutch population." I put on my overcoat. "It's time to get ready for today's transmission," I said. "Are you coming along?"

He looked me in the eye. "Yes," he replied.

Lauwers sent off the three messages, then received several messages which referred to previous reports. Heinrichs, of course, had one of his men listening to the transmission, his hand ready on the key of a jamming transmitter in case Lauwers should attempt to betray us. Nothing suspicious occurred.

(Editor's note: Lauwers stated after the war that London instructed him to make a deliberate mistake in every 16th letter of every message; lack of this "identity check" would indicate that he had fallen into enemy hands. He was able to conceal this device from his captors, and thus inserted a clear warning in every message he transmitted for the Germans. Incredibly, however, London missed these warnings.)

This was the beginning of what we named Operation Nordpol (North Pole).

How long could this radio link with London be maintained? If, unknown to us, there were supposed to be signs in the ciphering to confirm the genuineness of the operator, the bubble might well be pricked the next time we transmitted.

The second time we were on the air London had an urgent request: the preparation of a dropping zone for a large quantity of sabotage material and a new agent. The news upset Lauwers considerably. He said he would not operate RLS any longer; he could not be responsible for allowing comrades to fall into our hands.

"We can lay our hands on this man," I told him, "whether you coöperate or not. If you continue operating for us I hope to obtain a decision from the highest authorities that none of the captured agents will be given the death penalty. Think over your decision." Lauwers went back on the key.

(In spite of my hopes, out of 54 Dutch-English Nordpol agents, 47 did not survive the war. Investigations by the Dutch have revealed that they were shot in 1944 in Mauthausen camp. Their liquidation was one of the many crimes typical of Himmler's system, which cannot be justified by any necessities of war. The memory of these victims of an infamous breach of confidence, which I can remember only with shame and bitterness, has guided my pen in the writing of this story.)

The signal for that first drop came through on March 27, and at 11 that night a small string of cars with dimmed lights parked in a small wood near the dropping area, where three men with powerful red-beamed flashlights were stationed in a large triangle. We waited two hours. Had the British discovered our game? Were they on their way to our lighted triangle with a load of bombs, to plow us into the moorland with TNT?

Finally we heard the hum of aircraft engines and a plane swept overhead at hardly more than 600 feet. Suddenly directly above us there appeared in the wake of the aircraft several dark blobs. Four heavy containers, supported by parachutes, hit the ground with dull thuds. A fifth parachute carried an agent. The twin-engined bomber gained height, blinked its navigation lights in salutation and disappeared. Heinrichs and I shook hands in silent congratulation.

Directly after this drop we radioed London that the parachuted agent was well and in safe hands. A quiet interval of several weeks followed. This seemed ominous because we had proof that the Anglo-Dutch Secret Service was carrying out operations in Holland without our help. Among other things, a new transmitter was heard in the Utrecht area. And in April the body of a parachutist was found near Holten with a fractured skull; he had struck a stone water trough on landing. I became uneasy about our playback on RLS. Had London smelled a rat?

Certainly our first success could not have been maintained for long except for what happened now: by sheer chance all the channels through which London controlled the Anglo-Dutch Secret Service in Holland fell into our hands!

Without our knowledge, three pairs of agents, each pair with a radio set, had been dropped. In the drops, we learned later, one radio operator, Maartens, had been killed (it was his body that was found by the water trough) and only one radio landed without damage. So the agents linked up and reported through this sole functioning set, code-named Trumpet. When London instructed RLS to make contact with one of the Trumpet agents, the entire network became known to us.

Trumpet fell into our hands complete with signal plan and cipher material. We used it to open up a second Nordpol link with London and proposed a new dropping area for this group. We accepted the first drop there about a fortnight later.

Meanwhile the signal plan for the dead operator, Maartens, had been found on his teammate, Andringa. We reported to London via Trumpet that Andringa had discovered a reliable operator in the Underground who could carry out Maartens'

signal plan, using Maartens' repaired set. London gave this new recruit a trial transmission to test his efficiency. The German operator who took the test was quickly approved. Thus we established a third link with London.

About the middle of May, Heinrichs reported that he suspected Lauwers of having transmitted additional letters at the end of his last message. We waited anxiously to see if London's suspicions had been aroused. Apparently they had not. Nevertheless, we put an end to transmission by Lauwers by proposing "reserve" operators. Surprisingly, they were approved.

As more agents were arrested on arrival in later months, our men operated their transmitters from the outset. In this procedure we ran the risk that an agent's "fist" might have been recorded in London before departure. If so, no careful comparison was ever made. At various times we had as many as 14 radio links with London—worked by only six German operators!

From June on, the operation expanded unbelievably. The drops came in on almost conveyor-belt schedule. London's decision to send all future agents and material through existing contacts was the really dramatic error made by our enemy. Just a single control group, dropped "blind" and unknown to us, could have punctured Operation Nordpol.

In July London entrusted the RLS group with an important special task: a reconnaissance to see whether the masts of the Kootwijk radio transmitter, through which the German Admiralty communicated with U-boats in the Atlantic, could be blown up. Agent Thijs was to be in charge of the demolition unit. I sent out a reconnaissance party, then radioed its exact findings: the demolition of the masts would not present much difficulty; Thijs and his men were standing by for an order to go ahead. By the time the order came I had thought out reasons for "failure."

Two days later RLS passed this message to London: "Kootwijk attempt a failure. Our men ran into minefield. Five men missing. Thijs and remainder safe, including two wounded." And the next day: "Two of five missing men returned. Three others killed in action. Enemy has strengthened guard on Kootwijk and other stations."

London messaged back: "Much regret your losses. Method of defense is new and unforeseeable. Greatest watchfulness necessary. Report anything unusual."

I had a reference to the affair published in the Dutch press. The article stated that criminal elements had attempted to blow up a wireless station. Captured sabotage material had pointed to enemy assistance. I hoped that my opponents in London would receive this report by way of neutral countries. A fortnight later London sent RLS a congratulatory message for the attempt to sabotage Kootwijk.

The decisive phase of Nordpol from June 1942 until the spring of 1943 was its involvement in the Anglo-Dutch Operation Marrow. The leader of Marrow was an agent named Jambroes, whose task—we learned when "Underground representatives" welcomed him before we arrested him—was to establish contact with the leaders of the Dutch organization Ordedienst and get them to organize 16 sabotage and resistance groups, with 100 men in each group.

We did not know who the leaders of the Ordedienst were, so we told London there were signs of demoralization among the top ranks of the organization, that its leadership had been penetrated by German informers. We proposed that Jambroes make contact with other more reliable organization leaders.

The fictitious build-up of the Marrow organization began in August 1942. The 16 groups made such apparent progress that by November London had sent 17 agents through our hands, five of them radio operators with their own sets and frequencies. When we radioed that some 1500 men were now under training, we realized that this number of men would urgently need such articles as clothing, footwear, tobacco, tea. So we asked for supplies, and one night received a consignment totaling five tons!

From January to April 1943, 17 more agents dropped into our hands, including seven operators with independent radio links. Now I was faced with the problem of keeping London supplied with information about the activities of nearly 50 agents. We couldn't keep this up for long—our six radio operators couldn't stand the gaff. Accordingly, we got London's permission, "for reasons of greater security," to close down some of the Marrow transmitters.

We had a close call when an agent named Jongelie, cover name "Arie," was dropped by parachute. When we arrested him he declared that he must at once radio to London: "The express left on time," to confirm his safe arrival. This put his interrogators in a quandary. Was he trying to trick us?

I went to see Jongelie. Immobile, he repeatedly answered my questions with the statement that he must immediately pass the message, "The express left on time," or London would realize that he was in German hands. Finally I pretended to be convinced. Seemingly deep in thought, I said that we would pass his message—and then, as I suddenly raised my eyes, I caught a gleam of triumph in his. So he *was* pulling a fast one!

At the next routine transmission we sent the following message: "Accident occurred. Arie landed heavily and is unconscious. Doctor diagnoses severe concussion." Three days later we radioed: "Arie regained consciousness for short period yesterday. Doctor hopes for improvement." Next day: "Arie died suddenly. We hope to give him a worthy memorial after victory is won."

We were lucky: London was taking normal precautions, but had not allowed for the possibility that its *entire* communication network in Holland and *all* its agents were in German hands.

Shortly after this incident Anglo-Dutch headquarters began to press us to send the head of the Marrow groups, agent Jambroes, back to England for consultation. We had to keep finding excuses for holding him; the principal one was that the courier route into Spain was difficult and insecure. We substantiated this from time to time by reporting that an agent had departed for France but had never arrived—anywhere. When London demanded information about areas in Holland where planes could land to pick up Jambroes, we said we were unable to find a suitable spot, or else we would suddenly declare an appointed area unsafe when a special flight seemed imminent. Finally we took the only course still open to us: we reported Jambroes missing after "a German police raid in Rotterdam."

To remedy this situation, Group Golf was dropped into Holland. It aimed at preparing safe courier routes and escape lines through Belgium and France to Spain and Switzerland. We let about six weeks pass before Golf radioed to London that a reliable route had been established as far as Paris and that the courier would be an experienced man named "Arnaud." Actually Arnaud was our Unteroffizier Arno; posing as a refugee Frenchman, he had made Underground contacts before, and had effectively penetrated enemy courier routes.

In order to "test the reliability" of the Golf escape line we dispatched to Spain two English flying officers who were living underground in Holland. Three weeks later London confirmed that the men had arrived safely. Through this exploit Golf and Arnaud acquired much credit in London, and we were given details of three stations of the British Secret Service in Paris which were working on new escape routes. German counter-espionage took no action against these stations, adhering to the principle that intelligence—of which we proceeded to gather considerable—is more valuable than elimination.

In subsequent months Golf did render certain services to the Allies. Numbers of enemy flying personnel who had been shot down in Holland and Belgium were guided on an adventurous underground journey to Spain without knowing they were under the wing of German counter-espionage. We continually reported such departures, giving names and ranks, and when the men arrived in England we had achieved our purpose: to enhance the prestige of Golf without damaging Nordpol.

In the latter part of August 1943, Ubbink and Dourlein, two of the 50-odd agents held by us in a prison in Haaren, broke out and disappeared. I was convinced that these brave and determined men would somehow make their way back to England. If they did, they would betray our counter-espionage operation.

During the first 10 days of December London's messages suddenly became dull and colorless. Ubbink and Dourlein had apparently reached their objective. Now London would try to trick *us*. We gave no indication that we realized the great bubble had finally been pricked, but instead carried on normally.

The messages from London merely grew more and more trivial.

In March 1944 I proposed to Berlin that we should put an end to the hollow mockery of the Nordpol radio operation by means of a final message. To the men we knew to be at the head of the Anglo-Dutch Secret Service we radioed:

> Messrs. Blunt, Bingham & Co., London. We understand that you have been endeavoring to do business in Holland without our assistance. We regret this since we have acted for so long as your sole representatives in this country, to our mutual satisfaction. Nevertheless we can assure you that, should you be thinking of paying us a visit on the Continent on any extensive scale, we shall give your emissaries the same attention as hitherto, and a similarly warm welcome.

The plain-language text was radioed to England over all 10 channels on April 1. The date seemed particularly appropriate. Operation Nordpol was over.

Secret Mission to North Africa

By Frederick C. Painton

In his London headquarters General Dwight Eisenhower stared at the War Department cablegram marked "Most Secret." It put up to him the gravest decision he had yet confronted in his career. In essence, it said this: *A group of pro-Ally French officers in Algeria suggest that five officers from General Eisenhower's staff come secretly and at once to a rendezvous near Algiers with information as to what the Allies will do to help them face a threatened Axis invasion.*

The General reflected. On "D-day" at "H-hour" (November 8, 1942, at 1:00 a.m.) American and British troops would make amphibious landings in North Africa. A secret rendezvous with the French could get information that might save many lives. But there was a terrible risk involved. The mission might be discovered, thus warning both the Vichy High Command and the Nazis of what was afoot. In that case the great operation might end in disaster.

General Eisenhower turned to the man across the desk—six-foot-three Major General Mark Wayne Clark, his Deputy Commander. "I think you can do it, Wayne," he said quietly.

The decision made, Eisenhower and Clark went at once to 10 Downing Street. Prime Minister Winston Churchill heard the plan and welcomed the idea. It was an adventure after his own heart. "Done," he said. "You'll have our full coöperation."

Clark hastily departed to hand-pick the four men to go with him: Captain Jerauld Wright, United States Navy, a crack shot; Colonel Julius Holmes, who knew French and knew Algeria; Colonel Arch Hamblen, an expert on shipping problems; and Brigadier General Lyman Lemnitzer of G-3, the operations branch.

Each was instructed: "Leave your office as if you would be away no more than an hour. Take what a musette bag will carry. No papers of any kind. We leave tonight." Besides the musette bags they carried Garand-type carbines, tommy guns and about $2000 to be used in case of trouble. At 7:30 a.m., October 19, two big planes roared into the air. The historic mission had started.

Meantime, coded cables had flashed orders to Captain D. E. Fawkes at a British naval base to provide a sub and four so-called kayaks—small boats made of wood and canvas, which would be used to put the passengers ashore. The commandos contributed the services of three officers who were expert in this kind of business: Captains G. B. (Jumbo) Courtney and R. P. Livingston, and Lieutenant J. P. Foote.

Late in the afternoon the Clark party arrived at the base. Fawkes listened attentively as the scheme was outlined. Then he said bluntly: "It's very dangerous. We can put you ashore, no trouble there. But the kayaks are cockleshells. If a sea springs up, you can't launch them, can't get away." Clark nodded. This was a risk he had already considered and accepted. Fawkes continued: "General, this sounds like an Oppenheim secret-service thriller where the hero goes to a haunted farmhouse that shows a light at midnight."

Clark grinned. "How the devil did you know that?" For a farmhouse *was* to show light if the coast was clear to land.

The moon was rising as the five Americans and the three British commandos, led by the submarine's commander, Lieutenant N. L. A. Jewell, boarded a little 750-ton undersea craft. With them they took special flashlights—which would not throw beams observable from the side—to signal in Morse code after they landed; and a small portable "walkie-talkie" which they could use to communicate with the submarine. The diesels rumbled and the sub got under way.

At four a.m. of the second night they sighted the rendezvous signal light on the African shore. But it was too close to dawn to

risk a landing. They submerged again to wait for evening. Through the periscope Clark could see the old Moorish-type farmhouse perched on the edge of an abrupt slope. Behind the house was the main highway to Algiers. They could see no sign of life anywhere.

For 15 hours the tiny submarine remained below. Night fell at last, and the submarine surfaced. The men climbed to the conning tower and waited for the signal light to gleam again. Eight o'clock came, then nine o'clock. The farmhouse remained dark. There were a lot of praying words used in an unprayerful way. Would they have to take 24 hours more of this mechanized sewer pipe? Lemnitzer groaned, "Something's happened. There'll be no light." "There will be light," said Clark, "and I'll bet $10 on it." All but Holmes accepted his wager. Clark went below for a brief nap. At 11:10 Holmes shook him awake. "You win. The light just came on."

The crew got the kayaks through the torpedo hatch and launched them. Keeping close together, the party headed for shore. Some 500 yards from the beach they stopped. Suppose

the Vichy-controlled police had been warned and were lurking in the bushes ashore. Were they about to walk into a trap? Somebody had to go first and make sure of the ground.

Julius Holmes spoke French the best and knew some of the people ashore, so he and commando Captain Livingston headed in. If all was clear, the others would follow. Ten minutes later Holmes' boat grated on the gravel beach. Carbines ready, the two men got out and moved cautiously along the beach.

Suddenly they heard someone moving in the brush. They whirled, guns leveled.

A voice said in English, "Who's there?"

"Who're you?" countered Holmes.

"I'm Ridgeway Knight." Knight was an American vice-consul who had taken part in the arrangements for the rendezvous.

"I'm Julius Holmes. Where's Bob Murphy?" Murphy, the American Consul General in North Africa, had been instrumental in bringing about the meeting.

"He'll be along in a minute. Everything's okay."

Holmes turned to Livingston. "Make the signal." Livingston blinked his flashlight seaward. The signals were "K" for "kerrect" if all was well; "F" for "foney" if there was trouble. He made the "K" signal in Morse, and presently the other kayaks came out of the night and the other six men stepped ashore. Then the signal "All's well" was made to the submarine, and its diesel drone died away as it stood offshore.

To hide the boats, the wet shivering men hauled them up to the farmhouse and hid them in the courtyard. Then they shucked off their clothes, spread them out to dry, and after a slight meal—excited men rarely get hungry—dozed until the French party arrived at seven o'clock, and the conference began.

The information obtained was priceless. It included the tonnage capacity of the ports of Casablanca, Algiers, Oran, Tunis; the French Navy's plans for preventing a landing; a list of the places where French Army resistance would be tough, and where it would be only token. Special information on airport runways later proved to be of inestimable value.

But General Clark's luck was running out at last. Jerry Wright heard a sound that brought him quickly out of the house. The wind was whistling round the house's red-tiled roof. Waves as tall as a man were roaring against the shore. Wright knew that no kayak could be launched in that foaming tumult. He went gloomily back inside.

Meanwhile two Arab servants, who had that morning been dismissed by the owner of the farmhouse for safety's sake, had gone to a nearby town and visited the Commissioner of Police. They reported that they had seen strange men carry big bundles (the boats) to the farmhouse. The place had once been a smugglers' hideout; perhaps it was being thus used again. So presently a police car was humming along the highway toward the rendezvous. . . .

The discussions at the farmhouse had about reached an end. Only one point remained to be settled. One of the French officers said, "It will be necessary to have some leader here whom we will all follow." The name of General Henri Honoré Giraud was suggested. The General was in hiding in occupied France, and it was decided to smuggle him out and bring him to North Africa.

Then, in the next room, the telephone jangled. The conferees jerked erect, looked at each other. The house owner answered the call and a moment later came rushing into the conference room, his eyes wide with fright. "The police! They'll be here in five minutes!"

Most of the French officers—the top ones—hurried out. To be discovered here in these circumstances meant being shot for treason. Motors roared, gears clashed and they were gone.

Clark's men hastily stuffed maps and papers inside their undershirts. They were trapped between the Vichy police and the stormy sea. And now the police car roared up. Where could they hide? "There's an empty wine cellar," said Murphy. "You go down there. I'll get rid of the police."

Clark didn't like it: a cellar seemed like a rat trap—no room to maneuver. But there was now no time for anything else. They could hear the gendarmes piling out of their car. Gripping carbines and tommy guns, the eight officers filed down into the wine cellar. Murphy pulled the doors down flat, put boxes over them, then turned to meet the police.

He had one stratagem that might work. The conference table was littered with half-empty wine bottles and cigarette stubs. A French lieutenant in civilian clothes and the owner of the house, a Frenchman named Teissier, took their lives in their hands to pretend a drunken party with Murphy and Knight. They began singing snatches of drinking songs, laughing and talking loudly. That was the scene the Commissioner of Police walked in upon a moment later.

Down in the cellar—it was only 10 feet square—Clark disposed his party behind the stairway and along the walls so that casual observation from above might not discover them. But if the police did come down to take a look, then what? General Clark's whispered orders were blunt: his men were to shoot to kill. Upstairs the situation rapidly worsened. They could hear Bob Murphy arguing with the Commissioner. He and a few friends, Murphy protested, were having a little party. Since when was that a crime? What would Monsieur le Commissaire think if American police invaded the privacy of French citizens in New York? But the voices were coming closer, until they seemed at the very cellar door.

And now the tense silence in the cellar was broken by choking gasps. Jumbo Courtney was trying to suppress a fit of coughing. The strangling sounds seemed to his companions loud enough to be heard in Algiers. Jumbo struggled desperately. "By George!" he gasped. "I'm afraid I'll choke."

"I'm afraid you won't!" said Clark grimly. "But here, chew this gum."

Jumbo fumbled for the gum, chewed desperately. The spasm passed. Silence settled on the cellar. The men could hear their own hearts thudding.

Above, Murphy was still arguing vociferously. Snatches of drunken song came from the French lieutenant. Then the voices upstairs changed tone. The Commissioner of Police was not so brusque. Holmes heaved a sigh. "Bob's got him," he whispered.

The Commissioner had decided there was no smuggling going on. Nonetheless, he said, he'd have to report to his superior. And, yes, without a doubt his superior would return to look into the matter further.

Just then Jumbo started to have another spasm of coughing.

"Chew that gum," Clark whispered tensely.

"I am, sir, but all the sweetness has gone out of it."

"I don't wonder," whispered Clark. "I chewed it an hour myself before I gave it to you." This was considered very funny—but much later.

At last the footsteps faded away, and they heard the police car leave. Clark and his party ascended, anxious to get to the submarine. But the surf still pounded on the beach. Jerry Wright said, "I'd hate to have to launch a whaleboat in that sea."

Yet the mission was now a success—if they could only get away with the information. Clark said: "We'll try it." A wireless message was sent to the submarine: "Stand in as close as possible. We're in trouble and will embark immediately."

They carried the kayaks down to the wind-swept beach. It took a bold man even to consider going into that roaring sea with a fragile craft hardly bigger than a child's toy boat. Clark stripped to his underclothes and, carrying his outer garments, walked out into the breakers with Courtney. They managed to get into the heaving little boat and drove their paddles deep. Then a huge wall of water broke over them, the kayak upended and both men vanished into a white fury of foam.

A moment later, battered, turned end over end by the undertow, they came rolling along the beach, full of sand, salt water and artistic profanity. The others retrieved the kayak, but the paddles and the General's clothing were being carried away by the current.

Somebody yelled, "Get his pants!"

Wright shouted, "The hell with his pants. Get those paddles!"

They got the paddles. The pants remained in Africa.

Even Clark was forced to admit they couldn't launch a boat that night. And he realized that they might be stranded here for days if the wind continued. But he refused to return to the cellar, police or no police. They would take to the woods, where a man had a chance to shoot his way out. So they hid themselves and the kayaks among the palms, shivering in the bitter cold. The wind continued unabated, preventing escape.

The police returned at 11 that night. Murphy greeted them again, smiling his charming smile, talking rapidly and smoothly. In the end the police did not search the woods. They were not satisfied; they said they would return in the morning; but for the moment they were staved off.

By four a.m. the wind seemed to have lessened somewhat, though the seas were still mountainous. "We'll try it again," said Clark. His wireless to the submarine this time was imperative: "Stand in as close as you possibly can."

Knight, Teissier, Murphy and the French lieutenant steadied the first kayak. Clark and Wright climbed in. Cautiously the four walked the frail craft out into the pounding surf until Wright saw a comparatively smooth stretch. "Now!" he yelled. The four men heaved the boat forward, Clark and Wright paddled with all their strength. The light kayak climbed the side of an oncoming wave and hung for an endless space almost perpendicular—then suddenly it went over the hooked crest and cleared the surf.

Meanwhile the others were trying to float their boats. They all finally succeeded. Holmes was the last to reach the submarine, and just as he did so a gigantic wave caught the kayak, lifted it high and swept it down upon the sub. Crew members snatched Holmes clear and held him while the water poured in a torrent off the submarine's back. The wave broke the kayak in two and swept it away.

The danger was instantly apparent. A broken boat ashore with its contents scattered along the beach—it had contained letters, uniforms and a musette bag holding the money—would be a complete betrayal of the Americans' presence. A radio message was later relayed to Murphy, warning him to clear the beach. Murphy, Knight and the two Frenchmen searched the beach early in the morning and destroyed all the boat fragments and other debris.

The sub turned her bow north at a painful four knots—her top speed submerged. Clark, anxious to get his information to London as soon as possible, decided to risk breaking radio silence. He sent a message to the nearest British base, giving the sub's course, speed and position, and asking that a plane be sent out.

At 3:20 p.m. a Catalina flying-boat droned low overhead and landed on the sea. Clark and his men paddled over from the submarine. (See photograph on page 344.) An hour and a half later they landed at the base and flashed the news of the great success. Then they boarded planes for England. The plane carrying Clark ran into every kind of difficulty, as though Fate at the last minute was reluctant to see him through. For hours they were completely lost in fog. The plane iced up so badly that at one time it staggered along, barely aloft. The General was to recall this flight as "the biggest thrill of the trip."

In England, where the other plane had arrived right on schedule, there was consternation. But Clark's plane finally nosed safely down through the soup. You could have bought all that remained of her gasoline for a dime.

Later General Clark commented on the great value of the plans laid in the farmhouse and of the information the French had given them. The meeting "saved thousands of American and British lives," he told me when I visited him after the successful invasion of North Africa. "French troops are now fighting bravely and well on our front line because of plans made in that conference."

The Grand Surprise Campaign

By Don Wharton

On a Monday morning early in the summer of 1942, 12 Army officers were called to a secret meeting in Room 3045 in the old Munitions Building in Washington. They arrived singly and unobtrusively, without knowing why they were summoned. Two hours later they left as unostentatiously, carrying with them one of the biggest military secrets of our times: the decision to send an American expeditionary force to North Africa.

Back in their offices, these brigadiers and colonels set in motion the intricate machinery which made the North African campaign possible. They began developing the campaign's "logistics"—the art of getting the right men with the right equipment to the right place at the right time. Fifteen weeks later wonderfully equipped American troops from the U.S. and from the United Kingdom landed with split-second timing at a dozen different points in three separate areas of French North Africa.

Up to that time this was the biggest overseas landing force in world history. Only the Normandy landings have exceeded it. Services of Supply had to provide 700,000 different items— 22 million pounds of food, for example, and 38 million pounds of clothing and equipage. There were 10 million gallons of gasoline to go ashore in five-gallon cans carried by individual soldiers, or in 50-gallon drums, or landed in bulk from tankers. The Quartermaster supply list for the African expedition was an amazing document. It included 100 alarm clocks and 580 rat traps, stepladders and rubber stamps, butchers' uniforms and steel safes.

Every American soldier went ashore with his own individual

water-purifying equipment. If he filled his canteen from some questionable source, he had simply to drop in a tablet about one third the size of an aspirin. Every soldier also carried salt tablets to help combat Africa's heat. For sprinkling on wounds each soldier was provided with sulfanilamide crystals in special envelopes with shaker tops. He was given a pair of goggles especially designed for Africa with two kinds of removable lenses, one for dust, one for sun. Quartermaster devised a new type of fumigation bag for the battle with lice.

The immense supply job was complicated by the necessity to keep everything secret. For instance, manufacturers were asked to produce mosquito netting with an unusually small mesh. If that secret had leaked, the Germans would have known immediately that our troops were Africa-bound because so fine a mesh is used only where there are sand flies. The Quartermaster had to provide every soldier with a foot-square piece of wool cloth to be attached to the lining of his helmet to protect the back of his neck against the sun. This, again, would have given the enemy a clue. Officers referred to them as "the unmentionables." Tens of thousands were delivered to boats in boxes marked "Contents: XY." Even combat troops didn't know what was in those boxes until they were nearing Africa.

Keeping the movement secret was a tremendous job in itself. Besides the usual precautions, a great pretense was built up that whatever was going on was simply another movement to the United Kingdom. Key officers even used "Ireland" and "Britain" as code words for Morocco and Algeria. When General Patton was in Washington conferring with the planners, he said, "For every additional person who knows this secret you can wipe off 750 men." That turned out to be an exaggeration, but it probably tied some loose tongues. Only 10 men in the Quartermaster Corps knew, only nine in Transportation. There were all degrees of knowing. Some high officers knew only that a big movement was planned. Some knew the destination but not the size; some the size but not the destination.

Ingenious steps were taken to intensify the secret. To hide the assembling of 850 ships, many were put in dry dock, ostensibly laid up for repairs. To prevent anyone from estimating the destination by the length of voyage, the ships were provisioned for a great many more days than they were to be at sea.

Everyone in the know was on a registered list. There were offices into which only persons on that list could go. Some officers dispensed with dictaphones and secretaries, writing all messages in longhand. The Army goes in strong for duplicates, triplicates and such, but file copies carried no data on this operation.

The Transportation Corps went to infinite pains to hide its interest in the ports of Oran, Casablanca and Algiers. Two Transportation officers would be huddled over a desk with no one else in the room. Still they would never say Oran, Casablanca or Algiers. They had a separate pantomime gesture for the name of each port.

Engineer troops at a camp hundreds of miles inland for weeks practiced loading cargo onto what they called "the concrete ship." They loaded all types of equipment—beans to 32-ton tanks—from every type of freight car used in the United States. They worked against stop watches. When they had become expert, they were moved to ports of embarkation and tested their technique on several ships from the convoys-to-be. Then came the short night and half-day which produced the greatest loading job in modern war before D-day in Normandy.

Alternate rail and highway routes from troop concentration areas to ports of embarkation had also been selected. If saboteurs had destroyed three quarters of the bridges in the eastern United States, the troops would still have moved.

For the African operation the Engineers prepared and issued maps of more than 1000 different types. These were carried under guard to a warehouse at a port of embarkation. There an Engineer officer and 15 enlisted men made up packages for each combat unit. For security reasons these soldiers were given no leaves. They ate and slept with the maps. Everything was under lock, key and guard until loading night, when the maps were delivered on the transports to unit commanders in person.

The Ordnance Department redesigned old weapons for the

African campaign and developed some new ones. One of the most important secret weapons was a powerful new tank destroyer. It was only in the blueprint stage the day those officers met in Room 3045. Forty-eight hours later an Ordnance officer was in Michigan conferring with production experts at one of our great automobile plants. He asked them to do the impossible—and they did. The plant was tooled up in August and the first tank destroyers were completed in September. They were tried out, delivered to troops, tested in the field and on the way to North Africa by late October.

It has been estimated that 50 to 80 percent of the African landing was a Services of Supply job. SOS provided everything from postage stamps to 32-ton tanks. It supplied well-digging equipment, coal for Moroccan locomotives, and millions of dollars in gold, silver and various currencies for paying troops. While irresponsible people talked dramatically about bringing second-front pressure on generals, these unknown SOS planners were silently getting hundreds of thousands of uniforms impregnated against poison-gas attacks. They were secretly developing a new one-man package for getting supplies quickly ashore, and waterproof crates which could be floated in to support the first echelons.

Generally, officers were told no more than was necessary for the carrying out of their particular assignments. Some division commanders didn't know where they were bound until the eleventh hour. In all the United States only a small handful knew the day set for the landing: "D-day."

We Were Expecting You at Dakar

By Donald Q. Coster

One night late in 1942 the formidable German U-boat packs in the South Atlantic received an urgent order to make full speed for a rendezvous off Dakar. And within a few days well over 100 Nazi submarines were circling around Africa's western tip. Ashore, Vichy French troops manned the powerful coastal defenses which two years before had repelled the British-Free French assault led by General de Gaulle. The American invasion across the Atlantic was steaming into an ambush which would prove disastrous—so thought the German High Command.

On the night of November 7, however, German radio stations flashed the news: "Achtung! Achtung! A large enemy army is on the northern coast of Africa. . . ." Our invasion forces had surprised the Germans by landing some 2000 miles from where they were expected. The Dakar Cover Plan, one of the most effective ruses of the war, had been successful.

A most important link in the chain of deception was forged by Donald Q. Coster, a soft-spoken young New Yorker who had been an advertising-agency executive in private life.

In 1940 Coster was driving an American Field Service ambulance for the French Army. He was captured, spent several unpleasant weeks in German hands, was released and came home to join the Navy. His knowledge of French pushed him into the Office of Naval Intelligence, from which he was later transferred to Colonel William Donovan's Office of Strategic Services.
—Frederic Sondern, Jr.

One Sunday I was called into Colonel Donovan's office. "You are going to Africa; to Casablanca," he said. "It's the most important place in the world at the moment." I blinked. "French Africa will be invaded one of these days," he continued, "by either the Germans or ourselves. You are to help prepare for either eventuality. We must know the German plans."

"Yes, sir," I gulped.

"A German Armistice Commission is in Casablanca, enforcing the terms the Nazis imposed on the French in 1940. You might try to make them believe that, if and when we invade, we will come in through Dakar. I'll leave the method of doing that up to you." I swallowed hard as the full significance of the Colonel's casually spoken words sank in. "And you'd better stop by at London, Lisbon and Gibraltar to pick up what information you can from British Intelligence. That's all."

I felt like Little Red Riding Hood about to enter a whole forest of wolves—at midnight. Gestapo gunmen, super-spies and ingenious Nazi methods of assassination chased each other past my mind's eye.

A few days later I found myself a "vice-consul" in the pay of the State Department. Donovan used this cover to cloak his agents operating in officially neutral Vichy French territory.

In Washington I was rushed through a quick course of instruction in the code I was to use, and very little else. The elaborate spy school, which later trained our agents in everything from safecracking to the tricky technique of contacting another agent on a street corner in hostile country with minimum risk of detection, had not yet been set up. I didn't even know how to pry open a desk drawer. I was acutely conscious of my inexperience as I flew to London.

Then the first of Coster's Curious Coincidences took place. An English girl whom I met through friends somehow picked up a hint that I was going to North Africa. She begged me to try to find and help a very dear friend of hers—an Austrian named Freddy—who had been in the French Foreign Legion and was now probably in a Vichyite concentration camp near Casablanca. I was one very embarrassed spy. No one was supposed to know where I was going. But I promised halfheartedly that I would try to find the Austrian.

In London, Lisbon and Gibraltar I met the "heavy brass" of the British intelligence services. They were smooth, formidable-looking men who had a calm self-assurance which made me feel uncomfortably inadequate. They told me about General Theodor Auer, chief of the German Armistice Commission—evidently a sinister opponent. His counter-intelligence system was well organized and ruthless.

The Englishmen shook their heads dubiously over my chances of convincing the Herr General of anything important that wasn't true; he knew all the tricks. And I should be careful, they warned, of my health. The Germans had a way of handling troublesome people: they were lured into back alleys and knifed. Just before my plane took off from Gibraltar one Englishman patted me on the shoulder: "Good luck, old man. We'll be thinking of you." I thought I detected a rather funereal tone in his voice.

In Casablanca only a few of our top diplomats knew what Colonel Donovan's men were doing. The regular consular staff was continually irritated by their young and inexplicable assistants, who had little interest in regular consular duties and had a most unconsular way of talking to dock foremen, fishermen and other odd characters. We also had a hard time concealing from some of our inquisitive colleagues the radio transmitters with which we sent reports.

With a Croix de Guerre in my buttonhole, and my command of French, I found it easy to make friends and dig up information. A number of trustworthy anti-Vichy people helped in checking the reliability of our sources. The owner of a fishing fleet drew a chart for me of the practicable sea approaches to the Moroccan coast. A French architect, who had escaped from forced labor in Germany, arranged to follow me to church two Sundays and in the cover of a pew hand me drawings of the newest German flak towers—towers he had been compelled to help build. All this was valuable information, but I was getting no closer to General Auer.

Then, one evening, Coster's second Curious Coincidence occurred. Another "vice-consul" and I were sitting in a disreputable waterfront café, where we listened for information on ship movements. Two young men passed our table. "Walter," called out my companion. The newcomer stopped. "Meet a friend of mine—Donald Coster. He's in the Consulate too." The young men sat down. They were Austrians, they said, who had been in France when the Germans invaded. They had joined the Foreign Legion, been interned in a Vichy concentration camp and had managed to escape to Casablanca. "When suddenly, one day"—Walter was telling the story—"who should I see on the street but Teddy Auer, the general who runs the German Armistice Commission. I knew him in Paris before the war. Well," Walter concluded blithely, "we made a deal with him. We supply him with information, and he keeps us out of jail. We're both violently anti-Nazi, of course, and we want the Germans' hides."

My mind started turning over—fast. Either Walter and his companion had been set on my trail by Auer and this was a trap or it was a heaven-sent opportunity. I was still thinking, hard, when the Austrian whose name I had missed turned to me. "So you arrived recently from London," he sighed. "I have a most wonderful girl there. If only I could get back . . ." I had pulled out my wallet to pay the check. Suddenly the Austrian almost jumped across the table at me. "It's her handwriting!" he yelled, pointing at an envelope in the wallet. It was a letter I had received from the London girl, and the handwriting was large and distinctive. This, of course, was Freddy, the man she had asked me to find.

A definite scheme evolved in my mind that night. I would be a stupid loudmouthed playboy, and in my frequent cups feed the Austrians accurate but unimportant information which they would pass on to Auer. I had read about that in books, and I didn't think it had a prayer of succeeding. But I couldn't think of anything else.

A few days later it developed that Auer not only believed the Austrians when they reported their new acquisition but opened a bottle of champagne. "*Ja*. All fools, these Americans," said the General. "Make them drunk, and they talk."

Auer's first demands for information were not difficult. The General was apparently trying out his new source of information for its precision in small things. Then, one day, the two were unusually concerned when I met them. The Herr General had been very excited the night before. "You Austrian pigs," he had shouted. "You don't know this American at all. You have been stealing my money." Freddy and Walter assured him that they did know the American very well, and could prove it. "Then prove it, and soon, or I'll teach you what it means to cheat a German general."

I saw my plan tottering. Auer was suspicious. He would turn his counter-intelligence people loose on us, and our whole espionage operation—which had gone along with surprising lack of interference from the Germans—would be jeopardized. Then suddenly the light dawned. Why, tell the General that if he wants to see what good friends we are, he should come to that black-market restaurant overlooking the sea tomorrow night and watch us having dinner together. "I'll put on a show that will convince him," I added.

The color shot back into the Austrians' faces. "And the General will pay for the dinner," said Walter gravely.

I shall never forget that night. All of us equally jittery, we were just starting on our black-market steaks when the gaunt, blond unofficial ruler of French North Africa, flanked by the key members of the German Armistice Commission, stalked in and took places nearby. I kept feeling the General's stare right on the back of my neck. And then I got pretty fried. I banged on the table, told some indiscreet stories about the State Department, shouted for more wine, argued with the waiter, kept clapping Walter and Freddy on the back, leveled an occasional belligerent glance at the Germans and mentally held my breath.

Gradually the Austrians began to relax. "Very good," Walter murmured. "The Herr General is pleased. I know the signs. He is relaxing. He is impressed." To clinch it, we parked our car outside the German Consulate afterward and sang raucously.

The next day Freddy presented the General with a bill of several thousand francs for our dinner. Auer beamed with pleasure as he handed over the money, with a substantial bonus. "*Sehr gut, mein Junge*," he laughed. "Now you find out *important* things for me about the Americans from that fool."

I could hardly believe my good luck. The General now began to invite the Austrians to all his lavish parties. They heard much conversation on subjects that interested us deeply. German chemists were working on mass production of a new gas. The

High Command had given up the idea of invading French Africa through Spain. Every night we sent out such bits of information by radio and pouch.

I hinted to Freddy and Walter periodically that an American invasion was being set up. By July, Auer was obviously worried. He summoned the Austrians to his office for fresh instructions: they were to devote themselves entirely to finding out when and where the Americans would strike.

"Tell Auer," I said, "that the invasion plan is definitely settled. We will be landing at Dakar late this autumn." Then I spent a sleepless night. Would Auer fall for it? Had Freddy and Walter been planted by Auer to play the game on me that I wanted to play on him? If I had guessed wrong, I would be responsible for the loss of many Allied lives.

Next morning the Austrians were jubilant. Herr General had shouted with delight, "We'll catch the American swine! They'll walk into a beautiful trap. This news must go at once to the High Command!" He had pushed buttons and shouted for aides. And a long message had gone off to Wiesbaden. Then champagne had been broken out and innumerable toasts drunk—to Hitler, to the glory of German arms, to Auer's "staunch Austrian friends," and even to "the stupid American." Freddy and Walter had been rewarded with a large sum of money.

My contribution to the Dakar Cover Plan was complete. It was, of course, supported by other feints and intentional "leakages" of information, all designed to cast further suspicion toward Dakar.

A few months later I had the thrill of my life. I landed on D-day on the beach at Oran—1900 miles from Dakar. Operation Torch overwhelmed French North Africa with few shots fired and not a single ship of our huge armada sunk en route. Proceeding to Tafaroui airfield, where 600 prisoners were taken, I was instructed to contact the Vichyite commanding officer. His face got very red when I approached him. He pointed an accusing finger at me.

"Why are you Americans here?" he exploded. "We were expecting you at Dakar!"

Surreptitious Entry

Condensed from the book

By Willis George

One night, shortly after Pearl Harbor, I was on the duty watch of the Naval Intelligence unit of the Third Naval District in New York. At 11 p.m. the quiet of the office was broken by the chatter of the teletype. It was a message from Washington, and it started me off on what can only be described as a career of official burglary.

The message stated that attachés of a certain Embassy in Washington were believed to have burned their papers the previous day. Could we find out whether their Consulate in New York had done the same?

I asked my commanding officer for permission to try to get into this Consulate to investigate. Unlike many officers, he was willing to take long chances and to gamble his career for things he knew ought to be done.

"Go ahead," he said. "But remember that consulates are foreign territory. If you should get caught, it would be extremely embarrassing to the Navy Department."

I realized that only too well and tried to evolve a foolproof plan. First I saw the night superintendent of the building and showed him my credentials. He proved to be a Navy veteran and readily agreed to help. "There's no one on guard at night except the man on the Consulate's special elevator," he said.

I borrowed a suit of cleaner's coveralls and, thus disguised as a building employe, rode up in another elevator to two floors above the Consulate. Then I walked down the stairs to the Consulate and used the superintendent's passkey. Inside, I was greeted with the odor of burned paper. Every wastebasket gave evidence that papers had been destroyed. But there were a number of safes, a built-in vault and many filing cabinets, all locked. I was sure that important papers still remained.

I decided that, with or without permission, I was coming back to that office with whatever persons and tools might be necessary to open those safes and files. Once more my commanding officer was game, though this time he was acting without authority from Washington. And he knew, as I did, that it was one thing to smell a wastebasket in line of duty and quite another thing to crack a safe.

"I make only one condition," he said. "You must do your stuff in such a way that no one will suspect that you have been in those safes."

The next morning I began to assemble a crew: a locksmith, a safe expert, a linguist to tell us which documents were worth photographing and a first-class cameraman to microfilm them. British Security lent us an angular, mousy spinster of 50 who, with the aid of two armloads of pots, pans and steamkettles, could open any sealed package so that the job would defy detection even when examined under ultraviolet light. We also added a squad of security men to watch the building and warn us if any of the Consulate staff approached.

When my hastily assembled crew undertook its first surreptitious entry, we were amateurish indeed. We milled around in the Consulate, crowded from room to room to see just how locks were picked, and when the first safe was opened everyone tried to look inside at the same time. We were undoubtedly lax about removing traces of our visit, but somehow we escaped detection, and our searches continued nightly.

One night our camera fell to the floor with a resounding crash. Nothing happened, but the Consulate elevator operator must have reported the incident. On a subsequent night a sixth sense warned me that something was wrong and I decided to check before sending up the searching party. I put on cleaner's coveralls and, accompanied by the head of the cleaning staff, entered the Consulate. Immediately the light snapped on and we were confronted by the Consul and an armed guard, both with drawn guns. The cleaners' uniforms saved the situation, and the Consul apologized, saying he thought we were burglars.

After this, watching from an adjoining building, I observed that the guard arrived each afternoon at five and stayed all night. As long as he was there, further visits were impossible. I undertook to get rid of him. One night I sneaked up to the second floor and noisily crashed a chair near the elevator shaft. Then I hastily retreated to the basement with the chair. Half an hour later the Consul, who had been summoned by the guard, arrived by taxi-cab. From the adjoining building we watched him excitedly searching the Consulate. Several nights later I repeated the chair crash with identical results. This time the Consul was very angry. He was tired of being dragged out of bed on such foolish errands. Next day the guard failed to appear. Evidently the Consul had fired him.

We again took up our searches. Now, however, we were much more cautious, for we knew that the Consul was suspicious. We were learning the hard way. It took us 10 weeks to complete that job. When it was done, however, we had photographed every important document there. We possessed the Consulate codes, a card index of pro-Axis residents of the United States, and a wealth of material that showed that the Nazis had been using this Consulate for important espionage work.

In the next two years I made more than 150 such surreptitious entries—all without getting caught. Which is just as well, for we were completely on our own on these jobs. Operating outside the law, we could not hope for government support or recognition if we were caught.

When war came on December 7, everyone, including ourselves, became acutely spy-conscious. It seemed as if our telephones never stopped ringing. One night a light was seen to flash from the window of a penthouse atop a large apartment building. A spy sending code! We crashed the door of the penthouse and caught our "spy." The flashing code turned out to be an expensive aquarium placed near a window, equipped with an electric light that went on and off to warm the tropical fish.

Reports were telephoned to us about persons sending short-wave radio messages and about German submarines sighted in the Hudson River. These all proved wild stories, but each one had to be investigated.

It all seemed rather childish to me. I began to think wistfully of the secrets locked up in the files and safes of the hundreds of German-controlled corporations doing business in the United States. There—and not in the hands of individual crackpots— was the vital information our Intelligence must have. The idea of surreptitious entry—or, to put it more baldly, *burglary*—was already forming in my mind. Our initial success in searching the suspected Consulate had won approval of this method from higher quarters.

Indeed, our early success nearly ruined us. Although we knew how crude we still were, the higher-ups now felt that we could carry on surreptitious entries on a wholesale scale. We must train—presumably overnight—50 men to become expert lock-pickers and as many more to master the niceties of safe-opening.

Keeping our activities secret from our suspects was much less difficult than keeping them from our own people. The research laboratory we set up became uncomfortably popular with visiting officers. The technicians loved to show these gentlemen how easily filing cabinets could be opened with a piece of wire or a broken hacksaw blade; how locks were picked, letters opened, and whatever else we did in the course of a search. Too often reference was made to specific cases on which we were still working. The knowledge thus acquired later made fascinating dinner-table conversation. Officers and others who had never been members of a search team found this a splendid means of impressing their girl friends. Once, at a cocktail party, I was given full details about one of our searches by a young woman who had obtained them from a swivel-chair commando pretending to be a member of our team.

We improved our techniques and equipment to the point where we could duplicate our first job—which took us 10 weeks— in a single night. Planning and preparing for such a search, however, sometimes took a month.

Every important search was now preceded by careful sorting

of all scrap paper taken from the suspect's office by the cleaning staff. In many cases torn or burned scraps of letters established the fact that a complete search was worthwhile. One suspect tore up his letters and then burned the pieces, but a month later his private secretary tossed her stenographic notebooks into the wastebasket intact. Transcription of this shorthand gave us every important letter he had written for six weeks.

Under instructions from the mousy little British Security woman, we perfected our ability to open sealed envelopes. We learned to carry blackout curtains which would permit us to work with the lights on; to work in complete silence until we had located any possible microphones; to bring a dust-gun containing a mixture of charcoal and talc for redusting any disturbed documents or surfaces; to watch for traps; to sketch the contents of all safes before touching them, so that they could be replaced exactly. One of our squad cars was equipped with a short-wave radio sending and receiving set. Three other miniature two-way sets were built into suitcases that we could take with us. Only in trying to teach non-technical members of the team to open locks did we fail to make much progress. The techniques of lock-picking and safe-opening require a complete knowledge of the mechanism of locking devices and at least a year of constant practice.

One of our most rewarding searches was conducted in Chicago, in the elaborate 12th-floor suite of Stephen K. Ziggly. Ostensibly, Ziggly's business was banking and insurance, in both of which he had an international reputation. But American authorities suspected that he had another and more important business: operating a Nazi spy ring. He maintained his own banking and insurance business in a neutral European capital, but most of his connections were in Germany.

When Ziggly had taken the Chicago offices, he had insisted upon extensive alterations, rearranging the suite so that a visitor, to reach his private office, had to undergo the scrutiny of employes in four rooms. Soon after moving in, he complained to the building management that careless cleaning women had ruined a valuable document, and insisted on employing his own cleaning staff.

For three months we examined the scrap paper from Ziggly's office. He was an inveterate doodler, and his doodles were nearly always neat little pictures of guns and ships, of airplanes and bombs; and occasionally there appeared a design which bore a striking likeness to a radar apparatus. Finally we decided to effect a surreptitious entry.

As agent-in-charge I carried a revolver and blackjack; so did the three security men. Each of the others had a gas gun, pencil type. My first task was to obtain the coöperation of the superintendent. Both he and the owner, who had previously been investigated, were helpful. The owner insisted, however, that the searching party invent a reasonable excuse for entering the building. I suggested that the group take the cover of engineers who were testing the sway of the building.

"All buildings," I explained, "develop cracks at stress points from swaying, and the possibility of air raids makes it plausible for you to want the stress points tested. Also, using this cover, we can shut down the elevators during the search on the pretext that their vibration would affect the delicate testing instruments. That would help to prevent interruptions."

"Okay," said the owner. "You're the engineers."

The five building employes on night duty were investigated. One, whose background was not quite satisfactory, was transferred to day work. Meanwhile our radio experts selected parking places near the building, and two security men, in painters' coveralls, began to paint the hallway just outside Ziggly's suite. Two days later the "painters" reported that they could identify all of Ziggly's personnel.

Then my locksmith and I made a preliminary survey of Ziggly's premises. Very quietly—for we knew that if Ziggly were really a spy, there would be traps—the lock expert picked the intricate lock on the outer door. He had the door open in less than 15 minutes and, working just outside the doorway, began making a key.

Using a floor plan furnished by the owner of the building, I rapidly sketched in all of the partitions installed by Ziggly and noted the location of chairs, desks, file cabinets and other furniture. Then I searched for traps. On a window sill behind Ziggly's desk I found a large suitcase from which a concealed wire ran to a base plug. I disconnected the plug and opened the suitcase. It contained a sound-recording device with an extremely sensitive switch. This switch was thrown automatically whenever a word was spoken in the room, and the sound, picked up by microphones, was recorded silently on film.

One of the microphones was found on a shelf behind Ziggly's desk, and another was hidden beneath a small table in the center of the room. Ziggly's private office was found to contain a "burglarproof" safe. The handle number was noted. Before leaving the office we made a careful check to be sure that everything had been restored to its original position. The polished floor, which bore the marks of our rubber heels, was repolished. A thin layer of dust which had covered the suitcase was replaced with our dust powder of talc and charcoal. On the way out, I investigated all possible escape routes in case of interruption, and chose a washroom a few doors from Ziggly's office for camera work.

Three days after the preliminary survey, about one o'clock in the morning, our group of 11 men drove up to the building in several cars and a large enclosed delivery truck on which was lettered "The Northwest Engineering Company." We actually had rented a small office. The telephone number and address were listed in the Chicago directory. From the truck we unloaded a dozen boxes and suitcases, each stenciled with the name of the company, containing both search equipment and instruments for measuring building sway. Two men remained hidden in the truck—a radio operator and the security agent who could identify Ziggly's employes. A concealed slot in the side of the truck gave them a good view of the entrance of the building.

I approached the superintendent in the lobby as a stranger and showed him a copy of a contract for the sway tests signed by the owner. I asked that elevator service be suspended. Two of the elevators were requisitioned by the "engineers," who got off with their equipment at various floors and then walked up or down to the 12th. They left coats, hats and shoes in the elevator, telling the operator that even the thud of heels caused enough vibration to affect the instruments.

One of our men, with the key made by the lock expert, went ahead to open Ziggly's door and make certain that the group was not walking into a trap. If he found himself in trouble, he would pretend to be a burglar and escape as best he could. But the way was clear, so he immediately entered the room, disconnected the sound recorder, put up blackout curtains and turned on the lights. At his signal the rest of us entered, and each man went to work on his particular assignment. The radio operator established communication with the truck in the street, the cameraman set up his equipment in the washroom and the lock expert picked the lock of an office across the hallway. This was to be used if flight became necessary.

Some 15 minutes after the work started, the radio operator in the truck reported that one of Ziggly's employes had entered the building. Swiftly the men gathered up their equipment, retired to a room across the hall and from there re-established radio communication with the truck. In less than 10 minutes Ziggly's office was vacated, with nothing there to show that it had ever been entered.

Meanwhile the two security men in the lobby carried out a pre-arranged plan of delay. One insisted that Ziggly's employe identify himself to the superintendent, and wasted more than five minutes telephoning empty offices, trying to find that official. The other went into a highly technical explanation of the sway tests.

"You're interfering with an important job," our man complained. "Can't your work wait until tomorrow?"

"Well," said the employe, "the truth is I'm not going to work. I've got my girl in a bar around the corner, and I'm short of dough. I want to get a bottle of whiskey out of my desk. I won't be but a minute."

After much hedging, he was run up to the 12th floor and the elevator was held for him while he unlocked Ziggly's office and got his liquor. Then he left the building and was followed by one of our men until he joined his girl in the bar. We resumed work.

Our expert opened Ziggly's "burglarproof" safe in less than 20 minutes. My eyes went at once to a sealed package, dated in the purple ink of an office stamp and marked "Received 5:10 p.m." The date was the day before. Apparently the package had arrived so near closing time that Ziggly, knowing its contents, had thrust it into the safe unopened. I turned it over to the flaps-and-seals expert.

He wrapped the package in cellophane with holes cut in it to expose the seals. Then he mixed a small batch of the impression paste used by dentists. With this he took an impression of the exposed wax seals and then, using a heated pencil-point soldering iron, cut through the seal along the edge of the wrapping paper. The package contained a code book. The cameraman photographed each page, then returned the book to the flaps-and-seals expert for resealing. When the latter had softened the broken seals with a hot soldering iron and pressed them firmly into place with the matrices made of dental compound, the seals looked as they had originally and showed no indication that they had been tampered with in any way.

While this was going on, we had discovered in the safe what looked like a trap—a string laid in zigzag fashion atop a dust-covered tin box. It took us 20 minutes to sketch and measure the string and to make sure that it didn't lead to something else. Then the remaining contents of the safe were removed and examined by the evaluator. The same procedure was followed with the papers and documents taken from the desks and filing cabinets.

Everything judged to be important by the evaluator, who knew four languages and used all of them before the search was completed, was photographed. The camera expert worked at top speed. In a little less than four hours he made 2000 photographs of letters, codes, reports and other material.

After the search we gathered in the lobby of the building. There, for the benefit of the employes, we made a considerable show of packing away the sway-test instruments, and of jotting down elaborate calculations. We were about halfway through this job when Ziggly rushed in. The employe who had been there

earlier, befuddled by two hours of steady drinking, had finally telephoned him that a lot of men were prowling around the building with queer-looking instruments. The alarmed Ziggly hurried past the agents and demanded that he be taken upstairs immediately. Confident that he would find no traces of our visit, we ignored him.

Twenty minutes later Ziggly reappeared, jovial and smiling broadly; obviously he had found all his traps in place and suspected nothing. He showed great interest in the sway-testing instruments spread out on the lobby floor and seemed pleased when one of the "engineers" told him the building was safe. Presently he departed, whistling gaily. It may have been the last time he so whistled, for two days later government agents went quietly to his office and, still quietly, led him away.

We had obtained conclusive evidence that Ziggly operated a German espionage ring of a dozen agents in six large American cities. Some of the records in his safe contained the names and addresses of these agents. Others were instructions in the use of microfilm, invisible ink, disguises and so on. Within a month all of Ziggly's agents had been rounded up and the espionage ring smashed. But neither Ziggly nor any of his associates knew how it had been done.

By this time, in contrast to our first clumsy entry of the foreign Consulate, we had reduced our operations to a system which left nothing to chance. The Bata case perhaps illustrates better than any other the changes and refinements we had wrought in our technique.

One day a trusted and important employe of a western war plant, Gustav Jensen, was arrested when a routine security check disclosed in his coat pocket part of the plans of a new secret weapon. Jensen, an engineer in the department where the weapon was being developed, claimed that he had put the blueprint in his pocket while working and had forgotten it. As he had previously made several valuable contributions to the company's war effort, he was released with a stern warning. But the plant's security chief was not satisfied with Gustav's story and ordered him placed under surveillance.

Gustav Jensen was a naturalized American citizen, born in a country then occupied by the Nazis which maintained a government-in-exile in London. He was highly respected and considered strongly pro-American. But a neighbor, in giving a glowing account of his good qualities, furnished a clue that heightened the security chief's suspicions. "Gustav is a very smart man," he said. "He is not only a fine engineer, doing great work at the plant, but he can make all sorts of things for his own use. Just a little while ago he built a photostating machine and has it in his cellar."

A photostating machine? This seemed to point to espionage, and the case was turned over to our office. Jensen's dossier showed that in his application for employment he had used as a reference the name of Colonel Bata, an important official in the New York office of his former country's government-in-exile. Colonel Bata, we knew, had engaged in espionage during World War I, and it seemed worthwhile to check on him now. I was detailed to make a preliminary survey of the Colonel's office in New York.

"I'm glad you've come," the building superintendent said. "I've been worried about those people. They occupy the whole 10th floor and several offices on the 11th. There's a constant stream of visitors. And they've taken to burning papers up there in their baskets."

We examined the record book kept in the lobby and found that Saturday night would be the safest time for our preliminary search. On the following Saturday I met the superintendent, who admitted us to the 10th-floor offices. The cameraman, using infrared equipment which allowed him to take pictures in the dark, made photographs of the entire floor and office upstairs.

The office was huge. In one section alone I found 140 filing cabinets, all locked. I took the serial number of the lock of each cabinet and desk, as well as the make, type and size of each safe. The serial numbers would enable us to make keys, and the advance information concerning the safes would enable our safe expert to refresh his memory regarding the types on which he was to work.

I soon realized that this entry would be complicated and on a scale that would require all the men and equipment we had. We would need two photo-record cameras, the radio car, a portable radio for each floor and at least 20 men.

The security detail, acting as cleaning and repair crews, worked around the offices for days until they could recognize the principal employes at a glance. The radios were tested in the area to make sure that the building's electrical equipment would not interfere with sending and receiving.

As cover for this search we decided to use the building-sway technique again. We added several meaningless but impressive-looking instruments to make the building's night staff feel that they were "in" on important stuff. Armed with these props, our group was ready to make an impressive entrance.

The radio car was parked directly across the street, where the security men could watch the entrance. By arrangement with the superintendent, the steel door of the freight entrance rolled up and the two squad cars, carrying interior radio and camera crews, drove in. A minute later the doors rolled down. The men loaded their equipment into an elevator and went up to the 10th and 11th floors.

The two cars bearing the "engineering" group arrived at the front entrance, where they were met by the superintendent. Pausing just long enough to exhibit their elaborate props and make their reason for being there look plausible, they too made for the suspected floors.

The safe expert settled down to his task. Filing cabinets and desks were rapidly unlocked with the previously made keys. The evaluators went to work on the mass of material in the files. Within 10 minutes the first photographs had been taken.

Suddenly we were warned from the street that a light could be seen in one of the windows. We fixed the faulty blackout curtain and got a cheerful "O.K." from the radio car. Work went ahead quickly. In another 10 minutes the safe was opened. We worked without speaking. Silence was complete. No one was allowed to use drinking fountains or lavatories lest the slightest rumble in the plumbing pipes betray our presence. For five hours the searchers and evaluators continued at top speed. The cameramen took more than 6000 photographs. The job was done. We got ready to leave.

Everything was restored to its proper place. The dust that covered the contents of a small safe, evidently seldom used, was replaced with a dust-gun. Desks were polished, files wiped clean of fingerprints and carpets brushed free of footprints our stock-inged feet might have made.

When we returned to our quarters, the photographic labora-tory developed the rolls of 35-mm. film. As soon as they were dry, enlargements of the individual frames were made. Then we sorted and indexed the photographs. Now we could examine the fruits of the night's search.

What did we have?

First, we had Gustav Jensen's entire history. We knew he was a foreign agent, and knew each piece of information he had sup-plied. But, beyond that, we had uncovered an intelligence head-quarters that was collecting war secrets from every large city in North and South America.

The thoroughness of this network's intelligence operation stunned us. For instance, we found the plan of the Allied invasion of Sicily two weeks before it started!

Much of the credit for the success of our surreptitious entries should be given to the skilled technicians who aided us. These men were civilians who nightly risked their personal reputations as well as their lives to help us. Had they been caught during one of these entries, they could have made no defense. All of us were on our own—but these men chanced business or professional ruin as well. One of the best-known camera experts in the country repeatedly risked arrest as a housebreaker to help us with an es-pecially difficult photographic job.

Eventually I was transferred from my search team and became an instructor in the secret Office of Strategic Services schools, where I taught fledgling OSS agents the intricacies of lock-pick-ing and allied arts. Still later I took a safe-blowing squad into Germany, where we secured documents which were sent as evi-dence to the Nuremberg trials.

PART FOUR

1 9 4 3

CUNNING VS. CUNNING

NOW at last the tide of war was beginning to turn. In the Pacific, Guadalcanal fell to the American forces; the fearful task of island-hopping lay ahead. In the fall of the year, Italy was invaded and the Allies, fighting stubbornly against Nazi fire, advanced inch by inch over the ancient terrain.

As the fury of war mounted, the grand trumps of espionage were thrown down in a game of deception more imaginative than ever before. It was a time of hazardous missions and great hoaxes; of daring rescues involving thousands; of armed units secretly built up far behind enemy lines to harass the foe. It was a time when international thievery and intrigue flourished in Lisbon and Istanbul, those "neutral" centers of spies and diplomats.

Never before had psychological warfare been such a vital weapon. Axis propaganda, already successful in enslaving its own people, sent out malicious appeals, expert lies and demoralizing rumors. The Allies fought back with new devices of communication that could reach across the fields of battle.

The race of science for greater means of destruction was given the highest military priority, and each side ferreted out the other's dreadful secrets with spies and reconnaissance. Allied raiders made savage, suicidal attacks to destroy the enemy's experiments in weapons that could gain sudden victory.

By the year's end, none could tell whether sheer manpower or sheer wits might win the great struggle.

The Corpse
That Hoaxed the Axis

Condensed from the book The Man Who Never Was

By Ewen E. S. Montagu

In the graveyard of the Spanish town of Huelva, 130 miles north of Gibraltar on the Atlantic coast, there lies a British subject. He died of pneumonia in the foggy damp of England, never knowing he would lie forever under sunny Spanish skies. In his life he had done little for his country. After death he probably saved thousands of British and American lives.

In the autumn of 1942 the invasion of North Africa was moving forward steadily to victory. The decision had been tentatively made to strike next in Sicily. The Germans were bound to expect that Sicily would be an objective. How could we convince them otherwise, fox them into scattering their strength?

One member of our security team had a suggestion. The Germans knew that our officers were continually being flown around the coast of Spain to North Africa. Why not plant a body, carrying doctored papers, in the sea off Spain as if coming from a crashed plane? If it floated ashore, it was a good bet that the papers would fall into the hands of German espionage agents.

A practical question arose. A dead man does not breathe; if his body is placed in the sea, the lungs remain empty—so a post mortem might establish that the body was dead when it entered the water. The finder would then suspect a "plant."

We quietly opened inquiries in service medical circles to obtain a body whose cause of death could be confused with drowning. Finally a report came through: a man had just died from pneumonia, in which form of death there is liquid in the lungs.

Some of the dead man's relatives were alive. Without disclosing details we obtained their consent—on the understanding that the identity of the body would always remain secret. From that time forward the dead man became "Major William Martin, Royal Marines." His body was placed in cold storage.

From the outset it was decided that the document carrying the deception must be on a high level. I arranged for the Vice-Chief of the Imperial General Staff to write a letter to General Alexander, then commanding the 18th Army Group in Africa. The letter was an off-the-record explanation of why Alexander was not getting quite what he wanted from the Chiefs of Staff. By inference it carried the conclusion that the target we were planning to attack in the western Mediterranean was *not* Sicily.

In the letter we took care to plant two false targets as being our possible objectives—one in Greece, and the other, not actually identified in this letter, somewhere in the western Mediterranean. The letter also made it clear that we *wanted* the Germans to think that the landing would be in Sicily—that we were using it as the "cover" for our real target. Thus, if the Germans swallowed the trick, any real leakage about Sicily that reached them would be regarded as part of our deception.

In addition, we decided to give Major Martin a communiqué from Lord Louis Mountbatten to Admiral of the Fleet Sir Andrew Cunningham, Commander in Chief, Mediterranean. It explained Major Martin's mission and concluded: "I think you will find Martin the man you want. Let me have him back, please, as soon as the assault is over. He might bring some sardines with him—they are 'on points' here!" I thought the rather labored joke about sardines would appeal to the Germans—and help to pinpoint Sardinia as the target of the assault.

The next hurdle was Major Martin's identity card, with photograph. Any photograph of the body looked hopelessly dead. Then one day at a meeting I looked across the table and there, opposite me, was Major Martin's double. We persuaded the double to sit for the picture. (See photograph on page 347.)

Now we had to give our body a personality. We decided Martin was an expert on landing craft, hence the reason for his being flown to North Africa. He was, however, a little extravagant, and in his pocket was a letter from Lloyds Bank, dated April 14, 1943, calling on him to pay off an overdraft of nearly £80.

Every young officer had some romantic attachment and Major Martin had recently met a charming girl called Pam. He carried a snap of her and two letters from her in his wallet. These letters were folded and unfolded continually to look as though they had been read and reread. Probably his engagement was the cause of his overdraft, for he also had a bill for £53 in his pocket for an engagement ring. Major Martin had, of course, the usual effects and junk—identity disks, wristwatch, cigarettes, old bus tickets, scraps of paper, keys. We decided that he would probably take his fiancée to the theater on his last night in England. So the halves of two tickets to *Strike a New Note* for April 22 were put into his pocket before he left by submarine on April 19.

We decided to plant the body off Huelva, a small port near the Portuguese frontier. The Spaniards would, of course, hand over the body to the British Vice-Consul for burial. But we felt sure that the local German agent would get copies of the papers.

By good fortune, the submarine *Seraph*, commanded by Lieutenant N. L. A. Jewell, was due to sail for Malta at about the right date. Jewell had smuggled General Mark Clark in and out of North Africa in 1942 before the Allied landings. (See "Secret Mission to North Africa," page 216.)

Final approval was now sought from Prime Minister Churchill. We had to warn him that if the Germans saw through our deception Sicily would be pinpointed as the Allied target. Churchill gave his consent, and directed that General Eisenhower, in supreme command of the invasion of Sicily, be informed.

The *Seraph* sailed at six p.m. on April 19, 1943. On board was Major William Martin—in a six-foot metal canister packed with dry ice. For 10 days the *Seraph* surfaced only at night. On April 30 she was 1600 yards off Huelva, undetected and on schedule. At zero hour, 4:30 a.m., the canister was hauled aloft and Major Martin was slid out. Jewell inflated the major's Mae West and four young officers bent bare heads as their commander murmured the burial service. And then with a gentle push Major

Martin went to war. A half-mile away Jewell launched a rubber dinghy from one of our aircraft, with only one aluminum oar so as to simulate haste.

Early in the morning of April 30, 1943, a Spanish fisherman sighted the body close inshore. It was recovered by the authorities and a post mortem carried out: the verdict, "asphyxiation through immersion in the sea." The British Vice-Consul was duly informed, and on May 2, 1943, Major Martin was buried with full military honors.

So far so good. We had been given the body—*but we had not been told about the documents!*

On May 4 we sent an "Immediate Most Secret" signal stating that we had learned that Major William Martin was carrying papers, some of which were "of great importance and secrecy." Formal demand was to be made to the neutral Spanish government for all documents.

Meanwhile the German agent in Huelva had not let us down. He had learned of the existence of the envelopes and of the distinction of the addresses, and there is no doubt from what happened later that he alerted his superiors. Not until May 13 did the Chief of the Spanish Naval Staff hand over the documents to our attaché and inform him that "everything was safely there."

We then asked that a tombstone be placed over the grave. It is still there. (Pam sent a wreath.) Finally, we had Major Martin's name inserted in the casualty list which appeared in the London *Times* of June 4, 1943.

The success of the landing on Sicily in July was pretty good evidence that our ruse had succeeded, but proof positive was found later in captured enemy documents. One day after the war the British officer in charge of the examination of captured German naval archives reported to the Deputy Director of Naval Intelligence with horror in his voice. A very senior Army officer, he said, had sent some highly secret letters, apparently by an irregular route, and they had fallen into German hands.

Sure enough, they were the documents carried by Major Martin. There, in the German files, were photographic copies of the letters, with translations and intelligence reports. There was a file especially prepared for Admiral Karl Doenitz. Fourteen days after the body had floated ashore in Spain the German Naval Staff War Diary recorded that the Army Staff had definitely concluded that the documents were genuine, and that the main Allied assault would be not in Sicily but in Sardinia, with a subsidiary landing in Greece.

The German High Command moved a whole panzer division from France to the Peloponnesus in Greece, to cover communications to the two beaches—Cape Araxos and Kalamata—mentioned in the documents Major Martin carried. This was an enormous operation that kept the division out of the war for some time. The High Command also ordered the laying of minefields off the Greek coast, the installation of coastal batteries and the preparation of R-boat (German motor torpedo boat) bases, command stations and sea-patrol services. A whole group of R-boats was sent from Sicily to Greece in June.

The commander in the West, Field Marshal Wilhelm Keitel, himself signed an order from the Supreme Command of the Armed Forces ordering "reinforcement of Sardinia." A strong panzer force was sent to Corsica, and defenses were improved on the north coast of Sicily (where we did not land) against "a diversionary attack during the assault on Sardinia."

Even after the Sicily invasion had started, the High Command asked for a special lookout in the Strait of Gibraltar for convoys which would be going to attack Corsica and Sardinia. In other documents it was stated bitterly that the sending of R-boats to Greece had left a fatal gap in the defenses of Sicily.

The success of Major Martin's "mission" can be measured in the words of Field Marshal Erwin Rommel, whose personal papers reveal that when the Allies invaded Sicily the German defenses were led astray—"as a result of a diplomatic courier's body being washed up off Spain."

Hitler also must have seen the documents, for Admiral Doenitz recorded in his diary these words: "The Führer does not agree . . . that the most likely invasion point is Sicily. He believes that the discovered Anglo-Saxon order confirms that the attack will be directed mainly against Sardinia and the Peloponnesus."

Censors and Spies

By Mary Knight

I was a wartime censor—one of the 15,000 snoopers who for nearly four years opened mail, listened to telephone conversations and meddled with movies, reading matter and radio programs.

At first we suffered from a sense of guilt. We were doing a thing most of us hated to do—poking into other people's business. But we soon found how necessary Censorship really was. That became evident even before Pearl Harbor's ruins ceased smoking. One of the first letters opened in the bathroom-laboratory of an old house which Censorship immediately took over in Honolulu described in detail the results of the attack. The message, by a devious route, was headed for Japan.

Censorship was a double-edged weapon. It not only kept information from the enemy but in many cases gave us valuable data about the enemy. For example, by culling a bit from one business letter, a bit from another, and so on, a censor accumulated a picture of a Japanese trade route that enabled the Navy to sink seven merchant ships by lying in wait at one spot.

An overheard phone conversation revealed the whereabouts of a black-market hoard of badly needed quinine. A censored cable disclosed a German spy in Havana, posing as a dress-goods dealer, receiving money mysteriously through multiple banks. He was arrested, tried, convicted and shot. Ninety-one individuals were caught and convicted of spying against the United States during 1938–1945; censorship played a part in the majority of these cases.

When the chief of the Office of Censorship first went to work, he had only a borrowed room in Washington. Eventually his organization expanded into 90 buildings throughout the country and, with the United Kingdom and Canada, set up the first global censorship network.

Most censors had to be experts in some field. We needed decoders and translators, technical, legal and financial experts, even such specialists as philatelists. (A letter from one "stamp collector" to another enclosed a sheet of stamps which by an ingenious code revealed that the battleship *Iowa* was sailing from a certain port on a given date for a certain destination.) One Columbia University professor read nine languages, including Sanskrit, and could identify 95 others. Among the languages we encountered were Haitian Creole; Hindustani in Braille; Portuguese Romanized Japanese (Portuguese priests went as missionaries to Japan in the 17th century and romanized the language now used by groups of Japanese in Brazil); Papiamento (spoken in Curaçao and comprising Dutch, Spanish, Portuguese and English words picked up from sailors). We had linguists who could read shorthand in 300 languages.

Every day a million pieces of mail crossed our desks. Air mail could be delayed only 24 hours, surface mail not more than 48. Correspondence to and from the heads of our own and Allied governments was not to be opened, but we had to examine the envelopes carefully, for enemy agents counterfeited even envelopes of the State Department and White House. All mail was checked against a Watch List—persons we knew or suspected were enemies. This list fluctuated between 75,000 and 100,000 names. Such mail received special handling.

Other letters we immediately transferred to the examining tables. Each examiner used a bulky volume listing subjects on which government agencies wanted information—Treasury on financial deals, Commerce on business, Labor on working conditions, FBI on suspicious activities, etc.

Intercepted letters located stores of rubber, tin plate and mica. A clue from a censor traced a cargo of zinc on its way to Argentina; it was caught in mid-ocean and turned back. One letter showed that a New York firm was sending three million pounds of nickel scrap to Sweden to produce hard steel which eventually would reach Germany; another disclosed a German plan to sell a million bottles of champagne in Spain and thus bank abroad nearly $6,000,000. A German mother wrote her son in America that when he returned he could ride to work. That revealed a new railroad, which was promptly bombed.

At the borders of the country we censored papers carried by air and train passengers. One woman we caught had, hidden in a basket of flowers, a message revealing the date of an important ship departure. A secret-ink message from a Nazi agent that we intercepted complained that his activities had been paralyzed by Travelers' Censorship, which nailed him at a border.

Our suspicions were continually sharpened by new discoveries—such as attempts to smuggle diamonds in chocolate drops. In false-bottomed meat cans we found a report on a year's operations in the Western Hemisphere of the giant I. G. Farbenindustrie, which also conducted Nazi espionage.

Our greatest anxiety was messages in secret codes and inks. We scanned every letter for strange use of numbers or symbols, for awkward expressions; for paper that looked dried out or scratched. Even colorless scratches denoted paper fibers disturbed by invisible ink. We sent every letter bearing those or other suspicious indications, and almost every letter to or from anyone on the Watch List, to TOD.

Technical Operations Division was the intentionally vague name for the laboratory in Washington which tested for codes, ciphers and secret inks. Remote, windowless, its screened entrance admitted only a dozen or so men and women. They "stripped" each letter with swabs containing reagents to develop all common secret inks. They searched them with ultraviolet light. They found a German device whereby an entire page, typewritten in code and photographed, was reduced to a tiny dot and hidden in the flap of an envelope or in a typewritten mark of punctuation in an otherwise innocent letter. (See "The Micro-Dot," page 175.)

We detected thousands of codes and ciphers, of which we thought 4600 worth the further attention of the FBI or other intelligence services. The codes were "open" and "closed." The open code used a seemingly innocent message to conceal a dangerous one: "Mother arriving Bilbao seventh" may mean not mother but a convoy, not Bilbao but Gibraltar. The closed code substituted letters, numbers or symbols for words. They were less dangerous than open codes, for they always proclaimed themselves secret messages.

It took the most alert censors to check international telephone messages. Wearing headphones, the censor sat with pencil in one hand, the other hand on the switch which could instantly cut off either party. Most of the trouble was with high officials, especially in moments of crisis. After the Teheran conference, a general's aide itemized by name and rank—some very high— the passenger list and schedule of a transport plane, virtually inviting the enemy to ambush it.

Every cable filed in this country was teletyped to the nearest of our 12 cable stations. If we clearly understood its meaning and were certain it was harmless, we okayed it, but if in doubt we double-checked. A soldier was not allowed to cable his girl "Four pounds' worth of orchids." We made it "Four pounds flowering plant"—names of flowers might be a code. A censor changed "Father is dead" to "Father is deceased." Back to the cable-sender came a query, "Is father dead or deceased?"—a dead giveaway.

All told, censorship intercepted nearly 400 secret espionage letters of major importance. Early skeptics about "spy stuff" were flabbergasted when a harmless-looking personal letter from Europe to a woman in a New York hotel showed under the testing strip a long secret-ink message beginning: "Write or go to Theresa. She receives from Mr. Miller money. . . ." The recipient was not arrested immediately. We went on reading her mail. Sure enough, she unwittingly uncovered five accomplices. All six got stiff sentences.

Another woman spy had a clever plan of communication, but muffed it. She had built up a worldwide business of selling dolls. Her apparently normal business correspondence made ideal cover for her reports to Japan about the location and condition of Allied war vessels she observed on business trips to the Pacific coast. "I left my three English dolls at the doll hospital," she wrote. "In a few months they'll be completely repaired." That meant three British ships. "Siamese dolls" meant dual-purpose escort carriers.

These meanings might have gone unsuspected had she not signed some mail with the names of other people in the business and mailed her letters to an Argentine address she had got from the Japanese—but got wrong. The letters came back to the supposed senders, who told the FBI, who told us. We pounced on all letters about dolls, signed by Velvalee Dickinson or anyone else, and from this avalanche screened ample evidence to arrest her. Pleading guilty to censorship evasion, she got the works—a $10,000 fine and 10 years in jail.

A letter directed to an address in Portugal which was on the Watch List brought about the discovery and arrest of a foreign agent, Ernest Lehmitz, on Staten Island, N.Y. (See "The Hunt for a Spy," page 186, and photograph on page 334.)

Also on our Watch List was one Hirzel in Switzerland. A letter addressed to him, signed R. O. Gerson, seemed quite natural and convincing—but it covered a message in a new secret ink about our production of explosives. This was a big fish we were playing! Luckily, later letters showed "Gerson" scared—"May have to flee." He begged his superiors to stop writing. His good ink was running low. Next time he must use urine and sign "Peel." He did, giving some military information. The FBI arrested him. Confronted by the evidence, he confessed being a Nazi spy—Count von Rautter, a naturalized American citizen.

Through censored letters we discovered three spy trails leading to our new bases in Alaska: a Japanese woman's plan to go through disguised as an Indian; a spy planning to establish a radio station in the woods; and another who asked for some secret ink.

Our most complete success in suppression—thanks to cooperation of radio and press—was in keeping from the Japanese any knowledge of how their new weapon was working. This weapon was their now-famous paper balloon loaded with bombs, released when winds would blow it over our northwestern forests. The Japanese hoped it would start fires and shake civilian morale. One bomb found by Sunday-school picnickers in Oregon killed a woman and five children. Though the Forest Service found 334 of these bombs, our secrecy was so effective that the Japanese eventually decided the bombs were not even reaching us and they abandoned the project after launching 9,000 bomb-laden balloons.

Censorship of all kinds was surprisingly successful. In all we intercepted over a million dangerous letters and cables. Incidentally, we got to know a lot about Americans, overhearing their conversations and reading their mail. When they transgressed national security it was almost always unintentional, and many even thanked us when we interrupted their telephone calls to tell them to be careful.

Jungle of Hidden Friends

By Ralph E. Henderson

"**W**hen we volunteered for 'hazardous service,'" the bearded young captain told me in Burma, "we didn't know we were coming out here, and we certainly had never heard of a tribe called Kachins. Well, we know plenty about them now. The best damn jungle fighters in the world. It's lucky they happen to like Americans."

The American-Kachin Rangers, a detachment of OSS, did their fighting *behind* the Japanese lines. For that reason they were necessarily protected by a cloak of military secrecy. But I already knew something of the amazing record.

They had been ahead of General Wingate in February 1943, an advance screen when he led his "Chindits" in the first spectacular strike deep into Burma. Ahead of General Merrill in early 1944, guiding his "Marauders" on their 750-mile jungle march to seize the Myitkyina air strip. Ahead of the Stilwell Road, as its engineers came crashing through the mountains to build a land route to China. Ahead of General Willey's "Mars Force" in the operation which shook loose the last Japanese grip on the North Burma mountains.

Action enough, perhaps; and yet that is only a small part of the story of the Americans who made contact with wild tribesmen, and of the strange results of that fighting partnership.

"The first signing up," continued the captain, "was rather like getting a bid to join a fraternity. Officers from this outfit were looking for candidates in the training camps back home. They would tap you for a little talk: 'Would you like to see some quick action—hazardous, of course?' 'Are you pretty good at taking care of yourself?' And then a question that made you think twice: 'Are you willing to make a parachute jump behind enemy lines—alone?' I got my first hint as to where I might be sent when I was called into a room in Washington and asked to make a list of things I would want if I should find myself *alone in the jungle*. A few days later I was on a boat, and an officer told me where I was bound for."

The Burma hill country bordering Assam is one of the wildest areas on earth. From a plane it looks like a gigantic green plush carpet flung over a rock pile. From the ground there is usually no view at all, only a sense of sunless, choking vegetation. The few trails used by the hill folk seem to emphasize, rather than relieve, the impenetrability of the endless jungle.

Along these trails, early in 1942, the beaten Allied forces had made their escape from Burma into Assam. Along them, after that retreat, crouched the Japanese, denying any hope of a return. The Japanese conquest of Burma had, moreover, isolated China by choking off the Burma Road. Unless a new way could be found to send in supplies, China was doomed. The task of digging the Japanese from the North Burma mountains and securing a supply road nearly 1000 miles long was assigned to General Joseph W. Stilwell. As one of his units, the American-Kachin Rangers were to play a spectacular part.

On July 4, 1942, a small group had gone ahead to set up the Rangers' headquarters in Assam. There had been only 20 of them at first, a curious little army of 11 officers and nine men. A hand-picked group of specialists, including not only experienced Army officers but others whose attainments seemed peaceful enough: geographers, linguists, lawyers, even a jeweler (his skill with precision instruments was to prove invaluable in designing tiny, durable radios).

The plan of operations was simple; "crazy," some conventional military minds called it. A warlike hill tribe called the Kachins back there in the Japanese-held mountains was known to dislike the Japanese. The plan was for American volunteers to organize the Kachins in fighting units and supply them with weapons and leadership. At night, deep in enemy territory, an American volunteer would parachute down near a jungle village. A second chute would carry food, weapons, drugs, a few presents for the natives and a small radio sending set.

From the moment he leaped (often his first parachute jump) the volunteer would be irrevocably on his own. He must make friends with natives whose language and customs were totally unfamiliar to him. He must make himself their leader, trust them not to betray him for a high reward. Once he was securely established, the night-flying planes would bring him more food, weapons, supplies. And then he could begin his own little war, a campaign of raids and ambushes, against the enemy.

The plan certainly lacked nothing in audacity. It might have been regarded as foolhardy but for two important facts. First, the country was so wild and densely jungled that there were remote villages to which Japanese patrols had never penetrated. Second, Kachin refugees had reported that men of their race liked Americans as much as they hated Japanese.

The Kachin warrior, as many American boys were later to discover with something of a shock, does not fit the romantic picture of the noble savage. He is usually no more than five feet tall, with stringy hair, crooked teeth and a retiring manner easily mistaken for stupidity. His clothes look like something given to him, a long time ago, by destitute relatives, and he wisely refrains from washing them lest they disintegrate altogether. There is nothing in his appearance to contradict his history of blood-feuding within the tribe and robbery beyond its borders. Dr. Gordon Seagrave, the "Burma Surgeon," acknowledged his debt to the Kachins as the first willing candidates for his surgery: their general fondness for knives made them welcome any experiments in cutting, even upon their own persons. The Kachin's taste for bloodletting is hereditary and natural; his fondness for Americans was acquired.

In 1878, when Burma was ruled by King Thibaw, an American missionary named William Henry Roberts sought permission to enter a part of the country far to the north. Here lived the backward, warlike race known to the Burmese as "Kachins"— "robbers." No traveler was considered safe among them. King Thibaw consented. It was no concern of his if a foreigner wished to devote his life, which promised to be extremely short, to his own brand of religious lunacy.

Roberts' labors among the Kachins produced two notable results. First, he won the gratitude of a large number of tribes-men. Their first unselfish friend, the first foreigner willing to teach them and live among them, was from a distant land called America. With a simple and primitive logic, these hillmen extended that friendship to other Americans who followed Roberts, and gradually transferred it wholesale to a great country they had never seen. Second, Roberts gave the Kachins a written language. They had no alphabet of their own, and so he captured the sound of the native words, as nearly as possible, in our own letters, and set up village schools to teach the ABC's. Many Kachins, therefore, learned to read their language in our alphabet. That fact of an identical alphabet has made the training of Kachin radio operators very easy.

The first American volunteers to take the dark leap into the unknown were scared. They admitted it. Scared of being hope-lessly lost in the jungle; scared of injury, of snakes, of sickness; scared most of all of being caught and tortured by the enemy.

"My first jump," one of them told me, "went off all right. I landed safely near a Kachin village, and they found me next day. They were perfectly friendly and gave me boiled rice and eggs. But I knew an enemy force was nearby and I was about ready to cross off my life. I didn't know, then, that you could just hook your hand in the nearest Kachin's belt and he would take you to some place where no Japanese could ever find you. Perhaps he couldn't understand a word of the few phrases you had tried to learn—it didn't matter. He would hide you, and feed you, and stay with you till it was safe to move again."

The volunteers, at first, were not at all concerned with fighting. They had enough to do in learning to exist in the jungle, in setting up radio communications with their home base, in getting acquainted with the language and customs of their hosts. They familiarized themselves with all the jungle trails in their areas, the roads used by the Japanese, the tiny paths and game tracks which only the Kachins knew. The Japanese were aware of their presence by now, of course. Enemy patrols often chased them from place to place, but could never catch them.

The Kachins were joyfully willing to enlist as fighters. Gradually each American organized his own band of tough little warriors and began to equip a force. (See photograph on page 336.) The radios reported positions, called for supplies, and the transport planes dropped the packages on mountain rice-field clearings or into secret forest glades. The standard supply was one third of what would be required for usual Army units; Rangers were expected to live two thirds off the country.

To the Kachins, stripped of nearly all necessities by the years of war, the bounty from the skies was miraculous: rice, salt (unobtainable in the hills, and valued like silver), medicines, tobacco, lamp oil, machine guns, rifles and fine jungle knives.

Before long these forces were beginning to make contact with one another, and to infiltrate deep in enemy-held territory. They cleared small, hidden landing strips in the jungle, where tiny liaison planes could slip in to take out sick or wounded men. They began to repay their debt to the Air Force by rescuing pilots whose planes had crashed in enemy territory.

The American boys who had leaped into the unknown were now veteran campaigners; they had learned a lot about living in the jungle, and about Kachins. Take the experience of our young captain. About two months after his jump-in, he had been given the word, over the radio, to "start fighting."

"I had a platoon or so of Kachin fighters at my back by that time," he said, "and had picked up a pretty sound idea of the surrounding roads and trails. We began to ambush trails, dynamite bridges, blow up ammunition dumps. In a jungle ambush, the Kachins can do terrible things with sharpened bamboos. They fill the bushes on both sides with needle-sharp stakes, cleverly hidden. When an enemy patrol was fired upon and dived for the timber—well, I hardly like to talk about it. After a few ambushes like that, the Japanese never took cover when we fired on them.

"Of course the Japs tried reverse operations on us, and my life wouldn't have been worth a nickel if my men hadn't been about 10 times as alert as any Jap in the jungle. They just seemed to *know* when Japs were around. Only once, in months of hide-and-seek fighting, were we ever surprised by Japs. We were going to blow a bridge, and perhaps we were too busy with our own ideas. Anyhow, a volley of rifle shots came at us from very close range. How they missed us I'll never know, except that shooting in the jungle is tricky. And what saved us in the next few moments was even queerer.

"The Kachin is a born jungle hunter, and he has never had anything to hunt with but crude homemade muzzle loaders. He always shoots at the closest possible range and then *runs forward* to finish the wounded animal with his knife. So now, like hunters, every Kachin around me sprinted forward. The Japanese ambushers got confused and jumped to their feet to meet a charge. And then the Kachins dropped down and murdered them with their tommy guns.

"Even so, it wasn't only luck that saved us. The Japs had rifles; but every Ranger carried a quick-shooting automatic, so that the firepower of our small group was overwhelming. We always tried to give our Kachins the most modern weapons.

"I taught the Kachins a trick I could never master myself—to like K rations. We got Whitman's candy, once, in a tin printed

with the New York skyline. They loved the candy and talked for days about the big American pagodas shown in that picture.''

In February of 1944, when Merrill's Marauders, a force of specially trained American jungle fighters, struck toward the Japanese base at Myitkyina, the Rangers supplied an advance screen for the column. Three months later, when the Marauders closed in on their objective after a magnificent march, it was a Kachin guide who led them in. The Kachin had been bitten by a poisonous snake that morning, but he refused to get sick until he had taken the Americans, by one of those jungle trails which only a Kachin could follow, to surprise and seize the airfield. The desperate battle that followed, the agony of mud and blood in which the Rangers shared, was a turning point in the campaign. But Myitkyina fell, at last, because the airfield had been captured, and was never relinquished.

Files at headquarters gave other glimpses of individual Rangers in action. Here was a southern boy who had been in the jungle alone for months. Among other activities, he had captured 10 elephants from the Japanese. An elephant was extremely valuable because it took the place of truck and tractor combined in the jungle.

Here was an American sergeant who had become a specialist in blowing up bridges and even had a troop train to his credit. He had walked more than 1500 miles over the steepest trails, living for long periods on rice stolen from enemy food dumps.

One of the most heartening details of this whole amazing adventure was the excellence of the medical care, and the fact that Americans and Kachins were always treated exactly alike. Later a first-class hospital was established in Assam, staffed in part by former nurses of Colonel Gordon Seagrave's famous unit. Many of these fine nurses were Kachin girls. The pilots of the unit's tiny air force risked their lives as readily to bring out Kachin casualties as they did for Americans.

No one outside the organization would deny that the American-Kachin Rangers took high honors for gallantry; no one inside it would deny that, individually, they were strictly and wonderfully out of this world.

At headquarters I happened to fall into conversation with a tall, blue-eyed officer, fresh from the jungle. "Wasn't someone telling me that you have become rather interested in Kachin superstitions?" I asked. "Evil spirits, and divination with chicken bones, and that sort of thing?"

"Certainly," he said. "Anyone who has had any real experience with divination is bound to see that it makes a lot of sense. The Kachins use chicken bones to choose a safe trail, for instance; if I had disregarded them, we would have walked into a Jap ambush more than once. I don't go for all their evil spirits, but it's reasonable to throw a few coins into a river before crossing it."

"Uh, huh," I said. "But some of the boys really are a bit eccentric?"

"Some," he said, "are definitely jungle-happy. We've got one who says he's a member of the Confederate Cavalry. But what I have to watch out for, and worry over, is something entirely different. Lonely men can crack up in the jungle. The trees close in till you seem to be fighting for space, for light and air. All this gets worse in the monsoon months. You are wet most of the time; the leeches, mosquitoes, and a million other biting and crawling things get to work on you. You get sores on your legs, and perhaps fever chills, and you bleach out till you are an awful pure white. You don't have anybody to tell your troubles to, and it grows on you that nobody has ever gone through such hell before. . . .

"When things like that begin to happen you can detect it in a man's radio messages. Then it's time to get him out fast."

The Japanese were finally dislodged from their mountain strongpoints and driven south to the plains of Burma. Truck convoys began rolling over the completed Stilwell Road on the long pull to China. Many heroic workers and fighters contributed to that victory; indispensable among them, and hitherto unheralded, were the American-Kachin Rangers, prodding the enemy from his hidden lair, filling his own secret jungle trails with terror and sudden death.

"One of the most wonderful things about the operation,"

said the young officer, "was the amazingly low record of American casualties. Of all the boys who had gone behind the lines, only seven were killed. There was just one explanation for it—Kachin loyalty, and Kachin jungle craft. Why, they just wouldn't allow our boys to get hurt, and they spotted every Japanese ambush. People ask how they did it; I never found out. But I do know that we tried out war dogs, specially trained for patrol work. The dogs were wonderful, but the Kachins were keener. The Kachins deserved a special medal and they got one, the 'CMA' award."

The medal was created because an officer in the jungle misread a radio message. The message said that his Kachins, for a particularly gallant action, could be rewarded with food and new clothing. After the word "food" in the message appeared the letters CMA, the radio abbreviation for COMMA. So—the officer forgot that was just punctuation and joyfully held a little ceremony to decorate some of his leaders with the "CMA Award." The actual medal, he said, was on its way. When Headquarters heard about this, they were in a quandary. They couldn't break an American officer's promise to his soldiers, and they couldn't invent decorations—or could they? When someone suggested that "CMA" could stand for "Citation for Military Assistance," the thing was practically done. A handsome silver medal bearing those words, and worn from a green ribbon embroidered with white peacocks, became a special American award for Kachins only. Irregular, perhaps, but very highly prized.

The Kachin homeland was at last freed of Japanese, and the hillmen again planted rice and giant cucumbers in their highland garden patches and followed the wild boar and the sambar along the dim trails once more.

"When I was a boy," an old Kachin headman remarked, "I saw the first Americans come to our country. They came on foot, or riding little ponies, and they carried books. This was good. We were jungle dwellers, and our need for learning was very great.

"Again, when our country was in bitter trouble, the Americans came. They leaped from the skies and they carried weapons. This also was good. Our knives were of no use against the Japanese. Our friendship for the Americans is very strong."

The regard was mutual. Many a young American found among his jungle hosts not only wonderful fighters but steadfast friends. Several determined to take Kachin boys to America for schooling and technical training after the war. When those bright young Kachins got their first look at America they felt lost, bewildered, frightened. But no more so than the Americans who dropped into the Kachins' own land.

The Secret at Peenemünde

By Allan A. Michie

In the late evening of August 17, 1943, a fleet of 571 RAF heavy night bombers roared out across the North Sea. The next day the British Air Ministry's communiqué recorded that the research and development station at Peenemünde, Germany, had been attacked. Behind the deliberately vague language of that communiqué lay one of the most dramatic stories of the war. Unknown to all except a handful of men, the RAF's bomber command had won an aerial battle which was a turning point of the war.

By the spring of 1943 the Allied air offensive had opened gaping wounds across the face of Germany. The Luftwaffe was unable to penetrate Britain's defenses except for pinprick hit-and-run attacks. But there remained Hitler's promise of "secret weapons" with which to satisfy the German people's demand for reprisals. Orders went out from Hitler to complete quickly the experimental development of the secret weapons.

The main center for this was the Luftwaffe research station at Peenemünde, craftily tucked away in a forest behind the beach of the Baltic Sea, 60 miles northeast of Stettin and 700 miles from England. Electrified barbed wire kept away all snoopers. Into Peenemünde went a staff of several thousand of the best technical brains of the Luftwaffe and the top men in German aeronautical and engineering science. These scientists were set to working around the clock, for Hitler hoped to unleash his promised weapons during the winter of 1943–44.

Enthusiasts believed that the secret weapons would decide the war within 24 hours. More realistic Germans hoped that they would at least disrupt British war production and halt invasion preparations. Even if they failed to prove decisive, the reprisal bombing would bolster German morale.

By July 1943, British intelligence reports had definitely located Peenemünde as Germany's chief spawning ground for robot bombs and rockets, to become known as V-1's and V-2's. (See photograph on page 349.) A file of reports and aerial reconnaissance pictures was placed in the hands of a special British cabinet committee, which suggested that the RAF grant Peenemünde a high priority in its bombing attentions. Air Marshal Sir Arthur Travers Harris, Chief of Bomber Command, decided to stage a surprise raid during the next clear moonlight period.

The Germans had become overconfident about Peenemünde. RAF night bombers frequently flew over it on their way to Stettin and even to Berlin, and Germans working at Peenemünde used to watch British planes pass overhead, secure in the belief that the British did not know of Peenemünde's importance.

Special reconnaissance photographs for the raid were taken, with great care to avoid warning the Germans that the RAF was interested in Peenemünde. They were made during routine reconnaissance flights over Baltic ports, to which the Germans had grown accustomed. These photographs enabled planners of the raid to pick out three aiming points where the most damage would be done.

The first was the living quarters of the scientists and technicians. The second consisted of hangars and workshops containing experimental bombs and rockets. The third was the administrative area—buildings containing blueprints and technical data.

The night of August 17 was selected because the moon would be almost full.

The bomber crews were informed only that Peenemünde was an important radar experimental station; that they would catch a lot of German scientists there, and that their job was to kill as many of them as possible. After the briefing, a special note from Bomber Command headquarters was read aloud: "The extreme importance of this target and the necessity of achieving its destruction with one attack is to be impressed on all crews. If the attack fails to achieve its object, it will have to be repeated on ensuing nights—regardless, within practicable limits, of casualties."

The 571 four-motored heavies took off and roared down on Peenemünde by an indirect route. Peenemünde's defenders, apparently believing that the bombers were headed for Stettin or Berlin, were caught napping. Pathfinders went in first, swooped low over their target and dropped colored flares around aiming points. Bombers using revolutionary new bombsights followed. Scorning the light flak, wave after wave unloaded high explosives and incendiaries from a few thousand feet on the three clearly visible aiming points. In 40 minutes the area was an almost continuous strip of fire.

As the last wave of bombers flew homeward, the German night fighters which had been waiting in vain around Berlin caught up with them, and 41 British bombers were lost.

The next morning a reconnaissance Spitfire photographed the damage. Half of the 45 huts in which scientists and specialists lived had been obliterated, and the remainder were badly damaged. In addition, 40 buildings, including assembly shops and laboratories, had been completely destroyed and 50 others had been damaged.

In a few days, more detailed reports of the results began to trickle in. Seven hundred thirty-five people, including 178 scientists and technical men stationed in Peenemünde, were killed or missing. Dr. Walter Thiel, regarded as the most important scientist on the project, was killed, and also Chief Engineer Erich Walther.

Nazi reaction to the raid was violent. Gestapo men quizzed survivors and combed the countryside for traitors who might have tipped off the RAF to Peenemünde's importance. General Walther Schreckenback, of the black-shirted secret service, was given command of Peenemünde, with orders to resume work on the flying bombs and rockets.

But all Germany's plans had to be recast. With Peenemünde half destroyed and open to further attack, new laboratories had to be built deep underground. Other scientists and specialists had to be found to carry on. As a result of the delay, the Nazis were unable to launch their secret weapons when they had planned, and they had a difficult time nursing German morale through continued Allied air raids.

The Germans were further set back by Allied air attacks on launching ramps for flying bombs and rockets and on component-parts factories. (See "The Man Who Saved London," page 277.) The people were told that the secret weapons were intended as anti-invasion weapons, being saved to blast the Allies in the ports and on the beaches. D-day, however, caught the Germans still not ready. Not until seven days after the Allies invaded Normandy did the first flying bomb fall on London.

If Peenemünde hadn't been blasted as and when it was, the robot-bomb attacks on London doubtless would have begun six months before they did, and would have been many times as heavy. London communications, the hub of Britain and nerve center of invasion planning and preparation, would have been severely stricken. The invasion itself might have had to be postponed.

The Man
Who Saved London

By George Kent

Based on the book by George Martelli

It was October 1943—the fifth year of World War II—and Michel Hollard, a small, muscular, 45-year-old Frenchman, was getting ready to slip across the border into neutral Switzerland. Over his shoulder was a sack of potatoes, in his hands an axe. To all appearances he was a woodcutter.

The morning sun filtered through the trees as he moved swiftly forward. To make even a small noise could mean death, for in the woods and behind the hills were cocked listening ears—ears of German patrols, of German police dogs.

Hollard, an industrial designer who, to help his country, had become a spy, had made the crossing into Switzerland 49 times in all. Each time he carried military information to be relayed to England. He and his helpers had pinpointed secret Nazi airfields in France, located coastal batteries, discovered a plan for a submarine base at Boulogne, reported the movements of entire divisions—all intelligence of great value. None of these secrets, however, compared with the one he was carrying now.

This time, concealed among the potatoes, was a paper which was not only to save London from destruction but was to shorten the war by many months. Hollard was carrying a blueprint of the launching sites for Hitler's terrible new flying bomb, the V-1. It was Hitler's idea to drop 50,000 V-1's on London, at the rate of 5000 a month. Preparations for their launching had been enveloped in the thickest secrecy. The workers on the construction of the launching ramps were mostly Dutch and Polish laborers who could speak no French. These ramps were nearing completion in more than 100 places.

Now Michel Hollard, the only man among the Allies who knew the details of the plan, was closing in on the border. He began to run. Soon he was at the rolls of barbed wire that separated France and Switzerland. He had thrown his axe and sack across when suddenly, without a sound, his knee was seized in an iron vise—the jaws of a huge German police dog. The dog simply stood there and held. Hollard could not move. Yet he knew he had to move, for certainly in the near vicinity were the men who worked with the dog. Hollard carried no weapons. In his pose as a simple countryman, the possession of a weapon would arouse suspicion if he was searched. In panic, he looked around for something with which to pry the dog's mouth open. There, providentially, was precisely what he needed—a long, sturdy stick. Working it between the animal's jaws, he thrust it with all his strength deep into the windpipe. For a long minute nothing happened. Then the dog relaxed, rolled over dead.

As Hollard wriggled through the wire and snatched up his sack, he saw a Swiss guard with a gun at his shoulder. He was pointing it not at Hollard, however, but at two German soldiers who were about to shoot Hollard. The Germans lowered their rifles and walked away, muttering.

Not long after Hollard's eventful crossing, Allied bombers began striking at the V-1 emplacements. In five weeks 73 of the sites were either totally destroyed or so badly damaged that they could not be used again. Though others were built—smaller ones—the Nazis' grand plan for leaving London in ruins was shattered. Hitler succeeded in dropping not 50,000 bombs but fewer than 2500. And they fell not at the end of 1943, when their impact might have been fatal, but in the middle of 1944—too few and too late.

"It seems likely," wrote Dwight D. Eisenhower in *Crusade in Europe*, "that if the Germans had succeeded in perfecting and using these new weapons six months earlier than they did, our invasion of Europe would have proved exceedingly difficult, perhaps impossible."

The amazing part of this story is that Michel Hollard—who became one of World War II's most remarkable spies—did so strictly on his own initiative. No one asked him to become a spy. No one helped him to become one. When he had information to deliver, he simply crossed the border into Switzerland. Michel Hollard was the simplest of men, an underpaid employe of a research organization. When the Germans marched into Paris and his employers began working for them, he felt that a turning point had come. He quit his job in protest and got a new one as agent for a manufacturer of charcoal-burning gas generators for automobiles. This work was to prove invaluable in helping him perform the task he had decided to do for his homeland: it explained his frequent visits to wooded areas near the frontier—he was hunting for wood for charcoal.

One day he tried to sneak across the heavily guarded Swiss border to offer his services as a spy to the British. He was captured by the Germans, but he talked his way out. The second time he got across. The British asked him to identify German troop units and to report on their movements.

For the next three years Hollard was almost constantly on the run. He had a wife and three children whom he loved, but he saw them seldom, lest they suffer on his account. Over the months he recruited a number of Frenchmen to help him: railroad workers, truck drivers, bartenders, hotelkeepers. From a nucleus of five, his organization, *Réseau Agir*—Network for Action—grew until toward the end it numbered 120. Of these, 20 were captured and put to death by the Germans. Others suffered injuries, had some incredibly narrow escapes. Hollard himself, returning one night from Switzerland, was foolish enough to have a lighted cigarette in his mouth. When a German voice shouted, "Halt!" he dropped to the ground, reached up and pinned the still-glowing cigarette to a tree. As he crept off, two bullets buried themselves in the bark.

Hollard's most important achievement—tracking down the V-1 plans—began in a café in Rouen in August 1943. One of his agents there reported hearing two building contractors talk of some unusual construction being carried on by the Germans.

What amazed them was the extraordinary amount of concrete involved. A day later Hollard was in Rouen. Clad in sober black, he walked into the official employment office, saying that he represented a Protestant organization interested in the spiritual welfare of laboring men. He produced several Bibles and asked if there were any building enterprises in the region. He was told that there was one at Auffay, about 20 miles from Rouen.

An hour later he was at Auffay, wearing workman's blues. He came upon a large clearing and several hundred men. Concrete was being poured; buildings were going up. Hollard seized a wheelbarrow, loaded it with bricks and pitched in. No one stopped him. Most of the laborers could speak no French. Those who could told him that they were building garages. This was obviously not true. The buildings were too small. Besides, why garages miles from the nearest big city?

What fascinated him most was a 50-yard strip of concrete with a long guideline of blue string. Taking out his compass, he discovered that the strip—obviously the emplacement for some sort of ramp—pointed directly toward London. When he learned that the Germans were working the laborers in three shifts, around the clock, he left to report to the British.

In London the Allied leaders, including Winston Churchill and General Eisenhower, were deeply concerned over what the Germans were doing. Hints had come from Peenemünde of a "pilotless plane" being developed (see "The Secret of Peenemünde," page 273); and on a beach in Bornholm a Dane had discovered the wreckage of a curious weapon that had apparently descended from the sky. A new blitz appeared to be in the making, but what it would be and how serious, no one knew.

In this situation Hollard's report exploded like a bomb. The little Frenchman was ordered to drop all other work and concentrate on the mysterious construction. Hollard and four agents began a systematic tour of northern France on bicycles. They discovered in three weeks more than 60 such mysterious sites. By mid-November they had found 40 more, all of them in a corridor nearly 200 miles long, 30 miles wide, roughly parallel to the coast—and all pointing at London! But what were they?

In espionage, luck frequently plays an important role, and it was a series of coincidences that led Hollard to Hitler's best-kept secret. Hollard was conferring one day with one of his agents, who warmly recommended a friend. This was a youth named Robert, who wanted to get in some licks against the Germans. Hollard got Robert a job at an airport. Robert, in turn, persuaded a friend, André, to volunteer for a job which eventually took him to Bois Carré, another place where the strange building was going on. One week after taking his new position, André reported to Hollard with tracings of plans that had passed through his hands. Hollard instructed André to get a tracing of the master plan at any cost.

At Bois Carré, the German in charge kept the master plan in an inside pocket of his overcoat—and he wore the overcoat even in his office. The only time he took it off was at nine o'clock in the morning, when he left to go to the toilet. For several days André timed the German's morning absences. They varied between three and five minutes. So one day when the German shed his coat, André dodged in, made a swift tracing of the master plan and was back at his desk by the time the German returned.

At the end of the week, following Hollard's suggestions and using medicine that had been given him, André complained of severe stomach pains. The German doctor scoffed, but when André began vomiting, he signed a pass enabling André to go to Paris to see his "family doctor."

In Paris, André and Hollard began coördinating the tracing from the master plan with the other plans that *Réseau Agir* had obtained. Then they checked their drawings against on-the-spot observations. At last they had all the pieces in position, and there it was in beautiful detail—the layout of a V-1 base.

This was the paper that lay among the potatoes when the German police dog seized Hollard's leg at the frontier.

After Hollard had delivered this prize, a wire came from London, reading, "Booty received safely. Congratulations." Then the reaction set in. Hollard was tired—tired of being ever-lastingly on the run, tired of living every minute with fear. The British practically insisted that he linger in Switzerland, and he was tempted. Then he thought of stationmasters copying down lists of train movements at the risk of their lives, of men sneaking into airplane hangars and shipyards, of others sitting in church steeples watching German maneuvers.

He went back to France, where, a few months later, because of a slip by a colleague, he was captured in a bistro. Of the three men who were seized with him, one died in a concentration camp; the others were released after three months. Hollard was tortured horribly, but he gave the Nazis no information. Because no proof of complicity was found on him, he was not shot but was condemned to the Neuengamme concentration camp.

As the war neared its end, the Nazis emptied the camp, drove the prisoners into the holds of vessels and set them adrift in the North Sea, confident that they would be sunk by Allied bombers. Hollard, locked up with hundreds of others, was miraculously transferred at the last moment from one of the doomed vessels to a ship of the Swedish Red Cross. It took six weeks of hospital care before Hollard was able to get about. The RAF sent a plane to take him to London, where he was to receive the highest military decoration for which a foreigner is eligible in England, the Distinguished Service Order. But Hollard was already homeward bound and had to be decorated later, in Paris. The plane carrying him home passed low over Auffay, where he could see the mass of twisted girders and rubble—the remains of the first V-1 site he had discovered.

Of Michel Hollard's wartime activities Lieutenant General Sir Brian Horrocks, who was commander of the XXX Corps of the British Liberation Army, said: "No one can doubt that Hollard was entitled to the highest decoration for bravery. He was, literally, the man who saved London."

The Spy Who Double-Crossed Hitler

By J. Edgar Hoover

Albert Van Loop, a Dutchman, walked into the American Consulate in Madrid on April 6, 1942, and asked for visas for himself and wife. His story was that he was being sent by German Intelligence to spy on American troops and war industries. He had been ordered to set up a secret radio station and report regularly to Hamburg. To prove his story, he exhibited microphotographs showing how to build and operate a short-wave radio—lists of materials needed, plans for assembling, frequency tables, ciphers and a detailed code. He showed the Consul $16,230 in cash and checks.

Van Loop insisted that he had joined the Germans and taken his training at a Nazi spy school only as a means of escaping from Europe. He wanted to serve the Allies. If we would admit him to the United States, he would be willing to act as our agent while pretending to serve Germany.

The Consul said he would take Van Loop's request under consideration, and immediately informed us. We found Van Loop's record in our files in Washington: born in Holland, about 50 years old, married to a German national, engineer and jeweler, a spy in two wars. "Send him along," we wirelessed.

In the meantime Van Loop was closely watched. We knew that before he sailed he received these written instructions: "American scientists are working on atom-smashing from uranium. Stage of these experiments important for us." Names and addresses of several scientists engaged in atomic research followed. This, remember, was early in 1942, when few, even among government officials, knew we were working on the atomic bomb.

We met the Van Loops when they arrived on a Portuguese ship. Under very persuasive questioning we finally made him admit he had been a German spy in World War I and that he had served a prison term for stealing $7000 from a friend. We caught him in many lies, and he was badly shaken.

We put the Van Loops in a hotel; they were free to go where they pleased—but of course they were under the strictest surveillance. Our plan was to build the radio station and set up communication with German Intelligence in the name of Van Loop. One slip on our part would mean failure. For example, the Germans had a man named Vizetum who could identify the radio-sending style of anyone with whom he had once communicated—and he knew Van Loop's hand intimately.

We made phonograph records of Van Loop's radio sending, and three FBI agents practiced until they could imitate his style faultlessly. (His principal idiosyncrasy was that his dots were almost as long as his dashes.) Then they studied Van Loop's language—the odd expressions of a Hollander using German.

We set up the radio station on a secluded estate on Long Island, N.Y., and on February 7, 1943, we established our first contact with Germany: "Am now ready to operate. Necessary to be very careful, but feel I am safe. Will listen for you at 1900." Five days later came the reply: "Uncle is highly pleased. He declares his appreciation and well wishes."

We were jubilant. For more than two years—until May 1, 1945—we maintained unbroken communication with Hamburg. We fed the Germans military and industrial information, for the most part true. We gave them weather reports, the names of some ships in American ports, men-of-war under repair and newspaper reports of government appropriations for new ships and munitions.

We could not pretend that Van Loop knew too much. The Germans were well aware that the work of a solitary operative in America must necessarily be limited. But we did invent two

German shipyard workers, one in the Brooklyn Navy Yard, the other in Philadelphia, who made regular reports to him. Month by month, Van Loop's star rose higher and higher with the German High Command.

We were not just having fun. We wanted to find out whether any other spies were operating in America; Hamburg might tell Van Loop to get in touch with them. We wanted to know how the Germans paid their operatives in the Americas. And, most important of all, we hoped to mislead the High Command by feeding them false information.

We had Van Loop pretend again and again to be broke and unable to continue his work. His chief, a Nazi general, was driven almost frantic trying to keep him contented. First the Nazi offered to send $2000 to a Swiss bank, to be cabled to a bank in New York. To see what else the Germans would try, we vetoed that idea as too dangerous. Then the general tried to send rare stamps, via South America. Over a period of two years Van Loop received only two sets of stamps, worth not more than $150 a set. If the Germans had this much difficulty in sending money to a spy with the assistance of the FBI, how much more would they have had without it?

Meanwhile we continued to demand more money. At last the Germans sent a Dutch motion-picture magnate to America; one of his chores was to deliver to Van Loop $6000 worth of jewelry. When we heard the new spy was coming, we worried. If we arrested the man—call him Shubert—Berlin might become suspicious that he would betray Van Loop. If we let Shubert contact Van Loop and return to Germany, we feared Shubert might inform the Germans that Van Loop was a double spy.

Curiously, Shubert also went to the American Consulate at Madrid, offering to serve the Allies. I think he was sincere, for he coöperated with us in every way.

By radio instruction, Van Loop was to telephone Shubert at his hotel. One of our agents telephoned instead, saying: "This is Mr. Kliemann. I bring you greetings from Uncle. Have you anything for me?" Shubert said he had. Arrangements were made for them to meet in a hotel lobby. The jewelry would be delivered on the exchange of the password "Kliemann." Shubert gave us all the details so that we could watch and catch the man when he made the contact.

To Shubert's chagrin, he found the lobby packed with people. Someone murmured "Kliemann" in his ear, snatched the package of jewelry and vanished in the crowd. Shubert almost wept. Neither he nor, as he thought, the FBI agents had seen Van Loop. If Shubert had seen the man who whispered "Kliemann," he would have seen a Negro dressed in a chauffeur's uniform. He never would have been able to report to the Germans that we had seen Van Loop.

Now we were closing in for the kill. The Germans had asked Van Loop to concentrate on American plans for the invasion of Europe. They wanted descriptions of insignia on troops in New York, the serial numbers of military trucks, and so on. We gave them plenty of information. Slyly, we began to slip in bits about Iceland. By this time Van Loop was working in a jewelry store. "A friend of mine at the store," we radioed, "told me his son has just gone to Iceland." We drummed it incessantly—trivialities, always—Iceland, Iceland, Iceland.

Then on March 3, 1944, we sent a message to Hamburg to this effect: "Last Sunday at a hotel bar a group of officers were drinking and conversing. In reply to a joking remark about service in Iceland, an officer wearing a five-sided emblem told the others that they shouldn't laugh too soon because it was entirely possible that some of them might also be sent there, as, prior to his departure from Iceland, he had seen housing facilities being prepared for a large number of troops."

There hadn't been a German reconnaissance plane over Iceland for months, but the day after we sent this message, one appeared. The observer could see that Iceland camps had many barracks—fake ones—and the harbor was full of ships. Acting on this tip, the German High Command prepared against invasion in Norway.

We gave them lots of time, stalling them along with reports indicating that the invasion had been delayed. Then our Army and Navy struck Normandy.

Strangely, Van Loop did not lose face through his misleading reports. He was never reprimanded. We went right on sending more information, much of it suggestive of our growing naval power, which we knew Germany would relay to Japan.

Then, on April 27, 1945, we received this message from Hamburg: "Because of present situation, we must disrupt our connection, but stand by once a week. Uncle will protect your interest in the future, as before."

We stood by, day after day, waiting for a signal. None came. Uncle had fled. Germany was broken. Only Van Loop remained, a little Dutch jeweler who had played ball—with a pistol at his back.

The Brain Invasion

By Frederick C. Painton

One night during the invasion of Sicily an American artilleryman slammed a shell into a field gun trained on an enemy stronghold. The cannon blasted white flame, the shell screeched into the night. Presently in the distance there was a weak explosion. The gunner was irritated. He muttered, "It's a hell of a war when you fight with confetti."

That shell was stuffed with leaflets. They told the Italians that they were pawns of the Nazis, who would make their beloved Italy a battlefield; that their position was hopeless; that these leaflets were "surrender tickets" entitling them to good food and safety behind the Allied lines. Up where American GI's crouched in their foxholes, men who spoke Italian repeated the same message through loudspeakers that made the words echo in the hills.

Just before dawn American medium bombers dropped more "surrender tickets" behind the enemy lines. Annoyed pilots complained that blockbusters would have done a lot more good. But that morning scores of Italians came over from the enemy position. Each held up a white leaflet. "Ticket to surrender?" yelled one anxiously. The Americans welcomed them to a barbed-wire hoosegow and a can of C ration.

This was our Psychological Warfare Branch in action. It was part of the Information and Censorship Section of Allied Force Headquarters. At first it was scorned by professional soldiers. Shortly after the battle of El Alamein, General Montgomery said, "I won't have a propaganda van on my battlefield." But by the time the Allies were in Sicily, Monty himself was ordering barrages of leaflet shells.

It all started when the North African invasion was being planned. At that time America and Britain had a half-dozen organizations, civilian and military, that wanted to fight the enemy on the brain front, and each had its own ideas. Words flowed from the Office of War Information, the Office of Strategic Services, the British Political Warfare Executive, the British Ministry of Information, and from British and American Army and Navy intelligence services. The result was chaotic.

In October 1942, Eisenhower handed the whole problem to Colonel Charles B. Hazeltine, a tough-minded cavalry officer for 33 years and more recently commander of a mechanized infantry regiment. Hazeltine gathered men and women from all the various propaganda organizations to form the Psychological Warfare Branch of the Allied Forces. "I don't know anything about propaganda," he told them bluntly, "but I believe in its power. I know the Army and I understand organization. We're on trial until we produce the goods. So you write the words and I'll sell the Army on their value."

The PWB was divided into three sections: combat propaganda units that advanced with the front-line troops; occupation units that worked in newly captured territory; and base units that coördinated the propaganda effort of Allied Force Headquarters with that of London and Washington. Here is a typical example of how this setup worked: John Whitaker, formerly a widely known foreign correspondent, led a combat propaganda unit into Palermo, Sicily, and immediately seized the radio station and newspaper plants. Then he cabled PWB for an occupation unit. Within a few days the radio was broadcasting unbiased news to the Italian people and the newspaper *Sicilia Libertata* was giving Sicilians the first truths they had read in more than 20 years.

In the early days of its existence, PWB traversed a tough road. The organization was completed just when the Tunisian campaign looked critical, and nobody paid much attention. Moreover, pilots didn't want to carry the leaflets, and infantry patrols disliked going out behind enemy lines to plant them. A British captain rediscovered how to fill a cannon shell with leaflets and put in sufficient charge to break the casing without burning the paper; but the artillery didn't like shooting "duds."

Patiently PWB officers called on generals, selling their idea. Each week they managed to get more leaflets dropped, and at last the break came. Italians began to surrender by scores and hundreds, each holding up a leaflet as a safe-conduct. Telling about it, a PWB officer said, "Two Italians walked in one day with leaflets, and told us there were 60 more afraid to come in because they didn't have tickets. We sent out men to round them up. Another time an Italian came over, asked to have an extra leaflet and ran back to bring in his brother. I've been told that in the last days of the Tunisian scrap the Arabs actually ran a black market in leaflets, selling them as tickets of surrender to Germans as well as Italians."

A captured German captain told intelligence officers: "Your propaganda was disastrous. Even the little *Flugblätter* [leaflets]—after you read them you imagined you read the truth, that our government was lying to us."

Now, indeed, the combat generals took notice. Lieutenant General George S. Patton, then commanding the Second Corps, ordered pamphlets dropped in front of his positions. When the Northwest African Air Force decided to bomb military objectives in Rome, Lieutenant General Carl A. Spaatz ordered several million dropped to warn the city's residents.

PWB also used the radio to weaken the enemy's will to resist, and the power of this invisible weapon was soon demonstrated by a startling change in the outlook of German prisoners. In Tunisia the captured Nazis were full of Dr. Goebbels' fantasies. One said, "Now that Japan has invaded Siberia it's all up with the Russians this year, and we'll beat you and England next year." Another remarked, "I hope I'm shipped to America. I want to see what New York looks like, now that the Japanese have bombed it flat." They were very cocky.

But in Sicily many German prisoners were sullen and discouraged. They knew Germany's offensive in Russia had failed. They knew Sicily was lost, and thought Italy was also. Some officers admitted that Germany could no longer hope to win the war. These Germans had come mostly from reserves in southern France, which had been bombarded for 14 hours daily by PWB radio. So many German war vehicles were equipped with radio that it was impossible for the High Command to prevent broadcasts being received.

These PWB stations became siege guns broadcasting in Italian, German and French. The cardinal rule in preparing newscasts was: "Make it simple and tell only the truth. Our value is gone if the Nazis can point to one lie."

The radio pounded incessantly at Italy. Eisenhower used PWB's radio to announce the armistice with Italy to Italians. Later, PWB broadcasts to the Italians carried specific instructions on how to sabotage German communications.

"We started from scratch in a game we knew nothing about," said an official of the PWB. "But we soon found out that honest propaganda was as deadly as a bomber raid. And we were saving the lives of American soldiers; for every enemy who surrendered with one of our pamphlets in his hand was one less to shoot at our boys along the front."

Eleven Against the Nazi A-Bomb

By Frederic Sondern, Jr.

One morning in February 1944 the heavily laden railroad ferry *Hydro* was plunging through the choppy waves of Norway's Lake Tinnsjø. Suddenly the dull boom of an explosion sounded from belowdecks. The ship lurched to a stop. Five minutes later the *Hydro* had sunk, and with it Hitler's dream of possessing the first atom bomb. Behind that explosion lies the story of one of the war's most fantastic undercover operations.

As far back as April 1940 the international scientists' grapevine—notoriously indiscreet and uncontrollable—had indicated that the Kaiser Wilhelm Institut was conducting extensive experiments toward splitting the atom. Then, just as our Manhattan Project was being set up in 1942, the Intelligence Section of the British Ministry of Economic Warfare came through with electrifying information: the Germans had ordered the Norwegian electrochemical plant, Norsk Hydro—largest of its kind in the world—to increase its production of deuterium oxide ("heavy water") from 3000 to 10,000 pounds a year. That could mean only one appalling thing. Our physicists had discovered that heavy water was an ideal "moderator" to use in the preparation of uranium-235. Since the Allies did not possess sufficient heavy water, and since its refinement takes a year and a half, we finally and successfully used graphite for the process. But the British report confirmed that the Kaiser Wilhelm Institut was well along with its experiments.

The problem of paralyzing Norsk Hydro and destroying its stock of heavy water was given highest priority by Britain's War

Cabinet. The Air Staff reported that a bombing attack on this pinpoint objective, ringed by mountains, was not practicable with the planes then available. It was a Commando job.

Sometime earlier a group of Norwegian resistance men had seized the coastal steamer *Galtesund* and sailed her through the mine and submarine perils of the North Sea into Aberdeen. One of them had already organized a highly effective section of the Norwegian Underground.

Einar Skinnarland was immediately summoned to Special Forces headquarters in London. This intelligent, powerfully built man was a master on skis and an excellent shot—important qualifications for the job ahead. Still better, he had lived within a few miles of the Norsk Hydro plant almost all his life, had a brother and friends in important positions there.

At Special Forces headquarters Skinnarland met Dr. Leif Tronstad, who had developed the large-scale production of deuterium oxide. As a prewar personal friend of a great number of German nuclear physicists, he had more exact information about Germany's "atomic bomb" progress than any non-German alive. Late in 1941, Tronstad had been smuggled into Sweden by the Norwegian Underground and flown to London.

After a talk with Tronstad, Skinnarland was asked, "Do you think that Norsk Hydro can be put out of commission by sabotage?" He explained the situation with Scandinavian deliberation. The plant was a seven-story steel and concrete building, massively constructed. It and the equally solid hydroelectric power works nearby were perched on the brink of a 1000-foot gorge. All approaches and the plant itself were guarded by picked German troops. The mountains around it were almost impassable. It would be very difficult indeed. "But," he added, "we would certainly like to try."

Skinnarland was whisked off to Special Forces training center. He quickly learned to operate a powerful short-wave receiver-transmitter which fitted into a small suitcase. He was taught the necessary codes, made his parachute training jumps and was given his final orders. He was to return to Norway immediately, gather every available scrap of information about Norsk Hydro, send it to London and await the arrival of a reinforcing group.

On a moonlit night Skinnarland plummeted out of an RAF bomber into the mountains 20 miles from his home. Through his brother, he secured a job with Norsk Hydro on the construction of a new dam being built to increase the heavy-water output. With infinite care he organized his most trusted friends into a reliable grapevine which brought him every item of news about the factory. This information was flashed to British central intelligence.

Production of deuterium oxide was increasing rapidly, Skinnarland reported; stocks of it were being shipped monthly to Germany. The War Cabinet ordered Combined Operations to prepare a Commando assault on Norsk Hydro at once.

Combined Operations, with all their experience in suicidal exploits, faced one of their toughest jobs. Craggy mountains, over which violent air currents roar unpredictably, made Norway the worst country in Europe for parachute or glider attacks. But with the help of Dr. Tronstad, who directed the construction of exact models of the target and its inner works, and Skinnarland's precise reports, Operation Swallow was finally organized.

Four picked Norwegians, all expert skiers and natives of the area, were to be dropped first to reinforce Skinnarland and form a reception committee for a later Commando assault by British airborne troops. Twice a bomber took the Swallows over Norway, ready to jump, only to be forced back by impenetrable cloud. Finally on an evening in October 1942 they were bundled into their ship on a few minutes' notice and several hours later jumped into the night. When they took their bearings next morning, they found they were on a rugged mountainside more than 100 miles from their operation area. It took them two days to find their equipment in the scattered parachuted containers.

During the next 15 days the Swallows made one of the classic treks of the war. At 4000 feet altitude, in constantly subzero weather, a 60-pound pack was the maximum that one man could carry. That meant that each day each Swallow had to shuttle three times over the same route to move his 120-pound load.

The daily ration of each man was a small slab of cheese, a handful of groats and four biscuits.

At last, on November 9, the anxious officers of Combined Operations heard the long-awaited Swallow code signal. They were in position near Norsk Hydro, had made contact with Skinnarland and were ready to guide in the gliderborne sabotage party by radio and landing lights.

On November 19 two Halifax bombers, each towing a glider full of airborne troopers, took off from England. A few hours later an agent in Norway radioed that bombers and tows had crashed and that all personnel had been killed or captured.

Worse news was to follow. A German military-intelligence officer, searching the plane wreckage, had found a map with a red line drawn through Vemork, the town where the heavy-water plant was located. Josef Terboven, German Reichskommissar for Norway, and Commanding General von Falkenhorst rushed to Vemork to inspect its defenses personally. SS troops combed the neighborhood and arrested everyone in the least suspect of pro-British sentiments. But they did not find any of the Swallows.

In London, desperate Combined Operations started all over again. The idea of a glider attack was given up. Six Special Force Norwegians would be dropped by parachute. Dr. Tronstad went to work training them with maps and models. Time was growing short. The Swallows, with little food and the batteries of their radios running down, were hanging on under frightful conditions in their 4000-foot mountain eyrie. They were living in a tiny snow-covered hut and were forced to eat reindeer moss. Skinnarland, a few miles away, was running a close race with the Gestapo; but every few days he would leave his tiny camouflaged hut in the snow, ski down at dusk and meet his trusted informants around Vemork.

Soon Skinnarland radioed the almost unbelievable information that the Germans, for some reason, believed that the Commandos had not been after the Norsk Hydro plant itself, but the new dam being built nearby. One hundred new guards had been put on the dam, only 12 assigned to the factory.

By late December, Operation Gunnerside was ready to go.

The six Norsemen dropped one evening on the snow-covered ice of Lake Skryken, 30 miles north of the Swallow hideout. After that, events moved quickly. At the Swallows' hiding place, the Norwegians—there were now 11 of them—put their heads together. Skinnarland supplied the latest details on the positions of the guards and the times of their changing, which gates were locked and how. The attackers would have to descend several snow-covered miles of steeply sloping forest, clamber down into a 1000-foot gorge, cross a raging torrent and scale another 1000-foot, almost sheer wall of rock to reach a railroad embankment that led to the factory. At the slightest alarm the whole area would be automatically floodlighted.

At eight o'clock on February 27 nine men started out. Loaded as they were with sensitive demolition charges, their floundering descent through the treacherous snow to the bottom of the gorge was a nightmare. Then began the terrible climb up the rock face. Joachim, the party's leader, kept looking at his wristwatch; the precise timetable allowed for little delay. Inching their way up 1000 feet of almost perpendicular cliff, the Norwegians all knew that one slip would spell oblivion.

On top at last, they crept forward along the railroad embankment to within 500 feet of the factory. They could hear the hum of its machinery. Joachim, in a final whispered conference, made sure that everyone knew exactly what to do. One of the men, armed with powerful shears, went first—to the factory gate which had been chosen because it was secured with only a chain and padlock. Then came the sharp snap of cracking steel. The others froze in their tracks. But there were no sounds from within. Quickly they filed through the open gate. A group of five, their tommy guns ready, quietly took position around the barracks in which the 12 German guards were quartered. If the alarm sounded, they were to shoot down the soldiers as they streamed out.

So well had Dr. Tronstad done his work that it took the demolition squad of four, led by Joachim, only a few minutes to find the cable tunnel which led directly into a room adjoining the high-concentration section. Two of Joachim's men lost him in the darkness. But he and one other began to crawl through the maze of conduits.

The guard on duty in the all-important chamber suddenly looked up into the muzzles of two pistols and reached for the ceiling—silently. "He seemed frightened," the sober Norwegians' report reads, "but otherwise was quiet and obedient." Quickly Joachim made the rounds of the tanks, pipes and machinery, and fastened his charges—as he had been taught to do on their replicas in England—where the explosive would do the most damage. Then—a clatter of glass. Someone had kicked in a basement window. Joachim almost began shooting, but recognized in the nick of time that it was one of his strayed assistants clambering in the window. With shaking hands he finished setting the charges.

Still the wail of the alarm siren, which he had been fearing from moment to moment, had not sounded. He checked the 30-second fuses and lit them. He told the guard, a Norwegian, to run for it. Twenty yards outside the cellar door they heard the explosion, dull behind the massive concrete walls but shaking the ground under them.

By the time the siren began to shriek and the sleepy Germans came pouring out, Joachim and his men had vanished by the same perilous and—to the Germans—incredible route by which they had come. Meanwhile 1000 pounds of the priceless deuterium oxide had gushed from broken tanks onto the floor and into the factory's sewers.

Within a few hours General von Falkenhorst, the German commander, roared into Vemork. Surveying the damage, he exclaimed, "This is the best damned *coup* I have ever seen." Then the General erupted orders. A whole division of the Wehrmacht, 12,000 strong, converged on the area. Ski patrols and slow-flying reconnaissance planes combed the mountains. All roads and trails were blocked, while Gestapo and SS men made a house-to-house search. But of the raiders there was not a single trace to be found.

Five of the six Gunnerside men had started immediately for the Swedish border on skis; after incredible hardships they made

it safely and were flown back to England. The sixth, Knut, and the four Swallows stayed behind to take care of some other Underground work, playing tag on skis with Falkenhorst's patrols. Skinnarland retired to his cavelike lair, to report the sequel of the demolition and continue the watch on Norsk Hydro.

Late in 1943, Skinnarland radioed that the damage had been repaired and the plant was resuming production. Almost immediately bombers of the U.S. Eighth Air Force knocked out the factory's power station. Then the Germans decided to move all of Norsk Hydro's heavy-water equipment and stocks to an underground site in the Reich. Skinnarland requested permission to sink the ferryboat *Hydro*, which was to carry freight cars with these remaining stocks across Lake Tinnsjø on a certain day. Permission came speedily, and Skinnarland asked Knut, who was working with a Norwegian Underground detachment some 50 miles away, to join him. With forged papers Knut, masquerading as a Norsk Hydro employe, made an exploratory crossing on the *Hydro* to decide how she should be sunk so as to make salvage impossible. Just before she sailed, time charges were placed in her forepeak bilges.

In a short while the last of Germany's deuterium oxide was under the waters of Lake Tinnsjø. In desperate need of something that could be developed and used against the Allies quickly, Hitler and Goering turned to other weapons, and German experiments in atomic energy were slowed to a standstill.

The Highest-Paid Spy in History

By Robert M. W. Kempner

The secret conferences in Moscow, Teheran and Cairo in 1943 were not as secret as they were thought to be. Thanks to a spy employed in the British Embassy in Ankara, Hitler learned a great deal about these fateful meetings within a few days after they were held.

I learned about Operation Cicero, the cover name for the Ankara job, by accident. As chief prosecutor of Nazi diplomats at Nuremberg, I examined, among masses of other documents, the German Foreign Ministry's secret correspondence with the German Embassy in Ankara. My curiosity was aroused by the many references to Operation Cicero. On seeking further information I was told by Horst Wagner, the Foreign Office liaison with the intelligence service, that Cicero was the "biggest thing" in which his department had ever engaged. General Walter Schellenberg, the chief of civil and military intelligence, acknowledged that his "greatest success" had been due to Operation Cicero. It was not until I located Ludwig Moyzisch, however, that I learned the whole fantastic story.

Moyzisch, a slight, self-effacing little man, was a former Viennese journalist who joined the Nazi Party and was made Commercial Attaché in Ankara. One of his duties had been to direct the regional operations of German intelligence. He was suspected of being a war criminal because of a letter that Franz von Papen, German Ambassador to Turkey, had written to Gestapo chief Heinrich Himmler, commending Moyzisch for "excellent service." After being questioned by the British, he had gone into hiding in the French zone of his native Austria. Found again by my office, he was eager to clear his name. The deposition he gave me seemed incredible at first. Checked and rechecked, it turned out to be entirely true.

On the night of October 26, 1943, Moyzisch, who occupied a house in the German Embassy's compound in Ankara, was awakened by the insistent ringing of his telephone. Frau Jenke, wife of Ambassador von Papen's second-in-command, was on the line. Her husband wanted Moyzisch to come to the Jenke house at once. Meeting Moyzisch at the door, Jenke said: "There's a fellow in the living room who has something interesting in your line. He's an Albanian named Diello. When you've finished talking, see him out and lock the door."

In the living room Moyzisch found a small man with sharp, unpleasant features. (See photograph on page 332.) "I can do your government a valuable service," the man said. "But I want to be well paid for it. I can get you photographs of the most important documents in the British Embassy. My price will be 5000 pounds sterling for every document." Moyzisch told me that his first impulse was to show Diello to the door. Yet the man's boldness in demanding such a preposterous fee intrigued him.

"How do I know you're not a British agent?" asked Moyzisch. "Other people will pay me if you don't," said Diello with an impatient flourish in the direction of the Russian Embassy. "You'll have to take my word that what I'm offering you is worth the price."

He declined to talk it over further. "I know you can't come to a decision until you've talked with your Ambassador," he said. "I'll give you until the afternoon of the 28th to make up your minds." That was less than two days. Moyzisch protested that he would need more time, but Diello said that he would telephone exactly at five on the day named. If the answer was "Yes," he would meet Moyzisch in a certain park at 10 o'clock that night and hand over undeveloped photographs of four top-secret documents, in return for which Moyzisch would give him £20,000. With that, Diello left.

"How did you like my former butler?" Jenke asked Moyzisch the next morning. Moyzisch indicated his bewilderment. "Diello's now the butler of the British Ambassador," said Jenke with a smile. "I think he once wanted to be an opera singer. At any rate, he's much too clever to be a butler. That's why I let him go."

Jenke agreed with Moyzisch that £20,000—then more than $80,000—was a tremendous price to pay for unknown material. But he pointed out that if the documents were as good as Diello seemed to think, they could scarcely afford to pass them up. At Jenke's suggestion. Moyzisch submitted a memorandum on the subject to the Ambassador. Later that morning Von Papen dictated an urgent radiogram to Ribbentrop in Berlin, requesting him, if he approved, to forward £20,000 at once. The money arrived the next afternoon by plane.

Moyzisch met Diello the night of the 28th. The latter accepted the money without comment and handed over a small aluminum container of film. Moyzisch hurried back to his office and called in the photographer whom the Gestapo had assigned him for secret work. Von Papen and Jenke joined him.

When the enlarged photostats were ready, the trio found that the documents were indeed worth what had been paid for them. One was a list of British intelligence agents in Turkey. Another was a summary of an American report on the exact types and quantities of U.S. armaments thus far delivered to Russia. Another was a copy of a memorandum that Sir Hughe Knatchbull-Hugessen, the British Ambassador, had just sent to London. It gave full details of his latest conference with the Turkish Foreign Minister, whom he was trying to persuade to declare war on Germany. Last were photostats of a preliminary report on the decisions reached at the current conference of Allied foreign ministers—Hull, Eden and Molotov—in Moscow.

Von Papen's eyes lit up. "We seem to have employed a very eloquent little man," he said. "We can't call him Diello, because that happens to be his name. Cicero was an eloquent man too. Let's call him Cicero." And Cicero he was from that moment onward.

The photostats were sent to Berlin by special courier. Ribbentrop immediately showed them to Hitler, who said that he wanted to see all the material Cicero could obtain. Ribbentrop instructed Von Papen to employ him permanently—though, if possible, at more reasonable rates. After considerable haggling, Cicero agreed to take £15,000 for every 20 frames of film that were legibly exposed. This fee was later reduced to £10,000. But altogether, during the next five months, *he collected over $1,000,000 in pounds sterling.*

In answer to repeated questions, Cicero one day told Moyzisch how he was able to photograph so many secret documents. Knatchbull-Hugessen was a music lover. When Cicero told him that he knew a number of Italian operas by heart, Sir Hughe was highly pleased. He often asked Cicero, after that, to sing him certain arias. Cicero became his valet as well as his butler. One day when he was cleaning a pair of the Ambassador's trousers, he discovered a key in one of the pockets—the key to the Ambassador's safe. Realizing that he could make a fortune out of his employer's forgetfulness, he immediately had a duplicate key made.

Cicero bought a camera and began to photograph the most important-looking documents in the Ambassador's safe. He usually took his pictures when Knatchbull-Hugessen was out of town, but he sometimes operated at night when the Ambassador was asleep.

Moyzisch was both fascinated and repelled by Cicero's personality. He learned that Cicero's father had been killed by the British. But the man's sole interest was to make as much money as possible. He was a German spy simply because he thought that the Germans would pay more for British secrets than anybody else.

Cicero's information was invaluable to the Germans. His photostats of the British report on the Teheran Conference revealed the discussion about the Second Front. From photographs of Sir Hughe's memoranda on the Cairo Conference, Hitler learned that both the British and the Russians were determined to force Turkey into the war.

Von Papen's task was to combine bribes with threats to keep Turkey neutral. In carrying out this task he depended so much on Cicero's information that he overplayed his hand. Numan Menemencioglu, the anti-Nazi Turkish Foreign Minister, became increasingly suspicious, and finally he told Knatchbull-Hugessen that there must be a spy operating within the British Embassy.

Sir Hughe immediately coded a radiogram—a copy of which Cicero photographed and promptly delivered to the German Embassy—informing London of Menemencioglu's suspicions. Whitehall flew down an elaborate burglar alarm, which Cicero helped to install. In doing so he learned how to disconnect the alarm so that he could go on rifling the Ambassador's safe without being caught.

Suddenly, in April 1944, everything exploded in the German Embassy's face. The previous January, Moyzisch had hired a pretty new secretary, Nelly Kapp, daughter of a former German Consul in Bombay. On April 6 she disappeared. It was later discovered that she was an anti-Nazi and had been working for the British intelligence service. It was she who denounced Cicero to Knatchbull-Hugessen.

Shortly after the Normandy invasion, Turkey severed diplomatic relations with Germany and prepared at last to enter the war on the side of the Allies. Von Papen returned to Berlin—in disgrace, it was thought. But, shortly after, he was decorated—as was his attaché, Moyzisch.

Moyzisch told me that he saw Cicero only once after his expulsion from the British Embassy. It was later rumored that he had emigrated to a Latin-American country, where he was living under an assumed name.

Ludwig Moyzisch, who had confined himself to the accepted practices of espionage, was cleared of any suspicion of war crimes and returned to his little village in the Tyrolean Alps.

The story of the spy Cicero has an ironic twist. Most of the money (the equivalent of over $1,000,000) paid to him by the Nazis turned out to be worthless counterfeit English pound notes. (See "The Nazi Counterfeit Plot," page 507.)

Trapping the *Scharnhorst*

By C. S. Forester, author of Captain Horatio Hornblower

The Nazis knew about the presence of that convoy making its way to Murmansk round the most northerly point of Norway. That was why the *Scharnhorst* was sent out into the arctic night from her Norwegian fiord, wearing at her masthead the flag of Rear Admiral Bey.

For the purposes of a raid this 26,000-ton battle cruiser had all the desirable qualities. Designed for a speed of 29 knots, she was faster than any British battleship. With nine 11-inch guns she was more powerful than any British cruiser. And her enormous secondary armament would ensure that if she once got into a convoy she would sink ships faster than a fox killing chickens in a hen roost.

She left on the afternoon of Christmas Day, and at precisely the right time, just when the gloomy northern sea was beginning to be faintly illumined by the next dawn, made her contact with the convoy. There was up to half a million tons of shipping there. It was possible for her, in the next hour, to do as much damage as the whole U-boat navy could achieve in six months.

The British convoy was heading east some 150 miles north of North Cape. It was guarded against submarine attack by a ring of corvettes and destroyers, small craft. To guard against attack by surface vessels, Vice-Admiral Burnett had three cruisers, *Belfast*, *Norfolk* and *Sheffield*. He had stationed his squadron to the southeast of the convoy, and it was from the southeast that Bey arrived at 9:35 a.m.

The *Scharnhorst* and the British escort sighted each other at less than seven miles. Aboard the British ships, the unsleeping eye of radar that could see through the arctic night and through fog or snowstorm had been watching over their safety. It had given the first alarm, and now was reporting just where this almost certain enemy was to be found and whither she was headed. The guns were training in accordance with its observations, and the gunnery officers awaiting the moment to open fire. In obedience to the Commodore's orders, the convoy turned itself about while the *Norfolk*, the *Sheffield* and the *Belfast* went dashing forward to meet the enemy.

In a broadside the *Scharnhorst* could fire rather more than the weight of shells that could be fired by the three cruisers all put together. It would be a fortunate light cruiser that could sustain a hit from one of her 11-inch shells and live through it, while the armor over her own vitals would keep out the cruisers' shells at all but the closest range. The approaching conflict was unfair. Yet the three cruisers flung themselves upon the *Scharnhorst*.

In the twilight of that arctic morning—the sun would not all day long come above the horizon—the glittering white bow wave flung up by the speeding *Scharnhorst* could be seen even when her gray upper works were invisible. A gun was fired in the British squadron and a star shell traced a lovely curve of white light before it burst fairly over the battle cruiser, lighting up the sea for a mile around her. As it hung in the sky from its parachute the cruisers' guns opened fire.

The shells went screaming on their mission, and the spotting officer of the *Norfolk*, through his glasses, saw, just at that very second when the *Norfolk's* shells should land, a vivid green flash from the *Scharnhorst's* black hull. The *Norfolk* carried eight-inch guns, the other cruisers only six-inch. There was a chance that the *Scharnhorst* had been hurt.

The *Scharnhorst* spun about rapidly, so that the next salvo missed. Then she dashed out of the illuminated circle and vanished into the twilight. Admiral Bey was acting on a plan he had devised long beforehand. It was the convoy he was after. He knew now where were the main defenses of the convoy, and could guess with some accuracy where the merchant ships themselves were to be found. He could circle away, losing himself in the gloom, and make a fresh stab.

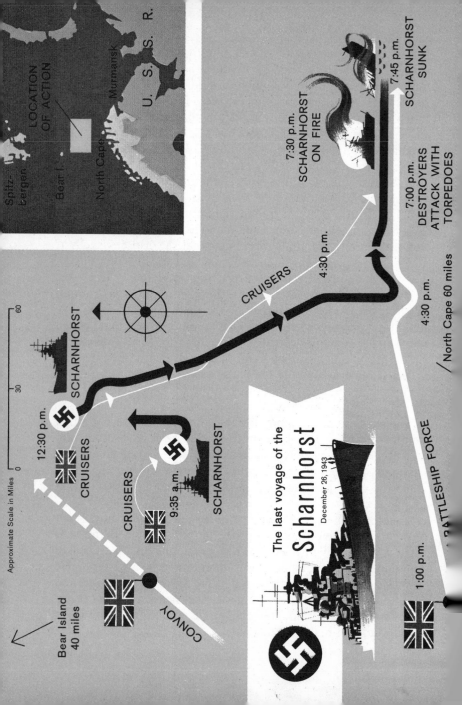

The last voyage of the **Scharnhorst**
December 26, 1943

LOCATION OF ACTION

Spitz-bergen

Bear I.

North Cape

Murmansk

U. S. S. R.

SCHARNHORST

SCHARNHORST

SCHARNHORST

12:30 p.m.

9:35 a.m.

CRUISERS

CRUISERS

CRUISERS

CRUISERS

4:30 p.m.

7:30 p.m.
SCHARNHORST
ON FIRE

7:00 p.m.
DESTROYERS
ATTACK WITH
TORPEDOES

7:45 p.m.
SCHARNHORST SUNK

4:30 p.m.

North Cape 60 miles

BATTLESHIP FORCE

1:00 p.m.

CONVOY

Bear Island
40 miles

Approximate Scale in Miles

0   30   60

Admiral Burnett, aboard the *Belfast*, had to guess what Bey would do next, where and when he would attack the convoy. A 29-knot battleship could circle the whole convoy in an hour. It might dash in from any direction and in 10 minutes sink many merchant vessels. So there was no margin whatever for miscalculation on the part of Burnett, standing there on the crowded and exposed bridge of the *Belfast*, with the spray flying aft as the cruiser steamed at top speed over the heaving sea.

At 12:30—three hours after the first contact from the southeast—the *Scharnhorst* reappeared from the northeast. She found Burnett and his cruisers right in her path. It was an extraordinary achievement on Burnett's part. What Bey thought of this apparition of three indomitable cruisers, when by all the laws of chance they should have been 20 miles away, can be guessed from his actions. There was a sudden flurry of salvos, during which a shell burst on the *Norfolk's* stern, and then Bey turned and ran for home.

He could not doubt that three hours ago hurried messages had been broadcast to the British Admiralty and to the main British fleet; nor could he doubt that the British were straining every nerve to send ships and aircraft to attack a ship as valuable as the *Scharnhorst*.

As a matter of fact, there was far more risk than he knew. Some 150 miles to the southwest of him and steaming fast to cut him off was a force which could make scrap iron of his ship. This was the *Duke of York* with her attendant cruiser, the *Jamaica*, and her screen of four destroyers. From her masthead flew the St. George's Cross of a full admiral—no less a person than Sir Bruce Fraser, commander of the Home Fleet.

Nobody outside a few favored persons knew how many times the Royal Navy had set that trap, how many times a battleship force had plodded along to Russia on a course parallel to, but well away from, that of the convoy, in the hope of intercepting any Nazi force sent out from Norway. This was the first time that patience and resolution were to be rewarded.

The *Duke of York* had been about 200 miles away when Burnett's first message came. The enemy had an advantage in speed of several knots. Fraser had to be sure of being able to interpose between the *Scharnhorst* and her base; any mere pursuit was doomed to failure before it started. He headed toward the strategical center of gravity—the nearest point of a straight line between the *Scharnhorst's* last known position and the German base.

When the next news came from Burnett, after the *Scharnhorst* had made her second appearance, Fraser knew her exact position again. She was still 150 miles away.

It was time for Burnett to distinguish himself once more. The *Scharnhorst*, after scoring her hit on the *Norfolk*, had headed south through the twilight. Burnett swung his ships in pursuit. It was of the utmost importance that Fraser should be kept informed of the German's course. So Burnett had to keep in touch with the *Scharnhorst*, but to keep in touch with a ship that mounts 11-inch guns is more easily asked than done. Those guns were capable of hitting a target clean over the horizon, and it needed only one salvo, landing square, to sink any of Burnett's cruisers.

All during that anxious afternoon Fraser did nothing to reveal his position. One whisper from his radio and the *Scharnhorst* would know of the presence of another British force to the southward. Then at 4:30 all doubts were suddenly resolved. The *Duke of York* broke her wireless silence with an order from Fraser to Burnett to "illuminate the enemy with star shell." Then they knew that Fraser was very close—the *Duke of York's* navigating officers had done a neat professional job. They had accurately tracked down their quarry.

It was quite dark. The *Scharnhorst* was on Fraser's port bow, and the *Belfast* was eight miles astern of the Nazi ship. A streak of white fire shot from one of the *Belfast's* guns and soared against the black sky. The shell burst high up, and then the tremendous white flare blazed out.

Right in the center of that blaze of light was the *Scharnhorst*, and the lookouts and spotters and gunnery officers in Fraser's force saw her upper works standing out boldly against the horizon. Five 14-inch guns roared out with the incredible loud din of their kind and sent three and a half tons of hot steel and high explosive at their mark. For a score of seconds the shells rumbled through the air; one of the destroyers in the *Duke of York's* screen under the arch of their trajectory heard them pass overhead like maddened express trains.

Then they landed, flinging up 200-foot splashes, and so closely had the range been estimated that this first salvo was registered as a "straddle." The next, half a minute later, recorded a hit. Bey turned his ship sharply to port and sent her wildly seeking safety in the eastward darkness. After her plunged the *Duke of York*. The *Scharnhorst* was hit and hit again, but was not wounded sufficiently to make any immediate difference to her speed. Before half past six she was out of range—battered, on fire, but safe for the moment from the *Duke of York*.

But hardly had the *Duke of York* ceased fire when a new blaze of gunfire lit the horizon far ahead. The *Scharnhorst* was having to defend herself against other enemies. The four destroyers of the *Duke of York's* screen, with their superior speed, had overhauled her—the *Savage* and *Saumarez* on the starboard side, the *Scorpion* and *Stord* (the last a vessel of the Norwegian Navy) on the port side. They were dashing in, and just in the nick of time to prevent Bey's escape.

The *Scharnhorst* opened fire with all the guns of her secondary battery. From a spectacular point of view her defense was dramatic enough. She was one vast glow from the orange-red flames of her guns, and from this central nucleus radiated the innumerable streaks of tracer shells. But destroyers charging in at 40 knots are hard to stop. Moreover, the *Scharnhorst* had been hard hit, with damage to her fire-control director and communications system. Her salvos were singularly ineffective. Only the *Saumarez* was hit. The destroyers pressed home their attack to the uttermost limit. They did not loose their torpedoes at 10,000 yards, nor at 6000 yards, which is the nearest a destroyer can hope to approach a well-defended capital ship. They pressed in to 2000 yards and less, launched their torpedoes and then sheered away from the doomed battleship.

Several of the torpedoes struck home, but the *Scharnhorst*

survived these underwater blows and maintained a tremendous volume of fire, comparatively ill-directed but impressive. One singular advantage which the German Navy had always possessed was clearly demonstrated at this crisis. As the weaker naval power, she had never had to design her ships for ability to remain at sea for long periods of time; swift and sudden blows were all she expected of them, with the result that habitability was not considered a necessity. They could lie in harbor with their crews on shore in barracks most of their time, so that they could be compartmented in a fashion impossible to British or American ships.

The *Scharnhorst*, however, had lost speed, and now the *Duke of York* came up in range again, and her 14-inch guns began to smash the *Scharnhorst* to pieces. The *Duke of York's* attendant cruiser, *Jamaica*, closed to point-blank range. At the same time there arrived on the scene two of Burnett's cruisers, the *Belfast* and the *Norfolk*, and four destroyers from the convoy escort. In the pitch darkness no fewer than eight destroyers, three cruisers and a battleship were tearing about at their highest speed round the *Scharnhorst*. It was time for the master hand to take control again. The signal sent out by the Commander in Chief was in plain English, owing to the urgency of the occasion: "Clear the area of the target except for those ships with torpedoes and one destroyer with searchlight."

All the ships but two sheered away. One destroyer trained her searchlights on the wreck—long, long pencils of intense white light reaching through the darkness—and the *Jamaica* came in for the kill. She swung round and a salvo of torpedoes leaped from her deck. There were tremendous explosions when they hit the mark. When the smoke cleared away, the *Scharnhorst* was revealed for the last time, on her side, with the flames of her ammunition fires spouting from her. Then the smoke closed round her again and she went to the bottom, while the British destroyers raced in to try to pick up survivors. Of almost 2000 men only 36 were pulled alive from the icy waters.

It is hard to criticize the Nazi tactics or strategy. Yet the fact remains that the *Scharnhorst* came out and was destroyed.

Conspiracy of Mercy

By George Kent

The universal revulsion created when the world learned how the Nazis killed six million Jews has an antidote. It is to be found in the decency and heroism of thousands of Europeans who risked death to save other Jews from Hitler.

This is the heartening story of the rescuers, men and women of every nationality—French, Dutch, Danes, Norwegians, Belgians, Italians, Portuguese and Germans, too—who could not stand idle while others suffered and died. These self-appointed protectors of the Jews smuggled to safety or kept alive in their homes no fewer than 200,000 refugees from Nazi persecution. In Berlin itself, 5000 Jews, passed from hiding place to hiding place, lived to the end of the war. This means that here, in the headquarters city of the Gestapo, at least 50,000 Germans must have taken part in the rescue.

Denmark saved practically its entire Jewish population. France saved at least half. The Netherlands rescued nearly 20 percent of its Jews. And Norway spirited thousands to safety.

The rescuers were all manner of people: clergymen, farmers, businessmen, waiters, schoolteachers, policemen, titled men and women. A Belgian countess concealed more than 100 women and children. An Italian officer smuggled 3000 Jews from Yugoslavia into Italy, where they lived out the war, unmolested, in a camp.

In Nice a Protestant minister saved more than 100 Jews, smuggling them into Italy and putting them on ships headed for North Africa. In Rome a Catholic priest established a printing plant to make false passports and birth certificates for Jewish fugitives. So many clergymen, in fact, devoted themselves to saving Jews that clerical garb became highly suspect to the Gestapo. (See "Shepherds of the Underground," page 191.) In Paris alone 49 priests who had aided Jews and worked in the Underground were arrested, and many of them shot.

At Bordeaux the Portuguese consul, Dr. Aristides de Sousa Mendes, defied orders from his government and issued visas to all Jews who applied for them. In three 15-hour days he stamped passports so that 9000 fugitives could enter Portugal from France. He also sheltered and fed scores while they waited for transportation, and then drove them to the railroad station in his own car.

In rowboats, trawlers, freighters, police launches, lighthouse tenders, even canoes, the Danes ferried to Sweden all but 472 of Denmark's total Jewish population of about 8000. Among the leaders of this "Little Dunkirk" were Copenhagen's doctors. They hid the fugitives in hospitals, giving them false names and hanging fever charts on their beds. Others were stowed away in nurses' quarters. When the rescue ships were ready, the doctors drove the Jews in canvas-covered trucks to lonely beaches, where they embarked for freedom. To support these rescue operations, Danes of every class contributed a total of about $2,000,000.

The doctors did not work alone. One shopkeeper doing business directly opposite Nazi quarters in Copenhagen became virtually a travel agent. Jews would tell him when they were ready to go, and he would arrange passage. The Swedes helped, too. No Swedish merchant vessel left Danish waters without at least a half-dozen Jews stowed in the bilges.

One of the most spectacular yet least-known stories concerns an extraordinary Dutchwoman, Truuss Wijsmuller, a social worker who concealed her love for her fellow human beings beneath a rough exterior. Mrs. Wijsmuller's rescue work began one day in 1938. Driving on a wooded road close to the German border, she spied a small boy limping along. She stopped and found his body covered with welts from a whip. "They killed my papa and mama. I saw it," he babbled. After taking the boy to a hospital she went back to the border and found five more little fugitives. On her return she hid three of them under rags in the back of the car; two huddled under her wide bell skirt.

When the British government decided to permit the entry of Jewish children, Mrs. Wijsmuller was one of the agents for the Dutch committee charged with assembling them. She went to Vienna, where she wangled an interview with Adolf Eichmann, then supervising anti-Jewish activity in Austria. Ushered into his presence, Mrs. Wijsmuller explained her mission.

Eichmann referred to his papers. "On Saturday you can have 600 of them," he said. "You arrange the transportation. If they get to England and England takes them, you can have the others."

The proposal was diabolic. Saturday was only five days away. It seemed an impossible task—to find places for the 600, arrange for feeding, escorts, customs and immigration clearance. But Truuss Wijsmuller, who in Amsterdam was affectionately called "the bulldozer," roared over all obstacles. On Saturday the train was ready, and the 600 children started their journey. It was the first of a series of trains that took more than 10,000 children out of Germany, Austria and Czechoslovakia to England.

The Dutch remember with particular fondness Mrs. Wijsmuller's exploit on the day their country surrendered, May 14, 1940. The jackboots were nearing Amsterdam when Mrs. Wijsmuller learned of a ship with steam up waiting in Ijmuiden for clearance for England. Quickly she rounded up five buses and filled them with 80 Jewish children from a municipal orphanage. As they rolled along, other Jews clambered aboard, clinging to steps and lying flat on roofs. By the time they reached the harbor there were 200. No one was left behind.

One Dutch schoolteacher, Joop Westerweel, guided many Jews into France. His last party was a group of 23 boys. When he left them, this devout Calvinist made the youths promise they would try to go to Palestine. Most of them made it, and today his memory is kept alive in Israel by a grove of trees planted in his name. Westerweel was not to see it. On his return to Holland the Gestapo put him to death.

Among the bravest of the rescuers were the Germans, for they performed their mercies under the very noses of the Gestapo. In Berlin, Dr. Franz Kauffmann, a non-Jew, worked day and night nurturing his fugitives, passing them on to friends. Associates warned him: "You must stop." His only reply was: "I know that sooner or later I will be caught, but I have taken my oath on the high altar, and I cannot stop helping the poor people." One day it happened. He was led out into a stony yard and shot.

In Kattowitz, Upper Silesia, the chief air warden built false walls in an empty barbershop and there kept three Jews in safety. Perhaps more remarkable was the SS officer whose living quarters were directly above an SS center in Berlin. He kept a Jewish couple concealed there until the end of the war.

Anton Schmidt, a German soldier stationed in Wilno, Poland, repeatedly warned Jews of impending Gestapo raids. He had three houses under his command, all officially the property of the German Army, and in the cellar of each he hid Jews who were wanted by the Gestapo.

Oskar Schindler, a German businessman who took over an enamelware plant in Cracow, Poland, gathered up every Jew he could find—1200 altogether—put them to work in his factory and had them classified as essential war workers. He paid large sums in bribe money to the SS.

One of the most moving stories of rescue in Poland concerns Dr. Alexander Mikolajkow, who lived with his wife in a three-story house in Debica. He hid 13 Jews in his attic until the end of the war. The attic was so low no one could stand erect in it. There was no toilet, no way of washing, no light. At midnight the Doctor or his wife would climb the ladder, leave food and remove the waste buckets. When at last Debica was liberated, the men and women stumbled down from their hiding place, shaggy, haggard, filthy—but alive. The Doctor, however, was not there to welcome them. When the battle for the city was going on, he had hurried out with his surgical kit to help the wounded. A burst of shrapnel ended his life.

Such are the stories of the men and women who could not

close their eyes to the distress of their fellow human beings. Nowhere, in any period of history, has the ennobling quality of compassion been more clearly demonstrated than in the humanity of the simple men and women of Europe who suffered and died to help the Jews.

Tunnel to Freedom

By Flight Lieutenant Paul Brickhill, Royal Australian Air Force, as told to Allan A. Michie

Stalag Luft III, at Sagan, Germany, halfway between Berlin and Breslau, held 10,000 captured airmen in the spring of 1943. Nearly all were from the RAF, although Americans were beginning to arrive in numbers. (See photograph on page 340.)

At the end of March the camp was enlarged by addition of a North Compound, and 700 of us were moved into it. Already prisoners in the working parties that helped build the compound had studied its layout and paced off its distances—with tunnels in mind. Escape was the one hope that had kept us going through the numbing months of captivity.

A few of the officers had dug tunnels at other camps, and around them we built "X," our escape organization. Head of "X" was Squadron Leader Roger Bushell, a tall South African who had been a fighter pilot until shot down over Dunkirk. Bushell had already made two remarkable escapes, and once had got almost to Switzerland before he was caught.

North Compound was a 1000-foot square enclosed by two tall barbed-wire fences, parallel and five feet apart, the space between crammed with barbed-wire coils. Ten yards inside this barrier was the warning wire; step across it and the guards shot. Numerous sentry towers, 15 feet high, each with searchlight and machine gun, were manned 24 hours a day. Twenty-five yards outside the wire on all four sides were dense pine woods which cut off any view of the outside world—but equally would cover an escape.

As soon as we moved in, notices were posted asking for volunteers to play cricket and softball. The notices were signed "Big X." Everybody knew what that meant, and 500 signed up for the tunnel work. It was decided to start three long tunnels, "Tom," "Dick" and "Harry," in the hope that one would be undetected. We never used the word "tunnels"; too many eavesdropping guards understood English.

Tom was to be dug from Block 123 to the wire, 150 feet away, and then on to the shelter of the woods. Dick was to be dug from 122 toward Tom, so that it could either be joined with Tom's shaft or be dug all the way to the woods. Harry was to begin from Block 104 and drive to the woods on the north.

Of course the tunnels would have to start from within our huts. Each hut was 100 feet long, with sleeping quarters, washroom and small kitchen. The Germans had built these huts about a foot off the ground, so that the guards could look underneath to see if we were up to any funny business. There were usually several of these "ferrets" around, easily spotted by their blue overalls. With torches and long steel probes they searched for hidden trapdoors and telltale sand from tunnels.

Three teams were organized, each under a veteran tunneler. Wally Floody, a Canadian mining engineer, was technician in chief. Every volunteer was interviewed by the "X" chief of his block. Miners, carpenters, engineers were assigned to tunnel. Tailors were organized to turn out disguises. Artists set up a forgery shop to fake papers. Any man who spoke fluent German was assigned to make friends with a ferret, keep him always in sight, cultivate him, eventually try to bribe him to bring in items needed from the outside.

One day a new ferret, a particularly zealous one, appeared on duty and we labeled him "Keen Type." Within a month, however, a contact had so cultivated him that he lost his zest for anti-escape vigilance. He would come into the compound, walk straight to his contact's room and say, "Keen Type here.

Can I come in?" and then settle down for tea and a biscuit.

Prisoners without any special skills were assigned either as "penguins," to dispose of sand from the tunnels, or as "stooges," to keep watch on ferrets. For the next year we had 300 stooges working in shifts every day. They reported to "Big S," the head security officer, a tall, rangy American colonel.

Once the security system was working we went ahead on the tunnels. The Germans had overlooked one detail. In each hut the washroom, kitchen and a small section where there was a stove had concrete floors and stood on brick and concrete foundations that had no openings through which the security guards could probe. These were the places from which we started work.

The first job was to build secret trapdoors. At any hour of the day or night the Germans would rush into a block shouting "*Aus, Aus!*" and then upset beds, pry into cupboards and rip up floor and wall boards, looking for tools, civilian clothing, buttons, nails, anything an escaper might use. Yet ingenuity, backed by three years of weary experience, built trapdoors they couldn't find.

By luck, we got hold of a little cement left over from building the camp. A Polish team cast a removable block to replace a slab about two feet square chipped from the floor of Block 123. When a little sand and dirt had been rubbed around the edges, nobody could spot it. This was Tom's entrance.

Dick's trapdoor in Block 122 was the most ingenious. In the washroom floor was an iron grating through which waste water ran into a concrete well three feet deep. The drainpipe that led from this sump was so placed that there was always some water in the well. While stooges kept watch outside, the Poles removed the iron grill, bailed out the well and, with a cold chisel acquired by bribing a guard, freed the whole concrete slab that formed one side of the well so that it was removable at will. When the slab was in place and the cracks were sealed with clay, the waste water rapidly accumulated, making everything look most unsuspicious.

Harry's entrance was also tricky. The tall heating stove in

Room 23 of Block 104 stood on tiles embedded in a concrete base about four feet square. The men moved the stove back, chipped the tiles free and reset them in a concrete trapdoor which looked precisely like the original base. Five of the tiles cracked in the process. They were replaced by tiles stolen from a cookhouse in East Compound and smuggled in to us. It had been risky business. Harry's floor was up for about 10 days in all, hidden from the ferrets only by a carelessly placed mattress, but we got away with it. (See diagram on page 340.)

Now we were set for the more dangerous business of tunneling. The distances, direction and angles of the three tunnels had been computed by rough trigonometry. We had learned that German sound detectors could hear nothing below a depth of 25 feet, so we decided to sink shafts 30 feet straight down from the three trapdoors before heading for the woods.

The light, sandy soil was easy to dig, but it needed almost solid shoring. As a start we made each man provide two bed slats. This first levy wasn't too bad, but by the time the fifth and sixth levies took more slats, it was hard to sleep.

Early in May 1943 the first sand was cut away. Teams worked from just after morning roll call right through to the evening roll call with only a short break for lunch.

The penguins had the troublesome job of disposing of the bright yellow sand, which showed up glaringly if dumped on the dun-colored soil above ground. Some of the sand could be stirred into the soil of our tiny gardens, but that didn't begin to solve the problem. So we took dozens of small towels and sewed them into sausage-shaped sacks. A penguin would hang one of these, filled with sand, in each trouser leg and wander casually out to the playing ground. There stooges would be staging boxing matches, volleyball games or pretended brawls. Once in among the men, the penguin, hands in pockets, would pull strings that freed pins at the bottom of the sausage sacks and let the sand trickle to the ground. Scores of scuffling feet would quickly discolor it and trample it into the surface. When we were going good, we kept 150 penguins busy and we disposed of tons of sand under the very noses of the ferrets.

The tunnels were scooped out with little coal shovels and iron scrapers made from our cookstoves. The bores were about two feet square and shored with box frames made of bed slats, notched to fit. We saved our few nails to build shaft ladders.

At the base of each shaft, chambers were dug for the use of carpenters and fitters and for the ventilating equipment. One day when three diggers were thus enlarging the base of Dick's shaft, a frame began to leak sand. In a matter of seconds the leak became an avalanche. The ladder held and two diggers scrambled up. The third, Wally Floody, was almost smothered before the other two got him out. Dick's shaft filled almost to the top. It was a bitter setback, but the job was grimly done over again.

Veterans had learned that you could not tunnel far without fresh air, and that holes poked up to the surface were not adequate. By luck, a copy of a modern-mechanics type of magazine came into camp and it contained an article which described a homemade air pump. We promptly set to work to make one.

Our "tin bashers" collected Red Cross dried-milk tins, cut off the ends and fitted the cylinders together to build pipe. They wrapped the joints with German propaganda newspapers. The pipe was laid in a ditch along the tunnel floor and covered with sand. At the far end was a nozzle, which delivered fresh air. The air was forced through the pipe by shifts of pumpers who operated a bellows constructed from kit bags. This first outfit worked perfectly and we promptly built two more. Now we could close the trapdoors and work without fear of interruption from the ferrets.

Our electrical specialists rounded up odd bits of wiring left behind by the builders. Then they surreptitiously rearranged the camp wiring, gaining a few score feet in the process. They wired the three shafts and made hidden connections to the camp circuit. We stole bulbs from corridors and had light to dig by. When sometimes the Germans neglected to switch on the power during the day, we used homemade lamps—tin cans with pajama-cord wicks burning in margarine. They were a bit smelly.

The digging teams evolved a rigid system. No. 1 digger lay full length on his side and one elbow, hacking away at the tunnel face and pushing the sand back toward his feet. No. 2 lay facing the other way, his legs overlapping No. 1's. He collected the sand in special boxes, which were placed on trolleys and hauled by homemade ropes back to the shaft.

These trolleys, strong enough to carry two sand boxes or one man, were first-class installations. They had carved flanged wooden wheels fitted with "tires" cut from tin cans. The hubs even had ball bearings, smuggled in by a tame ferret. The track rails were made from barrack moldings. When the tunnels became long, the diggers sprawled on the trolleys and pushed their way to the working face.

At times it was stifling hot in the hole. Men worked naked or in the hated long underpants issued to prisoners. Dirt stains on their outer clothes would have given the show away. Up above we rigged rough showers where the diggers could quickly wash off all telltale sand before roll calls.

By the end of May, a month after digging commenced, each of the three tunnels was about 70 feet long. We were nearly into summer, the best time for escaping, for we could sleep out and live off the land. The X leaders decided to concentrate on Tom, which had least distance to go. A week later they set up the first "halfway house" at the 100-foot mark. This was a little chamber built from the end frames of our wooden bunks. In it men could turn around without having to go back to the shaft. Calculations were that Tom's halfway house was just under the warning wire. That meant another 100 feet of digging to get just inside the woods.

Other X groups were busily preparing the equipment we'd need. Our forgery department of 50 men turned out phony passports and identity cards. Some of our guards could be tempted with a gift of coffee or chocolate, and once they had smuggled in one item they couldn't refuse more, because we might give them away to the Kommandant. In this way we got colored inks, pens, brushes, special types of paper, magnets to make com-

passes, radio parts to build our illegal receiver on which we got daily news bulletins, a camera and equipment to make photos for our fake passports, hammers, saws, pliers, nails and maps.

A few guards, smoothly cultivated by our linguists, were even persuaded to lend us their *Zahlbuch*, combined paybook and identity card, while our forgers made copies. The faking of documents was an incredibly finicky job. Whole sheets of simulated typewriting were drawn by hand, complete with strike-overs, imperfect letters and bad shifts. Other documents called for lines of close print or endless whorls of "engraving." Forgers ripped fine paper from Bibles and linen covers from books to make identification books. One document needed in crossing frontiers was so complicated that it would take a skilled forger five hours a day for a month to make one. Letterheads were "embossed" with toothbrush handles. German eagle and swastika stamps were cut from rubber boot heels. Altogether, the forgery department outfitted the escapers with more than 400 false documents.

An Australian pilot made compasses—the cases from melted phonograph records, the glasses from broken windows, the needles from sewing needles rubbed on a magnet.

In the tailor shop 60 men made civilian clothes out of RAF uniforms and turned out close copies of Luftwaffe uniforms. Escapers caught wearing exact copies would be shot as spies, but by the Geneva Convention we could use imitations.

Half a dozen map makers traced a variety of maps and ran copies off on a makeshift duplicator. They made the gelatin from fruit jello, the ink from the crushed lead of indelible pencils.

We learned that the Americans were to be moved in six weeks to a separate compound and they had put in a lot of work on the tunnels. So evening shifts were added to hurry things up. We had to take greater chances with sand. More of it was dug into our vegetable gardens and some scattered near the upturned soil around a new camp theater. One day a probing ferret turned over some bright yellow sand in a garden. This touched off a series of frantic but futile searches. The Germans dug a trench between Block 123 and the wire, but it was not deep enough to reveal Tom.

By the end of June we calculated that Tom had reached just under the edge of the wood, and we prepared to dig a shaft straight up to the surface. Suddenly a horde of Germans appeared and began to cut away the trees! It was actually mere coincidence; they had decided to build a new compound there. They chopped the trees back for 50 yards, but time for the Americans was short and it was decided to break Tom out anyway and let the escapers crawl the rest of the way to cover.

We had so much sand coming up that we were desperate. Someone suggested storing it temporarily in Dick. Every evening a stream of penguins carrying cardboard Red Cross boxes strolled across to Dick's hut and dumped sand down the shaft. Even that was not enough. The X leaders decided to store sand in Red Cross boxes under our beds and hope that the Germans wouldn't find it until it could be properly disposed of.

Tom was now 260 feet long, with a few yards to go to its goal. Bushell decided to lie low for a few days to allay suspicion. Then ferrets found the boxes of sand in our huts! Heavy transport wagons were brought into camp and trundled all around in an effort to collapse any tunnels we might have. They only wrecked our vegetable gardens.

A day or so later, in a last suspicious search of Block 123, a ferret accidentally jabbed his probe into the edge of Tom's trapdoor. That was the end of Tom. The ferrets couldn't find how to open the trap, so they broke it in. They dynamited Tom and incidentally blew up part of the roof of Block 123. They were so relieved at discovering Tom that they took no reprisals or even precautions.

A mass meeting decided that work would go ahead on Dick and Harry. However, it was deemed wise to do no more until winter, when we assumed vigilance would slacken because it is a bad season for escapes.

At the end of August 1943 the Americans were moved to their new compound and we threw a great party on home-brewed raisin wine as a farewell.

While we were waiting for winter, it was decided to try some above-ground escapes. For one of them, the carpenters made imitation German rifles out of wood—they got the exact measurements by sneaking up behind guards with calipers and measuring the parts. These they leaded with pencil to resemble metal and polished until you couldn't tell them from the real thing. Periodically the Germans escorted small parties of prisoners through the gates for delousing our clothes, and the idea was to stage an unofficial delousing party of our own. Three prisoners, disguised as Luftwaffe *Unteroffiziers*, took 24 other prisoners in tow, passed the inspection at the gate and made off into the woods. A few minutes later six senior officers, including the Battle of Britain fighter ace Bob Stanford Tuck, tried to get through but were detected. We were all forced to stand on parade for nearly seven hours while the three missing men were identified. Later all were rounded up.

We were ready to start tunneling again early in 1944. Dick was almost filled in with Tom's sand, and anyway the Germans had started to build a new compound where Dick was to have broken out. That left Harry. But snow lay deep on the ground and sand disposal stumped us. One of the tunnelers suggested we put it under the theater. He had noticed the Germans never looked there. We had built the theater ourselves and taken care to leave no openings for the ferrets to peek through. Underneath was a deep excavation which could take tons and tons of sand. Our engineers adjusted one seat so that it swung back on hinges, and under it they cut a trapdoor. Into this the penguins dumped kit bags full of sand every night.

Three teams, with 10 veteran diggers in each team, pushed Harry ahead up to 12 feet per day. By the end of January the first "halfway house" was built 100 feet out. The planners had calculated that 300 feet of tunnel in all would bring us into the shelter of the trees.

It was a long dig, and conditions were getting worse. The ground was cold and damp. Every digger suffered continuously from colds. Sand falls kept occurring nearly every day. But by mid-February another 100 feet had been dug and the second halfway house was put in. This was just about under the far boundary wire; there was 100 feet still to go.

The chief ferret again became suspicious. Wally Floody, our chief penguin, our security chief and half a dozen of the key diggers were suddenly transferred to a compound several miles away. That was a blow. It was bad enough losing key men, but it was worse that the Germans obviously knew we were up to something.

By March 8, 1944, the final 100-foot section was dug and a chamber excavated at the end. In four days four of the best diggers carved straight upward, fitting ladders to the side as they progressed, until they struck pine-tree roots. They estimated that they were about two feet below the surface, just inside the woods. They boarded over the top of the shaft and left the remainder to be dug on the night of the break. By March 14 the tunnel was ready. The trapdoor was closed and its sides were cemented up to wait for milder weather and a night suitable for our getaway.

The very next day the chief ferret sent his men to search Block 104. One of them even ran his probe around the cement that sealed Harry's trapdoor. It held.

About 500 men had worked on the tunnels, but we estimated that only 220 would be able to pass through it during the hours of darkness. The escape committee drew up a list of the men best qualified to make good their escape and the men who had done the most work on the project. The rest of the names were drawn out of a hat.

The lucky ones began their preparations. We had enough money to buy train tickets for 40 men; the rest were to walk across country. Bushell and other men who had been loose in Germany conducted lectures, giving hints and advice. A Czech pilot described the border mountains of Czechoslovakia, 60 miles away, for which most of the foot travelers intended to head.

After roll call on the morning of Friday, March 24, Roger Bushell announced that the escape would take place that night. There was six inches of snow on the ground, which was not good, but there would be no moon. Our meteorologist thought there would be a wind to drown suspicious noises.

The forgery-department boys filled in their documents and stamped them with the correct date, which of course couldn't have been done until then. Some escapers were to go as foreign workers, others as neutrals, others as German officials, soldiers and civilians—and each man's papers had to fit his story.

A digger went out to Harry's end to see how far we had to go to break through. When he jabbed a stick upward three inches he struck daylight, much to his surprise. At least, it seemed, there wouldn't be any difficulty in getting to the surface.

We laid blankets at the bottom of the shafts to deaden sounds and nailed planks on the trolleys so the escapers could lie on them and be pulled along. When darkness came the escapers put on their disguises. Our improvised iron rations were issued, a revolting but nourishing combination of grated chocolate, oatmeal, crushed biscuits, vitamin pills, barley, dried milk and other concentrated foods all boiled together.

By half past eight it was announced that all was ready. Ten minutes later the first escaper went down the ladder, well turned out in a civilian suit and carrying a homemade briefcase. The second, dressed as a workman, followed on his heels. Roger Bushell, carrying an attaché case and looking like a smart businessman in his gray herringbone lounge suit, black overcoat and dark hat, went down among the first five.

There was a bad wait when the first man was unable to pry the roof boards loose. It was almost an hour, an agonizing time for the men lying along the tunnel, before the swollen boards came loose and the earth was removed. Up above twinkled a few stars, and down the shaft came the sweet fresh air of freedom.

But when the digger cautiously stuck his head out he got a shock. Instead of being just inside the woods, the hole was 10 feet short of the trees and its gaping opening was a bare 15 yards from a sentry tower.

We were stunned when he broke the news. But the men were in no mood to be stopped. To go out now was risky. To wait a month for the next dark of the moon and in the meantime dig another 30 feet of tunnel was equally risky. Besides, the forged papers were all dated and would have to be redone. That was the deciding factor.

The first man up crawled to a brushwood fence, paying out a rope by which he could signal when it was safe for the next man to emerge. The sentry in the tower paid no attention to the woods, but played his searchlight on the barbed-wire fence and compound. Two other sentries patrolled back and forth along the wire. When both were out of sight the rope was tugged and the second man slipped across into the woods.

It took more than an hour for the first 20 to make it. They were all going by train, and they headed for the Sagan railway station a quarter of a mile away. From timetables smuggled in by guards we knew exactly when the trains were due.

Back in Block 104 the initial delay had been terrible. Escapers sat around, a queer collection of well-dressed civilians, workmen and a German corporal, hoping that ferrets would not appear. Just after half past nine the men at the trapdoor felt a blast of cold air. It could only mean that we'd broken out. A muffled cheer went around the block.

There were other interruptions. Two bad sand falls held up the show for about an hour and a half in all. Sometimes the trolleys left their rails—more delays. We were running far behind schedule. At midnight the air-raid sirens sounded and all lights, including our illegal ones in the tunnel, were switched off. It was obvious now that not more than 100 men would get away before daylight.

We heard the faraway sound of falling bombs and the huts rattled as RAF blockbusters fell crashing on Berlin, 100 miles away. At any other time we would have cheered, but that night we cursed. It was about two in the morning before the lights came on again. In the meantime, one by one, the escapers had been crawling silently from the tunnel mouth and away into the woods.

When it was almost five the RAF man in charge decided it was getting too light. "Get the next three men down," he said. "Then we finish. If all of them get away without detection the

Huns won't know a thing until morning roll call and the boys will have an extra four hours before the hunt is on."

The last three men quickly descended. Just as the third man vanished up the tunnel on the trolley, we heard the crack of a rifle.

Two escaping men had reached the rendezvous tree in the woods, another man, crawling, was halfway to it, a fourth man had just emerged from the hole when the rope signaler saw a guard approaching. If he kept on coming he was bound to step right into the hole. The men outside froze to the ground when they felt two sharp warning tugs on the rope. The German strode on. He was only seven yards away now and still hadn't seen the hole.

Left, right, he strode on, probably half asleep, and one foot came down a bare 12 inches from the tunnel mouth. His next step almost trod on the man lying doggo alongside the opening. He took one more pace, and then he snapped out of his daze. He didn't even notice the man lying at his feet, but he must have seen the black track across the snow. Then he saw the man lying halfway to the wood and raised his rifle to shoot. At that moment one of the escapers waiting by the tree leaped into sight and waved his arms, shouting, *"Nicht schiessen, Posten! Nicht schiessen!"* ("Don't shoot, sentry! Don't shoot!")

The sentry, startled, shot wild. The two men at the edge of the wood and the man who had crawled halfway came slowly forward, hands raised. And then, right at his feet, the last escaper, still unseen, rose slowly. The guard jumped back a yard and looked downward. There in front of him was Harry's gaping mouth. He whipped out a torch and flashed it down the hole into the face of the 81st escaper, hanging precariously on the ladder.

The sentry blew his whistle. In a moment guards came running from all directions. Harry's long life had ended.

In Block 104 there was a frantic scramble to burn our lists and papers, break up equipment and get rid of civilian clothes. The men in the tunnel were inching back along the trolleys, expecting a shot from behind. When the last man came up, the trapdoor was sealed down and the stove replaced.

In a few minutes there came a scratching sound from below. A ferret had worked back along the tunnel and couldn't get out. We let him stay there.

By six in the morning the compound was swarming with guards, machine guns covered the doors and windows, and ferrets combed Block 104 calling, "*Aus! Aus! Efferbody aus!*" As each man came out of Block 104, a ferret grabbed him and forced him to strip in the snow, boots and all, while every article of clothing was inspected.

While the search was going on an adjutant came running to implore us to open the trapdoor. The ferret was still down there and they were afraid he would suffocate. The other ferrets couldn't find the trapdoor. We opened it for them. The ferret down below was not a bad type—he was the only one with nerve enough to go down the tunnel.

In a matter of hours the whole countryside was roused in one of the biggest manhunts of the war. The radio warned all civilians to be on the watch. SS and Gestapo men, Luftwaffe men and even naval men from Stettin and Danzig were mobilized by the thousands for the search.

Back in the compound we waited for reprisals. Harry had broken the world's record for the number of escapers who got away, and we expected the Germans to take it out on us. The Gestapo arrived to investigate, but its agents, never liked by the regular Army, got no help from the ferrets and found nothing. We even managed to filch two of their flashlights.

Most of the 76 men who got away were nabbed within a day or so, although some got as far as Danzig and Munich. Many were taken to a filthy Gestapo prison in Gorlitz, 40 miles away. From Gorlitz 15 men were brought back to Stalag Luft III. We could learn nothing more.

Then, a fortnight after the break, our senior officer was called to the Kommandant's office. Stiffly the German read out the official report—of the 76 escaped officers 41 had been shot!

Our senior officer called a meeting and announced the dreadful news. Under the Geneva Convention, drastic penalties must not be inflicted upon prisoners who attempt escape. The Germans had never before done such a thing. We thought most likely the announcement was a bluff to dissuade us from further escape attempts. We held a memorial service in the compound, however, and every man defiantly wore a black diamond of mourning on his sleeve.

When the Germans posted the list of dead it contained not 41 but 47 names, among them the leaders—Roger Bushell; Tim Walenn, who ran the forgery factory; Al Hake, the compass maker; Charlie Hall, the photographer. For days the compound was shaken with grief and fury. Then three more names were added to the list of dead. The Germans never gave us any reason for the shootings or told us why they shot only 50 of 76. A couple of weeks later they brought in urns carrying the cremated ashes of the dead, which we placed in a memorial vault.

In June a letter arrived, written in Spanish and signed by a fictitious name. That was the signal that one escaper, a Dutch pilot in the RAF, had reached England. A postcard from Sweden, signed with two false names, revealed that two Norwegians had made it out. With 15 men sent back to Stalag Luft III and 50 shot, that left eight unaccounted for.

Not till long afterward did we learn that three had been sent to a concentration camp at Barth and five to the notorious Sachsenhausen concentration camp. Nobody had ever escaped from a concentration camp, the Gestapo boasted. Within a few months three had tunneled out of Sachsenhausen. They were eventually rounded up, but by then Germany was in the chaos of collapse and they were not shot.

If the Germans shot our 50 comrades to frighten us from building more tunnels, they made a psychological blunder. "X" was re-formed around two veteran tunnelers and we immediately began work on "George," which started under the theater. George was on as grand a scale as Harry and we were almost ready to break out when we were hurriedly evacuated. The Russians were only 30 miles away. We were forced to march for weeks half across Germany. We were at Lubeck on May 2, 1945, when tanks of the British Second Army swept forward and set us free.

THE SPY WHO OPENED THE WAR

Information secretly gathered by the master Japanese spy Takeo Yoshikawa (left) laid the groundwork for the surprise attack on Pearl Harbor. (See "The Last Instant of Peace," page 17.) The Japanese photograph (below) shows the attacking planes over "Battleship Row" during the early moments of the assault on December 7, 1941. Note the bomb splashes. (See Part I, "The Intrigue of Infamy," pages 13-43.)

SPIES ON BOTH SIDES

Igor Gouzenko, former Russian cipher clerk, in 1945 exposed a wartime Soviet spy ring in Canada. He wore a mask when interviewed.

The notorious spy "Cicero" was paid a great fortune by the Nazis for stolen information while he served as butler and valet to the British Ambassador in Turkey. (See "The Highest-Paid Spy in History," page 299.)

(Right) Joey Guerrero, daring secret agent for the United States in the Japanese-occupied Philippines. (See "Joey's Quiet War," page 180.)

(Below) Eric Erickson, the Allies' most valuable industrial spy in Germany, is shown, left, with Prince Carl Bernadotte. (See "The American Who Did Business with Himmler," page 451.)

THE GREAT NAZI SPY RINGS

After following slim leads for 16 months, agents of the FBI finally apprehended the Nazi spy Ernest Lehmitz (left) and his associate Harry DeSpretter (right) in 1943. (See "The Hunt for a Spy," page 186, and "Censors and Spies," page 258.)

Counter-spy William Sebold (back to camera) helped the FBI bring about another spy round-up in 1941, the largest in U.S. history.

In Sebold's office, members of the spy ring were photographed and their conversations recorded by hidden FBI agents.

One spy bragged of having sold information of a top-secret U.S. bombsight to Germany for $4000. (See "The Spy-Catchers," page 46.)

SECRET WARRIORS

Kachin tribesmen and Americans formed crack fighting units behind Japanese lines in Burma. (See "Jungle of Hidden Friends," page 263.)

Four of Italy's famous frogmen with a midget submarine which carried a detachable war head. (See "Human Torpedoes at Gibraltar," page 119.)

Members of the Paris Underground meeting secretly in a wine cellar before the fall of the city in August 1944.

During the hours before D-day the French Underground wrecked more than 500 railroad lines. (See "The Phantom Army," page 384.)

THE NAZI SABOTAGE PLOT

J. Edgar Hoover, director of the FBI (right), and an aide arrive at court
after the arrest of eight Nazi saboteurs, landed in the U.S. by submarine.
(See "Hitler's Undercover Invasion of the United States," page 154.)

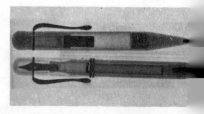

Among the invaders' tools of sabotage were an electric match (left)
for starting fires and incendiary bombs masked as a pen-and-pencil set.

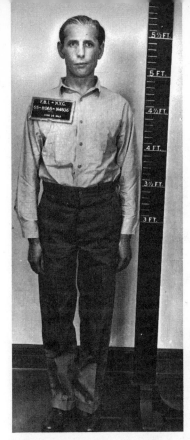

George Dasch (left), the informer, was sentenced to 30 years in prison. Peter Burger (right) got a life sentence. The other six were executed.

Also found in boxes buried by the saboteurs were an electric blasting cap (left) and an instrument for detonating dynamite.

ESCAPES AND CAPTURES

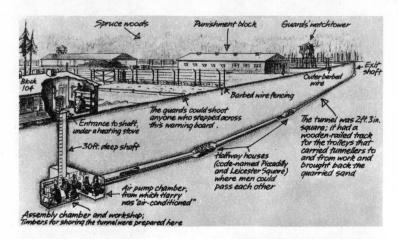

(Top) Diagram of the tunnel called "Harry," dug under Stalag Luft III at Sagan, Germany, by Allied prisoners of war, some of whom are shown in the photograph below. (See "Tunnel to Freedom," page 315.)

Anne Frank, the girl whose diary focused attention on the horrors of the Nazi regime. (Left) The Annex, where Anne, her family and others hid. (See "The Hidden Annex," page 479.)

The Italian dictator Benito Mussolini was held a prisoner at this mountaintop hotel until rescued by Colonel Otto Skorzeny and Nazi paratroopers. (See "The Most Dangerous Man in Europe," page 468.)

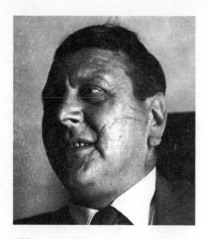

"The most dangerous" Nazi, Colonel Skorzeny, escaped in 1948 and was never recaptured. (See page 475.)

Father Chaillet saved 4000 Jewish children. (See "Shepherds of the Underground," page 191.)

Oberleutnant Franz von Werra, one of Hitler's most flamboyant fighter pilots, whose adventures in three daring escape episodes delighted the world. (See "The One That Got Away," page 90.)

Party from a U.S. warship shown boarding U-505, the first German submarine captured intact. (See "The Code Books of the Deep," page 375.)

Captured by the Germans in 1940, General Giraud (right) is shown being taken into custody. (See "Giraud's Brilliant Escape," page 201.)

MISSIONS AND MYSTERIOUS DEATHS

Wreckage of the plane in which Rudolf Hess flew from Germany to Scotland. (See "The Mystery of the Hess Flight," page 145.)

General Mark Clark leaving the submarine which had taken him to his hush-hush meeting. (See "Secret Mission to North Africa," page 216.)

Frau Rommel and son at the funeral of General Rommel, who died on Hitler's orders. (See "What Really Happened to Rommel," page 442.)

Hitler inspects the ruins of the Chancellery in April 1945 a few days before his disputed death. (See "Adolph Hitler's Last Days," page 514.)

HOAXES

(Right) Actor Clifton James' impersonation of General Montgomery (left) hoodwinked the Nazis. (See "I Was Monty's Double," page 352.)

Part of the great cache of fake English bank notes being recovered from an Austrian lake. (See "The Nazi Counterfeit Plot," page 507.)

(Left) The harbor of Hamburg, Germany, before camouflaging. (Right) The inner harbor is disguised by painted cloth mounted on floats. A dummy bridge spans the bay and painted roads cross the roof of the railroad station. (See "Fooling Enemy Airmen," page 111.)

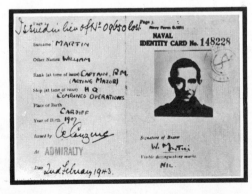

The bogus identity card carried by the dead man, "Major William Martin," in the brilliant British ruse to mislead the Nazi High Command into believing that the Allies were planning to invade Sardinia—not Sicily. (See "The Corpse That Hoaxed the Axis," page 252.)

SECRET WEAPONS

A two-man Japanese submarine captured after the Pearl Harbor attack. (See "Five Chances Missed," page 39.)

(Below) Four members of the crew of the plane that dropped the first atomic bomb. Left to right: Major Thomas W. Ferebee, bombardier; Col. Paul W. Tibbets, pilot; Capt. Theodore J. Van Kirk, navigator; and Capt. Robert A. Lewis, co-pilot. (See "The Secret That Won the War," page 529.)

A suicide attack on a U.S. warship by a Japanese kamikaze pilot in a bomb-laden Zero. (See "Death on the Wing," page 447.)

One of Hitler's terror weapons, the V-1 flying bomb, being taken to its launching ramp. (See "The Secret at Peenemünde," page 273.)

PART FIVE

1 9 4 4

STRIKING BACK

"YOU will enter the continent of Europe and, in conjunction with the other United Nations, undertake operations aimed at the heart of Germany and the destruction of her armed forces." So read the directive from the combined British and U.S. Chiefs of Staff to the Supreme Commander, General Dwight D. Eisenhower, on February 12, 1944.

No amount of secrecy could conceal from the enemy the subsequent build-up of troops, supplies and ships in England. Yet, if the invasion were to have a chance of success, the location of the landing and the date when the biggest amphibious operation in history would take place had to be cloaked in deepest mystery.

The brave acts of ordinary patriots, the quiet spying of clever individuals, the stealing of secrets, the captures and escapes — all were now related to the coming invasion. Elaborate bluffs and masquerades were perpetrated; misleading information was planted. Fakery was in the very air as false radio signals were dispatched and radar screens confused. Deep inside Nazi-occupied France, the scattered resistance fighters were welded into a one-army striking force, ready to slash the foe from within.

Then on D-day, June 6, 1944, the carefully contrived plans were sprung on the enemy. In a matter of hours Hitler's vaunted Westwall, with its bristling defenses, was breached and the Allies were thrusting swiftly toward Germany.

What plans had the Nazis themselves to counteract and throw back this mammoth Allied thrust? These, too, unfolded as the weeks went by.

After D-day the island bastions of the Pacific were, one by one, overwhelmed by the Allies. But the Japanese armies cut China in two.

I Was Monty's Double

Condensed from the book

By M. E. Clifton James

One late spring morning in 1944 the phone rang at my desk in the Royal Army Pay Corps office in Leicester. "Lieutenant James?" a pleasant voice said. "This is Colonel Niven of the Army Kinematograph section." I recognized the voice of David Niven, the film star. "Would you be interested in making some Army films?"

"Yes, sir," I answered, "I most certainly should."

"Good," Niven said briskly. "See if you can come up to London for a film test."

Slowly I replaced the receiver. Had the Army had a lapse into sanity? I had been an actor for 25 years, so when the war broke out in 1939 I volunteered my services as an entertainer. Instead I was given a commission in the Pay Corps, where I was a complete misfit. Now perhaps the mistake was to be corrected.

I went up to London in high spirits. At the Curzon Street address he had given me, David Niven greeted me cordially, then left me with a man in civvies who introduced himself as Colonel Lester.

"James," he said, "I am a member of MI 5, the Army intelligence branch, and I'm afraid I've got rather a shock for you. You are not going to make any films. You have been chosen to act as a double for General Montgomery."

I knew, of course, that I looked like "Monty." My friends had often commented on the striking resemblance. (See photographs on page 346.) And my picture had once appeared in the London *News Chronicle*, posed in a beret and captioned: YOU'RE

WRONG—HIS NAME IS LT. CLIFTON JAMES. But this assignment was a poser.

Colonel Lester studied me silently for some moments. Then he explained the plan. D-day was now imminent, he said. We had built up a mighty invasion force which would soon land in France and battle its way to Berlin. It was impossible to conceal this build-up from the Germans, and they could probably guess where we intended to strike. But they did not know the date of the expected attack, nor could they rule out the possibility of a surprise blow on some other front. Hence a deception plan had been formulated and approved by General Eisenhower. The idea was to pile up evidence that Monty—probable commander of the British invasion force—had left his post in England for a different part of the world. To do this I, after some hasty training for the part, was to *become General Montgomery.* "You must not breathe a word of this to any person whatsoever," Colonel Lester warned me. "Any questions?"

I shook my head. Either I would have to ask several dozen or none at all. After the interview I had a nightmarish feeling of stage fright. I had been a private in the last war and still had a schoolboy fear of senior officers—the idea of my impersonating the greatest of them all was grimly comic! From then on, however, I was allowed no time in which to brood.

During the next few days I studied newspaper photographs and watched newsreels of Monty. Colonel Lester and two of his junior officers drilled me in hundreds of details of the impersonation. And the need for secrecy was drummed into me so persistently that at first I was scared of talking to anyone at all. "I want you to look on this as a play we are producing for the benefit of the enemy," Colonel Lester said. "Our audience is not simple. We have to hoodwink the German High Command."

As further preparation for my role, it was arranged for me to spend several days on Monty's immediate staff where I could study him at close hand. To avoid inviting suspicion or awkward questions, I was assigned there in the guise of an Intelligence Corps sergeant. Only two members of the staff were in on the plot.

The first morning after I reported in with my strange IC sergeant's uniform and credentials, I found myself in a jeep directly behind the General's Rolls Royce. At dawn our line of vehicles, separated by gaps of exactly five yards, drew up before a country mansion near Portsmouth. There followed a five-minute wait of unmistakable tension, whereupon, at exactly timed intervals, Monty's immediate aides began to appear; and after they had each inspected us with ritualistic precision, Monty himself came out. The General looked exactly as I had imagined him. He was wearing his famous black beret and a leather flying jacket, and I noted that he had his own special salute—a slight double movement of the hand that made it more of a greeting than anything else.

When the line of cars took off, my driver kept the regulation five yards behind the Rolls. I kept my eyes glued to Monty. As we sped along the country roads, the few people who were about at this early hour stopped and stared. Then, suddenly recognizing the General, they would grin and wave wildly, receiving in return that friendly salute.

When we came within sight of the sea a marvelous spectacle met my eyes. I was attending a full-dress rehearsal of D-day. Offshore as far as the eye could reach were battleships, cruisers, destroyers and other ships. Huge landing craft were disgorging tanks, armored cars and guns by the hundred. Overhead the air was thick with planes, while infantry poured ashore from invasion barges.

After conferring briefly with the other Chiefs of Allied Command who were watching the operation from a hotel roof, Monty reappeared, and at once a small procession formed behind him. I slipped into place behind them, and as I watched him I forgot everything else. He strode along dominating the scene, but never interfering unnecessarily. Every now and then he stopped and fired questions at officers, NCO's and privates—checking up, offering advice, crisply issuing orders. What personality he had! The moment he appeared, before he even spoke, it hit people bang between the eyes. He would have made a fortune on the stage, I thought.

During the next few days I learned a great deal about the General. He was strictly a non-smoker, a teetotaler and a fanatic on physical fitness. When Colonel Lester once telephoned him to ask if there were any peculiarities about his diet that I should know, he snapped, "Certainly not. I take no milk or sugar with my porridge. That's all." At meals he chatted gaily about birds, beasts and flowers and quietly pulled his officers' legs if he found them ignorant of natural history. I never once heard him refer to war.

I watched him like a hawk, trying to catch his fleeting expressions. I observed his characteristic walk with hands clasped behind his back, the way he pinched his cheek when thinking, his sudden movements, his manner of eating, his habit of throwing out one hand as he hammered home a point. Finally I was confident I could impersonate him, as far as voice, gestures and mannerisms go. But, with my natural timidity, would I ever be able to imitate his unique personality, to radiate the feeling he gave of strength and quiet confidence? I doubted it.

As a final step in my study of him, I was given a private interview with the General. He was sitting at his desk writing, but he stood up with a smile when I came in. He was an older man than I, but the likeness was uncanny: it was like looking at myself in a mirror. There was no need for false eyebrows, padded cheeks or any other kind of artifice. He quickly found common ground between us to put me at ease—I had been brought up in Australia, he in nearby Tasmania. As he talked, I listened carefully, trying to record the incisive, rather high-pitched voice and the way he chose his words. He never used high-flown phrases; some people have even described his speech as dry and arid.

"You have a great responsibility, you know," he said before I left. "Do you feel confident?" When I hesitated, he added quickly, "Everything will be all right; don't worry about it." And in that moment, such was his ability to inspire confidence, my qualms vanished.

At the War Office a few days later I felt an air of tension.

"Now, James," said Colonel Lester, "it's time for the curtain to go up. Tomorrow evening at 6:30 you become General Montgomery. You will be driven to the airport and, in full view of scores of people, will take off in the Prime Minister's plane. At 7:45 a.m. next morning you land at Gibraltar. We have spread rumors all along the African coast that Monty may be coming to form an Anglo-American army for an invasion of southern France. You are going to travel all through the Middle East to give weight to these rumors. Every move of yours will be watched intently by Hitler's agents. We can tell you more or less what to do, but things never work out exactly as planned. You must paddle your own canoe. Always take command of the situation. Remember: from now on, senior officers are mere subordinates. If crowds cheer, it is only your due."

Next day the heavy feeling of zero hour hung over me as I donned my full general's battle-dress and the famous black beret with its Armoured Corps badge. But Colonel Lester seemed satisfied with the effect when I reported to him for inspection. "There's just one last thing," he said, and handed me some khaki handkerchiefs marked with the General's initials, B.L.M. "Drop these about as if by accident wherever you think fit. In this game it's the little details that count." He gripped my hand hard, wished me luck and went away.

Quickly I set my beret at the correct angle and, followed by Brigadier Heywood and Captain Moore, my two personal aides, I led the way downstairs. Outside were three Army cars. A crowd had gathered round the one which flew Monty's pennant. A cheer went up when I got in, and as the car moved off and I gave them a brilliant Monty smile and the famous Monty salute, I heard shouts of "Good old Monty!" I smiled and saluted until the muscles of my face were stiff and my arm began to ache.

At Northolt airport there were more crowds, and near my plane stood a formidable array of high-ranking officers, some of whom knew Monty intimately. My heart was pounding like a piston, but with a violent effort I stepped briskly out of the car, smiling a little. Followed by Brigadier Heywood, I slowly walked along the ranks of the top brass, inspecting them, while they stood stiffly to attention. Then I went over to the crew of the aircraft.

"How are you, Slee?" I asked the pilot. "D'you think we shall have a good trip?" We exchanged a few words about the weather reports. Then, after inspecting the aircrew, I went up the gangway, turned to give everyone a final salute and at last entered the plane, greatly relieved to have got through the first scene successfully. (I later heard that none of the brass who saw me off had any suspicions about my identity; one of them who knew Monty well remarked that the old man looked very fit but a bit tired.)

Next morning the plane landed at Gibraltar and the curtain went up on another scene. In the background rose the famous Rock. Before me stood two groups of officers and a line of cars. Among the usual airport crowd were some Spanish workmen—several of them known enemy agents. I heard Brigadier Heywood saying, "Let as many people see you as possible," and then the doors of the plane slid open. I stood there a moment; in the dead silence I gave the Monty salute, then walked briskly down the gangway.

After the welcoming ceremonies I was driven through the streets of Gibraltar while crowds of Spanish civilians watched. There were more crowds at Government House when we drew up there. A guard of honor presented arms and General Sir Ralph Eastwood—Governor of Gibraltar and an old friend of Montgomery's—smiled and held out his hand. "Hullo, Monty, it's good to see you again."

I had been thoroughly briefed for this meeting, and knew that Monty always called Sir Ralph by his nickname. "How are you, Rusty?" I said in Monty's breezy tones. "You're looking very fit." I took him familiarly by the arm as we walked in.

Sir Ralph led me into his study, looked down the corridor, then shut the door carefully and in dead silence just stared at me. Then a smile spread over his face and he shook me warmly by the hand. "I can't get over it," he exclaimed. "Why, you *are* Monty! For a few moments I thought he had changed the plan and decided to come himself."

I was ushered to my room and ate breakfast there alone. Afterward I stepped idly to the window. Happening to glance upward, I noticed a slight movement on the roof of the adjoining building. A workman perched there was pointing something which looked very much like a rifle straight at me. I had a very bad moment, but when I looked more closely I realized that my fears were exaggerated. The man was not aiming a rifle; he was trying to examine me through a thin telescope!

An aide now conducted me again to the study, where Sir Ralph explained the next moves. "Twelve minutes from now you and I will take a walk in the gardens back of the house. Two prominent Spanish financiers, acquaintances of ours—I would hardly describe them as friends—are calling to look at some ancient Moroccan carpets we have here. By pure chance they will meet you as they pass through the gardens on their way in." Presently he glanced at his watch and led me toward the gardens, remarking, "I haven't enjoyed myself so much since I was a boy."

The sun blazed down from a clear sky as we strolled slowly between the flower beds, stopping at intervals to discuss some point of horticulture. Turning down a side path, we faced the left wing of the house and I saw that a party of workmen, on scaffolding, was repairing the walls. One of them was staring at me intently, but when I caught his eye he at once looked away and went on with his job. I recognized him as the man who earlier had peered at me through the telescope.

We continued our stroll until suddenly the iron gates of the garden clanged. Two men were coming toward us down the center path—clean-shaven Spaniards in their late 30's, dressed in dark suits.

"Don't be nervous, James," Sir Ralph whispered hoarsely as they drew near. "Just keep your head."

Pretending not to notice the two strangers, I began to talk about the War Cabinet and "Plan 303." The Governor touched me on the arm as if to caution me, and I broke off abruptly, registering surprise at their approach. Sir Ralph greeted them cordially and they bowed in the Spanish manner. I was intro-

duced, and both of them stood looking at me with evident awe
and respect. I was polite but aloof, and as I spoke I kept my
hands clasped behind me in Monty's characteristic manner.

One of the Spaniards, who looked as sinister as any spy in
thriller fiction, kept his snake's eyes fastened on me, while the
other pretended to be interested in what Sir Ralph was saying;
but I noticed that at odd moments his eyes traveled over every
inch of my figure. Both listened with ludicrous intentness to
my babble of talk about the weather, the flowers and the history
of Government House. When I judged they had seen enough of
me I said briskly: "Well, I only hope the weather holds, I have
a lot more flying in front of me." And I half turned away. At
once they took their leave of me, and Sir Ralph ushered them
into the house. It was all over very quickly, and yet in that brief
space of time the fate of those two spies and perhaps of many
thousands of our soldiers was profoundly changed.

As I heard later, these Spaniards were two of Hitler's cleverest agents, Gestapo-trained. As a result of MI 5's carefully
circulated rumors, they had been given faked papers and false
names in Berlin, and had then hastily entered Spanish society as
bankers and taken up residence in Gibraltar—all for the express
purpose of spying on me. They had also planted two underlings;
one, posing as a workman, had been employed on the buildings
of Government House; the other got a job at the airport. Each
of the four spies was to file a separate report giving every detail
that he had observed.

The Spaniards must have worked pretty fast. Two hours
after they left Government House, Hitler's representatives in
Madrid had the news that General Montgomery had arrived
in Gibraltar and was proceeding to Africa by air. Soon Berlin
received the frantic appeal: "At all costs discover nature of
Plan 303. Have you any information? Very urgent." And at
once the German counter-espionage department ordered its
men to concentrate on this problem.

My departure from Gibraltar was very much like my arrival.
Bayonets flashed in the sun and a flight of Spitfires came over
the airport, dipping their wings in salute. When the usual for-

malities were over I took Sir Ralph by the arm and we strolled up and down by the airport canteen, for it was here that the Gestapo agent was employed. Near the open canteen window I began faking an intensely preoccupied and urgent military dis- cussion. "Now about these harbor defenses, Rusty," I said. "I've told the PM that C4 is perfectly safe. But I want the naval end tied up so that the armor can be shipped without any time lag." Then, pointing across the bay, "If we take about three o'clock right of the cape, the engineers can alter it to fit Plan 303." I continued in this vein, all of it arrant twaddle, and at one point I could almost swear the Governor gave me a suspicion of a wink.

My next stop was Algiers, where carefully planted rumors were circulating that Monty was arriving on an important mis- sion—perhaps to form an Anglo-American army for invading the south of France. At the airport I was greeted by members of General Maitland Wilson's staff, after which I made the usual inspections. Nearby a big polyglot crowd of civilians, lured by the calculated leaks about my "top-secret visit," were waiting to catch a glimpse of General Montgomery.

Among them were two Italians, ostensibly pro-Ally but known to be employed by the Gestapo, and a mysterious French major who was their immediate boss. The major had turned up in Algiers the week before posing as a member of the French Intelligence; but, as our people knew, he was really an ace enemy agent. Almost immediately he had expressed a strong de- sire to meet Monty if he should happen to come to Algiers, and it was now arranged to gratify this wish.

Before we left the airfield the French major was introduced to me by a colonel on General Wilson's staff. I have seldom met a more sinister-looking man. With his glittering dark eyes, his pale face across which ran a livid scar, and his cruel mouth, he looked capable of anything. I couldn't help watching his move- ments suspiciously, lest he be planning to shoot me. But we merely shook hands and exchanged polite greetings without incident.

An American colonel accompanied me into Algiers from the airport. When we entered our car, the beautiful blonde driver, who wore a marvelously cut Wac uniform, saluted and at once asked for my autograph. Having foreseen just such an emergency in my contacts with the autograph-conscious Americans, Colonel Lester had provided me with photographs of the General signed in Monty's own hand. Without a smile—for Monty's aversion to women in the theater of war was well known— I handed one of the photos to the Wac, remarking coldly, "I hope this one will do."

As long as I live I shall never forget that drive from the airport to Algiers. My American escort had been warned that an attempt might be made on Monty's life and, as no troops could be spared to guard the 12-mile route, it was decided to drive hell-for-leather and hope for the best. So we shot out of the airport like a stick of rockets and, with sirens screaming, maintained a headlong pace all the way to Algiers. All through this hectic drive I kept up a Monty conversation with the colonel— who, of course, was in the know—for the benefit of our lovely driver. I was relieved when we finally turned through large gates and pulled up before a white stone mansion, General Wilson's GHQ. As its welcome doors closed behind me, the curtain came down on another completed scene.

The next few days passed in a sort of recurring dream—landings, official receptions, guards of honor, bogus talks on high strategy; crowds of civilian spectators, no doubt with enemy agents among them; the streets lined with cheering troops. I had dreaded most of all the prospect of meeting high-ranking officers at close quarters, since I could not hope to keep up a conversation on highly technical military affairs. But MI 5 had planned my tour so cleverly that I always took my meals in private and was carefully prevented from meeting officers (except the few who were in on the plot) who were likely to know the General personally.

I was, however, continually thrown in the path of enemy agents. I remember Brigadier Heywood bringing up one of them, an elderly civilian whose goatee, shabby black suit and big sombrero made him look like a broken-down tragedian. "Excuse me, sir," Heywood said, "Professor Salvadore X— would take it as a great favor if you would allow him to pay his respects. As an archaeologist he is, of course, famous. And he's a loyal Italian," he added, seeing my dubious expression. For a moment I wondered why I should waste my time talking to an archaeologist. But I knew that Heywood had been with MI 5 for many years, that he had been specially chosen for this ticklish job, and that he never did anything without good reason. So I exchanged a few words with the Professor and when he had bowed himself out of my presence and withdrawn a few yards I turned to Heywood and began a rather loud discussion of cryptic military plans.

As the days went by I slipped into my role so completely that to all intents and purposes I *was* General Montgomery. Even when alone I found myself playing the part.

Once, just as we were about to land at an airport, Heywood asked, "How are the nerves?" In the precise Monty tone I snapped: "Nerves, Heywood? Don't talk rot!"

"Sorry, sir," he replied with a perfectly straight face.

At the end of a week I returned to Algiers knowing that I had carried out my task without any serious mishap. So far as we knew, nobody had doubted that I was General Montgomery.

D-day was now only a few days away and my job was done. I drove up to General Wilson's headquarters in a final blaze of glory, changed back into my lieutenant's uniform and was quietly smuggled out the back door. My likeness to the General had now become an embarrassment, for until the invasion was actually launched there was always the danger that my secret might leak out. So the following afternoon I was stealthily put on a plane to Cairo—the only city nearby which was big enough to swallow me without a trace—and kept there under wraps until after D-day.

For a long time I wondered how useful my efforts had been. Not until after the war was I told how the deception had helped mislead the enemy, drawing away Rommel's armored divisions, and so contributing to the success of the invasion.

I also learned later how potentially dangerous the mission had been. When the news of Monty's intended journey to the Middle

East first reached Berlin, the German High Command had ordered my plane shot down en route; or, if this plan miscarried, for Monty to be assassinated somewhere in Spain or Africa. But at the last moment the Germans decided to make sure that I really *was* Monty; and when they had satisfied themselves on this point, the Führer intervened to save my life. Hitler ordered that Monty was on no account to be killed until they discovered just where he was intending to launch his invasion. And this the Germans never did discover until the dawn of June 6.

The Golden Sphinx: The Army's Counter-Intelligence

By Thomas M. Johnson

Popular in military circles during World War II was the story of a general in the Pacific area who, when told that his CIC detachment was reporting for duty, exclaimed: "CIC? What in hell are they?" It could have happened. The Army's Counter Intelligence Corps was long the least-understood part of G-2— Army's intelligence organization.

Organized in 1942 to succeed the old CIP (Corps of Intelligence Police), the CIC quickly became a unique force of soldier spy-hunters. By intercepting thousands of spies and saboteurs, foiling scores of dangerous plots, the CIC saved us countless lives and dollars during World War II. General MacArthur said that the corps shortened the war in the Pacific by six months.

A Filipino CIC agent spent three years in Manila disguised as a peddler. He sold fruit to Japanese officers and collected information which was radioed to MacArthur. When the Americans landed, the "peddler" greeted them with a map showing enemy troop dispositions. Then he ripped off the sole of his shoe, disclosing his CIC credentials.

The corps included at various times a forestry expert, a dance-band leader, a Syrian rug dealer, a poet. One difficult investigation required a man with 13 qualifications, among them that he be a Negro and an Elk and speak French. CIC produced him.

One anthropologist was sent to persuade the natives of wild northern Australia not to kill Allied airmen or Japanese spies but to bring them in. Knowing the aborigines' love of shiny things, he distributed large metal sunflowers inscribed "Vote for Landon" and was virtually adopted by the tribesmen.

During the war the only known member of a spy ring operating from an Italian dive in Melbourne was the tavern proprietor. If he were arrested, the others would scatter, then resume from a new hideout. So Sergeant Frank Colucci, in civil life a Ph.D.,

determined to get himself accepted by Melbourne's Little Italy. For a week nothing was heard from him. Scouting the neighborhood, a CIC colonel found his agent, in dirty uniform, unshaven, stinking of stale wine, outside the pub.

The officer put on an act. "Are you a soldier or a drunken bum?" he demanded loudly.

"Who in hell wants to know?" the sergeant retorted, lurching into the pub.

Through the open door the officer roared after him, "I'll be back with the MP's to get you, you—deserter!"

That night the colonel's telephone rang and a low voice said, "Thanks! They were a little suspicious, but that brawl with you fixed me up." Colucci was soon accepted into the Italian ring, and before long all the spies were gathered in.

In Eritrea in 1943 we had a big air base about which the local Italian espionage organization was very curious. Their headquarters was a hotel whose Italian-American proprietor had papers proving the U.S. Army did not want him because of his Fascist leanings. Actually, he was a CIC agent, and all of the rooms in his hotel were equipped with microphones. This spy trap was so valuable that CIC didn't spring it until the mob turned from espionage—which CIC could limit and direct—to sabotage.

One CIC agent, screening refugees returning to newly liberated Manila, stopped a fat, barefooted youth, apparently a Filipino. "Explain those big toes," he challenged. "They spread out as if you'd been wearing Japanese Army sneakers with the big toe separate." A search revealed a pistol, a grenade and sabotage matches hidden in his clothing, together with a Japanese questionnaire with blanks for the number of American troops, tanks and trucks the spy had seen, and their location. He confessed also that he was reconnoitering for others who were plotting to kill General MacArthur.

All counter-intelligence organizations relied heavily on interception of enemy radio messages. Ships leaving Africa's Gold Coast with cargos of manganese, indispensable to American steel manufacture, were often sunk by waiting Nazi submarines. A clue to the information leak came when British monitors detected a wireless transmitter sending information to the Nazis from Accra. A "fix"—two listening posts taking bearings on the suspicious transmissions—pointed to Accra's only white dentist, an anti-British Irishman. CIC dispatched an agent to have his teeth examined—and to complain about the trouble Americans were having with their ore ships. He gave the dentist fake names and departure schedules. An hour later the interceptors heard the suspected radio flash the fake information to the Nazis. The dentist was seized, and messages in his code were used to lure the submarines to a rendezvous, where they were sunk.

The most delicate trick in counter-espionage is to catch a spy and "double" him—turn him around to send misleading information to the enemy. This can be done only by convincing the spy that his life depends upon his ability to double-cross his former master. His radio messages must be concocted with utmost skill, combining harmless truth with the desired falsehood. And the "doubled" operator must himself send them, for the receiver, knowing his "fist," will immediately detect an impostor. Also, the "doubled" operator must be watched closely, lest he slip in a prearranged code warning: "This stuff is phony. They're making me send it!"

CIC's most successful turn-around was the Italian spy Alpha Primo, who in May 1944 flashed word to his former bosses that the British Eighth Army was preparing to attack Italy's east coast. As a result, the Germans massed reserves there. A few days later the American Fifth Army, reinforced by British troops, staged its all-out offensive in the west-coast sector and ultimately plunged through to Rome.

D-day security was perhaps CIC's most trying job and its biggest victory. The Nazis never learned the time and place of the Normandy landing until it had happened, and the American part of the big secret was kept primarily by the work of 2000 CIC agents in the British Isles. They were tireless in plugging possible leaks, in silencing careless talk of GI's and officers in pubs and night clubs. They even intercepted secret invasion papers mailed accidentally to a woman in Chicago. They also assisted in the quiet sequestration of a carpenter who innocently popped into a room whose walls were papered with top-secret invasion maps.

CIC won many successes in battlefield detective work by its "ragpicking" operations. The term covered everything from searching a Japanese cave for papers to seizing the files at German-Italian Armistice Commission headquarters in North Africa—a feat accomplished by CIC agents amid splintering glass and flying brick from American and French shellfire. This exploit yielded valuable information on German intelligence methods, locations of supply depots which our Army found most useful, and lists of Frenchmen who had collaborated with the Germans.

Near Oran, CIC caught a cadaverous Nazi who possessed maps showing all the Vichy French minefields in North Africa. That find saved so many American lives and so speeded our advance that thereafter CIC agents regularly accompanied attacking troops under fire. In Sicily, CIC men captured a map showing the whereabouts of every Italian troop unit in Sicily and Italy.

In the Pacific, CIC's ragpicking first paid off in the Admiralties. Landing with the troops on what was intended as a hit-run raid, CIC agent Barney Strachan found documents revealing that only a relative handful of Japanese held the islands. General MacArthur saw the papers and said, "Hang on!" And the islands were captured at little cost.

One of the corps' toughest jobs was to teach Americans security. Lonely officers who confided military secrets to sympathetic dance partners were so dangerous that when CIC suspected one it assigned an attractive Wac or nurse to date him. If he blabbed, he was transferred to some less sensitive post. CIC also helped postal censors detect and delete the numerous passages, unintentionally dangerous, whereby soldiers tried to tell wives and sweethearts their whereabouts in private code.

The emblem of these dedicated, anonymous men of the Army's Counter Intelligence Corps, appropriately enough, includes a golden sphinx—for silence.

The Idol of San Vittore

By Indro Montanelli
Translation and adaptation by Erwin C. Lessner

My story begins on that day in March 1944 when His Excellency General Della Rovere, intimate of Marshal Badoglio and technical adviser to Britain's General Alexander, was brought to San Vittore Prison and put in the cell across from mine. The Italian Underground was attempting, at that time, to disrupt the flow of German reserves to the fighting front in the south. The General, I learned, had been captured by the Germans in a northern province when he was put ashore by an Allied submarine to assume command of guerrilla operations there. I was impressed by his aristocratic bearing. Even Franz, the brutal German overseer of the prison, stood at attention before him.

Of all the German-operated "confession" factories in Italy, San Vittore was the worst. Captured Italian Underground fighters who stood up under primary "routine" questioning were brought here. Then Gestapo Commissar Mueller and his bunch of picked SS men—by methods now celebrated in the annals of refined torture—usually squeezed desired information out of even the toughest customers.

Six months had passed since my own arrest. I had been "interrogated" several times, and I was exhausted and discouraged. I sometimes wondered how much longer I could hold out. Then, to my astonishment one day, Ceraso, one of the Italian guards, unlocked my cell door and told me that General Della Rovere wished to see me.

The General's door was unlocked, as always. Moreover, he had a cot, whereas the rest of us slept on bare planks. Immac-

ulately groomed, monocle in his right eye, he greeted me courteously. "Captain Montanelli? I knew before I landed that you
were here. His Majesty's government is keenly interested in your
fate. We are confident that even when you fall before a German
firing squad you will fulfill your duty, your most elementary duty
as an officer. But make yourself at ease, pray." Only then did I
realize that I had been standing at attention—heels touching,
thumbs against trouser seams.

"We officers all lead provisional lives, do we not?" he asked.
"An officer is, so to speak, a bridegroom of the Goddess of
Death." He paused, polishing his monocle with a white handker-
chief, and it occurred to me that names often reflected the bear-
ers' personality. Della Rovere means "of the oak." Here, surely,
was a man of solid timber.

"They have already sentenced me," he continued. "How
about you?"

"Not yet, Your Excellency," I replied, almost apologetically.

"They will," he said. "The Germans are rigorous when they
expect a confession, but they are also chivalrous in their esteem
for those who refuse to confess. You have not talked. Well done!
That means that you will be honored by being shot through the
chest, not through the back. I urge you to persist in your silence.
But should you undergo torture—I don't mean to question your
moral strength, but there are limits to physical endurance—I
suggest that you give them just one name: mine. Tell them that,
whatever you did, you were acting under my orders. . . . By the
way, what are the charges against you?"

I told him everything—unreservedly. His Excellency listened
like a father confessor. From time to time he nodded approv-
ingly. "Your case is as clear-cut as mine," he said when I had
finished. "We were both apprehended carrying out official
orders. Our only remaining duty is to die fighting on the field of
honor. It should be easy to die decently."

When Ceraso was locking me back in my cell I implored him
to send me a barber the following day. And that night I folded
my trousers and creased them on the window lattice before
stretching myself out on my plank to sleep.

During the following days I saw many prisoners visit the General's cell. When they came out, they all seemed to hold themselves more erectly, they no longer looked dejected. Noise and disorder in our isolated sector abated. No. 215, who had rent the air with cries for his wife and children, fell silent and showed great composure when he was called for interrogation. Ceraso told me that after talking with the General almost everyone asked for the barber, and for a comb and soap. Prison guards took to shaving daily. Even Mueller, when he inspected the place, grudgingly commended the general improvement in discipline and dignity.

Best of all, the "confession factory" no longer produced confessions. The men persisted in a stubborn silence. From his own great store of courage Della Rovere gave them strength to endure. From his own experiences under arrest he gave them invaluable advice. "The most dangerous hours are in the early afternoon," he would warn them. "The mere longing for distraction could make you confess." Or, "Don't stare at the walls. Close your eyes from time to time and the walls will lose their power to choke you." He reprimanded them for neglecting their appearance: "Neatness builds morale." He knew that the military formalities they observed with him strengthened their pride. And he never stopped reminding them of their duty toward Italy.

After a while a rumor began to sweep through the prison that the General was a counter-spy, a German stool pigeon. The Italian guards, even though drawn from the dregs of Mussolini's old regime, felt there were limits to the humiliations they would take. They agreed among themselves to watch the General constantly; if he turned out to be a stool pigeon, they were determined to strangle him.

Next morning Della Rovere received No. 203, a major who was supposed to have more than the usual amount of information and who had not talked. Ceraso lingered near the cell door, and other Italian guards watched nearby. "You will undergo extreme torture," they heard the General say to the major. "You must confess nothing. Keep your mind blank, force yourself to believe that you know nothing. Even thinking of the secrets you are guarding might bring them to your lips." The major listened, ashen-faced, as the General said to him what he had said to me: "If you are driven to speak, tell them that whatever you did you did on my orders."

That afternoon an apologetic Ceraso brought His Excellency a few roses, a gift of the Italian prison guards. The General accepted the flowers graciously; he seemed not to have the slightest notion that he had been distrusted.

One morning the Germans came for Colonels P. and F. Before being led to the courtyard, the officers were granted one last wish—to say farewell to the General. I saw them at his cell door, standing at attention. I couldn't hear what the General said to them, but both officers smiled. He shook their hands—something I'd never seen him do. Then, as if suddenly aware of the Germans present, he stiffened, raised his hand and saluted. The men returned the salute, turned on their heels and walked to their deaths. We learned later that both shouted "Long live the King!" as they faced the firing squad.

That afternoon I was questioned again. Commissar Mueller told me that my fate would depend on the results of this interrogation. If I were to persist in my silence . . . I stared at him with wide-open eyes, yet I could hear nothing; I couldn't even see him. I saw instead the pale, composed faces of Colonels P. and F., the smiling face of His Excellency. After the Germans had questioned me in vain for two hours the interrogation came to an end. I was not tortured, but even if I had been, I think I would have been able to conceal everything. On my way back I asked Ceraso to let me stop at His Excellency's cell.

The General put aside the book he was reading and looked at me searchingly as I stood at attention. Then, before I spoke, he said, "Yes, that's what I expected you to do; you couldn't have done differently." He rose. "I cannot put all I would say into words, Captain Montanelli, but since there is no one else to report on us, let this upright Italian guard be a witness to what we say in these our last days. Let him listen to every word. I am well satisfied, Captain. I am pleased indeed. Bravo!"

That night I was truly alone in this world. But my beloved

country seemed nearer and dearer and more real than ever before.

I never saw the General again. Only after the liberation did I learn about his end. One of the survivors of Fossoli told me the story.

Fossoli was a notorious extermination camp where the ways of dying were intricate and of great variety. When General Della Rovere was transferred there by armored train, together with hundreds of others, he maintained his dignity. Throughout the trip he sat on a heap of knapsacks the others had gathered to provide him with a couch. He refused to rise when a Gestapo officer inspected the train. Even when the officer slapped him across the face and shouted, "I know you, you swine, Bertoni," he remained unperturbed. Why should he explain to this blundering German that his name was not Bertoni but Della Rovere, that he was a general of an Army corps, intimate friend of Badoglio and technical adviser to Alexander? Unruffled, he picked up his monocle and squeezed it on again. The German walked away, cursing.

At Fossoli the General no longer enjoyed the privileges granted him in San Vittore. He was quartered with everyone else in a single barrack and, like everyone else, he was put to work. His fellow prisoners sought to spare him the lowliest chores, took turns substituting for him. But he never tried to evade his tasks, difficult as they might be for a man who was no longer young. And at night he reminded his comrades that they were not convicts but officers. Facing his glaring monocle and listening to his voice, they stood a little straighter.

The massacre at Fossoli on June 22, 1944, may have been in reprisal for the Allied victories near Genoa. At any rate, on orders from Milan, 65 names were drawn from a total of 400 inmates. As a Lieutenant Tito read the list, the doomed men had to step forward from the ranks. When he called the name Bertoni, nobody stepped forward. "Bertoni!" he roared, staring at Della Rovere. His Excellency did not budge.

Did Tito want to show indulgence to a doomed man? No one could say. In any case, he suddenly smiled. "All right, all right," he said. "Della Rovere, if you wish." Everyone held his breath, watching the General. He pulled his monocle from his pocket and with a remarkably steady hand squeezed it against his right eye. "*General* Della Rovere, if you please," he said calmly as he joined the waiting group.

The 65 were handcuffed and led to the wall. All were blindfolded except His Excellency, who steadfastly refused, and they granted him his wish. While four machine guns were brought into firing position, His Excellency stepped forward, his bearing proud and determined. "Gentlemen, officers," he called in a firm, resounding voice. "As we face the ultimate sacrifice, may our thoughts turn faithfully toward our beloved country. *Long live the King!*"

Tito shouted, "Fire!" and the machine guns rattled.

The true story of General Della Rovere, which I learned after his death, is one of heroism and an impersonation almost beyond belief. For the idol of San Vittore was no general. Neither Badoglio nor Alexander had ever heard of him. And his name was not Della Rovere.

He was one Bertoni, a native of Genoa, a thief and confidence man with a long prison record. The Germans had arrested him for some petty crime and during the questioning had realized that the man·was a superb natural actor. They believed that his unscrupulous outlook coupled with his talent for acting would make him an excellent agent for tricking information out of guerrilla prisoners.

Bertoni was ready for a deal. He would do as requested in return for preferred treatment in prison and early release. The Germans invented the Della Rovere story and coached him in his part. When Bertoni was sent to San Vittore, he asked for and was granted a brief period during which he would gain the trust of the men he would later victimize. But Bertoni was shrewder than they knew; he was determined to trick no one but the Germans!

And then came the amazing transformation. Acting General Della Rovere's part, Bertoni *became* Della Rovere. He undertook a superhuman task—to make San Vittore confession-proof and its inmates strong enough to meet their fate. And by his commanding presence, his impeccable grooming, his high courage and faith, he brought a new dignity and sense of personal worth to the poor devils who were incarcerated there.

But, finally, he knew his time was running out. Commissar Mueller grew more and more impatient with his delays: why weren't the confessions coming through? When "Della Rovere" spoke to me that last day in his cell and asked the guard to be a witness, he knew that it was all over, that this was the only way the outside world might learn his story, the only way that Italy might know he had kept his trust.

On June 22, 1945, the first anniversary of the massacre at Fossoli, I stood in the Cathedral of Milan and watched the Cardinal-Prince-Archbishop of that city consecrate the coffins of the heroes of Fossoli. The Cardinal knew whose body lay in the coffin marked Della Rovere. He knew, too, that no one had a better right to the title of general than the occupant of that coffin, the former thief and jailbird Bertoni.

The Code Books
of the Deep

Condensed from the book Clear the Decks!

By Rear Admiral Daniel V. Gallery, USN

As commander of an Atlantic task group in 1944, I took part in one of the most spectacular exploits of World War II— the capture of a German U-boat. Not since 1815 had the U.S. Navy boarded and captured an enemy man-of-war on the high seas. In fact, so unprecedented was the move that first reports of our success were greeted with incredulity in Washington, especially when they heard that we were bringing our prize home on the end of a towline. (See photograph on page 343.)

Our ship was the *Guadalcanal*, a homely baby flat-top of 11,000 tons, nicknamed the *Can Do*. We had four little Nazi swastikas painted on our bridge, the last a proud emblem of our biggest haul to date—the sinking of the crack German sub U-515.

Hashing over the battle with the U-515, we remarked on one thing: *The U-Boat didn't fight back;* she didn't blow herself up. The captain and crew, when brought to bay, had just one urge— to save their skins. We asked ourselves: *Why then couldn't we board and capture a submarine we had fetched up from the depths?* Why couldn't the cry "Away boarders!"—never heard in the modern Navy—ring out again?

When a cornered sub surfaced, sometimes she came up fighting. Other times the hatches popped open and small black figures plunged over the side. But you couldn't stand on ceremony and wait for the enemy to initiate negotiations leading to a possible surrender. Your destroyers charged in at full speed, zigzagging wildly and blazing away with everything they had. Your planes swooped down with machine guns snarling. Depth charges, rockets, armor-piercing projectiles and torpedoes ripped into the surfaced sub from all directions. Maybe that U-boat had come up to surrender, but you couldn't afford to jump to any conclusions; the penalty for being wrong was too severe.

A wounded sub within five miles of you was an extremely dangerous animal. Her torpedoes, fired just as the crew abandoned the sub, could turn a fine ship into a blazing shambles. So we well knew that attempting to board and capture a sub would be dangerous business. But if we could get her code books, it would be worth taking long chances. The Naval Communications Office in Washington could then set a watch on the Nazi submarine frequency and read their operational orders. This would be like sticking your head into the opponent's huddle in a football game. The Nazi radio operators at naval headquarters in Berlin would all become U.S. intelligence agents!

At our next departure conference I outlined my plan. The Washington experts were skeptical. But we finally agreed that there was no need to fire lethal stuff at a sub after she had surfaced, because the Nazis would pull the plug on it themselves.

Our plan was to get the crew off with small fire, then board the sub ourselves and put the "plug" back in.

On the morning of Sunday, June 4, we were 100 miles off Cape Blanco, French West Africa, when suddenly the radio loudspeaker announced: "U.S.S. *Chatelain* to Task Group Commander. I have a possible sound contact." All sound contacts are treated with respect, so the *Guadalcanal* swung away at full speed while the two nearest destroyers broke off to assist the *Chatelain*. A carrier right at the scene of a sound contact is like an old lady in a barroom brawl. She has no business there.

Now the skipper of the *Chatelain* was reporting: "Contact evaluated as sub. Am starting attack." Our two Wildcat fighters, which had streaked over to the *Chatelain's* position, circled overhead until they sighted the long dark shape of the submarine running fully submerged. Then the *Chatelain*, following directions from the air, swung around and delivered her Sunday punch of depth charges. As the depth charges were subsiding, Ensign J. W. Cadle, flying one of the Wildcats, clamped down on his transmitter to shout, "You've struck oil! Sub is surfacing!"

Just 12½ minutes after the destroyer's original report, the sinister black hull hove in sight. As the sub broke surface, the *Chatelain*, *Pillsbury* and *Jenks*, according to plan, opened fire— but only with their small-caliber anti-aircraft guns. From above, the Wildcats swooped down, their .50-caliber machine guns blazing and sending torrents of hot steel ripping across the sub's deck. All this gunfire was harmless so far as the pressure hull of the U-boat was concerned.

We found out later that the Nazis were just sitting down to Sunday dinner when the depth-charge explosions dumped everybody into the bilges under a heap of crockery and food. Convinced the boat was sinking, the Nazis rushed for the escape hatch when the stunned skipper gave the order to surface, scuttle and abandon ship. We fished them all out of the water eventually, and they watched the rest of the show grimly from the deck of the *Chatelain*.

As the sub surfaced I thought, "This is where we come in." I grabbed the mike, and the ancient call, "*Away all boarding*

parties!" boomed out for the first time over modern loudspeakers. Our crazy plan worked to perfection. The Germans
got off so fast they didn't even stop the engines, but left the sub
circling at eight knots. Whaleboats plopped into the water.
Lieutenant A. L. David from the *Pillsbury* was the first to leap
aboard the sub.

David and his party had every reason to believe that they
would be greeted by a blast of machine-gun bullets when they
started down the hatch. They also knew that German subs were
usually fitted with 14 time-fused demolition charges—and they
couldn't read the German clocks. But they plunged down the
conning-tower hatch nevertheless, ready to fight it out with the
Nazis—only to find, to their amazement, that the boat was all
theirs. All theirs, that is, if she didn't blow up! (David was later
given the Medal of Honor, one of two awarded in the Battle
of the Atlantic. His helpers got Navy Crosses.)

In the main control room the boys found a six-inch stream of
water pouring into the hull through an open sea connection. A
few more minutes and she would have sunk, but the boarders
found the missing cover, slapped it back in place and stopped
the water.

The *Guadalcanal* now signaled, "Stop engines and we will take
her in tow." As soon as the motors subsided, the sub started to
submerge, stern first, and we lost no time in pulling alongside
and passing a tow wire to our lads. The U-boat's ugly snout,
with its four loaded torpedo tubes, was almost touching the side
of our ship. I said a fervent prayer: "Dear Lord, I've got a bunch
of inquisitive young lads on that submarine. Please don't let any
of them monkey with the firing switch." As we started off with
our prize in tow, the sub's stern came up again.

The boarding parties worked fast, disconnecting electric leads
from demolition charges, looking for booby traps and passing
up on deck all secret papers so that we would have something
to show in case we still lost the sub.

Though our maverick was securely roped, she was not broken
to the halter. Instead of towing meekly astern, she wanted to
circle to the right. I suspected her rudder was jammed, and this

fact, coupled with a report from the boys that they'd found a booby trap, made me decide to go aboard myself. As self-designated "officer in charge of booby traps," I itched for an excuse to get on her, and here was a legitimate one. I found the suspected trap attached to the watertight door of the sub's after torpedo room in such a manner that the door could not be opened without springing it. We had to get into that room in order to manipulate the hand steering gear. Correct bomb-disposal protocol called for clearing everyone else out of the boat while I operated on the suspected mechanism, but time was short, and, besides, it's nice to have company when you're doing a job like that. So, with a couple of our boarders anxiously kibitzing, I carefully sprang the trap. Broad grins spread across all faces as we eased the door open.

When I climbed back out of the escape hatch I saw that our hard-working painter had been busy. Daubed in big red letters on the conning tower was our sub's new name, *Can Do, Junior*. We soon shortened this and she became *Junior* to all hands.

Back on the *Guadalcanal*, we hoisted the traditional broom at our masthead (Navy signal for "Have made a clean sweep") and squared away for Bermuda.

Washington clamped a super-duper top-secret label on our news. Addressing the crew on the subject of security, I pointed out that if we could keep the capture secret it could be one of the turning points of the war. We had five of the acoustic torpedoes which had been raising hell with our ships: our technical people would soon know how to counter them. But, more important than that, we had the Nazi code books and it was absolutely vital to prevent word of this capture from reaching Germany because the Germans would immediately change the code if it did.

"There is no use whatever," I said, "in having a souvenir unless you can show it around and brag about it. So, all those having souvenirs will turn them in tomorrow and no questions will be asked."

Next day the executive officer was inundated with the damnedest collection of junk you've ever seen. I don't know how the boys had time to close valves, pull wires off time bombs and still collect that mountain of stuff. I know most of them would rather have turned in their right hands than those Lugers, binoculars, cameras and officers' caps.

We arrived in Bermuda on June 19 and the task group subsequently received the coveted Presidential Unit Citation. I was especially proud of the way those boys kept our great secret, particularly since we were all just full of the best story of our lives when we got back to the States. The secret was so well kept, in fact, that some of the histories of the war don't even mention it yet.

When the U-505 code books reached Washington, our experts were able to watch U-boat frequencies and read their messages as easily as if they were written in plain English. We got possession of every chart, publication, general order and code book that an operating submarine carried. Although the Nazis changed their codes periodically, the key to the changes was in the code books too. From the point of view of Naval Intelligence, it was the greatest windfall of the war.

"Baggy Pants"

By William E. Brougher, Brigadier General, USA, Retired

It was two o'clock of a June morning in 1944 when suddenly our prison barracks came ablaze with light. In an instant Japanese officers and guards were everywhere. It was a surprise inspection; we would have no opportunity to hide, destroy or otherwise dispose of anything that might be considered contraband or incriminating. As we groggily stood at attention, they ransacked our belongings and took any papers or books they found.

I was thoroughly alarmed. In the two years since my capture I had been scribbling down events, thoughts, feelings in a series of notebooks. I had even put together a little book of verse, harmless enough on the surface, but reflecting the grim experiences of prison life. To write had become an obsession with me, an absorbing interest, something to keep my hands busy, my mind occupied. In conditions of degradation and wretchedness it was my way of holding on to sanity.

It was a reckless pastime. General Jonathan M. Wainwright, who was a prisoner in the same camp, warned me of the risk I was taking in putting such things on paper. Our captors were extremely quick to resent anything we did or said that was uncomplimentary to them. And their resentment frequently took the form of violent reprisals. Naturally there was much in my pathetic scribblings that was considerably less than praise for the Japanese.

As I saw my notebooks carried off, I knew I was in for a rough time. From that moment on I trembled every time I caught sight of the camp commandant or of his lieutenant, whom we called "Baggy Pants."

Baggy Pants was the incarnation of everything we despised about our barbed-wire existence—the bad food, filth, punishments, the very humiliation of having been captured in the first place. A big hulk of a man, he wore his pants bagged down over the top of his boots and had a kind of shuffling gait. He spoke English fairly well, and we suspected he was on to our familiar reference to him.

It wasn't long before the Japanese began summoning the prisoners whose papers they had taken. Being extremely methodical, they started with men whose names began with A, then worked into the B's. A British Army brigadier whose papers turned up something our captors didn't like was thrown into solitary confinement on bread and water for three days. A U.S. Army colonel was terrifyingly beaten, then ordered to return each day for more of the same. It wouldn't be long before my name was reached.

To quiet my anxiety I spent as much time as possible in the postage-stamp-size garden I had been allowed to cultivate inside the prison compound. Only 10 by 20 feet, that garden was now my sole diversion—and a great source of pride. My 12 tomato plants were eight feet tall and heavy with ripe fruit. My white radishes, cabbage, kohlrabi might have taken prizes at a county fair back in the States.

I was hoeing around the roots of the tomato plants one afternoon when I heard a shuffle behind me. A voice asked crisply: "Your name is Brougher?" It was Baggy Pants! I was sure my turn for punishment had come! I dropped my hoe, stiffened my arms at my side and bowed low in the approved manner. Baggy Pants had a large envelope in his hand, and his face was intensely serious.

"Yes, I am Brougher," I answered.

"I have your books here," he said. "I read." He pulled one of my notebooks from the envelope, his expression still severe. "You write poetry?" he asked.

Here was something new in the way of booby traps. "Well," I answered cautiously, "I try to write verse."

"You write poetry a rong time?" he asked. Like many Japanese, he usually substituted *r* for *l*.

"Well," I said, trying to appear casual, "I've worked at it off and on most of my life."

He opened the notebook and moved close to me. "You write some very beautifu' things. Are you great poet in America?"

I searched for the note of sarcasm in his voice, the smirk of ridicule on his face. But he was completely serious. "Oh, no," I assured him. "I'm no poet. I'm a soldier. I merely fool around with verse. Did you really read my pieces?"

"Yes, yes, I read many times," replied Baggy Pants.

What was this leading to? I would open my mouth and put my foot in it for sure. But I could not hold back the eager question that every would-be poet must ask of one who has read his verse: "Did you—did you like any of my pieces?"

"Yes," said Baggy Pants. "Some pieces I rike very much. I no judge poetry, you know, but I rike."

By this time I was peering over his shoulder at my notebook, forgetting that I was supposed to remain at attention with heels together. "Which piece did you like?"

Baggy Pants' tough face actually smiled. "I rike best the one you write about your wife. And this one you write about famiry. This one I have—how you say—memorize?"

He had the book open at a small verse containing only 38 words. Without looking at the text he began to recite it. Its sentiment suffered little by being spoken in his peculiar English. But he faltered after a few lines and handed me the book. "My Engrish no good to read poetry. You prease read it to me."

My defenses were completely down. Here I was, a poet with an appreciative audience! Never was there a greater thrill than mine as I stood in my drab prison garb, flanked by tomato plants and cabbages, and read my composition:

> When twilight falls and silence calls
> To evening prayer,
> Fair forms appear and hover near
> About my chair.
> Soft hands entwine themselves in mine,
> Lips touch my face;
> Then miles are not, and time's forgot,
> As souls embrace.

"That good! That good!" applauded Baggy Pants. "I not see my famiry now rong time. I rike you piece."

"You like poetry?" I said, still baffled.

"Oh, yes, yes. We Japanese rove poetry. The Emperor make it. Great Japanese make poems."

I was in this deep now, unmindful of the dread reason for his visit. "Well, that's most interesting," I said. "Have you maybe written some yourself?"

Baggy Pants fumbled and blushed like a bashful schoolboy. "Yes, I try," he admitted hesitantly. "I try, but I no good. I not make nice poetry rike you. I no good poet."

All caution gone, I took the final fatal plunge. "Would you, perhaps, show me one of your verses?"

"You read my poem?" he asked with surprised and humble pleasure. "It no good—no good. But maybe you make better transration in Engrish?"

He handed me a sheet of paper with a few lines typed on it. I read it aloud:

> The moon is high in the autumn sky,
> The light is like silver snow on the grass,
> My body is weary with much striving,
> My soul is at peace.

My voice broke slightly as I spoke the last line. I was not far from choking up. "Why, Bag—" I stopped short.

He laughed. "Baggy Pants! Yes, I know. Okay, okay, Baggy Pants, yes." He shrugged and looked down at his trousers. Then he looked at me. "You rike my poem?"

"It's beautiful," I said, and I meant it. "Don't change it."

"Thank you, thank you." He carefully folded the paper, put it back in his pocket and handed me the envelope containing my confiscated scribblings. "Your papers—Genera'."

As he spoke my title, he made an instinctive motion as if to stiffen up and salute. Then he turned and started to walk away, but paused and came back.

"You have nice vegetab'es. We Japanese rove beautifu' garden. Beautifu' garden; beautifu' poetry. You shake hand?"

I would. And I did.

The Phantom Army

By Blake Clark

The nine-o'clock BBC newscast on the evening of June 1, 1944, was followed by a dry British voice quoting a line from a poem by Paul Verlaine: "*Les sanglots longs des violons de l'automne*" (The long sobs of the violins of autumn). On June 5 the next line was broadcast: "*Blessent mon coeur d'une langueur monotone*" (Wound my heart with a monotonous languor).

Then followed coded messages that meant nothing to most listeners, including the Germans; but for more than 200,000 armed Frenchmen they were long-awaited secret calls to action. That night, before a single Allied soldier had set foot in Normandy, all over France bridges collapsed, dams burst, steel rails leaped from ties, locomotives raced down wrong tracks, trees crashed across roads, flames rose from fuel dumps, telephone lines plummeted to earth.

By the next day, D-day, German troops and supplies were slowed to a walking pace. The formations sent to repel the landings in Normandy were delayed an average of 48 hours—precious time to the Americans and British. And later, after the break-through, French guerrillas constantly informed General Patton of the exact location of each German column and protected his flank, helping him make one of the speediest drives in the history of warfare.

The role played by British, American and French Underground organizers in setting off this powder keg of French resistance was new in warfare. All operations were directed by a joint command, established by General Eisenhower.

As early as 1941 the first groups of secret operatives sent to France by the British had got in touch with local saboteur groups which were spontaneously rising all over the country. These groups were persuaded to abandon sporadic acts of violence that brought only murderous reprisals, and to accept assignments from London headquarters. (See "We Organized the French Underground," page 127.) By 1944, with invasion plans nearing completion, the experienced British fighters known as SAS (Special Air Service) were given a unified command together with resistance operatives of the American OSS (Office of Strategic Services) and other operational branches. The French Underground was directed to strike German supply lines and later to help clear the enemy from every part of France. To aid them to organize quickly, headquarters parachuted special groups of soldiers into enemy-occupied territory. One type (known as Jedburghs or Jets) was a team made up of three officers or noncommissioned officers, one of whom could operate a radio, and a few other men. These teams consisted of three nationalities—British, American and French.

The three major Underground plans for D-day drawn up by the French were known as the Green, Violet and Blue plans. The objectives were to silence communications, blast railroads and attack electric-power plants.

It was necessary to contact, train and arm thousands of the FFI (French Forces of the Interior) under the very eyes of the Gestapo. To implement the Green Plan, operatives arranged a meeting of representatives of a million railway workers. For the Violet Plan, French operatives were slipped into key spots of the telecommunication system; for the Blue Plan, villagers were instructed in explosives and mine-laying.

The average operative dropped in with arms for the resistance could expect to live three to four months—if he was lucky. He had to keep files of information, and these were sometimes found by the enemy. He was forced to trust a few persons, any one of whom could be a spy. If he was a British or American agent, he had to be on constant guard against slips that might give him away. At mealtimes he had to remember to tuck his napkin in his collar, French fashion. He was careful not to ask for shaving cream or toothpaste, which had been absent from French stores for two years.

The Gestapo set traps to try to make the operative reveal himself. In one city, riding two abreast on bicycles was arbitrarily prohibited. In another, no bar could serve red wine on Tuesday or Friday afternoon, and bartenders were instructed to report anyone who asked for it. But, despite such traps, some operatives led double lives with amazing success, opening tobacco shops, bookstalls and secondhand-furniture stores where various "customers" traded without arousing suspicion.

Escapes were narrow. Operative George, an American agent wounded in a gunfight with the Gestapo, was handcuffed and tossed unconscious into the back of a staff car. Regaining consciousness, he took out a pistol concealed in his sock and shot each German in the back of the head. Frenchmen filed off his bonds and he continued his work in another section of France.

Operative Michel, a De Gaulle worker, was in a hotel room when the Gestapo raided the place. He ran to the top floor, but could find no escape to the roof. He darted into a room, and found a maid sorting sheets. Frantically he explained that he was running for his life and said, "Quick—get in bed with me." "No!" she protested. "Don't be a fool," he said, "I've got more important things on my mind!" The Gestapo men shoved open the door and turned on the light. The couple in bed pretended to be annoyed. The Gestapo leader laughed. "Have an enjoyable evening," he said, and closed the door.

Indispensable to the success of the secret organization was the radioman, who maintained regular communications with London or Algiers, ordering arms and explosives and directing the landings of new operatives. The wireless-telegraphy operators, one of whom was an American girl, were the unsung heroes of French resistance. The operators who transmitted from Paris were in constant danger of being pinpointed by 36 German direction finders continually combing the ether. So efficient were these direction finders that 20 minutes after an agent came on the air the patrol car would be at his door. Many a radioman climbed out a back window only seconds ahead of the Gestapo, leaving his equipment behind.

Before D-day the score of this phantom army totaled 750 locomotives destroyed or damaged in less than four months, indicating that a stepped-up program could seriously impair German supply lines on D-day. By March 1944, through the efforts of nearly 3000 secret operatives, the full strength of every effective resistance group in France was thrown into work on the Green, Violet and Blue plans. To each group, headquarters in London or Algiers dispatched detailed maps of the unit's particular area, indicating specific local objectives. Special instructors were parachuted in and held classes for two or three villages at a time, showing them how to blow up railroads and bridges. By June 1 the maps of France on the walls at the two headquarters were covered with red dots, each indicating where patriots were trained, supplied and ready for the signal to attack assigned objectives on D-day and later.

After the signal came for action on the evening of June 5, the railroads of France were blasted in more than 500 places. And, thanks to strategically placed French operatives, London knew every important train movement two days in advance, so Allied planes were able to swoop down on almost all troop trains headed for Normandy.

Certain agents had become conversant with the operations of the booster stations in France's long-distance telephone system. Now, equipped with German passes, they went to the booster stations and blew up many of them.

Thousands of villagers planted mines and littered roads with tire-busters which blasted German truck tires. The most optimistic hope had been to hold up the German reinforcements for 12 hours, but the operatives delayed them two days.

Most Jedburghs were in the mountainous regions helping the Maquis (French guerrillas), who now numbered over 100,000. In four months thousands of tons of American guns, grenades and medical supplies were flown over. On July 14, in a daring daylight mission, 324 American B-17's dropped 500 tons of equipment, enough to supply 36,000 men.

In Brittany, as the Allied forces broke through in August, some 30,000 FFI, organized around the veteran SAS, now members of the French Fourth Parachute Battalion, ambushed the enemy and protected the Allied routes.

The OG's—Operational Groups—were the hell-raisers of the secret army. Specialists in demolition and close-in fighting, they were dropped into France in groups of 15 to 30 to carry out jobs calling for exceptional skill. Eleven groups parachuted into southern France, where most of the Maquis were concentrated. Over 200 men organized and trained French units, and in combined operations with them killed 461 Germans, wounded 467 and took thousands of prisoners. The first group landed in the Department of Lot, where Germans were strong. Organizing three battalions, they ambushed 1000 Germans, blew railway bridges and viaducts, and closed the entire Department to German movement. (See photograph on page 337.)

As the Germans retreated, OG tactics changed. One group of

25 went in to save the great hydroelectric plant at Eguzon, the most important electric installation in France. The Germans had 500 men there ready to demolish the plant when it became necessary to pull out. The officer in command of the OG's arranged a meeting with the enemy commander, spread his uniformed men through the ranks of the Maquis and permitted them to be glimpsed by the Germans while he negotiated. He threatened attack by 1500 U.S. Army paratroopers and offered safe-conduct to another city. The frightened Germans pulled out, leaving the power plant intact.

To a man, the soldiers of the secret army give full credit to the patriotic French people who risked everything to help liberate France. Many were continually hunted, and lived without adequate food or shelter. Operating in small bands or singly, some had carried on the fight for four years, dedicating their lives to the struggle against the Germans. Their valor will always be an inspiration to freedom-loving peoples.

Fakery in the Air

By Allan A. Michie

Ever since the 1942 dress rehearsal at Dieppe the Germans had boasted of what they would do to an Allied invading force. Yet when the invasion came, on June 6, 1944, some 6000 Allied ships sailed to the Normandy coast unmolested and began landing troops before the Germans even knew they were there. At the critical hour the enemy radar operators were fooled into thinking that we were invading the Pas-de-Calais, 200 miles up the coast from the real invasion beaches. This ingenious D-day ruse was the climactic episode of the war in the ether—the top-secret radio battle, fought for four years alongside the shooting war between the Allied Air Force and the German Luftwaffe.

The tremendous speed of air combat in World War II made both sides vitally dependent on radio-telephone and wireless communications, which were necessary to assemble and direct bomber fleets as well as to lead intercepting fighters to enemy bombers. And the mainstay of both German and British anti-aircraft defenses was radar, which detected and located approaching aircraft. Consequently, the objective of the ether war was to disrupt the other side's radio communications and radar-detection devices.

Radio counter-measures, abbreviated in official jargon to RCM, began quietly in the autumn of 1940 when Goering's bombers undertook night raids against Britain's cities. The German bomber crews were guided to their targets by narrow radio beams, sent out from French and Belgian bases and sometimes intersected by cross-directional beams, transmitted from Holland or Norway, which gave the signal that they were approaching the target.

The British decided to interfere with these signals. Because the Germans often switched on their beams hours before a raid, the British operators had time to find and duplicate them. Thus they were able to retransmit the beams and gradually to "bend" them away from the intended target city. A two-degree deflection was enough to lead the enemy bombers almost nine miles off over a 250-mile course and cause them to drop their loads in open country.

After the Germans caught on and abandoned the beam system, substituting wirelessed directions from home bases, the British added a new wrinkle to the radio war. When a German navigator wirelessed for a bearing to determine his bomber's position, the British operator working on the Luftwaffe's frequencies would cut in and give him a false bearing. German pilots often got so muddled with false navigational instructions that they flew around, hopelessly lost, until daylight and then landed in southern England in the belief that it was France.

It was the Germans who scored the first success in jamming radar. In February 1942 the German warships *Scharnhorst*, *Gneisenau* and *Prinz Eugen* sneaked out of Brest and headed up the Channel. The British radar experts manning coastal stations noticed a jamming which, slight at first, increased almost imperceptibly in intensity. By the time the German flotilla reached the Dover Straits the jamming was continuous, preventing British ground controllers from seeing and directing their ships and planes. The German warships completed their dash up the Channel in safety.

About the same time the British discovered that the enemy's radar was subject to interference. High-powered transmitters, set up along the south coast of England, began jamming the enemy's early-warning radar. Parallel with this interference, the RAF also began jamming the Luftwaffe's vital ground-to-air radio-telephone and wireless communications.

There was never a dull moment in the war in the ether. In their search for new wave lengths, the Germans frequently modified or replaced their radar and communication equipment. But almost as soon as the new equipment was operating, the British brought out their own new devices for jamming it.

One of these, perfected after almost insurmountable technical difficulties, was an airborne jammer light enough to be installed in jammer bombers. This jammer, code-named "Airborne Cigar," was so successful that the Germans were forced to resort to a very high-powered transmitter to radio-telephone spoken instructions to their night fighters. The RAF then set up a high-powered station to broadcast on the same frequency, and "ghost voices" began heckling the German ground controllers, broadcasting contrary instructions and misleading information to the German night fighters. The "ghosts" not only spoke idiomatic German but trained themselves to mimic perfectly the inflections of the German controllers.

This technique, called Operation Corona, was first used on the night of October 22-23, 1943, when RAF bombers made a heavy attack on Kassel. During the raid the Germans caught on that something had gone wrong and RAF radio monitors heard the German controller telling his night fighter pilots to "beware of another voice," warning them "not to be led astray by the enemy." After a particularly violent outburst by the German controller, the "ghost" voice said: "The Englishman is now swearing." The German shouted: "It is not the Englishman who is swearing, but me!" Soon the German pilots were so confused that they were yelling abuse at each other.

The RCM experts anticipated that the Germans might suddenly attempt to beat the "ghost voice" by putting a woman on the microphone. So three German-speaking Waafs were coached and kept standing by. A week or so later, when the Germans actually did put on a woman announcer, one of the Waafs quickly mimicked her and Luftwaffe pilots were just as confused as before.

One of the most effective and spectacular radio countermeasures was the use of aluminum foil strips, known as "Window," to confuse the German radar operators. RAF scientists found that a number of strips dropping close together, but not touching, would simulate the reflections of an airplane on radar-indicator equipment. If enough strips were dropped at intervals, they would either black out the enemy's indicator screens or cause so many false "echoes" that the radar operators would not be able to identify the genuine aircraft "echoes."

Window was initially used on the first of the four massive raids which virtually obliterated Hamburg in the last week of July 1943. Each of the 791 bombers sent out that night dropped one bundle of 2000 foil strips every minute along a planned route to the target. Assuming that each bundle showed an echo for 15 minutes, the total number of echoes on the enemy's screens during the raid represented 12,500 airplanes! The effect on the German radar-based defenses was immediate and devastating. Bomber crews reported that the radar-controlled searchlights waved aimlessly about the skies, while the predicted flak fire, directed by radar, gave place to hit-or-miss barrage fire, sent blindly up in the direction of the profusion of echoes. The German night fighters who depended on ground radar for their general direction and airborne radar for the final interception were helpless. The 12 RAF bombers lost that night—a mere 1.5 percent of those sent out—were caught only by chance interception or blind flak hits.

With their radar-direction largely nullified by Window, the Luftwaffe's night fighters were thrown back to a system of free-lance interceptions, guided partly by ground observers who plotted the bombers by sight and sound, and assisted by such visual aids as flares and searchlights operated with sound locators. This defense was rudimentary compared to the pre-Window system, and its weak spots permitted Air Chief Marshal Sir Arthur Harris, commander of the RAF's Bomber Command, to begin bombing the bull's-eye target of the war, Berlin.

By the spring of 1944 the Germans were so bedeviled by the Anglo-American jamming offensive that their fighter controllers were sending messages simultaneously on 20 wave lengths in the hope that at least one could be heard.

The pay-off to the whole RCM campaign came during the critical hours before H-hour, D-day. Although preliminary air attacks had seriously reduced the efficiency of the German coastal radar system, many of the more than 100 known major pieces of radar equipment between Cherbourg and the Schelde were still functioning on the eve of the invasion. To ensure the success of our landings, it was essential that these radar watchers be blinded or bluffed. In the area to be invaded the enemy's radar had to be blinded, for the initial success of the invasion depended largely upon the element of surprise. And in certain other areas the German radar operators had to be made to see things that would suggest an invasion force coming in.

To accomplish these ends, RCM experts produced and rehearsed a complicated scheme of deception. On the night of June 5-6, while the real invasion fleet sailed straight across the English Channel toward the Cherbourg peninsula, the hoax went simultaneously into operation.

The Germans were convinced that the Allies would attempt to land above Le Havre, probably in the Pas-de-Calais, and it was on this conviction that the success of the spoof operation depended. Eighteen small ships of the Royal Navy steamed at seven knots toward Cap d'Antifer, just above Le Havre, to create the impression of an intended landing on that part of the French coast. Each ship towed several low-flying balloons which would produce a "big-ship echo" on the enemy radar screens. But because the enemy radar operators could quickly size up the limited strength of this force, each of 12 aircraft flying low above the ships dropped a bundle of Window foil at one-minute intervals to give the impression of a large convoy slowly heading toward France. Jammers in each plane were kept going continuously to prevent German radar from getting a clear recognition of the Window deception. Meticulous timing and careful adherence to a schedule were necessary, but for three and a half hours the planes flew a continuous orbit over a 12- by 8-mile area.

Simultaneously a like deception was carried out in a direction heading for Boulogne, and in the area between these two feints 29 Lancaster planes shuttled back and forth for four hours off the enemy coast in order to lure German night fighters from the real landing areas. And these 29 bombers continuously jammed the enemy radar from no fewer than 82 airborne jammers. A secondary reason for this operation was the hope that the Germans would mistake the patrolling planes as top air cover for the "invasion."

At the same time another operation, designed to distract the Germans while airborne troops were coming down in Normandy, was getting under way. Just before the real airborne landings began, a small force of RAF planes flew in above Le Havre and dropped scores of dummy parachutists which floated down into the areas around Fécamp. At the same moment other planes were releasing dummy paratroops across the peninsula behind Cherbourg, on the right flank of the real airborne landings. Enough Window was dropped with the dummies to give the harassed enemy radar operators the impression that the dummy parachute attack was 20 times larger than it was.

Meanwhile the real invasion armada was concealed behind the most intensive radar-jamming operations yet attempted. Twenty-four RAF and U.S. bombers, equipped with jammers, flew back and forth at 18,000 feet along a line 50 miles from the enemy coast, jamming the German radar stations on the Cherbourg peninsula for hours on end. This barrage not only concealed the Allied bombers coming in to give the Normandy coastal defenses a last-minute pounding and hid the long train of troop-carrying planes and gliders, but it also prevented enemy detection of the invasion fleet. Once the ships came within range, they too joined in the jamming barrage.

The deception worked to perfection. The Germans mistook the operation near Boulogne for a genuine threat and opened up with all available guns and searchlights. Torpedo boats rushed out to intercept the imaginary mighty convoy. Most of the available German night fighters went up to engage the 29 Lancasters under the impression that they were protecting the invading fleet. This, the most important diversion of the night, drew most of the enemy night fighters from the Normandy areas where the vulnerable troop-carrying planes and gliders were operating. The mock airborne drops also brought a speedy enemy reaction. While the Germans rushed to round up the wooden parachutists, the real airborne forces were able to consolidate the flanks east and west of the landing beaches. The combination of jamming from planes and ships threw the German radar system into hopeless confusion. Only when German observers actually saw the Allied fleet did they know where and when the invasion had come.

A Question of Courage

By Dorothy Cameron Disney

At a rather stiff military luncheon in England, where nobody knew anybody else, I sat next to an American paratrooper of the 101st Airborne Division, the heroes of Bastogne. He was perhaps 20 years old, but his breast blazed with more ribbons than I could remember seeing on anyone else of less rank than a general. He was shy at first and not very talkative. But after a while he lost his constraint and he told a story. Here it is:

On D-day minus one—24 hours before the invasion of France—picked men were dropped into Normandy, this youngster among them. Unfortunately he hit the ground some distance from the designated rendezvous. It was barely dawn. He could find none of the landmarks that had been carefully described in advance. None of his comrades was in sight. He blew the shrill police whistle that was supposed to bring the group together. No other police whistle sounded. He knew then that the plan had gone wrong, that he was alone and on his own in enemy-held country.

He realized that he must seek cover at once. He had landed near a stone wall in a neat, beautifully kept orchard. Not far away in the gray dawn light he saw a small red-roofed farmhouse. Whether the people who lived there were pro-Ally or pro-German he didn't know, but it was a chance he had to take. He ran toward the house, rehearsing the few phrases of French he had been taught for such emergencies.

Answering his knock, a Frenchwoman of about 30—"she wasn't pretty and didn't smile much, but she had kind, steady eyes"—opened the door. She had just stepped from a big kitchen fireplace where the morning meal was cooking. Her husband and her three small children—the baby in a high chair—stared in wondering surprise from the breakfast table.

"I am an American soldier," said the parachutist. "Will you hide me?"

"Yes, of course," said the Frenchwoman and drew him inside.

"Hurry! You must hurry!" said the husband. He pushed the American into a large wood-cupboard beside the fireplace and slammed the door.

A few minutes later six men of the German SS arrived. They had seen the parachute coming down. This was the only house in the neighborhood. They searched it thoroughly and swiftly. Almost immediately the parachutist was found and pulled from the cupboard. The French farmer, guilty only of hiding him, got no trial. There were no formalities, no farewells. He tried to call to his wife as he was dragged from the kitchen, but one of the Storm Troopers struck him in the mouth and his words were lost. The Germans stood him in the farmyard and shot him at once. His wife moaned; one child screamed.

The Storm Troopers knew what to do with a French civilian who had dared to shelter an enemy, but apparently there was an argument as to the disposition of their prisoner. So, for the time being, they shoved him into a shed in the farmyard and bolted the door.

There was a small window at the back of the shed. Skirting the farm were woods. The chutist squeezed through the window, ran for the woods. The Germans heard him go. They rushed around the shed and after him, firing as they came. The bullets missed him. But now the attempt at escape seemed quite hopeless. He had hardly got into the woods—carefully tended French woods with little underbrush—when he heard his pursuers all around, shouting to one another. They had scattered. Their voices came from all directions as they searched systematically. It was only a matter of time until they would find him. There was no chance.

Yes, there was one last chance. The parachutist nerved himself and accepted the risk. Doubling on his tracks, ducking from tree to tree, he left the woods and fled into the open again. He ran back past the shed and on through the farmyard where the body of the murdered French farmer still lay. Once again the American stood at the silent farmhouse, knocking softly at the kitchen door.

The woman came quickly. Her face was pale, her eyes dulled with tears. For perhaps a second they faced each other. She didn't look toward the body of her husband, which she hadn't dared yet to touch. She looked straight into the eyes of the young American whose coming had made her a widow and orphaned her children.

"Will you hide me?" he said.

"Yes. Be quick!"

Without hesitation she returned him to the cupboard beside the fireplace.

The Storm Troopers never came back to the farmhouse. It didn't occur to them to search that house again because they did not understand the kind of people they were dealing with. They

could not comprehend, perhaps, that human beings could reach such heights. Two kinds of courage defeated them—the courage of the American boy who out-thought them, the courage of the French widow who unhesitatingly gave him a second chance. After three days that part of Normandy was freed and the parachutist was able to rejoin his division.

I was fascinated by the two protagonists in this true tale. I thought about them often. I told the story many times to groups of American soldiers in France and Italy. But I lacked eloquence. I never could express fully what I thought of these two remarkable people. It was not until after VE-day, as I was preparing to come home, that I met an Air Force general who put into words exactly what I felt.

"The young parachutist had the courage of desperation," he said. "In a box, he saw and seized the only way out. A brave, smart boy. But the woman had the courage that is with you always, that never lets you down. She was a fortunate woman."

"Fortunate?" I looked at him in astonishment.

"Yes, fortunate," repeated the general. "She knew what she believed in."

The Longest Day

Condensed from the book
By Cornelius Ryan

The village was silent in the damp June morning. Its name was La Roche-Guyon and it had sat undisturbed for nearly 12 centuries in a great lazy loop of the Seine midway between Paris and Normandy. For years it had been just a place that people passed through on their way to somewhere else. Its only distinction had been the castle of the dukes of Rochefoucauld.

But now the village had attained a distinction of another kind.

For behind its pastoral front La Roche-Guyon was really a prison—the most occupied village in all of occupied France. For every one of the 543 villagers, there were more than three German soldiers. One of these soldiers was Field Marshal Erwin Rommel, commander in chief of Army Group B, the most powerful force in the German West. His headquarters was in the castle. From here Rommel was preparing to fight the most desperate battle of his career. Although Rommel did not know it, that battle—against the Allied invasion—would begin in 48 hours. For this was Sunday, June 4, 1944.

Under Rommel's command more than half a million troops manned defenses along a tremendous length of coast line—stretching almost 800 miles, from the dikes of Holland to the Atlantic-washed shores of the Brittany peninsula. His main strength, the 15th Army, was concentrated about the Pas-de-Calais, at the narrowest point of the Channel between France and England. Night after night Allied bombers hit this area. Bomb-weary veterans of the 15th Army joked bitterly that the place for a rest cure was in the zone of the Seventh Army in Normandy. Hardly a bomb had fallen there.

For months, behind a fantastic jungle of beach obstacles and minefields, Rommel's troops had waited. But the blue-gray English Channel had remained empty of ships. Nothing had happened. From La Roche-Guyon, on this gloomy and peaceful Sunday morning, there was still no sign of the Allied invasion.

In his ground-floor office Rommel was alone, working by the light of a single desk lamp. Although he looked older than his 51 years, he remained as tireless as ever. This morning, as usual, he had been up since before four. Now he waited impatiently for six o'clock. At that time he would breakfast with his staff and then depart for Germany—his first leave at home in months.

On Rommel's shoulders lay the enormous responsibility for repulsing the Allied assault the moment it began. Hitler's Third Reich was reeling, from one disaster after another. Day and night thousands of Allied bombers pounded Germany. Russia's massive forces had driven into Poland. Allied troops were at the gates of Rome. Everywhere the Wehrmacht was being driven back and destroyed. Germany was still far from beaten, but the Allied invasion would be the decisive battle—and no one knew it better than Rommel.

Yet this morning Rommel was going home. For months he had hoped to spend a few days in Germany the first part of June. Also, he wanted to see Hitler. There were many reasons why he now believed he could leave, and although he would never have admitted it, he desperately needed rest. Only one person really knew the strain that Rommel was under. To his wife, Lucie-Maria, he confided everything. In less than four months he had written her more than 40 letters, and in almost every other letter he had made a new prediction about the Allied assault.

On April 6 he wrote: "Here the tension is growing from day to day. . . . It will probably be only weeks. . . ."

On May 6: "Still no signs of the British and Americans. . . . Every day, every week . . . we get stronger. . . . I am looking forward to the battle with confidence. . . . Perhaps it will come on May 15, perhaps at the end of the month."

On May 19: "I am wondering if I can spare a few days in June to get away from here. Right now there isn't a chance."

But there was a chance after all. One of the reasons for Rommel's decision to leave at this time was his own estimate of the Allies' intentions. Before him now on the desk was Army Group B's weekly report—due to be sent the following day to Field Marshal Gerd von Rundstedt's headquarters at St.-Germain, outside Paris—and from there to Hitler's headquarters. Rommel's estimate read in part that the Allies had reached a "high degree of readiness" and that there was an "increased volume of messages going to the French Resistance." But it went on, "According to past experience, this is not indicative that an invasion is imminent. . . ." Rommel had guessed wrong again.

Now that May had passed—and it had been a month of perfect weather for the Allied attack—Rommel had reached the conclusion that the invasion would not come for several more weeks. He now reasoned—as did Hitler and the German High Command—that the invasion would take place either simultaneously with the Red Army's summer offensive or shortly thereafter. The Russian attack, they knew, could not begin until after the late thaw in Poland, and therefore they did not think the offensive could be mounted until the latter part of June.

In the west the weather had been bad for several days, and it promised to be even worse. The five a.m. report for June 4 predicted increasing cloudiness, high winds and rain. Even now a 20- to 30-m.p.h. wind was blowing in the Channel. To Rommel it seemed hardly likely that the Allies would dare launch their attack during the next few days. He opened the door of his office and went down to have breakfast with his staff. Outside in the village of La Roche-Guyon the bell in the church of St.-Samson sounded the Angelus. Each note fought for its existence against the wind. It was six a.m.

Rommel had been in France since November 1943. To the humiliation of Von Rundstedt, the aristocratic 68-year-old field marshal who was responsible for the defense of all of western Europe, Rommel had arrived with a *Gummibefehl*, an "elastic directive," ordering him to inspect the coastal fortifications—Hitler's much publicized "Atlantic Wall"—and then to report directly back to the Führer's headquarters.

The Atlantic Wall was one of Hitler's relatively new obsessions. Up to 1941 victory had seemed so certain to the Führer and his strutting Nazis that there was no need for coastal fortifications. After the collapse of France, Hitler had expected the British to sue for peace. They didn't; and as time passed, the situation rapidly changed. With U.S. help Britain began staging a slow but sure recovery. Hitler, by now deeply involved in Russia—he attacked the Soviet Union in June 1941—saw that the coast of France was no longer an offensive springboard. It was now a soft spot in his defenses. And in December 1941, after America had entered the war, the Führer ranted to the world that "a belt of strongpoints and gigantic fortifications runs from Kirkenes [on the Norwegian-Finnish frontier] to the Pyrenees [on the Franco-Spanish border] . . . and it is my unshakable decision to make this front impregnable against every enemy." It was a wild, impossible boast. Discounting the indentations, this coast line stretches over 3000 miles.

In 1942, as the tide of war began to swing against the Germans, Hitler thundered at his generals that the wall must be completed at top speed. Thousands of slave laborers worked night and day to build the fortifications. Millions of tons of concrete were poured—so much that all over Hitler's Europe it became impossible to get concrete for anything else. Staggering quantities of steel were ordered, but this commodity was in such short supply that the engineers were often forced to do without it. By the end of 1943, although over half a million men were working on it, the wall was far from finished.

What Rommel saw when he inspected the wall in November 1943 appalled him. In only a few places were the fortifications completed, and at some places work had not even begun. True, even in its present state the Atlantic Wall was a formidable barrier. Where it was finished, it fairly bristled with heavy guns. But there were not enough of them—or of anything—to suit Rommel. To his critical eye the Atlantic Wall was a farce. He denounced it as a "figment of Hitler's *Wolkenkuckucksheim*" (cloud cuckoo-land).

Von Rundstedt heartily concurred with Rommel's scathing denunciation. (It was probably the only time that he completely agreed with Rommel on anything.) The wise old Von Rundstedt had never believed in fixed defenses. He had masterminded the attack outflanking the Maginot Line in 1940 that had led to the collapse of France. To him Hitler's Atlantic Wall was an "enormous bluff . . . more for the German people than for the enemy." It would "temporarily obstruct" the Allied attack, but would not stop it. Nothing, Von Rundstedt was convinced, could prevent the initial landings from being successful. His plan to defeat the invasion was to hold the great mass of his troops back from the coast and to attack *after* the Allied troops had landed.

With this theory Rommel disagreed completely. He was positive that there was only one way to smash the attack: meet it head on. There would be no time to bring up reinforcements. He was certain that they would be destroyed by air attacks or naval or artillery bombardment. Everything, in his view, from troops to panzer divisions, had to be held ready at the coast or just behind it.

Captain Helmut Lang, his 36-year-old aide, well remembers a day when Rommel summed up his strategy. They stood on a deserted beach and Rommel, a short, stocky figure in a heavy greatcoat with an old muffler around his throat, stalked up and down waving his "informal" marshal's baton, a two-foot-long, silver-topped black stick with a red, black and white tassel. He pointed to the sands and said, "The war will be won or lost on the beaches. We'll have only one chance to stop the enemy, and that's while he's in the water, struggling to get ashore. Reserves will never get up to the point of attack and it's foolish even to consider them. Everything we have must be on the coast. Believe me, Lang, the first 24 hours of the invasion will be decisive. . . . For the Allies, as well as Germany, it will be the longest day."

Hitler approved Rommel's plan in general, and from then on Von Rundstedt became merely a figurehead. In a few short months Rommel's ruthless drive changed the whole picture. On every beach where he considered a landing possible he ordered crude anti-invasion obstacles erected. These obstacles—jagged triangles of steel; saw-toothed, gatelike structures of iron; metal-tipped wooden stakes and concrete cones—were planted just below high- and low-tide watermarks. Strapped to each one were explosives. Rommel's strange inventions (he had designed most of them himself) were both simple and deadly. Their object was to impale and destroy troop-filled landing craft or to obstruct them long enough for shore batteries to zero in. More than half a million of these lethal underwater obstacles now stretched along the coast line.

Still Rommel was not satisfied. In the sands, in bluffs, in gullies and pathways leading off the beaches, he ordered mines laid—all varieties from the large pancake type, capable of blowing off a tank's tracks, to the small S mine, which, when stepped on, bounded into the air and exploded level with a man's midriff. Over five million of these mines now infested the coast. Before the attack came, Rommel hoped to have a total of 50 million.

Overlooking the coast line, back of this jungle of mines and obstacles, Rommel's troops waited in pillboxes, concrete bunkers and communication trenches, all surrounded by layers of barbed wire. Every piece of artillery that the Field Marshal had been able to lay hands on looked down on sands and sea, already sighted in to give overlapping fields of fire.

Rommel took advantage of every new technique or development. Where he was short of guns, he positioned batteries of rocket launchers or multiple mortar throwers. At one place he even had miniature robot tanks called "Goliaths." These devices, capable of carrying more than half a ton of explosives, could be guided by remote control from the fortifications down onto the beaches and detonated among troops or landing craft.

Never in the history of warfare had a more deadly array of defenses been prepared for an invading force. Yet Rommel was not content. He wanted more pillboxes . . . more beach obstacles . . . more mines . . . more guns and troops. Most of all he wanted the massive panzer divisions which were lying in reserve far from the coast. But now, at this crucial moment, the Führer insisted on holding these armored formations under his personal authority. Rommel needed at least five panzer divisions at the coast. There was only one way to get them: he would see Hitler. Rommel had often told Lang, "The last man who sees Hitler wins the game." On this leaden morning in La Roche-Guyon, as he prepared to leave for Germany and the long drive home, Rommel was more determined than ever to win the game.

At 15th Army headquarters near the Belgian border, 125 miles away from La Roche-Guyon, Lieutenant Colonel Hellmuth Meyer sat in his office, haggard and bleary-eyed. Meyer had a frustrating, nerve-racking job. He headed the only counter-intelligence team on the invasion front. The heart of his setup was a 30-man radio-interception crew whose job was to listen, nothing more. But each man was an expert who spoke three languages, and there was hardly a stutter of Morse code whispering through the ether from Allied sources that they did not hear.

Meyer was good at his job. Several times a day he sifted

through sheaves of monitored reports, always searching for the suspicious, the unusual—even the unbelievable. During the night his men had picked up the unbelievable. The message, a high-speed press cable, had been monitored just after dark. It read: URGENT PRESS ASSOCIATED NYK FLASH EISENHOWER'S HQ ANNOUNCES ALLIED LANDINGS IN FRANCE.

Meyer was dumfounded. His first impulse was to alert head-quarters. But he paused and calmed down: because Meyer knew the message had to be wrong. There were two reasons why. First, there was a complete absence of any activity along the invasion front. (He would have known immediately if there had been an attack.) Second, in January Admiral Wilhelm Canaris, then chief of German Intelligence, had given Meyer the details of a two-part signal which he said the Allies would use to alert the Underground prior to the invasion.

Canaris had warned that the Allies would broadcast hundreds of messages to the Underground in the months preceding the attack. Only a few of these would actually relate to D-day; the remainder would be fake, deliberately designed to mislead and confuse. Canaris had been explicit: Meyer was to monitor all messages in order not to miss the important one. At first Meyer had been skeptical. It had seemed madness to him to depend entirely on only one message. But on the night of June 1 his men had intercepted the first part of the Allied message—exactly as described by Canaris. It was not unlike the hundreds of other coded sentences that were read out to the Underground after the regular BBC news broadcasts. Most of the messages—given in French, Dutch, Danish and Norwegian—were meaningless: "The Trojan War will not be held." "Molasses tomorrow will spurt forth cognac." "John has a long mustache."

But the message that followed the nine p.m. BBC news on the night of June 1 was one that Meyer understood only too well. "Kindly listen now to a few personal messages," said the voice in French. There was a pause, and then: "*Les sanglots longs des violons de l'automne*" (The long sobs of the violins of autumn). There it was—the message that Canaris had warned them to expect. It was the first phrase of the poem by Verlaine which

was to be the signal. When the last half of the message—
"Blessent mon coeur d'une langueur monotone" (Wound my
heart with a monotonous languor)—was broadcast, it would
mean, according to Canaris, that "the invasion will begin within
48 hours."

Immediately on hearing the first phrase from Verlaine, Meyer
informed the 15th Army's chief of staff, Brigadier General
Wilhelm Hofmann. "The first message has come," he told
Hofmann. "Now something is going to happen." Hofmann gave
the alarm to alert the 15th Army.

Meyer meanwhile sent the message by teletype to Hitler's
headquarters. Next he telephoned Von Rundstedt's headquarters and Rommel's headquarters (Army Group B).

At Hitler's headquarters the message was delivered to General Alfred Jodl, chief of operations. The message remained on
Jodl's desk. He did not order an alert. He assumed Von Rundstedt had done so; but Von Rundstedt thought Rommel's
headquarters had issued the order. (Rommel must have known
about the message; but from his own estimate of Allied intentions it is obvious that he must have discounted it.) Along the
invasion coast only one army was placed on readiness: the 15th.
The Seventh Army, holding the coast of Normandy, heard
nothing about the message and was not alerted.

On the nights of the 2nd and 3rd of June the first part of the
message was again broadcast. Within the hour after the message
was repeated on the night of June 3 the AP flash regarding the
Allied landings in France was picked up. If the Canaris warning
was right, Meyer knew that the AP report must be wrong. The
flash turned out to be the weirdest kind of security leak. During
the night an AP teletype operator in England had been practicing
on an idle machine in an effort to improve her speed. Through
an error the perforated tape carrying her practice "flash" somehow preceded the usual nightly Russian communiqué. It was
corrected after only 30 seconds, but the word was out.

After his first moment of panic Meyer had bet on Canaris.
Now he was weary but elated. The coming of the dawn and the
continued peacefulness along the front more than proved him

right. Now there was nothing to do but wait for the last half of the vital alert, which might come at any moment.

As Meyer settled down to wait, the commander of Army Group B, 125 miles away, was preparing to leave for Germany. At seven a.m. the Field Marshal's car, with Rommel in the seat beside the chauffeur, drove through the village and turned left onto the main Paris road. Leaving La Roche-Guyon on this particular dismal Sunday morning of June 4 suited Rommel fine. The timing of the trip could not have been better. Beside him on the seat was a cardboard box containing a pair of hand-made gray suede shoes, size five and a half, for his wife. There was a special and very human reason why he wanted to be with her on Tuesday, June 6. It was her birthday.

In England it was eight a.m. (there was one hour's difference between British Double Summer Time and German Central Time). In a house trailer in a rain-washed wood near Portsmouth, General Dwight D. Eisenhower, the Allied Supreme Commander, was asleep after having been up nearly all night.

Eisenhower and his commanders had done everything to ensure that the invasion would have every possible chance of success at the lowest cost in lives. But now, after all the years of military and political planning, Operation Overlord, the code name for the invasion plan, lay at the mercy of the elements. The weather was bad. All Eisenhower could do was to wait and hope that conditions would improve. But now, on Sunday, June 4, no matter what happened, he would be forced to make a momentous decision: to go—or to postpone the assault.

On May 17 he had decided that D-day would have to be one of three days in June—the 5th, 6th or 7th. Meteorological studies had shown that two of the vital weather requirements for the invasion could be expected for Normandy on those days: a late-rising moon and, shortly after dawn, a low tide.

The paratroopers and gliderborne infantry who would launch the assault needed some moonlight. But their surprise attack depended on darkness until they arrived over the dropping zones. Thus their critical demand was for a late-rising moon.

The seaborne landings had to take place when the tide was low enough to expose Rommel's beach obstacles. On this tide the timing of the whole invasion would depend. And to complicate the meteorological calculations further, follow-up troops landing much later in the day would also need a low tide—and it had to come before darkness set in.

These two critical factors of moonlight and tide shackled Eisenhower. Tide alone reduced the number of days for the attack in any one month to six—and three of those were moonless. But that was not all. There were many other factors. First, all the services wanted long hours of daylight and good visibility. They wanted light to be able to identify the beaches; for the Navy and Air Force to spot their targets; and to reduce the hazard of collision when the mass of ships began maneuvering almost side by side in the Bay of the Seine. Second, a calm sea was required. Apart from the havoc a rough sea might cause to the fleet, seasickness could leave the troops helpless long before they even set foot on the beaches. Third, low winds, blowing inshore, were needed to clear the beaches of smoke so that targets would not be obscured. And, finally, the Allies would require three more quiet days after D-day for the quick build-up of men and supplies.

Of the three possible days for the invasion, Eisenhower had chosen the 5th. Now, on Sunday, June 4, at five a.m.—about the time that Rommel got up at La Roche-Guyon—he made a fateful decision: because of unfavorable weather conditions the Allied invasion would be postponed 24 hours. If conditions improved, D-day would be Tuesday, June 6.

Shortly before 9:30 that night of June 4, Eisenhower's senior commanders and their chiefs of staff gathered in the library of Southwick House. Standing about the room in little groups, the staff officers talked quietly. Near the fireplace Eisenhower's chief of staff, Major General Walter Bedell Smith, conversed with the pipe-smoking Deputy Supreme Commander, Air Chief Marshal Sir Arthur Tedder. Seated to one side were the fiery Allied Naval Commander, Admiral Sir Bertram Ramsay, and, close by, the Allied Air Commander, Air Chief Marshal Sir Trafford Leigh-

Mallory. Only one officer was dressed informally, General Smith recalls. The peppery Bernard Law Montgomery, who would be in charge of the D-day assault, wore his usual corduroy slacks and roll-neck sweater. These were the men who would translate the order for the attack when Eisenhower gave the word. Now they and their staff chiefs—altogether there were 12 senior officers in the room—waited for the decisive conference that would begin at 9:30.

At exactly 9:30 the door opened and Eisenhower, neat in his dark-green battle-dress, strode in. There was no need for a preamble: everybody knew the seriousness of the decision that had to be made. Almost immediately the three senior Overlord meteorologists, led by their chief, Group Captain J. N. Stagg of the RAF, came into the room. There was a hushed silence as Stagg opened the briefing. Quickly he sketched the weather picture of the previous 24 hours, and then he said quietly, "Gentlemen, there have been some rapid and unexpected developments in the situation. . . ." All eyes were on Stagg now, as he presented the anxious-faced Eisenhower and his commanders with a slender ray of hope.

A new weather front had been spotted which, he said, would move up the Channel within the next few hours and cause a gradual clearing over the assault areas. These improving conditions would last throughout the next day and continue up to the morning of June 6. After that the weather would begin to deteriorate again. During this promised period of improved weather the winds would drop appreciably and the skies would clear—enough at least for bombers to operate on the night of the 5th and throughout the morning of the 6th. By noon the cloud layer would thicken and the skies would become overcast again. In short, what Eisenhower was being told was that a barely tolerable period of fair conditions, far below the minimal requirements, would prevail *for just a little more than 24 hours*.

For the next 15 minutes Eisenhower and his commanders deliberated. The urgency of making a decision was stressed by Admiral Ramsay. The American task force for Omaha and Utah beaches under the command of Rear Admiral A. G. Kirk would have to get the order within a half-hour if Overlord was to take place on Tuesday.

Eisenhower now polled his commanders one by one. General Smith thought that the attack should go in on the 6th—it was a gamble, but one that should be taken. Tedder and Leigh-Mallory were both fearful that even the predicted cloud cover would prove too much for the air forces to operate effectively. It might mean that the assault would take place without adequate air support. They thought it was going to be "chancy." Montgomery stuck to the decision that he had made the night before when the June 5 D-day had been postponed. "I would say— go," he said. It was now up to Ike. The moment had come when only he could make the decision. There was a long silence as Eisenhower weighed all the possibilities. As General Smith watched, he was struck by the "isolation and loneliness" of the Supreme Commander as he sat, hands clasped before him, looking down at the table. The minutes ticked by. Then Eisenhower, his face strained, looked up and announced his decision. Slowly he said, "I am quite positive we must give the order. . . . I don't like it, but there it is. . . . I don't see how we can do anything else."

Eisenhower stood up. He looked tired, but some of the tension had left his face. Tuesday, June 6, would be D-day.

As the night closed in, the invasion forces all over England continued to wait. Keyed up by months of training, they were ready to go, and the postponement had made them jittery. They did not know that D-day now was barely 26 hours away; it was still much too early for the news to filter down. And so, on this stormy Sunday night, men waited—in loneliness, anxiety and secret fear—for something, anything, to happen. They did precisely what the world expects men to do under such circumstances: they thought of their families, their wives, their children, their sweethearts. And everybody talked about the fighting that lay ahead. What would the beaches really be like? Would the landings be as rough as everybody seemed to think? Nobody could visualize D-day, but as the hours passed, each man prepared for it in his own way.

Monday, June 5, 1944, was quiet and uneventful for the Germans. The weather was so bad that in Paris, at the Luftwaffe's headquarters, Colonel Professor Walter Stöbe, the chief meteorologist, told staff officers that they could relax. He doubted that Allied planes would even be operational this day. Antiaircraft crews were promptly ordered to stand down.

Next Stöbe telephoned Von Rundstedt's headquarters in St.-Germain. Von Rundstedt slept late that day as usual, and it was almost noon before he conferred with his chief of staff and approved his staff's "Estimate of Allied Intentions" so that it could be forwarded to Hitler's headquarters. The estimate was another typical wrong guess. It read: "The systematic and distinct increase of air attacks indicates that the enemy has reached a high degree of readiness. The probable invasion front still remains the sector from the Schelde [in Holland] to Normandy . . . and it is not impossible that the north front of Brittany might be included . . . [but] . . . it is still not clear where the enemy will invade within this total area. Concentrated air attacks on the coast defenses between Dunkirk and Dieppe may mean that the main Allied invasion effort will be made there . . . [but] . . . imminence of invasion is not recognizable. . . ." With this vague estimate out of the way—an estimate that covered almost 800 miles of the invasion coast—Von Rundstedt and his son, a young lieutenant, set out for the Field Marshal's favorite restaurant, the *Coq Hardi* at Bougival nearby. It was a little after one o'clock; D-day was 12 hours away.

All along the chain of German command the continuing bad weather acted like a tranquilizer. The various headquarters were quite confident that there would be no attack in the immediate future. Their reasoning was based on carefully assessed weather evaluations of the Allied landings in North Africa, Italy and Sicily. Conditions had varied, but meteorologists had noted that the Allies never attempted a landing unless the prospects of favorable weather were almost certain—particularly for covering air operations. To the methodical German mind there was no deviation from this rule: the weather had to be just right or the Allies wouldn't attack. And the weather wasn't just right.

At Rommel's headquarters in La Roche-Guyon the work went on as though the Field Marshal were still there; but the chief of staff, Major General Dr. Hans Speidel, thought it was quiet enough to plan a little dinner party. He had invited several guests, among them Ernst Juenger, the philosopher and author. The intellectual Speidel was looking forward to the dinner. He hoped they'd discuss his favorite subject: French literature. There was something else to be discussed: a 20-page manuscript that Juenger had drafted and secretly passed on to Rommel and Speidel. Both of them fervently believed in the document: it outlined a plan for bringing about peace—after Hitler had been either tried by a German court or assassinated.

In St.-Lô, at the headquarters of the 84th Corps, Major Friedrich Hayn, the intelligence officer, was making arrangements for a party for the corps commander, General Erich Marcks. His birthday was June 6. They were holding the surprise birthday party at midnight because Marcks had to leave for the city of Rennes in Brittany at daybreak. He and all the other senior commanders in Normandy were to take part in a big map exercise that was to begin early on Tuesday morning. Everyone thought the *Kriegsspiel* would be interesting: it dealt with a theoretical "invasion" which was supposed to take place in Normandy.

The *Kriegsspiel* worried the Seventh Army's chief of staff, Brigadier General Max Pemsel. It was bad enough that his senior commanders in Normandy and the Cherbourg peninsula would be away from their commands all at the same time. But it might be dangerous if they were away overnight. Rennes was a long way off for most of them, and Pemsel was afraid that some might be planning to leave the front before dawn. He believed that if an invasion ever came in Normandy, the attack would be launched at first light. He decided to warn all those due to participate in the games. The order he sent out by teletype read: "Commanding generals and others scheduled to attend the *Kriegsspiel* are reminded not to leave for Rennes before dawn on June 6." But it was too late. Some had already left.

One by one, senior officers had left the front on the very eve of the battle. All of them had reasons, but it was almost as though a capricious fate had manipulated their departure. Rommel was in Germany. So was Army Group B's operations officer, Colonel Hans George von Tempelhoff. Major General Heinz Hellmich, commanding the 243rd Division, holding one side of the Cherbourg peninsula, departed for Rennes. So did Major General Karl von Schlieben of the 709th Division. Brigadier General Wilhelm Falley, of the tough 91st Air Landing Division that had just moved into Normandy, prepared to go. Colonel Wilhelm Meyer-Detring, Von Rundstedt's intelligence officer, was on leave. The chief of staff of one division was off hunting with his French mistress.

(After D-day the coincidence of these multiple departures from the invasion front struck the Germans so forcibly that there was actually talk of an investigation to see whether British secret service could possibly have had anything to do with it! The fact is that Hitler himself was no better prepared for the great day than were his generals. The Führer was at his Berchtesgaden retreat in Bavaria. Hitler got up late, held his usual military conference at noon and then had lunch at four p.m. Besides his mistress, Eva Braun, there were a number of Nazi dignitaries and their wives. The vegetarian Hitler commented to the ladies on his meatless meal with his usual dinnertime remark: "The elephant is the strongest animal; he also cannot stand meat." After lunch the group adjourned to the garden, where the Führer sipped lime-blossom tea. He napped between six and seven, held another military conference at 11 p.m.; then, a little before midnight, the ladies were called back to listen to a couple of hours of Wagner, Lehár and Strauss.)

At this point, with the officers in charge of beachhead defenses dispersed all over Europe, the German High Command decided to transfer the Luftwaffe's last remaining fighter squadrons in France far out of range of the Normandy beaches. The fliers were aghast. The principal reason for the withdrawal was that the squadrons were needed for the defense of the Reich, which for months had been coming under increasingly heavy round-the-clock Allied bombing attack. Under the circumstances it just did not seem reasonable to the High Command to leave these vital planes on exposed airfields in France where they were being destroyed by Allied fighters and bombers. Hitler had promised his generals that 1000 Luftwaffe planes would hit the beaches on the day of invasion. Now that was patently impossible. On June 4 there were only 183 day fighter planes in the whole of France; about 160 were considered serviceable. Of the 160, one wing of 124—the 26th Fighter Wing— was being moved back from the coast this very afternoon.

Of all the millions who watched and waited throughout France, less than a dozen men and women actually knew that the invasion was imminent. They went about their affairs calmly and casually as usual. Being calm and casual was part of their business: they were the leaders of the French Underground.

Most of them were in Paris. From there they commanded a vast and complex organization so secret that leaders rarely knew each other except by code names, and never did one group know what another was doing.

In the previous days the Underground's high command had picked up hundreds of coded messages which had been broadcast by the BBC. One had been the first phrase of the Verlaine poem. For the Underground at large, however, the real tip-off would come when the Allies ordered the prearranged sabotage plans to go into effect. Two messages would trigger the attacks. One, "*It is hot in Suez*," would put into effect the sabotaging of railroad tracks and equipment. The other, "*The dice are on the table*," would call for the cutting of telephone lines and cables. On this Monday evening, the eve of D-day, one message was broadcast by the BBC at 6:30 p.m. The announcer said, "*The dice are on the table. . . . Napoleon's hat is in the ring. . . . The arrow will not pass*." The other vital message came a few minutes later.

Resistance groups were quietly told the news by their immediate leaders. Each unit had its own plan and knew exactly what had to be done. Albert Augé, the stationmaster at Caen, and his men were to destroy water pumps in the yards, smash the steam injectors on locomotives. André Farine, a café owner from Lieu Fontaine near Isigny, had the job of strangling Normandy's communications: his 40-man team would cut the massive telephone cable feeding out of Cherbourg. Yves Gresselin, a Cherbourg grocer, had one of the toughest jobs of all: his men were to dynamite a network of railway lines between Cherbourg, St.-Lô and Paris. Everywhere along the invasion coast, from Brittany to the Belgian border, men prepared.

Off the French coast a little before nine p.m. a dozen small ships appeared. They moved quietly along the horizon, so close that their crews could clearly see the houses of Normandy. The ships went unnoticed. They finished their job and then moved back. They were British minesweepers—the vanguard of the mightiest fleet ever assembled.

For now, back in the Channel, plowing through the choppy gray waters, a phalanx of ships bore down on Hitler's Europe— the might and fury of the free world unleashed at last. They came, rank after relentless rank, 10 lanes wide, 20 miles across, 2727 ships of every description. There were fast new attack transports, slow rust-scarred freighters, small ocean liners, channel steamers, hospital ships, weather-beaten tankers, coasters and swarms of fussing tugs. There were endless columns of shallow-draft landing ships—great wallowing vessels, some of them almost 350 feet long. Many of these and the other heavier transports carried smaller landing craft for the actual beach assault: more than 2500 of them.

Ahead of the convoys were processions of minesweepers, Coast Guard cutters, buoy layers and motor launches. Barrage balloons flew above the ships. Squadrons of fighter planes weaved below the clouds. And surrounding this fantastic cavalcade of ships packed with men, guns, tanks, motor vehicles and supplies was a formidable array of more than 700 warships.

There was the heavy cruiser U.S.S. *Augusta*, Rear Admiral Kirk's flagship, leading the American task force—21 convoys bound for Omaha and Utah beaches. Nearby, steaming majestically with all their battle flags flying were the battleships: H.M.S. *Ramillies* and *Warspite;* U.S.S. *Texas, Arkansas* and the proud

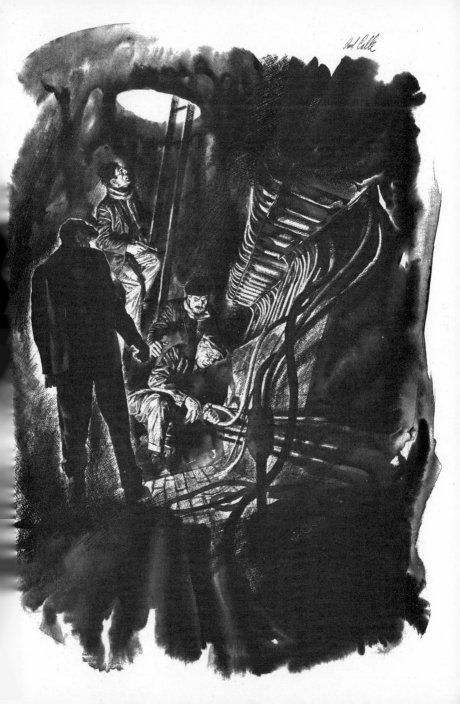

Nevada, which the Japanese had sunk and written off at Pearl Harbor.

Leading the 38 British and Canadian convoys bound for Sword, Juno and Gold beaches was the cruiser H.M.S. *Scylla*, the flagship of Rear Admiral Sir Philip Vian, who had helped track down the great German battleship *Bismarck*. And close by was one of Britain's most famous cruisers—H.M.S. *Ajax*, one of a trio which had hounded the *Graf Spee* to her doom in Montevideo harbor. There were many famous cruisers: the U.S.S. *Tuscaloosa* and *Quincy*, H.M.S. *Enterprise* and *Black Prince*, France's *Georges Leygues*—22 in all.

In lines, along the edges of the convoys, were a variety of ships: sloops, corvettes, powerful gunboats—like the Dutch *Soemba*—anti-submarine patrol craft, fast PT boats and everywhere sleek destroyers. Besides the scores of American and British destroyer units there were Canada's *Qu'appelle*, *Saskatchewan* and *Restigouche;* Free Norway's *Svenner;* and even a contribution from the Free Polish forces—the *Piorun*.

Slowly, ponderously, this great armada moved across the Channel. It followed a staggered minute-by-minute traffic pattern of a kind never attempted before. Ships poured out of British ports and, moving down the coasts in two-convoy lanes, converged on the assembly area south of the Isle of Wight. There they sorted themselves out and joined with the forces heading for one of the five beaches to which they had been assigned. Out of the assembly area, which was promptly nicknamed "Piccadilly Circus," the convoys headed for France along buoy-marked lanes. And as they approached Normandy these five paths, like a network of highways, split up into 10 channels—two for each beach, one for fast traffic, the other for slow. Up front near the head of these dual channels and lying behind the spearhead of minesweepers, battleships and cruisers were the command ships—five attack transports bristling with radar and radio antennas. These floating command posts would be the nerve centers of the invasion.

Everywhere there were ships, and to the men aboard, this historic armada was "the most impressive, unforgettable sight" they had ever seen. For the troops it was good to be on the way at last—despite the discomforts and the dangers ahead. Men were still tense, but some of the strain had lifted. Now everybody simply wanted to get the job over and done with. On the landing ships and transports men wrote last-minute letters, played interminable games of cards, joined in long bull sessions, and, as Major Thomas Dallas of the 29th Division recalls, "Chaplains did a land-office business."

Before they had been in the Channel very long, many men who had spent hours worrying about their chances of survival couldn't wait to reach the beaches. Seasickness had struck through the 59 convoys like a plague, especially in the rolling and heaving landing craft. Each man had been supplied with anti-seasickness pills, also an article of equipment which was listed in the loading sheets with typical Army thoroughness as "Bag, Vomit, One."

Some men tried to read—books that were odd and curious, books which, for the most part, had nothing to do with the situation that these men now found themselves in. Chaplain Lawrence E. Deery of the First Division on the transport H.M.S. *Empire Anvil* was amazed to see a British naval officer reading Horace's *Odes* in Latin. Deery himself, who would land on Omaha Beach in the first wave with the 16th Infantry Regiment, spent the evening reading Symonds' *Life of Michelangelo*. Nearby on a landing craft Captain James Douglas Gillan, a Canadian, opened a volume which made sense to everybody this night. To quiet his own nerves and those of a brother officer, he opened his Bible at the 23rd Psalm and read aloud, "The Lord is my Shepherd; I shall not want. . . ."

It was a little after 10:15 p.m. when Lieutenant Colonel Meyer, counter-intelligence chief of the German 15th Army, rushed out of his office. In his hand was probably the most important message the Germans had intercepted throughout the whole of World War II. Meyer now knew that the invasion would take place within 48 hours. He burst into the dining room where General Hans von Salmuth was playing bridge with his

chief of staff and two others. "General!" Meyer said breath-
lessly. "The message, the second part . . . it's here!" Von Salmuth thought a moment, then gave the order to put the 15th
Army on full alert.

Like his fellow paratroopers, Private Arthur B. "Dutch"
Schultz of the 82nd Airborne was ready, waiting on the airfield:
he was in his jump suit, with a parachute, unfastened, hanging
over his right arm. His face was blackened with charcoal, his
head shaven except for a narrow tuft of hair running back the
center of his scalp which made him look like an Iroquois. All
around him was his gear. Suddenly someone yelled, "Okay, let's
go!" The trucks began to move toward the waiting planes.

All over England the Allied airborne armies boarded their
planes and gliders. The pathfinder planes had already left. Over
at the 101st Airborne Division's headquarters at Newbury,
General Eisenhower, with a small group of officers and four
correspondents, watched the first planes get into position for
take-off. He had spent more than an hour talking to the men.
He was more worried about the airborne operation than any
other phase of the assault. Some of his commanders were
convinced that the airborne assault might result in upward of
75-percent casualties.

Eisenhower stood watching now as the planes trundled down
the runways and lifted slowly into the air. One by one they
followed each other into the darkness. Above the field they
circled as they assembled into formation. Eisenhower, his hands
deep in his pockets, gazed up into the night sky. As the huge
formation of planes roared once more over the field and headed
toward France, NBC's "Red" Mueller looked at the Supreme
Commander. Eisenhower's eyes were filled with tears.

Minutes later, over the Channel, the men of the invasion fleet
heard the roar of the planes, too. It grew louder by the second
as wave after wave passed overhead. The formations took more
than an hour to pass. Then the thunder of their engines began
to fade. On the decks of the ships the men gazed up into the
darkness. Nobody could say a word. And then as the last forma-

tion flew over, an amber light blinked down through the clouds on the fleet below. Slowly it flashed out in Morse code three dots and a dash: V for Victory.

Vague and contradictory reports began to filter into the German Seventh Army command posts all over Normandy, and everywhere officers were trying to assess them. They had little to go on—shadowy figures seen here, shots fired there, a parachute hanging from a tree somewhere else. Clues to something—but what? How many men had landed—two or 200? Were they bomber crews that had bailed out? Was this a series of French Underground attacks? Nobody was sure—and on the basis of information at hand nobody at the headquarters of the Seventh Army or of the 15th Army in the Pas-de-Calais area was willing to raise the alarm—an alarm that later might be proved wrong. And so the minutes ticked by.

Although the Germans didn't recognize it, the appearance of paratroopers on the Cherbourg peninsula was the clue to the fact that D-day had begun. These first American troopers—120 of them—were pathfinders. They had been trained in a special school set up by Brigadier General James M. "Jumpin' Jim" Gavin, assistant division commander of the 82nd Airborne. Their mission was to mark "drop zones" in a 50-square-mile area of the peninsula back of Utah Beach for the full-scale American paratrooper and glider assault that would begin one hour later. "When you land in Normandy," Gavin had told them, "you will have only one friend: God."

The pathfinders ran into difficulties at the very beginning. German flak was so intense that the planes were forced off course. Only 38 of the 120 pathfinders landed on their targets. The remainder came down miles off. All over the area pathfinders tried to get their bearings. Moving silently from hedgerow to hedgerow, bulky with guns, mines, lights and fluorescent panels, they set out for rendezvous points. They had barely one hour to mark the drop zones for the full-scale American assault.

Fifty miles away, at the eastern end of the Normandy battlefield, six planeloads of British pathfinders and six RAF bombers towing gliders swept in over the coast. The sky stormed with vicious flak, and ghostly chandeliers of flares hung everywhere when the jumps began.

Two of the British pathfinders plunged out of the night sky squarely onto the lawn before the headquarters of Major General Josef Reichert, commanding officer of the German 711th Division. Reichert was playing cards when the planes roared over, and he and the other officers rushed out—just in time to see the two Britons land. It would have been hard to tell who were the more astonished, the Germans or the pathfinders. The astounded Reichert could only blurt out, "Where have you come from?" To which one of the pathfinders, with all the aplomb of a man who had just crashed a cocktail party, replied, "Awfully sorry, old man, but we simply landed here by accident." Reichert hurried into his headquarters and picked up the phone. "Get me 15th Army Headquarters," he said. But even as he waited for the call to be put through, the drop-zone lights in both the British and American sectors began to flash on. Some of the pathfinders had found their zones.

For most of the paratroopers it was an experience they would never forget. Lieutenant Richard Hilborn, of the First Canadian Battalion, remembers that one paratrooper crashed through the top of a greenhouse, "shattering glass all over the place and making a hell of a lot of noise," but he was out and running before the glass had stopped falling. Another fell with pinpoint accuracy into a well. Hauling himself up hand over hand on his shroud lines, he set out for his assembly point as though nothing had happened.

Rommel's anti-paratroop precautions in the British zone paid off well: he had caused the Dives valley to be flooded, and the waters and swamps were death traps. The number of men who died in these wastes will never be known. Survivors say that the marshes were intersected by a maze of ditches seven feet deep, four feet wide and bottomed with sticky mud. A man plunging into one of these ditches, and weighed down with guns and heavy equipment, was helpless. Many drowned with dry land only a few yards away.

In Ste.-Mère-Eglise the sound of bombing was very close. Alexandre Renaud, the mayor and town pharmacist, could feel the very ground shaking. He herded his wife and three children into their makeshift air-raid shelter—a heavily timbered passageway off the living room. It was 12:10 a.m. He remembers the time because just then there was a persistent, urgent knocking at the street door. Even before Renaud reached the door he could see what the trouble was—M. Hairon's villa across the square was blazing fiercely. At the door was the town's fire chief, resplendent in his polished, shoulder-length brass helmet. "I think it was hit by a stray incendiary," he said. "Can you get the commandant to lift the curfew? We need help for the bucket brigade." The mayor ran to the nearby German headquarters and got permission. Then he and others went about banging on doors, calling for the inhabitants to help. Soon more than 100 men and women in two long lines were passing buckets of water from hand to hand. Surrounding them were 30 German guards armed with rifles and *Schmeissers*.

In the midst of this confusion, Renaud remembers, there came the droning of planes, coming straight for Ste.-Mère-Eglise. With the steadily mounting roar came the approaching racket of anti-aircraft fire as battery after battery picked up the formations. Then the German guns in the town began firing and the roaring was on top of them. The aircraft swept in through a crisscrossing barrage of fire. In wave after wave the formations flew over—the first planes of the biggest airborne operation ever attempted: 882 planes carrying 13,000 men of the U.S. 101st and 82nd Airborne divisions, heading for six drop zones all within a few miles of Ste.-Mère-Eglise.

The troopers tumbled out of their planes. Caught by a heavy wind, Private John Steele saw that instead of landing in a lighted drop zone, he was heading for the center of a town that seemed to be on fire. Then he saw German soldiers and French civilians running frantically about. Most of them, it seemed to Steele, were looking up at him. The next moment he was hit by something that felt "like the bite of a sharp knife." A bullet had smashed into his foot. Then Steele saw something that alarmed him even more. Swinging in his harness, unable to veer away, he was heading straight toward the tower of a church at the edge of the square. Steele's parachute draped itself over a corner of the tower and he dangled there helplessly. He heard the shouts and the screams. He saw Germans and Americans firing at each other in the square and the streets. And he saw, on a roof only a few yards away from him, German machine-gunners firing at everything in sight. Steele decided that his only hope lay in playing dead. He hung so realistically "dead" in his harness that Captain Willard Young of the 82nd, who passed by during the height of the fighting, still remembers "the dead man hanging from the church." Steele was to dangle there for two hours before being taken captive by the Germans.

The first invaders of D-day, almost 18,000 Americans, British and Canadians, were on the flanks of the Normandy battlefield. In between lay the five invasion beaches, and beyond the horizon, steadily approaching, only 12 miles out, was the first of the mighty invasion fleet—over 5000 vessels, including the landing craft.

And still the Germans remained blind. There were many reasons. The weather, their lack of reconnaissance (only a few planes had been sent over the embarkation areas in the preceding weeks, and all had been shot down), their stubborn belief that the invasion *must* come at the Pas-de-Calais, the section of the French coast nearest Britain, all played a part. Even their radar stations failed them this night, confused by Allied planes flying along the coast dropping strips of tinfoil which snowed the screens. Only one station had made a report. It saw only "normal Channel traffic." (See "Fakery in the Air," page 390.)

More than two hours had elapsed since the first paratroopers had landed. Only now were the German commanders in Normandy beginning to realize that something important might be happening. The first scattered reports were beginning to come in.

General Marcks, 84th Corps commander, was still at his birthday party when his phone rang. The man who was calling was Major General Wilhelm Richter, commander of the 716th Division holding the coast above Caen. "Parachutists have

landed east of the Orne. . . . The area seems to be around
Bréville and Ranville. . . ." This was the first official report of
the Allied attack to reach a major German headquarters. The
time was 2:11 a.m.

Marcks immediately telephoned Major General Pemsel, chief
of staff of the Seventh Army, who wakened the Seventh's commanding officer, General Friedrich Dollmann. "General," said
Pemsel, "I believe this is the invasion. Will you please come over
immediately?" As Pemsel waited for Dollmann, the 84th Corps
reported again: ". . . Parachute drops near Montebourg and
Marcouf . . . troops engaged in battle." Pemsel promptly alerted
Major General Speidel, chief of staff for the absent Rommel.

These were strange, confusing minutes at Rommel's headquarters. Reports now came piling in from everywhere—reports
that were often inaccurate, incomprehensible and contradictory.
Luftwaffe headquarters in Paris announced that "50 to 60 two-
engine planes are coming in" over the Cherbourg peninsula and
that paratroopers had landed "near Caen." Admiral Theodor
Krancke's headquarters confirmed the British paratroop landings and added that "part of the parachute drop consists of straw
dummies." Within minutes of their first message the Luftwaffe
also reported parachutists down near Bayeux. Actually none
had landed there at all. Other reports came in saying that the
airborne troops were only "dolls disguised as paratroopers."

The observation was partly right. The Allies had dropped
hundreds of paratrooper-like rubber dummies south of the
Normandy invasion area. Attached to each were strings of
firecrackers which exploded on landing, giving the impression of
a small-arms fight. A few of these dummies were to have an
effect on the course of the Omaha Beach battle later in the day.
They were to deceive General Marcks into believing that he was
being attacked from the rear. He would send troops, who could
have been committed at the beachhead, south to meet the make-
believe attack.

At Rommel's headquarters men tried desperately to evaluate
the rash of red spots sprouting over their maps. If this was the
invasion, was it aimed at Normandy? Were the attacks simply a

diversion intended to draw attention from the real invasion? Hashing the situation over, the German officers came up with conclusions which, in the light of what was actually happening, seem incredible. When Major Doertenbach, acting intelligence officer of Von Rundstedt's headquarters, called Rommel's headquarters for a report, he was told that "the chief of staff views the situation with equanimity" and that "there is a possibility that parachutists who have been reported are merely bailed-out bomber crews."

The Seventh Army didn't think so. At three a.m. Pemsel called Speidel to report that the naval station at Cherbourg was picking up offshore ships on its sound-direction apparatus. Speidel's answer was that "the affair is still locally confined, and for the time being is not to be considered a large operation."

Probably the most baffled men in Normandy this night were the 16,200 seasoned troops of the tough 21st Panzer Division— once a part of Rommel's famed Afrika Korps. Clogging every small village, hamlet and wood in an area just 25 miles southeast of Caen, a major British objective, these men were sitting almost on the edge of the battlefield. Ever since the air-raid alert they had been standing alongside their tanks and vehicles, engines running. But, after the alert, no further word had come. With growing anger and impatience, they continued to wait.

It was nearly dawn—the dawn that 18,000 paratroopers had been fighting toward. In less than five hours the airborne armies had confused the enemy, disrupted communications and now, holding the flanks at either end of the Normandy invasion area, they had to a great extent blocked the movement of enemy reinforcements.

In the British zone gliderborne troops were firmly astride the vital Caen and Orne bridges, which they had captured in a daring attack just after midnight, and paratroopers were in position on the heights overlooking Caen. By dawn the five German-held crossings over the Dives would be demolished. Thus the principal British assignments had been completed and, as long as the various arteries could be held, German counter-attacks would be slowed down or stopped altogether.

At the other end of the invasion beaches the Americans had done equally well. The men of the Allied airborne armies had invaded the Continent and secured the initial foothold. Now they awaited the arrival of the seaborne forces with whom they would drive into Hitler's Europe. For U.S. ground troops, H-hour—6:30 a.m.—was exactly one hour and 45 minutes away.

Everywhere men waited for this dawn, but none so anxiously as the Germans. For by now a new and ominous note had begun to creep into the welter of messages pouring into Rommel's and Von Rundstedt's headquarters. All along the invasion coast Admiral Krancke's naval stations were picking up the sound of ships—not just one or two as before, but ships by the score. For more than an hour the reports had been mounting. At last, a little before five a.m., the persistent Major General Pemsel telephoned Major General Speidel and said bluntly, "Ships are concentrating between the mouths of the Vire and the Orne. An enemy landing and large-scale attack against Normandy are imminent."

Field Marshal von Rundstedt, at his headquarters outside Paris, had already reached a similar conclusion. To him the impending Normandy assault still looked like a "diversionary attack" and not the real invasion, but, even so, he had moved fast. He had already ordered two massive panzer divisions—the 12th SS and the Panzer Lehr, both lying in reserve near Paris— to assemble and rush to the coast. Technically both these divisions were not to be committed without Hitler's specific approval. But Von Rundstedt had taken the chance; he could not believe that Hitler would countermand the order. He sent an official request for the reserves.

At Hitler's headquarters in Berchtesgaden, in the balmy, unrealistic climate of southern Bavaria, the message was delivered to the office of General Jodl. Jodl was asleep and his staff believed that the situation had not yet developed sufficiently for his sleep to be disturbed. The message could wait.

Three miles away, at the "Eagle's Nest," Hitler's mountain retreat at Obersalzberg, the Führer and Eva Braun were also asleep. Hitler had retired as usual at four a.m., and his personal physician, Dr. Morell, had given him a sleeping draught (he was unable to sleep now without it). At about five a.m. Hitler's naval aide, Admiral Karl Jesko von Puttkamer, was awakened by a call from Jodl's headquarters. Puttkamer's caller said that there had been "some sort of landings in France." Nothing precise was known yet—in fact, Puttkamer was told, "the first messages are extremely vague." Did Puttkamer think that the Führer should be informed? The men hashed it over and then decided not to wake Hitler. Puttkamer remembers that "there wasn't much to tell him anyway and we both feared that if I woke him at this time he might start one of his endless nervous scenes which often led to the wildest decisions." He decided that the morning would be time enough to give Hitler the news.

In France the generals at Rommel's and Von Rundstedt's headquarters sat down to wait. They had alerted their forces and called up the panzer reserves—now the next move was up to the Allies. Nobody could estimate the magnitude of the impending assault. Nobody knew—or could even guess—the size of the Allied fleet. And although everything pointed toward Normandy, nobody was really sure where the main attack would come. The German generals had done all they could. The rest depended on the men holding the coastal fortifications. There the soldiers of the Reich looked out toward the sea, wondering if this was a practice alert or the real thing at last.

Major Werner Pluskat in his bunker overlooking Omaha Beach had heard nothing from his superiors since one a.m. To be sure, the very fact that his phone had remained silent all night was a good sign—it must mean that nothing serious was happening. But what about the paratroopers, the massed formations of planes? Pluskat began another slow sweep of the horizon with his binoculars. Everything seemed peaceful. Behind him his officers, Wilkening and Theen, were talking quietly. Pluskat joined them. "Still nothing out there," he told them. "I'm about to give it up." But he decided to make another routine sweep. Wearily he swung the glasses over to the left again. Slowly he tracked across the horizon. He reached the dead center of the bay. The glasses stopped moving. Pluskat tensed, stared hard.

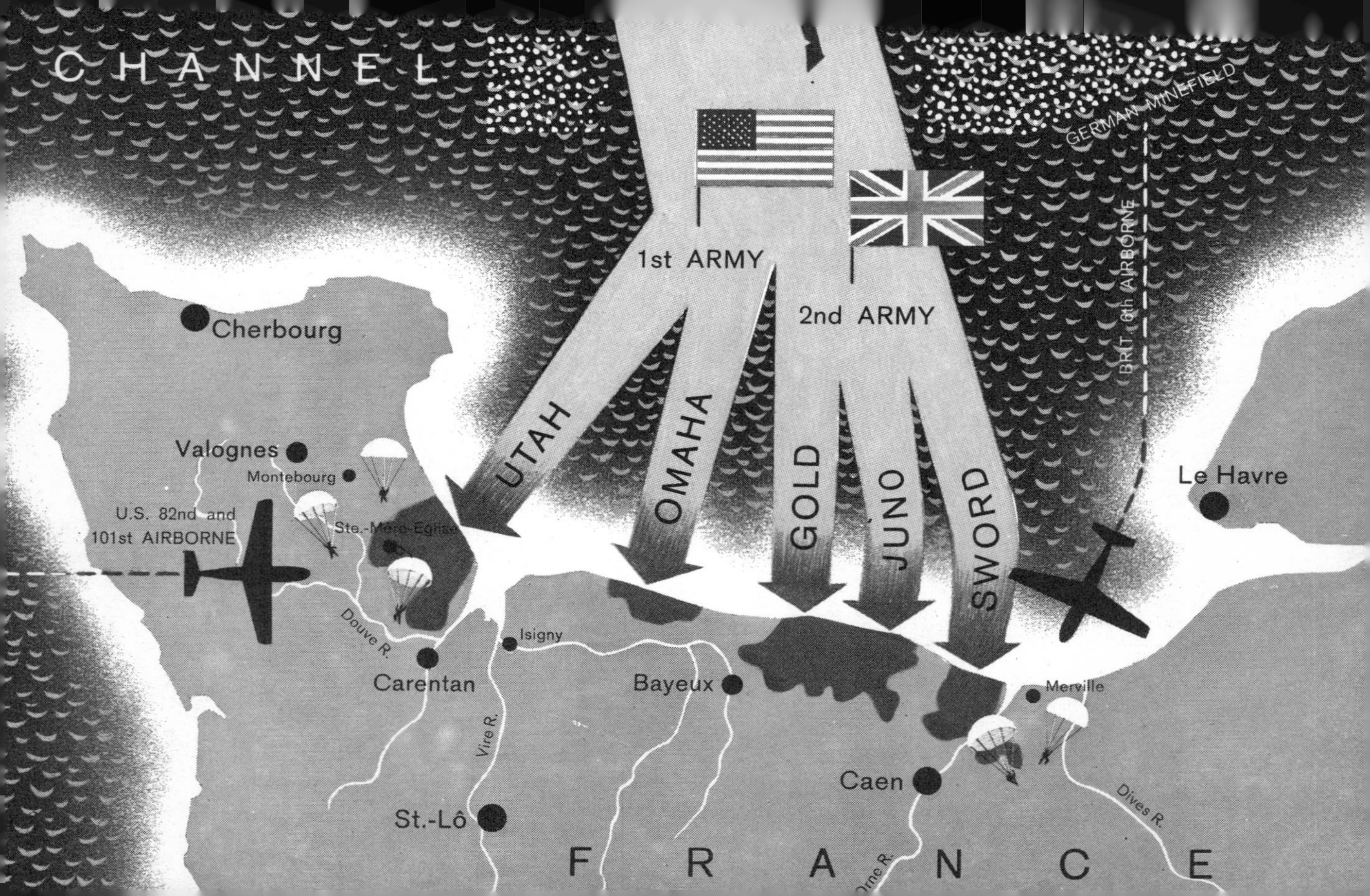
CHANNEL
GERMAN MINEFIELD
1st ARMY
2nd ARMY
BRIT. 6th AIRBORNE
Cherbourg
Valognes
Montebourg
U.S. 82nd and
101st AIRBORNE
Ste.-Mère-Église
UTAH
OMAHA
GOLD
JUNO
SWORD
Le Havre
Douve R.
Isigny
Carentan
Bayeux
Merville
Vire R.
Caen
Dives R.
St.-Lô
Orne R.
FRANCE

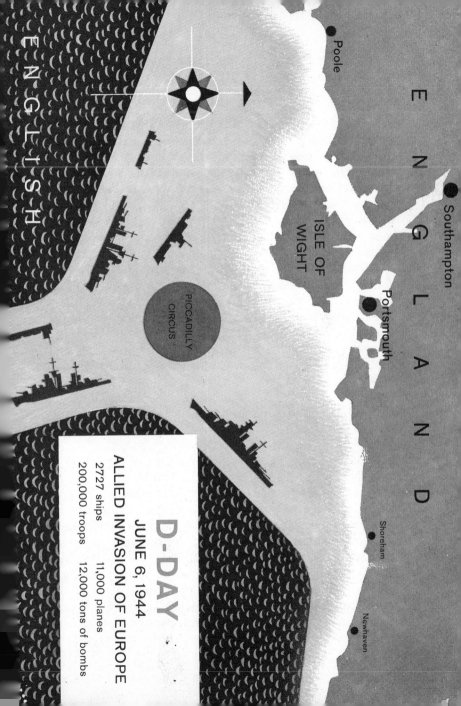

Through the scattering, thinning mist the horizon was mag-
ically filling with ships—ships of every size and description, ships
that casually maneuvered back and forth as though they had
been there for hours. There appeared to be thousands of them.
It was a ghostly armada that somehow had appeared from
nowhere. Pluskat stared in frozen disbelief, speechless, moved as
he had never been before in his life. At that moment the world
of the good soldier Pluskat began falling apart. He says that in
those first few moments he knew, calmly and surely, that "this
was the end for Germany."

He turned to Wilkening and Theen and, with a strange detachment, said simply, "It's the invasion. See for yourselves." Then
he picked up the phone and called Major Block at the 352nd
Division's headquarters. "Block," said Pluskat, "there must be
10,000 ships out there." Even as he said it, he knew his words
must sound incredible. "Get hold of yourself, Pluskat!" snapped
Block. "The Americans and the British together don't have that
many ships. Nobody has that many ships!" Block's disbelief
brought Pluskat out of his daze. "If you don't believe me," he
suddenly yelled, "come up here and see for yourself. It's fantastic! It's unbelievable!" There was a slight pause and then
Block said, "Where are the ships heading?" Pluskat, phone in
hand, looked out the aperture of the bunker and replied, "Right
for me."

Never had there been a dawn like this. In the murky, gray
light the great Allied fleet lay off Normandy's five invasion
beaches. The sea teemed with ships. Battle ensigns snapped in
the wind all the way across the horizon from the edge of the
Utah area on the Cherbourg peninsula to Sword Beach near the
mouth of the Orne. Outlined against the sky were the big battle-
wagons, the menacing cruisers, the whippet-like destroyers.
Behind them were the squat command ships, sprouting their
forests of antennas. And behind these came the convoys of
troop-filled transports and landing ships, lying low and sluggish
in the water. Circling the lead transports, waiting for the signal
to head for the beaches, were swarms of bobbing landing craft,

jam-packed with the men who would land in the first waves.

More and more troop-filled boats joined the churning assault craft endlessly circling the mother ships. Sodden, seasick and miserable, the men in these boats would lead the way into Normandy. Loading the boats in the heaving swells was a complex and hazardous operation. Soldiers carried so much equipment that they were barely able to move. They had rubber-tube life preservers, weapons, musette bags, entrenching tools, gas masks, first-aid kits, canteens, knives, rations and extra .quantities of grenades, explosives and ammunition—often as much as 250 rounds. In addition, many men were burdened with the special equipment that their particular jobs demanded. Some men estimate that they weighed at least 300 pounds as they waddled across decks and prepared to debark.

The first wave of assault troops could not yet see the misty shores of Normandy. They were still more than nine miles away. Some warships were already dueling with German naval coastal batteries, but the action as yet was remote and impersonal for the men of the first waves—nobody was firing directly at them. Seasickness was still their biggest enemy.

On the flagship *Augusta*, lying off the American target beaches, Lieutenant General Omar N. Bradley plugged his ears with cotton and then trained his binoculars on the landing craft speeding toward the beaches. His troops, the men of the U.S. First Army, were moving steadily in. Bradley was extremely worried. A few hours earlier he had learned that elements of a tough German division, the battle-tested 352nd, had moved into position along Omaha Beach. The information had come too late for the assault troops to be notified. Now the naval bombardment which he prayed would make their job easier was about to begin. The time was 5:50 a.m. The British fleet had been firing at their beaches for more than 20 minutes. Now the bombardment began in the American zone. The entire invasion area erupted with a roaring storm of fire. The maelstrom of sound thundered back and forth along the Normandy coast as the big ships slammed steadily away at their pre-selected targets.

Off Omaha, the big battleships *Texas* and *Arkansas*, mounting

between them a total of ten 14-inch, twelve 12-inch and twelve
5-inch guns, pumped 600 shells onto the coastal battery position
atop Pointe du Hoc in an all-out attempt to ease the way for the
Ranger battalions even now heading for the 100-foot-high sheer
cliffs. Off Sword, Juno and Gold the British battleships *Warspite*
and *Ramillies* lobbed tons of steel from their 15-inch guns toward the powerful German batteries at Le Havre and around
the mouth of the Orne. Maneuvering cruisers and destroyers
poured streams of shells into pillboxes, concrete bunkers and
redoubts.

Now a new sound throbbed over the fleet. Slowly at first, like
the rumbling of some giant bee, and then building to a great
crescendo of noise, the bombers and fighters appeared. They
flew straight in over the massive fleet, flying wing tip to wing
tip, formation after formation—11,000 planes. Spitfires, Thun-
derbolts and Mustangs whistled in over the heads of the men in
the assault boats. With apparent disregard for the rain of shells
from the fleet, they strafed the invasion beaches and headlands,
zoomed up, swept around and came in again.

Crisscrossing above them were the Ninth Air Force's B-26
medium bombers, and above these, out of sight in the heavy
cloud layer, droned the heavies—the RAF's Lancasters and the
Eighth Air Force's Fortresses and Liberators. It seemed as
though the sky could not possibly hold them all.

By now the long bobbing lines of assault craft were less than a
mile from Omaha and Utah beaches. For the Americans in the
first wave, H-hour was just 15 minutes away.

Overhead, like a great steel umbrella, the shells of the fleet
still thundered. And rolling out from the coast came the boom-
ing explosions of the Allied air forces' carpet bombing. Strangely,
the guns of the Germans' Atlantic Wall were silent. Troops saw
the coast line stretching ahead and wondered about the absence
of enemy fire. Maybe, many thought, it would be an easy landing
after all.

Closer and closer the boats pressed in . . . 500 yards . . . 450
yards. Still no enemy fire. Through waves that were four to five
feet high the assault craft surged in and now the great bombard-

ment began to lift, shifting to targets further inland. The first boats were barely 400 yards from the shore when the German guns—the guns that few believed could have survived the raging Allied air and sea bombardment—opened up. Through the din and clamor one sound was nearer, deadlier than all the rest—the sound of machine-gun bullets clanging across the snoutlike steel noses of the boats. Then artillery opened up; mortar shells rained down—and all along the four miles of Omaha Beach, German guns pounded the assault craft.

It was H-hour.

They came ashore on Omaha Beach—the slogging, unglamorous men that no one envied. They would call this beach "Bloody Omaha." Some boats wandered along the beach seeking a less heavily defended spot. Others, doggedly trying to come in at their assigned sectors, were shelled so badly that men plunged over the sides into deep water where they were immediately picked off by machine-gun fire.

Misfortune piled upon misfortune for the men on Omaha. Soldiers discovered that they had been landed in the wrong sectors. Some came in almost two miles away from their landing areas. The special Army-Navy demolition engineers who had the job of blowing paths through the beach obstacles were not only widely scattered—they were brought in crucial minutes behind schedule. These frustrated men set to work wherever they found themselves. Working with desperate haste, the demolition parties were impeded at every turn—infantrymen waded in among them, soldiers took shelter behind the obstacles they were about to blow, and landing craft, buffeted by the swells, came in almost on top of them. (See "The Frogmen," page 476.)

It was seven a.m. The second wave of troops arrived on the shambles that was Omaha Beach. The story was the same—men splashed ashore under the saturating fire of the enemy. Landing craft joined the ever growing graveyard of wrecked, blazing hulks. Each wave of boats gave up its own bloody contribution to the incoming tide. Piling up along the shore were the flotsam and jetsam of the invasion. Equipment and supplies were strewn everywhere. The twisted wrecks of landing craft canted up crazily out of the water. Burning tanks threw great spirals of black smoke into the air. Bulldozers lay on their sides among the obstacles.

Into the chaos, confusion and death on the beach the third wave came—and stopped. Men lay shoulder to shoulder on the sands, stones and shale. They crouched behind obstacles; they sheltered among the bodies of the dead. Pinned down by the enemy fire which they had expected to be neutralized, confused by their landings in the wrong sectors, bewildered by the absence of the sheltering craters they had expected from the air-force bombing, and shocked by the devastation and death all around them, the men froze on the beaches. They seemed in the grip of a strange paralysis. The shock would not last long. Even now a few men here and there, realizing that to stay on the beach meant certain death, were on their feet and moving.

Ten miles away, on Utah Beach, it was a different story. Here the men of Major General Raymond O. Barton's Fourth Division were swarming ashore and driving inland fast. The third wave of assault boats was coming in and still there was only light opposition. Amphibious tanks had been a big factor in the success of the landings. Yet there was another reason why the Utah forces had met so little opposition. By a fortunate error they had been landed in the wrong place. Confused by smoke from the naval bombardment, caught by a strong current, a solitary control boat had guided the first wave into a landing more than a mile south of the designated beach. Instead of invading the beach opposite Exits 3 and 4—two of the five vital causeways toward which the 101st Airborne was driving—the entire beachhead was now astride Exit 2.

Rather than fighting for the planned objectives, the Fourth would drive inland on the single causeway and take out German positions when and where they found them. Everything now depended on moving as quickly as possible, before the enemy recovered from the initial shock of the landings.

On the beaches named Sword, Juno and Gold the British and Canadians were landing. For almost 15 miles—from Ouistreham at the mouth of the Orne to the village of Le Hamel on the west—the shore line was choked with landing craft disgorging troops. The waters offshore became a junkyard of assault craft. Waves of boats began to pile up almost on top of one another. By and large, however, the British and Canadian troops encountered less resistance in their assault than did the Americans on Omaha. Their later H-hours had given the British fleet more time to saturate the coastal defenses, and the soldiers poured onto their beaches and moved inland. The British and Canadians would make D-day's greatest advances, but they would fail to capture their principal objective—Caen. The tough 21st Panzer Division would deny them this important Normandy city for the next five weeks.

Berchtesgaden lay quiet and peaceful in the early morning. The clouds were low on the surrounding mountains, and at Hitler's retreat all was still. But at the Führer's headquarters two miles away, General Jodl had begun to study early reports of the Normandy invasion. He did not think the situation was serious as yet.

The deputy chief of operations, General Walter Warlimont, phoned. "Von Rundstedt is requesting the release of the panzer reserves," he said. "He wants to move them to the invasion areas as soon as possible."

As Warlimont recalls, there was a long silence while Jodl pondered the request. "Are you so sure of all this?" Jodl asked. "I'm not certain this is the invasion. I do not think that this is the time to release the reserves. . . . We must wait for further clarification of the situation."

Warlimont was shocked by Jodl's literal interpretation of the Hitler edict concerning the control of the panzers. As he was later to recall, "Jodl's decision was the one he thought Hitler would have made." Now the decision to release the panzers would depend on the whim of one man—Hitler. And on this day, when the defeat of the Allied invasion depended on power and speed, that decision would come too late—not for another eight and a half hours.

Meanwhile the man who had anticipated just such a situation

and had hoped to discuss it with Hitler was less than an hour's drive from Berchtesgaden. Field Marshal Erwin Rommel was at his home in Herrlingen, Ulm. The time was 7:30 a.m. There is no record in the meticulously kept Army Group B War Diary that the Field Marshal had as yet even been briefed on the Normandy landings.

Even now—although the invasion had actually been in progress for seven and a half hours—the full scope of the Allied attack could not be gauged by the staffs of Von Rundstedt's and Rommel's headquarters. Everywhere along the front the vast network of communications had broken down. The paratroopers had done their work well. As the Seventh Army's General Pemsel put it in a call to Rommel's headquarters, "I'm fighting the sort of battle that William the Conqueror must have fought—by ear and sight only. My officers ring and say, 'I hear sounds and see ships,' but they cannot give me a true picture of the situation."

In Seventh Army headquarters at Le Mans, however, the officers were enthusiastic. It looked as though the tough 352nd Division, counter-attacking in the area of Omaha Beach, had already smashed the landing. Their spirits were so high that when a message came in from the 15th Army offering reinforcements, the Seventh operations officer turned them down. "We don't need them," he said.

At Rommel's headquarters in the Duke de la Rochefoucauld's old castle at La Roche-Guyon, there was a similar air of optimism. Colonel Leodegard Freyberg recalls that "the general impression was that the Allies would be thrown back into the sea by the end of the day." Vice Admiral Friedrich Ruge, Rommel's naval aide, shared in the general elation. But Ruge noticed one peculiar thing: the Duke's household staff was quietly going through the castle taking down from the walls the priceless Gobelin tapestries.

In England it was 9:30 a.m. General Eisenhower had paced the floor all night waiting for each new report to come in. There was no doubt now that a foothold had been achieved on the Continent. Although the hold was slight, there would be no need for him to release the message that he had quietly scribbled out just 24 hours before. In case the Allied attempt was defeated, he had written: "Our landings in the Cherbourg-Havre area have failed to gain a satisfactory foothold and I have withdrawn the troops. My decision to attack at this time and place was based upon the best information available. The troops, the air and the Navy did all that bravery and devotion to duty could do. If there is any blame or fault attached to the attempt, it is mine alone."

Instead, at 9:33 a.m. (3:33, New York time) a far different message was broadcast to the world. It read: "Under the command of General Eisenhower, Allied naval forces, supported by strong air forces, began landing Allied armies this morning on the northern coast of France."

At 10:15 the phone rang in Rommel's home at Herrlingen. The caller was his chief of staff, Major General Speidel. The purpose: the first complete briefing on the invasion. Rommel listened with sinking heart.

It was no longer a "Dieppe-type raid." It was the day he had been waiting for—the one he had said would be the "longest day." It was clear to Rommel, "the realist," that, although there would be months of fighting, the game was up. It was only midmorning, but the "longest day" was all but over. By an irony of fate the great German general had been on the sidelines during the decisive battle of the war. All Rommel could say when Speidel had finished was, "How stupid of me! How stupid of me!"

What Really Happened to Rommel

By Countess Waldeck

General Erwin Rommel was 49 years old when he catapulted into fame in May 1940 as commander of the Seventh Panzer Division during the German sweep across France. Two years later, when his Afrika Korps stood only 70 miles from Alexandria, his name was a household word all over the world. That was the year Hitler made him a field marshal, and the British called him the ablest general of the war.

When the Tommies of the British Eighth Army which opposed him in Africa spoke of "doing a rommel," they meant doing a superb job. His cunning and talent for improvisation earned him the sobriquet "Desert Fox." Once, hard pressed by the British, he frightened them off by convincing them of his superior strength. Knowing that every day the RAF photographed over the German lines, he ordered every available vehicle to drive incessantly for two whole nights, tracks over tracks, in the surrounding desert. The resulting photos, with added German propaganda, led the British into overrating the German forces, and they retreated.

Rommel had a quality which might be called military sex appeal. It was in the cocky set of his cap; it was in his peasantlike cunning. To his men, who saw him rising out of the turret of his tank in the front battle line, he was the god of battle. "Stay close to me," he once said to one of his officers while they were under fire. "Nothing ever happens to me." But something did happen to him, in the end.

What are the little-known facts about his mysterious death?

The official German story was that he died of injuries received when his command car was strafed near Livarot, south of Le Havre, at the time of the Normandy invasion. But the truth is far more dramatic—and revealing.

It was during the losing battles of the African campaign that Rommel first came to realize Hitler's abysmal contempt for the individual human being. Rommel knew that the campaign was lost beyond redemption, owing to the German lack of gasoline and equipment and the greatly reinforced British strength. He demanded that Hitler withdraw the German troops as the only means of saving the lives of thousands of men. Hitler replied excitedly: "Triumph or death!"

"I neither died nor triumphed," Rommel later commented dryly.

Before the surrender in Tunisia in May 1943, Hitler had ordered Rommel's return to Germany to become part of the Führer's entourage—so that he would not be identified with the defeat. The months that followed were bitter ones. Rommel had never joined the Nazi Party, never was decorated with the golden party emblem. And, preoccupied with self-aggrandizement, he had heretofore ignored the wholesale killings, the slave labor, the concentration camps, the Gestapo terror in the occupied areas. Now he was horrified by what the Nazis did in the name of the German people. "I conducted a clean war," he said, "but they soil my uniform." Later, when Hitler released his notorious order to shoot hostages at the ratio of 12 to 1, Rommel was one of the few German commanders who threw it in the wastebasket. What pained Rommel most was the realization, at last, that Hitler would drag all Germany into the abyss with him rather than give up.

To bolster the confidence of the German people and impress the Allies, Hitler assigned to Rommel the ground command of the anti-invasion forces in Normandy. The General soon foresaw that a full-scale invasion could not be repelled with the meager supply of matériel and troops at his disposal. In April 1944 he conferred with General Karl Heinrich von Stülpnagel, military governor of France and a leader of the German resistance to

Hitler, about ways and means of ending the war in the West at once and overthrowing the Nazi regime.

In the hope of gaining something a little better than the unconditional surrender proclaimed as Allied policy, Rommel wished to offer an armistice to Eisenhower and Montgomery without the knowledge of Hitler. Its basis was to be the withdrawal of German troops behind the Westwall. In return the Allies were to stop bombing German cities at once. In the East, however, the Germans were to continue fighting on a shortened front—Rumania, Lemberg, the Vistula, Memel—"in defense of Western civilization." Rommel proposed to have Hitler seized by reliable panzer units and tried before a German tribunal. He did not believe in making a martyr of Hitler by killing him outright.

Following the successful Allied invasion of Normandy, Rommel sent an ultimatum to Hitler in which he demanded the immediate opening of armistice negotiations.

On the evening of July 17, 1944, Rommel, returning from the front, reached the outskirts of Livarot. Suddenly two planes with British markings headed directly toward him. One, flying only a few yards above the ground, strafed the left half of the car. Rommel was knocked unconscious and thrown out of the car. As he lay on the road, the second plane swooped down and opened fire. Rommel was so seriously wounded—a skull fracture, two fractures of the temple, a broken cheekbone, an injury to the left eye, a concussion of the brain—that doctors doubted he would live.

This was the first of two severe blows to befall the anti-Nazi plot. The second came on July 20. "Operation Valkyrie," the conspiracy of German Army leaders and anti-Nazi civilians to assassinate Hitler (into the preparations for which Rommel had previously been drawn by Stülpnagel), missed fire at the Führer's Prussia headquarters. The bomb went off two yards from Hitler, wrecked his headquarters, injured 20 men and killed four. But Hitler miraculously escaped. Nazi revenge hunted down the known conspirators. Those who were caught were executed.

By the end of summer Rommel had made a brilliant recovery;

except for a partial paralysis of his left eye, he was as good as new. On October 14 he rose early in his villa in Herrlingen, near Ulm, to meet his 16-year-old son, Manfred, who was arriving home for a brief Army furlough. But another, less welcome visitor was expected at noon that day. A telephone call the previous night had informed Rommel that General Wilhelm Burgdorf was being sent by the Führer to discuss with him his "reassignment to a new command." The Marshal remarked to Manfred at breakfast: "Burgdorf's coming may be a trap."

At 12 o'clock General Burgdorf arrived, accompanied by General Ernest Maisel. Rommel, with his wife and son, greeted the visitors. They kissed Her Excellency's hand. There was the usual exchange of platitudes about the lovely autumn weather and everyone's health, including the Field Marshal's splendid recovery. Presently Frau Rommel and Manfred withdrew.

A little after one o'clock Rommel came upstairs to his wife's room. "What is the matter?" Frau Rommel exclaimed, alarmed by the look on her husband's face.

"In a quarter of an hour I shall be dead," Rommel said absently, as though tasting the words for their meaning.

He told her quickly: The testimony of Stülpnagel (who had been strangled after he blinded himself in a suicide attempt) had left no doubt about Rommel's participation in the July 20 plot. Hitler now gave him the choice between death by poison immediately or a trial before a people's court. The two generals had made it quite clear that if Rommel insisted on standing trial, reprisals would be taken against Frau Rommel and Manfred; if he let himself be poisoned, his family would be spared and would receive all honors and pensions due the family of a German field marshal. The Führer was determined to keep from the German people the fact that their most popular general had plotted to overthrow him and to make peace. With ghoulish precision Burgdorf had outlined for Rommel the last fine details of the plan. On the drive to Ulm a poison would be given him. Within three seconds he would be dead. His body would be delivered to a hospital in Ulm. A message would go to the world that he had died suddenly of the aftereffects of his July 17 injuries.

In that upstairs room Rommel divulged details of the diabolic plot to two others—his aide, Captain Aldinger, and Manfred. Then these three went downstairs. Rommel let himself be helped into his greatcoat, then put on his cap, a little jauntily as usual. Manfred and Aldinger handed him his gloves and baton. Then he walked out to the car where his assassins waited, and drove off.

In all the annals of the Third Reich no scene exposes more flagrantly the psychological climate on which Hitler thrived. Here was no poor Jew helpless in the hands of the Gestapo. Here was a German field marshal, complete with baton, the glory of his army, a legend over all the world for his courage and his cunning. Yet this man let himself be taken away to his death.

At 1:25 General Burgdorf and General Maisel delivered Rommel to the hospital at Ulm. He was already dead. The chief physician proposed an autopsy, but Burgdorf said quickly: "Do not touch the body. Berlin has arranged for everything."

Exactly what happened on that drive will probably remain a mystery forever. Burgdorf perished with Hitler in the cellar of the Reich Chancellery. Maisel and the SS driver later insisted that they were made to leave the car for a moment and on their return found Rommel dying.

At the state funeral on October 18 the assembly, studded with Nazi chieftains and high officers, behaved with solemn decorum. (See photograph on page 345.) Field Marshal von Rundstedt delivered the oration in Hitler's place. Frau Rommel, pale and grim, had refused Von Rundstedt's arm. A nameless tension threatened to burst through the thin veneer of well-bred punctilio. Only a few of those present, however, knew that they were attending the final act of a murder.

Death on the Wing

By Captain Rikihei Inoguchi and Commander Tadashi Nakajima,
Former Imperial Japanese Navy
Translated by Commander Masataka Chihaya and Roger Pineau

On October 17, 1944, when the Philippines were in Japanese hands, an American force landed at the entrance to Leyte Gulf. Even before that date U.S. carrier planes were swarming over targets from Luzon to Mindanao. The Japanese fleet had suffered overwhelming defeat in the Battle of the Philippine Sea; naval air strength was at a low ebb. Everyone was aware that it would take a miracle to save the Japanese from disaster.

As dusk settled over Mabalacat Field, Luzon, on October 19, a black sedan drew up in front of the command post of the 201st Japanese Air Group and Admiral Takijiro Onishi stepped out. Commander of the First Air Fleet, he was regarded as Japan's foremost exponent of aerial warfare. Now he summoned the 201st's staff officers into immediate conference and said:

"The situation is so grave that the fate of the entire empire depends on the successful defense of the Philippines. A naval force under Admiral Kurita is to penetrate Leyte Gulf and there annihilate enemy surface units. The First Air Fleet has been designated to support that mission by rendering enemy carriers ineffective for at least one week. But our position is such that we can no longer win by adhering to conventional methods of warfare. *In my opinion, the enemy can be stopped only by crash-diving on their carrier flight decks with Zero fighters carrying 250-kilogram bombs.*"

The listeners were electrified by the Admiral's words as his sharp eyes surveyed the crowded room. It was apparent that the purpose of his visit was to inspire suicide attacks.

When Admiral Onishi had finished, Commander Tamai, the executive officer, asked permission to consult with his squadron leaders on a matter so grave as this. He was confident that most of his pilots would dedicate themselves as human missiles when they heard of the plan. "They said little," he reported later, "but their eyes spoke eloquently of a willingness to die for their country."

It was decided that Lieutenant Yukio Seki should lead the attack. He was a man of outstanding character and ability, a graduate of the Naval Academy at Eta Jima. When told of the assignment by Commander Tamai, Seki leaned forward at the table, supporting his head in his hands, his eyes closed. The young officer had been married just before leaving the homeland. For several seconds he sat motionless except for the tightening of his clenched fists. Then, raising his head, he smoothed back his hair and spoke in a clear, quiet voice. "Please do appoint me to lead the attack."

Shortly after sunrise on October 20 Admiral Onishi summoned the 24 kamikaze (divine wind) pilots and addressed them, his voice shaking with emotion: "Japan faces a terrible crisis. The salvation of our country is beyond the power of ministers, the General Staff and lowly unit commanders like myself. It is now up to spirited young men such as you." Tears came to his eyes as he concluded: "I ask you to do your utmost and wish you success."

Similar recruiting of kamikaze pilots was taking place at other air bases. At Cebu all hands assembled at six p.m. on October 20. "Each volunteer for the 'special-attack' corps," said the commanding officer, "will write his name and rank on a piece of paper and insert it in an envelope and seal it. Enclose a blank paper if you do not wish to volunteer. You have three hours in which to give the matter serious consideration." At nine o'clock sharp the senior petty-officer pilot gathered up the envelopes and delivered them to the commander's quarters. Of the more than 20 pilots, only two turned in blank pieces of paper.

On October 25 the first successful kamikaze-unit attack was

carried out; six planes took off at dawn from Davao in southern Mindanao and damaged at least three enemy escort carriers. That same morning Lieutenant Seki led a successful attack from Mabalacat.

One of the four escorting pilots furnished a report of the action: "Sighting an enemy force of four carriers and six other ships, Lieutenant Seki dived headlong into one of the carriers, which he rammed successfully. A colleague crashed into the same ship, from which there arose a great column of smoke. Successful hits were also scored by two more pilots, one on another flat-top, the other on a light cruiser."

News of the kamikaze successes flashed throughout the Navy. A total of 93 fighters and 57 bombers had been flown in conventional attacks that day, inflicting no damage on the enemy. The superiority of the suicide attacks was manifest. Admiral Onishi was convinced that further employment of these inhuman tactics was unavoidable. He pressed this opinion on Vice Admiral Fukudome, commander in chief of the Second Air Fleet: "Nothing short of all-out use of special attacks can save us. It is time for your air fleet to adopt these tactics."

Thus the kamikaze tactics were given full play, and young men volunteered freely for the opportunity to add to the intensity of the "divine wind." Reinforcements poured out from the homeland eager to take their turn in crashing upon enemy warships.

Time was running out, however. Day by day the situation around Leyte Island became more hopeless. As the tempo of the invasion increased, so did the intensity and number of kamikaze attacks. But the supply of planes was dwindling, and on January 5 the last large-scale suicide attack from a Philippine base was launched. Fifteen fighter-bombers struck the invasion forces at Lingayen Gulf, damaging one cruiser and four transports. (See photograph on page 349.)

(Editor's note: American Navy accounts of the battle of Lingayen Gulf indicate that the kamikaze attacks were apparently even more effective than the Japanese themselves realized. Not one but two cruisers were damaged, as well as an

escort carrier and a destroyer. The threat of the kamikaze campaign was so great that U.S. carriers which had been scheduled to attack Formosa on January 7 were retained to continue
the attack at Luzon.)

Further Japanese defeats followed quickly after the fall of the
Philippines. The mighty enemy invaded Iwo Jima in February
1945 and Okinawa in April, trapping Japan in a grip of death.
This inspired kamikaze tactics on an unprecedented scale—even
training planes were mobilized.

Now a new suicide weapon was proposed. A rocket-powered
1800-kilogram missile would be attached to a "mother" bomber.
Within sight of the target the missile would be released with a
volunteer suicide pilot to crash it on an enemy ship. The group
of pilots trained to man this weapon was called *Jinrai Butai*
(divine thunderbolt unit). "Baka [foolish] Bomb" was the nickname it earned among the Allies.

Baka Bombs were used in the big attack on Okinawa on
April 12. The pilot of the first missile to score a hit was remarkably composed. In his non-flying hours he was supervisor of a
junior officers' billet. His last words before climbing into the
mother bomber were: "Keep an eye out for the new straw mats I
ordered for the billet." He napped peacefully during the journey
toward Okinawa and had to be awakened to start his flight to
eternity.

In the Okinawa campaign alone there were more than 1800
suicide flights. By the time Japan surrendered, a total of 2519
men and officers of the Imperial Japanese Navy had sacrificed
themselves.

A few hours after the Imperial proclamation of August 15,
1945, calling for immediate cessation of the war, the Fifth Air
Fleet commander, Admiral Ugaki, chose the same death he had
ordered for so many of his pilots. He stripped the insignia of
rank from his uniform and spoke to his assembled officers and
men: "I am going to take off for a crash attack upon the enemy
at Okinawa. Those who wish to follow me are requested to raise
their hands." There were more volunteers than there were
planes available. Of the 11 planes that took off, seven—includ-

ing Admiral Ugaki's—radioed that they were "diving on target."

That evening Admiral Onishi, who now was vice chief of the Naval General Staff in Tokyo, penned a note: "To the souls of my late subordinates I express the greatest appreciation for their valiant deeds. In death I wish to apologize to these brave men and their families." Then he plunged a samurai sword into his abdomen. Refusing medical aid or a *coup de grâce*, Admiral Onishi lingered on in agony until six o'clock the following evening. His choice to endure prolonged suffering was obviously made in expiation for his part in one of the most diabolical tactics of war the world has ever seen.

The American Who Did Business with Himmler

By Edwin Muller

Early in the war Mr. Eric Erickson of Stockholm was posted on the Allied blacklist, accused of trading with the enemy and aiding the German war effort. Allied Intelligençe had reported that Erickson was dealing in German oil, making regular trips to Germany, and that he was on intimate terms with high-ranking Gestapo officials.

The disclosure was a stunning shock to Erickson's family. His old friends, all strongly pro-Ally, now crossed the street when they saw him coming. His wife was ostracized. Although he was a Swedish citizen, Erickson had been born and brought up in Brooklyn, graduated from Cornell. Now he got scathing letters from his family in the United States. But nothing stopped him.

"Red" Erickson was the American salesman type. He had gone into the oil business because it was exciting and got you places. The "oil crowd" in the '20's and '30's was an international clan. You'd see a man in Shanghai one year, in London or Teheran the next. One year you might be competing ruthlessly with him, the next you'd both be on the same side of the fence. American, English, Dutch, German, they lived in an atmosphere of adventurous gambles and deals whose strings were drawn across national frontiers. Erickson became manager for The Texas Company in Sweden. Then he became a Swedish citizen and started his own company, to import American oil products.

Soon after the war began, he saw an opportunity to do business with the Nazis. Germany then had oil to export, and it was absurd to suppose that the Allies could ever affect the supply materially by bombing. So Erickson began to play around with German businessmen. He joined the German Chamber of Commerce in Stockholm. He drew away from most of his old friends, but kept on good terms with Prince Carl Bernadotte, nephew of the King of Sweden. (See photograph on page 333.)

Erickson knew that Gestapo Chief Heinrich Himmler would make the final decision in the oil deals. So the prospect on whom Erickson did his heavy work was Herr Finke, Himmler's chief representative in Sweden and a fanatical Nazi. Finke's weak point was a snobbish susceptibility to royalty. Prince Carl helped make the contact and Erickson did the cultivating. Soon he was entertaining Herr Finke at his place in the country. Other prospects, however, didn't come along—notably Herr Ludwig, commercial attaché of the German Legation. He didn't like Erickson at all. But despite Ludwig's aloofness, Erickson got permission to visit Germany in September 1941, with letters of introduction from Finke and others.

At Bromma Field, outside Stockholm, the plane to Berlin was held up while Erickson was ordered off by the Swedish police. They made a brusque and thorough search of him and his baggage. But nothing incriminating was found, and he was allowed to proceed. In Berlin an official car took him to Gestapo headquarters. There he met two men who had been on the plane with him—Gestapo agents. They agreed that the incident at Bromma had been the work of Allied representatives.

Erickson made his contacts with German oil men, especially in Hamburg. He visited refineries there, talked with the managers, discussed the terms of the contracts he wanted. He also looked around for some of the oil crowd he used to know. First he found a Junker who had had part of his education in England and had at one time been associated with Shell Oil. Since Erickson hoped to keep his deals secret, his talks with the Junker were very hush-hush. Another contact was Herr von Stürker, an oil banker, of an old Hamburg family. Erickson took pains to let neither of the men see him with the other.

Soon after Erickson went back to Sweden, the first deliveries of German oil began. It was then that the Allies put him on the blacklist. His alienation from his old friends was complete. Some of them would get up and leave a restaurant if he entered it. His Swedish wife suffered intensely. She was still anti-Nazi, yet she had to entertain her husband's new friends.

In the months that followed, Erickson made other trips to Germany and continued to cultivate his friends in the Gestapo. He was invited to their homes and he brought their wives butter and leather coats and other presents from Sweden. And he continued to make deals, though it became harder to get oil from Germany as the Allied bombings were stepped up. Once, after he had inspected a big refinery, the managing director asked him to stay to dinner. He hesitated but found it hard to decline. The meal was served in the director's office. It was nearly midnight when the party broke up, and just after midnight when Allied bombers arrived. When they finished their work, there wasn't any plant left. The Allies then and there almost put an end to Erickson's trading with the enemy.

The Allied attack on German oil was increasingly effective, yet in the latter part of 1944 a substantial portion of the industry was still functioning. Repairs were made more rapidly than the Allies had thought possible. Moreover, many refineries had been so well concealed that they were still untouched.

In the autumn of 1944 the Allied war effort was moving toward the climactic Battle of the Rhine. Erickson had to work fast if he wanted to make more deals. He had long been anxious to make an inclusive tour of the German oil industry. Now was the time for it. He figured that it was one of those cases in which a salesman had to get to the man at the top—in this case Heinrich Himmler.

Erickson worked out a grandiose "big deal," the kind that any high-pressure salesman would love. He proposed to construct a huge synthetic-oil refinery in Sweden, to cost $5,000,000. It would be financed by both Swedish and German capital. This proposal was calculated to appeal to the Germans for two reasons. First, it would put a source of oil for Germany in a neutral country, outside the reach of Allied bombers. Second, it offered a way of planting Nazi funds in a neutral country if Germany should be defeated.

Erickson prepared a prospectus and took it to Finke, who was delighted. The Nazi big shots in Germany expressed keen interest. There was one dissident voice—that of Herr Ludwig. He maintained that Mr. Erickson was a phony. Ludwig was a Foreign Office man, one of Ribbentrop's faction. More and more, as the war went on, that faction had come into collision with the Gestapo—in other words, with Heinrich Himmler. Himmler usually won. And so in this case Ludwig was overruled. Erickson was acceptable to the Gestapo, and the way was cleared for him to see Himmler.

It was October 1944. Once more Erickson took the plane from Bromma Field and flew over the gray waters of the Baltic and the dreary plains of northern Germany to Templehof Airdrome. He was given a suite at the best hotel in Berlin not yet smashed by Allied bombs, and in the morning the big black car with its Gestapo guards called for him.

At Himmler's headquarters the Gestapo chief greeted him cordially: "We have heard great things about you from Herr Finke." They talked at length of the refining plan, and of the need for Erickson to see, first hand, the operation of German plants. Then they went on to discuss other matters.

"What would happen," Himmler asked suddenly, "if the Wehrmacht were to invade Sweden?"

"The Swedes would fight like hell," Erickson replied.

He figured that the way to impress Himmler was not to kowtow. He was right. The result of the interview was that he was given a unique document which certified that he should be allowed to go anywhere and see anything in the oil industry. He was given a car and a generous allotment of gasoline.

Erickson covered central Europe from Cologne to Prague. He inspected Leuna, Annendorf, Halle—all the big plants. He talked with managers, found out what they were doing and proposed to do. Like a salesman covering a new territory, he got the whole picture. And took it back to Sweden.

When the war was over, the American Legation in Stockholm gave "Red" Erickson a big luncheon. All his old friends were invited. With innumerable toasts and congratulations he was put right with his world.

It was told how a representative of Allied Intelligence had called on him soon after the beginning of the war. How Erickson had agreed to act as a spy, but had refused any pay for his services. How at his own suggestion he was put on the blacklist. How Prince Carl Bernadotte, with whom he had worked, was also an agent for the Allies. How the oil which had been delivered to him from Germany was turned over to Vacuum Oil and British Petroleum and was eventually used against the Germans. How he had had to give Von Stürker and his other contacts signed letters acknowledging their services as secret Allied collaborators, for use after Allied victory. How each such paper was another sword hanging over his head, so that he could hardly sleep during his visits to Germany, waiting tensely through the long nights for the knock that would mean the Gestapo and death.

His information—and that of others in his hazardous line of work—paid off. In those months before the Battle of the Rhine the offensive against German oil rose to its climax. Our pilots knew the exact location of the refineries, big and little. They knew the location of the fighter strips, the ack-ack batteries and the smoke-screen installations that defended each refinery. After they had put one of these plants out of commission they knew how long the repairs would take. On the day when it was scheduled to resume production they went back again. The supply of fuel to the Wehrmacht and the Luftwaffe was cut to a trickle. When our last great assault began, many gasless German tanks stood helpless in the fields, many gasless German planes were grounded.

The Allies made good on Erickson's promises to Von Stürker and the others. Herr Ludwig, however, ended up as a prisoner, with leisure to reflect on the soundness of his judgment concerning Erickson. Herr Finke was finally caught, after months of masquerading in Denmark under a false name. As for salesman Erickson, he has retired from his life of adventure and now lives with his wife in Stockholm.

A Private Truce

By John Hereward Allix

After the excitement of D-day in 1944 and the weeks following, it came as an anti-climax when my bomber squadron was transferred from England to the shores of Lough Foyle in Northern Ireland. Our assignment—long-range night patrols in search of surfaced U-boats—promised to be monotonous; the odds against finding a submarine were great.

Soon after arrival my crew went on standby, which meant we slept in flying clothes, prepared to take off at 30 minutes' notice. One night about three a.m. I was shaken awake by the operations-room orderly. The enemy had struck right at our doorstep! In five minutes my crew and I—six yawning men— were assembled in the briefing room. Twenty minutes later we were airborne. As I headed the lumbering Wellington out to sea I saw a brilliant flash to westward, followed by the red glow of a torpedoed ship afire. In quick succession, as I watched, three ships were stricken.

All I could think of was getting that U-boat. Unluckily, it never surfaced. A Royal Navy ship picked up its echo and pursued the sub until it took refuge in the neutral waters of the Irish Republic—near the mouth of Lough Swilly, a long arm of the sea stretching deep into County Donegal. After that, though the area was patrolled constantly, the U-boat struck again and again. Each time it escaped to its neutral shelter.

A few weeks later my crew broke up and I was temporarily free from flying duty. I got a two-day furlough and headed across the Irish border for Buncrana, a small town on the shore of Lough Swilly. It was, of course, "irregular" for an officer of His Majesty's forces to enter Ireland, but almost all our men stationed near the border did it—in civilian clothes, with the tacit consent of the border guards on both sides. Food was plentiful and unrationed in Ireland, and liquor was cheaper. It made a nice change.

On my arrival at Buncrana I went to the bar of the inn to have a drink before supper. It was unoccupied save for a fair-haired man smoking a pipe, with a bottle of stout before him. I ordered stout for myself and struck up a conversation. One had to be careful what one said at Buncrana—we could be interned if our status were challenged. The fair-haired man was careful, too, and we avoided mentioning our units, the war, anything controversial.

He was pleasant, knowledgeable and easy to talk with. But there was something indefinably different about him. I knew instinctively that he was not an RAF man, nor could I picture him in either the Royal Navy or the British Army. When we finished our drinks, we played darts, and all the while the problem of who he could be kept picking away at the back of my mind. His English was of the kind normally associated with Oxford and Cambridge. I studied his clothes. His tweed jacket and flannel slacks were well cut. Perhaps I only imagined that nobody I knew in Britain would wear them. But what did it matter? He was good company. I invited him to join me for supper. He accepted.

"By the way," I said, "we haven't introduced ourselves. My

name's John Stewart." I thought it wiser not to give my real surname.

He hesitated a second before he offered his hand. His name, he said, was Charles Hamilton.

During the meal I asked him a number of leading questions, which he answered naturally enough. Obviously he knew central London well, Oxford even better. His knowledge of England did not appear to be recent, however, and references to wartime changes seemed to make him nervous. By now I was convinced that there was something wrong about him. Suddenly my suspicion crystallized: he *must* be German.

Once my mind had leaped this barrier it was easy to elaborate. He could be on the staff of the German Embassy in Dublin. But if so, what was he doing in Buncrana? Then I thought of the U-boat. Of course. That was it! A minor Embassy official sent to exchange signals with the U-boat? A member of the boat's crew? He might even be the sub's commander!

Suddenly I realized that Charles was looking at me rather oddly. I hadn't been listening. "I'm sorry," I said, "what were you saying, Karl?"

I hadn't meant to do anything so clumsy, but the effect of the German version of "Charles" was electric. His jaw dropped, and the blood drained from his face. I was so surprised myself that my mind momentarily refused to accept its own wild surmise as a reality, and I must have looked as alarmed as my companion. I realized that I was grinning foolishly at him. Evidently it was the best thing I could have done, for the color returned to his face and he managed a smile.

In as normal a voice as I could muster, I said: "That was a pretty silly trick. I'm sorry."

"All right, you win," he said. "What are you going to do about it?"

I didn't know, so I said nothing. My companion regained his composure more quickly than I did, and before I had sorted out my tumbling thoughts he was grinning at me amiably. "I begin to see," he said slowly. "You too!"

"Yes, I'm not in a much better position than you are. We

could both be interned!" The situation seemed so ridiculous that I laughed. "I take it that you're the commander of the U-boat out there in the lough?"

That shook him a bit, and he shot back, "What are you talking about?"

"It's fairly obvious, isn't it? I'm a member of an anti-submarine squadron, and we've been out for your blood for weeks."

He relaxed again. "You're perfectly right. I think I'd like another drink, my friend. How about you?"

I needed time to think what I ought to do, so while the drinks were coming I strolled to the fireplace and pretended to look at the picture that hung above it, meanwhile filling my pipe. Should I call the police and have Karl arrested? If I did, they would make me show my identification papers, and then both he and I would probably be imprisoned for the duration of the war. Should I take the attitude that this neutral ground gave us temporary immunity, just as churches did in olden times?

Suppose I did inform the police who he was, and we were both knocked out of the war. My service to my country would be ended. As for Karl, his place would be taken by the second in command, and the U-boat would continue its raiding. I made my decision—to honor the sanctuary this neutral ground gave us.

Turning to Karl, I said I saw no point in getting on a high horse just because, a few miles away, in different circumstances, we would be trying to kill each other. He agreed.

We took our drinks outside and sat on a bench under a chestnut tree. There I learned how Karl came to speak English so well. His father had been head of the London office of a German firm, and Karl had been educated at one of our public schools and at Oxford. He had returned to Germany only a year before war broke out. I asked him how he had come ashore. He told me the U-boat had surfaced during the previous night and two members of his crew had paddled him ashore in a rubber dinghy two or three miles up the coast. They were to come back for him after midnight.

"I spent the morning buying eggs at farms with the English

pound note I'd been keeping as a souvenir," he said. "The food gets pretty dull in a submarine, and the men haven't seen fresh eggs for months. I've got quite a store hidden in the bracken down the road."

When it was almost dark, Karl said he must be going. I walked with him as far as the end of the village. Beyond the last house I stopped.

"I hope you get through, Karl."

"So do I," he said wryly, "and the same to you."

"Then you'd better keep out of my way," I said. "I wouldn't like to have to blow you up."

"Don't worry," he replied, "you won't get the chance!" And he walked slowly away.

I stood there, the feelings inside me quite mixed as I listened to the crunch of his footsteps dying away on the gritty Irish road that led to the sea.

They Carried Our Top Secrets

By Frederic Sondern, Jr.

During wartime as well as in days of peace, urgent brief communications between the State Department and its embassies and consulates all over the world were flashed in code by cable and radio. But detailed secret and top-secret reports and orders and classified maps and charts were delivered by couriers of the U.S. Diplomatic Service. As one ambassador on a sensitive post remarked, "What our electronics can do, another country's electronics might be able to undo. I feel safer when one of these boys is carrying the secret mail."

This sentiment was reinforced by a historic fact: the U.S.

Courier Service had never failed to deliver a single message, except those few destroyed in crashes and wrecks.

The highly secret messages were sealed in a so-called safehand pouch which the courier either carried or kept within easy reaching distance at all times. He usually slept with one rock-like bag as a pillow and the handles of several others chained to his wrists—so that none of them could be touched without waking him. In hotel rooms abroad, where bolts are seldom found and locks are primitive, a courier often barricaded the door with furniture.

The contents of safehand pouches must, according to regulations, be destroyed if the courier feels his plane might crash or his ship sink and that he might die. One courier was in a plane over a South American jungle. The pilot was lost, the tanks were empty and a crash seemed inevitable. The courier broke the sacrosanct seal on his briefcase, opened it and started shredding documents—to the horror of the crew, to whom this signified that all was now really lost. A few minutes later, by a miracle, a stretch of firm, level ground opened out below them and they came in for a comfortable landing. "Nuts," said the courier. "Now that I'm alive I'll have to explain to my supervisor why I tore up these messages."

The Courier Service had its share of bad moments during World War II. Courier Henry Coleman was carrying highly classified material from Washington to London when his ship was torpedoed by a German submarine in mid-Atlantic. The State Department gave him up for lost. But four days later a haggard individual tottered into the American Embassy in London. Coleman had spent half a day in a lifeboat in heavy seas and several days on a Norwegian freighter which had picked him up and put him ashore in Scotland. The courier was a weary wreck. The pouch was in good condition.

One of the classics of the Service is the memorable trip of Courier Horton Telford in the autumn of 1940. The Hitler-Mussolini combine had started its push toward Greece and Turkey; the United States was trying to stem the tide by diplomatic pressure. In Courier Telford's possession were top-secret instructions from Secretary of State Hull to the U.S. ambassadors in Athens and Ankara. For these papers the Axis governments would have paid a high price.

Telford picked up his pouches in Bern; his plane had hardly touched down in Rome when Radio Roma announced Mussolini's declaration of war on Greece. Telford's mail was now hotter than ever. Couriers are not told what they are carrying, but they often make a pretty shrewd guess. All planes to Greece were grounded. Telford caught a train to Venice, bribed his way aboard a ship across the Adriatic to the Yugoslav coast and got by rail to the Greek frontier. The Greek border guards respected his diplomatic passport and let him cross; then they informed him that he could get a train to Athens at Quevali—12 miles away over a rough mountain road. Telford hired two porters and walked.

Just as he arrived in Quevali, Italian fighter planes snarled down to strafe the railhead, and the courier spent a nasty half-hour with his precious pouches in a rain-filled ditch. Finally, soaked, cold and starved, Telford got aboard a jam-packed train and reached Athens with his secrets intact. He hoped for a short rest, but at the Embassy he was ordered to leave immediately for Istanbul.

An Embassy car, taking him 400 miles to a railroad station across the Turkish frontier, bogged down in mud 20 miles short of his destination, and Telford made the rest of the way by ox-cart. At last, a staggering, gray-faced man arrived in Istanbul. "I had a few difficulties," he said as he delivered his pouches.

Today Courier Service people cringe at screen and TV versions of their supposedly glamorous job, complete with beautiful blonde spies and high adventure. "You should see our regulations!" said one. The couriers' regulations, enforced with Draconic severity, cover everything from how to speak to a foreign customs official to what to eat and drink the night before a trip.

"Members of the traveling public," the Courier's Handbook says, "may wish to discuss with a courier his itinerary and duties. Such conversations shall be terminated as promptly as possible, and answers to casual questions shall be entirely noncommittal." An American commercial-airline pilot who has flown many couriers over various runs remarks, "They're the most polite—and the most unfriendly—guys in the world."

Regulations require every courier to be equipped, wherever he goes, with an alarm clock in good order. He has standing instructions to be at airport or railroad terminal 45 minutes or more before train time or plane deadline. Missing his transportation, except in rare circumstances, is unforgivable.

There are rigid rules about the abuse of diplomatic immunity. Couriers are strictly forbidden to carry anything except official correspondence and supplies and a bare minimum of personal effects. They have orders to report anyone, including an ambassador, who asks them to take a gift, a letter or anything else besides the pouch. Smuggling anything for themselves—even a pair of stockings or a box of cigars—is punishable by immediate dishonorable dismissal.

Couriers are never armed. Their security depends primarily on a long-standing unwritten agreement between all governments not to interfere with each other's diplomatic messengers. Diplomatic pouches are never opened by customs authorities. Even espionage agents do not touch pouches in transit, as long as they are under a courier's care, and no American diplomatic messenger has ever been attacked by a spy.

"They have been trained in a hard school," one high Department official said. "And they never fail to deliver the goods."

PART SIX

1 9 4 5

VICTORY BEHIND THE LINES

WITH the noose tightening around Adolf Hitler's "Thousand Year Reich," Germany struck out desperately. Beaten back in France, she launched a fierce counter-attack spearheaded by fake "American" troops. She rushed toward completion a secret scheme to bankrupt the British Empire by vast counterfeiting of money. Her scientists believed that they were far ahead in the race for atomic power.

Secrecy was also a potent weapon of the Allied forces. From the underwater activity of the U.S. Navy's elite corps of frogmen to the operations of the OSS cloak-and-dagger boys in the passes of the Alps, the foe was harassed by surprise sorties and attacks.

Hidden in his Berlin bunker, Hitler issued orders that all Germans must resist "to the last man." But with shells pulverizing the Nazi capital, Hitler committed suicide and the war in Europe ended. Now the Allies turned their full attention to the Pacific, where they faced the prospect of awesome bloodletting before the Japanese islands could be conquered.

Suddenly from Potsdam an ultimatum was broadcast to the Japanese people—surrender or face "prompt and utter destruction." As yet few men knew that Allied science had harnessed the atom. The ultimatum went unheeded and the war's greatest weapon—the hidden labor of 600,000 people—burst upon the world.

In spite of the unbelievable devastation brought by the first atomic bomb, the Japanese warlords in secret conclave still debated the question of capitulation. A second bomb forced them to a decision.

"A great tragedy has ended," said General MacArthur, the Supreme Commander for the Allied powers. "A great victory has been won. The skies no longer rain death. . . . The entire world is quietly at peace."

Perhaps never will all the secrets, all the hush-hush schemes of World War II be revealed. Nor will all the stories of spies and saboteurs be written down. Yet, what is already known gives a fascinating picture of the great acts of espionage and daring that crowded the war years.

The Most Dangerous Man in Europe

By Thomas M. Johnson

A brown-haired giant with a handsome face scarred from left ear to chin strode into an American headquarters near Salzburg, Austria, on May 17, 1945. He snapped a saluting hand to his jaunty cap that bore the death's-head insignia of Hitler's Elite Guard. "SS Lieutenant Colonel Otto Skorzeny gives himself up," he said. (See photograph on page 342.)

Surrendering Germans had become as common as K rations to the GI on duty. He jerked a jaded thumb. "Okay, Otto. G'wan over to the cage."

The officer glared, then wheeled. The light fell upon serried medals, upon cold, ice-blue eyes. An intelligence officer, inconspicuous in a worn uniform, stared at the German's wrist. "Mussolini's watch," he observed quietly to the GI. "He's *the* Skorzeny, foremost enemy secret agent on our grab list."

The Army's spy-hunters had no foeman more menacing than this six feet four inches and 220 pounds of scheming, daring adventurer. He had led the largest-scale sabotage operation ever directed against American forces, an adroit trick by which Nazis in U.S. uniforms had spread confusion behind our lines at the Battle of the Bulge and, under menace of assassination, had coerced General Eisenhower's staff into keeping the irate Allied Commander in Chief almost a prisoner in his own headquarters for 10 days.

Over a year earlier, with a little more than 100 men, Skorzeny had snatched an astounded and delighted Mussolini from his 400 Italian guards atop a mountain peak. (See photograph on page 341.) This abduction, by glider and small plane, enabled the Duce to set up a new government in northern Italy and helped the Germans prolong resistance. Mussolini gave Skorzeny an engraved wristwatch; Hitler gave him the Knight's Cross— and further delicate jobs.

In October 1944, German spies had reported that Regent Nicholas Horthy of Hungary was about to renounce his partnership with Hitler and join Stalin. Skorzeny, at the head of a small force, stormed Horthy's castle, but found the Admiral had escaped after broadcasting Hungary's surrender. Someone revealed Horthy's hideout, and while the Russians were sweeping across the borders, Skorzeny rushed him to Munich and captivity.

It was after the Horthy incident that Hitler called on his favorite strong-arm man for his crowning performance. The Führer was planning a final frenzied stroke. Against the thinly held American front in the rugged Ardennes he would hurl his last strategic reserves, led by elite armored divisions. These units would dash northward, encircle half the American, British and Canadian troops in Europe, seize their enormous supplies and their one good port, Antwerp. The United States and Britain would be paralyzed long enough, Hitler hoped, for the Germans to produce sufficient V-bombs, jet planes and new-type submarines to win the war after all.

"But there is an obstacle," Hitler confessed to a few leaders in secret. "How shall we seize the bridges over the Meuse so our panzers can cross? . . . I have it! Bring me Skorzeny!"

In a secret war-room on October 22, his face still pale and drawn from the July bomb explosion intended to kill him, the Führer confided to Skorzeny his daredevil stratagem. Skorzeny was to choose from all services a special unit of some 3000 bravos, all able to speak English. They would wear uniforms taken from American prisoners and be sent through American lines as spies, saboteurs and spreaders of demoralization. They were to seize and hold the bridges over the Meuse for the main body to cross. Skorzeny must be ready in less than two months.

Assembling his men at Friedenthal, near Oranienburg,

Skorzeny familiarized them with American equipment and weapons, American drill, rank and customs. "Don't be too military," he commanded. "No heel-clicking." He had them taught the American way of opening a package of cigarettes; they were given U.S. brands. They learned American swearwords and slang. "Okay, Butch!" became a password. They were supplied with American identification cards, American money and even letters and snapshots from the United States. The operation was dubbed Greif, meaning "grab."

But the operation could not be utterly hidden. American First Army Intelligence captured an order for English-speaking soldiers to report to Skorzeny. Skorzeny's reputation being known, Colonel Benjamin A. Dickson reported on December 10 that the order "obviously presages special operations for sabotage, attacks on headquarters and other vital installations by infiltrated or parachuted specialists." He added: "An extremely intelligent prisoner of war, whose other observations check exactly with established facts, stated all means possible are being gathered for a coming all-out counter-offensive." High Allied intelligence officers, however, were dubious. We sent no more troops to the Ardennes front. And on December 16 the Nazis struck.

As 17 German divisions, followed by 12 more, were crunching forward into one of the greatest battles in American history, thousands of German guns blasted a way through the rugged, snow-clad Ardennes. Meanwhile Skorzeny's "Americans," in captured American jeeps, were running wild. Giving other German units prearranged signals by raising helmets or blinking colored flashlights, they rode into or through our front, spotting air strips and supply dumps and scouting the routes whereby our reinforcements were struggling to come up. This helped the German artillery inflict heavy casualties. They strewed roads with cut-down trees, cut telephone wires. They snarled our traffic by mixing up road signs, and destroyed trucks by removing warnings from minefields. One Greifer, uniformed as an American MP, stood at a crossroad and thumbed an American regiment along the wrong road.

At first, few Americans realized that disguised enemies were

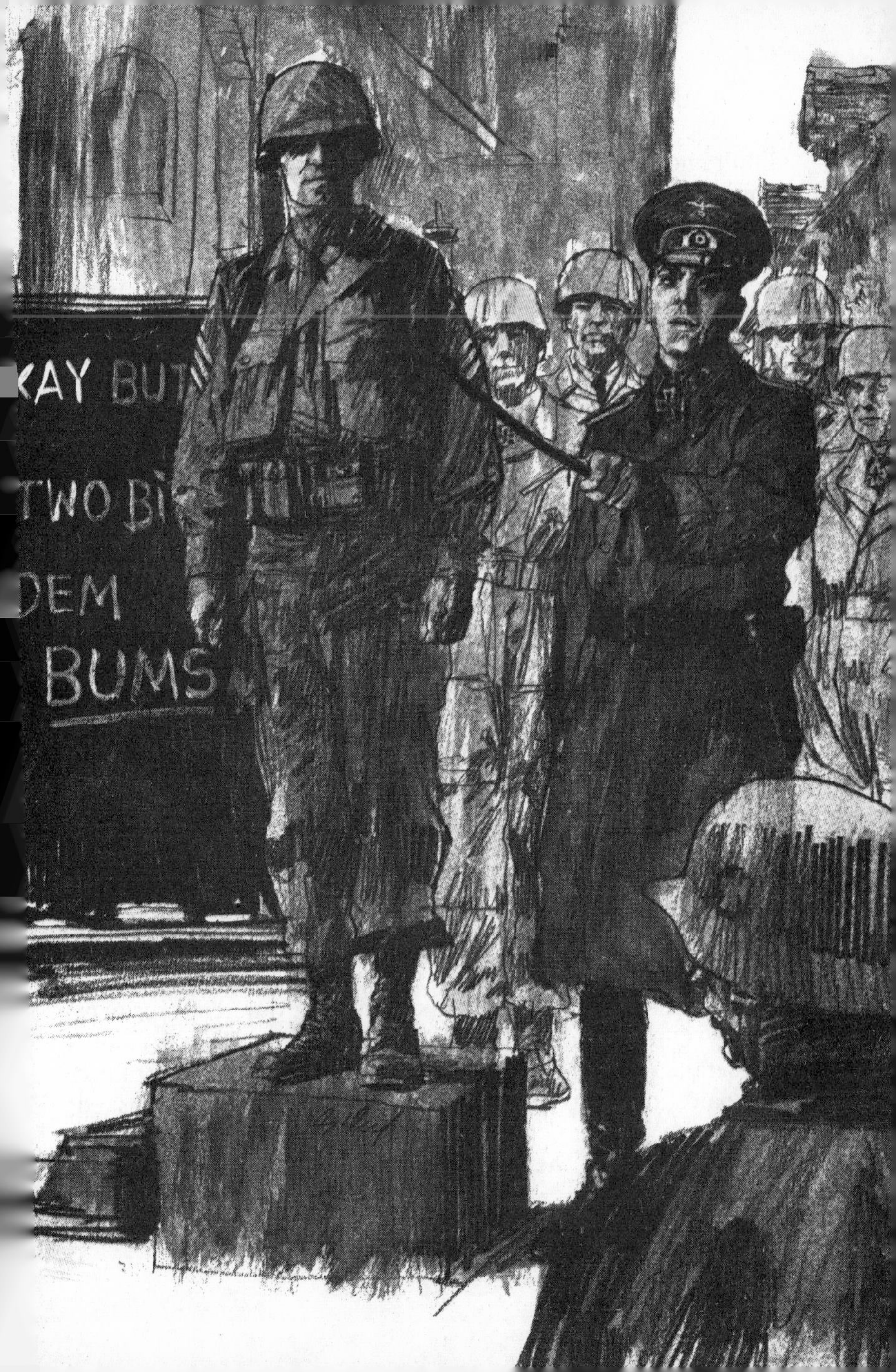
KAY BUT
TWO BI
DEM
BUMS

among them, doing such mischief. But on December 18, at
Aywaille, Belgium, MP's challenged three GI's in a jeep who
didn't know the password. They had papers indicating they were
from the Fifth Armored Division and told persuasive stories, but
they were "too damn polite." That alone delivered them to the
tender mercies of Lieutenant Frederick Wallach, Dachau escapee
and former German judge, now enthusiastically cross-examining
captured Nazis for our First Army. His strategy with the trio
was to shame them for wearing any uniform but that of the
German Army. It worked.

"Their story checks with that captured order," Wallach reminded his superiors. But to many of our officers the plot
seemed "too fantastic."

Soon officers of the Counter Intelligence Corps found a German radio and code book in a recaptured jeep, and American
radiomen heard jeep teams sending in their reports of damage
done us under cover of our own uniforms. That began a colossal
spy hunt. Passwords were useless—the Germans might have
learned them. So grim-faced MP's and CIC agents stuck guns
into the ribs of all in jeeps or other vehicles whose Americanism
seemed dubious and asked: "What's the Brown Bomber?
Where's the Windy City? Who's 'The Voice'? Who are Dem
Bums? Say 'wreath.'" (Almost any German would use the *t*
sound for *th*.) These new tests were applied at myriad roadblocks throughout front and rear, especially to the back-seat
riders, who, it was now known, spoke the worst English.
Some drivers, panicked by the questions, revealed themselves
by trying to speed away; others, by trying to rush roadblocks.

On December 19, CIC agents spotted two apparent American
second lieutenants in a jeep just watching our reinforcements
rush by. Questioned, they produced dogtags, inoculation records
and detailed stories of their Army experiences. They had trained,
they said, at Camp Hood. Almost satisfied, one agent asked:
"Ever been in Texas?" "No," said one German, "never." "Put
'em up!" snapped the agent, drawing his gun. "Camp Hood's
in Texas!"

Then at Liège—a Meuse River crossing, one of Skorzeny's

special goals—a jeep team boldly inquired for headquarters, Communications Zone. Instantly the men were surrounded by heavily armed MP's. Wallach was summoned to apply the "shame" technique, and a stubble-faced blond lieutenant was soon naming and describing all of Skorzeny's officers and giving further details: the 150th Panzer Brigade, also under Skorzeny, was pretending, in captured American tanks, to be American armor retreating until it could seize the Meuse bridges.

Taken to First Army headquarters for further interrogation, the lieutenant at first said he had told all he knew. "Okay," headquarters said, "we'll give you to the Commissar." Like most Germans, the lieutenant dreaded Russians, and before a giant in Red Army uniform who roared questions in German with an outlandish accent (being an American from Milwaukee), he paled and confessed hoarsely: "We're after Eisenhower, too. Skorzeny and a party will impersonate American officers taking captured German generals to your Supreme Headquarters at Versailles for questioning. They will drive in American cars. Once inside, they will turn their weapons on your staff and Eisenhower will be kidnaped or killed by Skorzeny himself."

The story might have been a fake, but SHAEF (Supreme Allied Headquarters), knowing about Skorzeny, had to play safe. The Trianon Hotel and other buildings that housed SHAEF were ringed with barbed wire, tanks and nearly 1000 well-armed MP's and GI's who examined passes at outlying roadblocks and greeted all who got closer with challenges and tommy guns. Five CIC agents saw that all visitors to General Eisenhower were identified by an aide. The General moved to a house within the enclosure whose doors, windows and roof were guarded. He did not step outside for several days, for CIC was afraid of long-range snipers. Then his active spirit rebelled and he exclaimed, "Hell's fire! I'm going out for a walk." But he yielded to his staff's entreaties when he learned that unless he remained inside still more troops, needed elsewhere, would be used in "trailing me around."

Meanwhile, in the Bulge, some of the 50 American tanks of the 150th Panzer Brigade had caught an American armored battalion unaware and wiped out half of it. The alarm spread: "Our own tanks are firing on us," and MP's were ordered to report all unscheduled tank movements. Boat traffic on the Meuse was stopped, both banks were patrolled and anyone who tried to cross was seized and examined. By this means 54 Germans in Allied uniforms or civilian clothes were caught.

Spreading news of defeat, Greifers of the disguised 150th Panzer Brigade were about to reach our last defense line in advance of the Meuse. At Malmédy, Skorzeny found American artillery ready. So, before attacking, he sent men afoot to find out from the gunners how many guns they had and what sort. The alerted gunners grabbed the impostors, and then the guns gave the answer. The stolen American tanks were ruined, and from the wreckage were extricated numerous Germans, dead and living, all in American uniforms.

First Army began on December 22 to try its Greif prisoners in a military tribunal. All were convicted of violating the laws of war in wearing an enemy's uniform behind his lines to deceive and commit espionage and sabotage. The sentence of death was carried out by a firing squad.

No one knows how many hundred Greifers were killed in action. But it is known that some 130 were executed after trial. First Army counter-intelligence officers broadcast their names from Radio Luxembourg with particulars of Operation Greif and a description of officers still uncaptured, especially Skorzeny. The massive Austrian had waited so close to the fighting that a shell fragment wounded him. He hoped for a chance to drive forward what remained of his 150th Panzer on its mission of deceit and death. The broadcast was final proof that the chance had slipped away. Reluctantly Skorzeny told his disappointed desperadoes to take off their American uniforms. Operation Greif was *kaput*.

One of the last things Skorzeny did after this was to design and distribute the poison capsules with which a number of bigshot Nazis, including Goering and Himmler, committed suicide.

When Skorzeny surrendered to the Americans, he said he had never really intended to kill Eisenhower. That was a tale he had cooked up to inflame his men. He knew that some of his men would be captured, tell the story and add to our confusion. He said politely but firmly: "Had I planned it, I would have tried; had I tried it, I would have succeeded."

Before a nine-officer court at Dachau, the prosecutors of Skorzeny withdrew some charges, including implication in the notorious Malmédy massacre of American prisoners. The strapping deceiver swore that many others besides his Greifers, including British and Russian soldiers, had worn enemy uniforms, and that he had told his men to use theirs to sneak through our lines but to doff them before firing a shot. On September 8, 1947, the tribunal, after only two and a half hours' deliberation, freed Skorzeny and seven of his aides. "I have had a fair trial," said Skorzeny, "and no physical ill-treatment, although I was 22 months in solitary. My only complaint is that someone 'liberated' the wristwatch Mussolini gave me."

As an SS officer, Skorzeny now faced a German denazification trial. In his German prison he received fan letters from America, including offers of aid, apparently resulting from newspaper stories of his acquittal which had aroused compassion in some minds here. The morning of July 27, 1948, his German jailers found him gone.

"This man has many followers who are at liberty," said his outraged prosecutor, Colonel Alfred J. Rosenfeld. "They are believed to have formed an underground and to be awaiting his leadership. He is the most dangerous man in Europe."

The whereabouts of the handsome, scar-faced giant, so easily recognizable, was for years a mystery. He was recently reported to be residing in Madrid, and to have attended a requiem mass for Mussolini on the 18th anniversary of the Italian dictator's death.

The Frogmen

By Edwin Muller

Any day along a southern California beach near Coronado you could see a group of sun-tanned, muscular young men in swim trunks who seemed to be having a lot of fun. They dived into the surf, swam long distances underwater, rode in on the crests of the waves. If the surf was treacherous, all the better. It looked like great sport—but actually these men were engaged in an especially rugged form of military training. For these were the Navy's UDT: Underwater Demolition Teams, known as the "frogmen."

During World War II the frogmen were a top-secret unit. Their job was to spearhead amphibious landings—go in ahead of ground troops, chart the approach, clear the beach and off-shore water of mines and other obstacles. They saved thousands of lives—at high cost to their own.

The need for UDT came home in blood and horror at Tarawa. Along the approaches to that island the Japanese had set up rows of "hedgehogs"—steel rails set on end in concrete, projecting in all directions just under the surface. As our landing craft raced for the shore, boat after boat became impaled. The Marines, crowded together on board, were helpless against the deadly machine-gun fire from the beach. Eventually the Marines took Tarawa. But the troops who took it waded through the bodies of hundreds of their comrades. The Navy determined that no such disaster would happen again.

On June 24, 1945, an amphibious group of the Seventh Amphibious Force lay off the coast of Borneo, ready for an assault on the beach. At 7:30 a.m. a roaring U.S. bombardment began. At eight o'clock seven small boats crowded with men in swimming trunks slipped away from the fleet and headed full speed toward the beach. The men wore underwater masks, and rubber fins on their feet. Three boats were hit by Japanese guns, but none was put out of action.

Five hundred yards offshore the boats swung parallel to the beach. Each boat put over a rubber raft alongside and towed it. At a signal the frogmen tumbled onto the rafts, two by two. Then, every 50 yards, a pair of men rolled into the water and started toward the beach. They swam breast stroke, which makes no splash and exposes less of the body to fire than an over-arm.

The men rode in on the crests of the long rollers. A little way offshore they came to the line of obstacles: four rows of 10-inch-thick piles driven into the coral bottom; the tops, just under water, were interlaced with barbed wire.

Each pair of frogmen was assigned to a 50-yard area. Each had a Plexiglas slate and a pencil tied around the neck. They dived deep, stayed under one minute. When they surfaced, they scribbled the pattern of the barrier on the slate, then dived again. In the midst of their work Japanese mortar fire found them. Then came splashes of machine-gun bullets. The swimmers stayed below the surface as much as possible and kept to the wave troughs. The reconnaissance finished, the frogmen headed out to sea. The boats came in at top speed, towing their rafts. One by one the frogmen were pulled from the sea. Later, far out in the fleet, staff officers studied the data on the slates.

Next came the job of demolishing the obstacles. Again the little boats headed in. This time, as each pair of frogmen dived, a heavy bundle was thrown into the water. This was the explosive, 100 pounds of it in five packages, each package floating on an inflated rubber bladder. The swimmers towed their bundles gingerly toward shore. A near-miss by a mortar shell would blow them to bits. At the barrier the pairs got to work, fast and systematically. Along the tops of the piles they strung a trunk line made of "prima-cord," which has a continuous core of explosive. Then they attached the bundles to the bottom of the piles and tied each bundle to the trunk line above. Within half an hour they mined half a mile of obstacles, then headed out to the boats—all but two "triggermen," who waited behind to set the fuse. They timed it for 15 minutes, then raced after the others. Probably the fastest swimming of the war was done by outbound triggermen. Then it came. In an ear-shattering blast half a mile of sand, water and logs leaped high in the air and crashed back into the ocean. The frogmen went back to work clearing away more death traps.

The assault took place on July 1. With heavy bombardment overhead and with UDT boats guiding them, the swarm of landing craft took the beach.

Borneo was typical of a dozen major amphibious landings prepared and led by UDT. At Guam the chief obstacle was a coral reef, 300 yards offshore, covered by one to three feet of water. Using 10,000 pounds of explosives, UDT blasted a broad, safe passage through. When the first wave of Marines headed for the beach—some bloody, all sweating, ducking machine-gun fire—they found set up on the reef the first of those signs that became famous in the Navy: "Marines, welcome to Guam. Beach open courtesy of UDT. USO two blocks to the right."

The frogmen suffered their highest casualties during the Normandy landing, at Omaha Beach. Broad and gently sloping, the beach has an 18-foot tide—you have to move at a dogtrot to keep ahead of it as it comes in. Between low- and high-tide marks the Germans had set three rows of posts, interlaced with barbed wire. They figured that the first assault boats would get ashore at low tide. Then the quickly rising water would cover the obstacles. Boats coming later would be caught and held. The troops already on the beach would be cut off.

UDT wasn't allowed to reconnoiter the Normandy beaches— that would have given away the show. But they had accurate information on the beach defenses from French Underground reports, from aerial reconnaissance and from photographs taken through submarine periscopes. The frogmen went in with the first wave of troops, paddling through the surf in rubber boats. The fire of the German 88's was deadly. When a shell hit a rubber boat loaded with high explosive, the boat and the men in it vanished. The boats that got through reached the beach as the tide began to come in. Hurrying ahead of the tide, the frog-men got to the first line of posts and wire. The sand around them was leaping with shell bursts. Every now and then a man carrying his deadly pack would disappear.

In one sector the frogmen blew all three lines of obstacles, row by row, in 45 minutes. And in that landing 41 percent of them were killed or wounded.

Today the Underwater Demolition Teams are again top-secret units. Few of the frogmen themselves know just what sort of amphibious operations they are preparing for. All they know is that if U.S. troops are ever called on to go ashore on any hostile coast, they must be preceded by men who can clear the way.

The Hidden Annex

By Louis de Jong

And how do you know that the human race is *worth* saving?" an argumentative youngster once asked Justice Felix Frank-furter. Said the Justice: "I have read Anne Frank's diary."

How this diary of a teen-age girl came to be written and saved is a story as dramatic as the diary itself. No one foresaw the tremendous impact the small book would have—not even her father, who had it published after Anne's death in a Nazi concentration camp.

When Hitler came to power, Otto Frank was a banker, living in Germany. He had married in 1925. In 1926 his first daughter, Margot, was born and three years later his second, Annelies Marie. She was usually called "Anne," sometimes "Tender One." (See photograph on page 341.)

In the autumn of 1933, when Hitler was issuing one anti-Jewish decree after another, Otto Frank decided to emigrate to the hospitable Netherlands. He started a small firm in Amsterdam. Shortly before the outbreak of war he took in a partner, Mr. Van Daan, a fellow refugee. Mostly they traded in spices. Trade was often slow. Once Otto Frank was forced to ask his small staff to accept a temporary cut in their modest wages. No one left. They all liked his warm personality. They admired his courage and the evident care he took to give his two girls a good education.

As a pupil Anne was not particularly brilliant. Most people believed with her parents that Margot, her elder sister, was more promising. Anne was chiefly remarkable for the early interest she took in other people. She was emotional and strong-willed—"a real problem child," her father once told me, "a great talker and fond of nice clothes." Life in town, where she was usually surrounded by a chattering crowd of girl friends, suited her exactly. This was a lucky fact because the Frank family could only rarely afford a holiday. Nor did they own a car.

When the Nazis invaded the Netherlands in May 1940, the Franks were trapped. Earlier than most Jews in Amsterdam, Otto Frank realized that the time might come when he and his family would have to go into hiding. He decided to hide in his own business office, which faced one of Amsterdam's tree-lined canals. A few derelict rooms on the upper floors, called the "Annexe," were secretly prepared to house both the Frank and the Van Daan families. (See photograph on page 341.)

Early in July 1942, Margot Frank was called up for deportation, but she did not go. Straightway the Franks moved into their hiding place, and the Van Daans followed shortly afterward. Four months later they took into their cramped lodgings another Jew, a dentist. They were eight hunted people. Any sound, any light might betray their presence. A tenuous link with the outside was provided by the radio and by four courageous members of Otto Frank's staff, two of them typists, who in secret brought food, magazines, books. The only other company they had was a cat.

While in hiding, Anne decided to continue a diary which her parents had given her on her 13th birthday. She described life in the "Annexe" with all its inevitable tensions and quarrels. But she created first and foremost a wonderfully delicate record of adolescence, sketching with complete honesty a young girl's thoughts and feelings, her longing and loneliness. "I feel like a songbird whose wings have been brutally torn out and who is flying in utter darkness against the bars of its own cage," she wrote when she had been isolated from the outside world for nearly 16 months. Two months later she had filled every page of the diary, a small book bound in a tartan cloth, and one of the typists, Miep van Santen, gave her an ordinary exercise book. Later she used Margot's chemistry exercise book.

Her diary reveals the trust she puts in a wise father; her grief because, as she feels it, her mother does not understand her; the ecstasy of a first, rapturous kiss, exchanged with the Van Daans' 17-year-old son; finally, the flowering of a charmingly feminine personality, eager to face life with adult courage and mature self-insight.

On a slip of paper Anne wrote fake names which she intended to use in case of publication. For the time being, the diary was her own secret which she wanted to keep from everyone, especially from the grumpy dentist with whom she had to share her tiny bedroom. Her father allowed her to put her diaries in his briefcase. He never read them until after her death.

On August 4, 1944, one German and four Dutch Nazi policemen suddenly stormed upstairs. (How the secret of the Annexe had been revealed is not known.) "Where are your money and jewels?" they shouted. Mrs. Frank and Mrs. Van Daan had some gold and jewelry. It was quickly discovered. Looking round for something to carry it in, one of the policemen noticed Otto Frank's briefcase. He emptied it on the floor, barely giving a glance to the notebooks. Then the people of the Annexe were taken into arrest.

In the beginning of September, while the Allied armies under Eisenhower were rapidly approaching the Netherlands, the Franks and Van Daans and the dentist were carried in cattle trucks to Auschwitz—the Nazi death camp in southern Poland. There the Nazis separated Otto Frank from his wife and daughters without giving them time to say farewell. Mrs. Frank, Anne and Margot were marched into the women's part of the camp, where Mrs. Frank died from exhaustion. The Van Daans and the dentist too lost their lives.

Anne proved to be a courageous leader of her small Auschwitz group. When there was nothing to eat, she dared to go to the kitchen to ask for food. She constantly told Margot never to give in. Once she passed hundreds of Hungarian Jewish children who were standing naked in freezing rain, waiting to be led to the gas chambers, unable to grasp the horrors inflicted upon them in the world of adults. "Oh, look, their eyes . . ." she whispered.

Later in the autumn she and her sister were transported to another camp, Bergen-Belsen, between Berlin and Hamburg. A close friend saw her there: "cold and hungry, her head shaved and her skeleton-like form draped in the coarse, shapeless striped garb of the concentration camp." She was pitifully weak, her body racked by typhoid fever. She died in early March 1945, a few days after Margot. Both were buried in a mass grave.

In Auschwitz, Otto Frank had managed somehow to stay alive. He was freed early in 1945 by the Russians, and in the summer he arrived back in liberated Amsterdam. A friend had told him that his wife had died, but he kept on hoping that Anne and Margot would return. After six weeks of waiting he met someone who had to tell him that both had perished. It was only then that Miep, his former typist, handed him Anne's diaries.

A week after the Frank family had been arrested, Miep had boldly returned to the Annexe. A heap of paper lay on the floor. Miep recognized Anne's handwriting and decided to keep the diary but not to read it. Had she read it, she would have found detailed information about the help she and other people had given the Frank family at the risk of their own lives, and she might well have decided to destroy the diary for reasons of safety.

It took Otto Frank many weeks to finish reading what his dead child had written. He broke down after every few pages. As his old mother was still alive—she had emigrated to Switzerland, where other near relatives lived—he started copying the manuscript for her. Some passages which he felt to be too intimate or which might hurt other people's feelings were left out by him. The idea of publishing the diary did not enter his mind. He gave one typed copy to a close friend, who lent it to a professor of modern history. Much to Otto Frank's surprise, the professor devoted an article to it in a Dutch newspaper. His friends now urged Otto Frank to have Anne's diary published, as she herself had wished; in one passage she had written: "I want to publish a book entitled *The Annexe* after the war. . . . My diary can serve this purpose." When Anne's father finally consented to publication, the manuscript was refused by two well-known Dutch publishers before a third decided to accept it.

Since then it has been published in at least 22 languages, has sold close to three million copies. A play made from the diary has been produced in more than 20 countries, and a motion picture about Anne has been shown everywhere. So many letters were sent to Otto Frank from all over the world that he was forced to retire from business. The care of his daughter's diary has become his passion, his mission in life. He now lives modestly in Switzerland. (He still does not own a car.) All royalties are devoted to humanitarian projects which, he feels, would have been approved by Anne. All letters are answered by him personally. Every day new ones sadly remind him of the losses he has suffered, but he feels that there is truth and consolation in what the headmistress of one of England's largest schools wrote to him: "It must be a source of deep joy to you—in all your sorrow—to know that Anne's brief life is, in the deepest sense, only just beginning."

The most remarkable response came from Germany. When the book's first printing of 4500 copies came out in Germany in 1950, many booksellers were afraid to put it in their windows. Since then sales of the German pocket-book edition have totaled close to a million.

When the play opened in seven German cities simultaneously, no one knew how the audiences would react. The drama progressed through its eight brief scenes. No Nazis were seen on the stage, but their ominous presence made itself felt every minute.

Finally, Nazi jackboots were heard storming upstairs to raid the hiding place. At the end of the epilogue only Anne's father was on the stage, a lonely old man. Quietly he told how he received news that his wife and daughters had died. Picking up Anne's slim diary, he turned back the pages to find a certain passage and, as he found it, her young, confident voice was heard, saying: "In spite of everything, I still believe that people are really good at heart."

Packed audiences received Anne Frank's tragedy in a silence heavy with remorse. In Düsseldorf people did not even go out during the interval. "They sat in their seats as if afraid of the lights outside, ashamed to face each other," someone reported. The Düsseldorf producer, Kuno Epple, explained: "*Anne Frank* has succeeded because it enables the audience to come to grips with history, personally and without denunciation. We watch it as an indictment, in the most humble, pitiful terms, of inhumanity to fellow men. No one accuses us as Germans. We accuse ourselves."

In West Berlin an Anne Frank Home was opened, devoted to social work for young people. The people of Berlin had chosen her name "to symbolize the spirit of racial and social tolerance." Elsewhere in Germany an organization was set up, named after her, to combat remaining vestiges of anti-Semitism.

Anne's brief life is indeed only beginning. She carries a message of courage and tolerance all over the world. She lives after death.

The Great Ambush

By William L. White, author of They Were Expendable,
Queens Die Proudly *and other books*

Slowly losing altitude, the big plane droned through the night.
Now four hours from its base at Bari in southeastern Italy,
it was 300 miles deep into enemy territory behind the lines, which
were then south of Bologna. It was the night after Christmas,
1944. The three men who were to jump peered down into the
blackness, looking for the signal fire the partisans had lit at the
designated spot near the village of Trichiana in the foothills of
the Italian Alps. Then, as the plane banked, they saw the tiny
signal fire on the snow.

First to jump was the leader, Captain Howard Chappell, of
the Office of Strategic Services (OSS), 26 years old, a graduate
of Ohio State and Western Reserve Universities. American-born
of Prussian descent, he spoke German but not Italian. However,
Sergeant Farbrega, his interpreter, spoke Italian and several
other languages. Sergeant Silsby, the radio operator, veteran of
two OSS missions in Yugoslavia, jumped last. Before the three
men bailed out, big parachute containers packed with rifles,
ammunition and uniforms for the partisans were tossed out.

When Captain Chappell picked himself up he found about 30
partisans, wearing a nondescript motley of Italian and German
uniforms, waiting there. Others were out gathering the containers of equipment, because any not recovered by dawn would be
found by the Germans.

Bolzano, headquarters of the German SS troops in Italy, was
only 60 kilometers (about 38 miles) away, and every big town
was heavily garrisoned. There were many Germans in this area,
for nearby were the two great mountain passes—the Brenner and

another east to Vienna. Only through these passes could the
Germans supply their armies fighting in Italy, or later evacuate
them. Chappell's mission was to organize partisans who could
block these escape routes.

At the nearby town of Belluno, Captain Bennucci, another
OSS agent, already was operating, and the three stayed five
days with him. They taught the partisans how to make booby
traps to leave in barracks, hotels or taverns frequented by the
Germans.

"My first job," Chappell related, "was to try to get to Cortina,
where we hoped to land a parachute drop of 12 more Americans
to help organize the partisans. The snow was so deep we knew
we would have to stick to the highway, where the Germans had
many roadblocks. We thought of going in a truck, riding standing up in plain view. To make it more plausible, the partisans
gave me two Austrian deserters from the 20th Luftwaffe Division, who still had their German uniforms. They would appear
to be guarding us. The partisans said these deserters were loyal
to our side. Our papers, forged by the partisans in their secret
press in Belluno, would show us to be laborers being transported
to work on German fortifications in the Brenner Pass.

"About this time the 20th Luftwaffe Division was moved into
our area, and I noticed that the two Austrian deserters began to
get impertinent and furtive. I told Sergeant Farbrega to keep an
eye on them. They didn't know he spoke German. He reported
that they were homesick for their old outfit, and now that it was
back in the neighborhood they planned to rejoin it and turn us
in for a reward. So we had to do away with them.

"I decided to postpone the Cortina move. Meanwhile I had
been talking things over with Captain Brietche, a British secret
agent who was working in this area, and we agreed to split the
zone between us. I would take over two brigades of the partisans'
so-called Nanette Division.

"This was a Communist outfit. I found myself in command of
an army of generals. There were plenty of commanders, vice-
commanders, division and brigade commanders and political
commissars, but not many ordinary partisans to do the tiresome

and dangerous work. Many of the Communists who had maneuvered themselves into key positions in the Underground were about 20 percent for fighting Nazis and 80 percent for Russia. We soon found that they were burying the German arms they had captured, to save them for use when the war was over and the Americans had pulled out of Italy. What the Italians did after the war was their own business, but we were dropping weapons to the partisans for the purpose of saving American lives. I wanted our weapons used for this.

"Many of the rank-and-file partisans, however, were fine and brave. One Communist girl, whose battle name was Maria, became my private messenger. She carried messages for me through the German lines, in her pants and brassiere. Maria had been planted by the Communists to watch me, but she grew to like me, and when they plotted to kill me she tipped me off.

"Every night I sent radio reports to our OSS base at Bari, giving the location of ammunition and petrol dumps which our Air Corps could bomb, telling them what German units were moving on the road and from the Brenner Pass, and relaying whatever I picked up about German morale and food supplies.

"I was giving sabotage training to the partisans. One of the most successful things we had was a steel road spike with four sharp points, one of which was always straight up. Even children could place these things along the highways. Because of our Air Corps dive bombers, all German traffic moved at night, and these spikes split a lot of tires wide open. We also stretched black wires across the road, rigged to mines, and made booby traps by covering mines with horse manure. We had the Germans frantic. They even tried driving dogs down the road ahead of them to set off these mines. But did you ever try to drive a dog down a straight road?

"By day we were in hiding, living with the partisans or in deserted houses or haystacks or in our sleeping bags, hidden in the bushes.

"There were four British and American missions in the field in this area, all supplied by parachute. We were acquiring a lot of shot-down American pilots (we presently accumulated 21), and one of my assignments was to get them back, through Underground channels, as soon as possible.

"When they parachuted down, my partisans would try to get to them before the Germans or Fascists, who would often kill our airmen when they landed. The pilots, therefore, usually whipped out their revolvers as soon as they scrambled to their feet. It was sometimes difficult for the partisans, few of whom spoke any English, to let the pilots know they were friendly. They brought in one pilot who told us that when a couple of tough characters had come running toward him across a field he had whipped out his .45 and was about to knock them off when one began yelling a string of oaths, names of cigarettes and American slang. So the pilot put his gun away. The Germans parachuted spies into this region disguised as shot-down American airmen, so we never trusted anyone until we had radioed his name and number to our base and got back confirmation that such a man was missing from his unit.

"We knew the Germans had spotted some of the parachute drops coming into this zone, that a clean-up would be coming soon and that it would be hard for us to hide so many airmen. I put pilots and partisans to work clearing away the snow from an old soccer field on which I hoped a big C-47 could land and take the airmen out. I radioed to base that I needed more men, especially a medical man with full equipment. We couldn't send our wounded to the local hospitals: a gunshot wound is a giveaway, and the Germans would execute them. Two days before the Fascist round-up, my reinforcements arrived. They were Erik Buchhardt, a hospital corpsman; Charles Ciccone, an expert weapons man; and Gene Delanie, a demolitions man. The last two spoke perfect Italian. Buchhardt brought along sulfa, morphine, iodine, gauze and instruments. In this zone, which was about 60 miles long and 20 miles wide, he set up a chain of dispensaries, each in charge of a partisan who knew a little about medicine.

"The work on the air strip was half done when I got word that the Fascists were starting a big sweep of the neighborhood. This meant we would have to hit for the hills, and I had to move fast.

I sent half my pilots over to Captain Brietche, the British agent, so he could forward them along the escape route through Yugoslavia. But another snowstorm blocked the route. They couldn't travel on the highways or fight the 15-foot drifts in the hills, so they spent the rest of the war with Brietche.

"The Fascists gathered a force equipped with heavy machine guns, mortars and rifles, so we moved over into another valley and dug in on the crest of a mountain. Our organization in the towns was working well: whatever the Fascists did down there was reported to us within five hours. We got word that the Fascists had moved 120 militiamen into a tiny town at the foot of our mountain and were using as their headquarters a shop which had been providing us with bread, butter, wine and cheese. Our supplies were now cut off, so I decided to strike.

"I took 20 partisans and at midnight we surrounded the Fascist garrison. The partisans had Sten guns, two automatic rifles and a bazooka. We first fired the bazooka through a window and called out to the garrison to surrender. A Fascist militiaman came to the door to ask our terms, but when one of our men advanced to talk it over with him the Fascist opened up with a machine gun, so we poured the rest of our bazooka rounds into the house. I'm sure no one escaped from it. We estimated the next morning that we had killed 80.

"Our attack caused tremendous repercussions. It was the first time this region had experienced the bazooka. The Fascists wanted to get the hell out, and the morale of the partisans soared. The 20 who had taken part in this attack were now heroes, known all over the Lower Alps, and everybody wanted to join us.

"Yet we were in real danger. Only three kilometers away was a German garrison equipped with armored cars. I knew they wouldn't take this attack lying down, so I gathered my Americans, including six Air Corps boys who were left, got food and ammunition, and with 30 partisans moved back up the highest mountain of the region—the Col de Moi, which towers 3000 feet above the Po valley. We hid in three shepherds' huts on its crest and waited.

"Soon about 120 Fascists came toiling up the zigzag mountain trail. We killed 20 of them with our machine guns, and the
rest ran down the mountain. Presently a partisan courier
crawled up gulleys through the Fascist lines to report that there
were now 3000 Fascists spread out through the zone and they
would soon close in. I told Silsby to radio our base that we were
surrounded, and wanted canned beef, five automatic rifles, two
American machine guns and a 47-mm. cannon. Two hours later
Silsby contacted base again and found that Captain Matterazzi
of our headquarters in Bari had already packed the order and
loaded it into a plane. It was coöperation like this which made
it possible for us to work in the field; we knew that we would
be backed up.

"Toward evening several Fascist trucks came up the road
about five kilometers away. We waited until the first truck entered a short tunnel through the opposite mountain, both ends
of which were in our field of fire. When the truck started to
come out we gave it a burst, whereupon they backed it into the
tunnel. For an hour we played cat and mouse with it, giving it
a burst of fire whenever it tried to leave either end of the tunnel.
Finally we disabled it and they left it there, blocking the narrow
mountain road.

"We were only a handful surrounded on a mountain, and
darkness was coming on. If they had the nerve to attack at night,
how could we handle them? I sent a messenger to the village for
Maria, who knew the Alpine trails as well as any mountain goat
and could take the Air Corps men to safety. That night she led
them 30 miles through the mountains to Captain Brietche.

"We discovered at dark that the Fascists were even more
alarmed than we were and had pulled out. Then we loaded our
arms on a sled and sneaked off to another mountain 15 miles
away. For the time being the Fascists had had enough. Our
spies told us that they appealed to the Germans for help and
were told to go to hell.

"And on the basis of this report we asked our base for 'black'
propaganda to distribute. They sent us a leaflet printed as
though it had been issued by the Germans, saying that Fascists

were all cowards and it would be best to send them quickly to the front. We distributed copies among the Fascists and it caused many desertions. Another leaflet, supposedly printed by the Fascists, charged that the Germans were deserting the Italians. Except for the distribution of these leaflets, we stopped all partisan activity in our new hideout. I wanted to let the area become peaceful again so I could bring in more men from base.

"Farbrega, Silsby, Buchhardt, Ciccone, Delanie and I lived in two deserted stone houses, along with three partisans. They were Porthos, a 22-year-old boy from Bolzano, whose parents had been killed by American bombs and whose brothers had been shot by the Germans; Victor, who presently was to betray us; and a kid called Brownie, whose parents had been killed by the Germans and who had more courage than them all. With another partisan Brownie walked into Belluno; spotting two German machine guns in the armory there, he disarmed the guards, threw the machine guns into a German truck, made four trips back into the armory for other weapons and drove the truck up the mountain to us.

"Farbrega now set to work to prepare caves in which we could bury the spare radio, gas, oil, food, clothing and ammunition in case we were suddenly chased away.

"One of our best operators, an Italian whose battle name was Sette, was a chauffeur at SS headquarters at Belluno. Through a chain of runners he kept us posted on exactly what the Germans were doing with the hostages they had taken, when they planned to raid us, and such things. He was a great help to us. Many times he had witnessed executions of our partisans in the courtyard of the Germans' headquarters. He would see men with whom he had been working walk up to the firing squad. Sometimes their eyes would meet and Sette would give the partisan a wink of encouragement, to remind him that his death would be avenged. None ever betrayed him.

"One day we got big news from Sette: the great General Albert Kesselring was making an inspection tour in this neighborhood and would be due the next morning at Trichiana, six kilometers away. Delanie, Brownie and I spent most of that damned day chasing around through the hills with two automatic rifles, trying to catch up with Kesselring. Even if we had known that he was about to be appointed the Germans' Supreme Commander on the Western Front we couldn't have tried any harder. But we were hampered by the deep snow, and he always kept two jumps ahead.

"That night I met Captain Bennucci in a tavern at Sant' Antonio, near Trichiana, and we talked over plans until three in the morning. Then I took him to my hideout for the night. I told him about the turkey the partisans had brought in. We were looking forward to eating it in the morning. We'd been living on cornmeal for days.

"Next morning I got up early and was brewing tea, looking now and then at the turkey cooking. Silsby was just setting up his radio so we could get our messages off. Suddenly there was a knock at the door. It was one of the peasant girls who had promised Brownie to warn him. 'Germans!' she whispered. 'They've surrounded you!'

"I told Silsby to pack up his radio quick and bury it. Bennucci was waking the other men. I ordered Farbrega to get all the surplus material into his caves. Bennucci and I took a couple of automatic rifles and went up on the rise above the house, as a guard. I guessed that they had finally called out the SS troops. I didn't know then that there were more than 1000, with a certain Major Schroeder in charge.

"Bennucci was sweeping the back ridge with the binoculars. 'There's some up there!' he called. I grabbed the glasses. They seemed spread out completely around us and were closing in. We'd have to get the hell out. The girl had gone because, of course, it wasn't safe to be around. We took off, running up the creek bed in water about to our knees. It was in plain view of the Germans, but for some reason they didn't spot us until we had run 1000 yards. Then a machine gun opened up on the four of us. Farbrega hit the dirt. I hollered to him, but there was no answer and I ran round the bend.

"Just as I turned this bend I picked up a Browning automatic which a partisan had dropped, and fired a few rounds to keep the

Germans from closing the ring on us; then I threw the rifle away and ran up the creek 400 yards. Here I found Buchhardt and Silsby, completely exhausted. I now saw more Germans—one firing from across the creek and another on a knoll about 25 yards away.

"'Captain,' said Buchhardt, 'they're going to get us.' I took Buchhardt's arm, pulled him up the creek and boosted him over a waterfall. 'Now get the hell out,' I said, and went back to Silsby. Both Germans were now shooting at us. Silsby was too exhausted to get up and run, so I hollered, '*Kamerad!*'

"'Captain, get out of here,' Silsby said. 'Don't stay with me.' I still had my .45, but I couldn't fight because they would be sure to shoot Silsby if I did. One German advanced and the other stayed back to cover us. I quickly shoved under a rock $1000 in Swiss francs and gold louis d'or which I had with me. I knew if they found all that money I couldn't argue that I was only a poor shot-down airman.

"The German came up and took my pistol, ordered me to lift Silsby to his feet and marched us to a road which led to Trichiana, three miles away, where there was a German garrison of 800. Once we arrived there, all hope of escape would be gone.

"Silsby was getting his breath back. When we reached a certain bend in the road, I knew Trichiana was not far away, so I whispered to Silsby that we must make a break soon. Just then I saw a stable with one door near the road and one just opposite. In back was a ravine. I told Silsby that when we got just opposite he was to dart into the front door of the stable and out the back; I would run around the stable and catch the guard just as he ran out its back door after Silsby.

"When we reached the stable I shouted 'Now!' and started to run around it. But, not hearing Silsby, I ran through it and down into the ravine. Luck was with me because the guard was so busy covering Silsby that he couldn't fire. I ran about 400 yards and walked a mile. Then I hid behind a boulder in the creek bed until dark, wondering what had happened to the others.

"To bring them up to date: After I had boosted Buchhardt up that waterfall, he ran on up the creek until he found a hole.

Ciccone, Delanie and Bennucci had also found holes, and all hid until dark. Farbrega wasn't quite so lucky. Three Germans found him hiding in some bushes, loaded him into a truck and took him to SS headquarters at Belluno for questioning. There he caught a glimpse of Silsby. Through Sette, Silsby warned Farbrega to stick to the story that they were only shot-down airmen. Sette was in and out of the place all the time, of course, with complete freedom; the Germans trusted him. They tortured Farbrega, but they couldn't break down his story.

"Then they brought in two of our partisans they had captured—Porthos and Victor. Porthos wouldn't talk, but Victor told on all of us and even led the Germans to the cave where we had buried our equipment. After he talked, they hanged him and Porthos.

"When they learned from Victor that Farbrega was not an Air Corps man but the sergeant in charge of our operations, and that he had understood everything they had been saying, they beat him some more in an attempt to find out about our radio. But Farbrega wouldn't give. Finally they gave up and told Farbrega he was to be sent to the Bolzano prison. They put him, handcuffed, into the back seat of a car. Sette had talked himself into the job of driver. 'Now's our time,' he said. 'I'll give you a chance to escape. I'll open the door and we'll both run into the hills and join the partisans.' Farbrega shook his head. 'Why not?' said Sette. 'You're much more valuable to us here in the Germans' headquarters than you would be with the partisans in the mountains,' said Farbrega. Which was true, but it was also a brave thing to say.

"Brownie, meanwhile, had run on up the creek. Spotting 15 Germans beating the bushes, he killed about 10 of them with his automatic rifle. But he was wounded in an arm and a leg and could neither run nor shoot, and another group captured him. We never saw him again. We got this story from villagers.

"I myself had been hiding behind a boulder, and at dark I went to a house. The people in it were sympathetic (they all were, outside the cities), and they fed me. Then I went to a house where a partisan named Cherbro was living, and while he was bandaging up my leg I heard that Silsby and Farbrega were being held prisoner at the schoolhouse in Sant' Antonio. I arranged to have four girl partisans who owned bikes start rounding up information about Buchhardt, Ciccone and Delanie.

"About midnight I borrowed a pistol from Cherbro, sneaked into town and snooped around for three hours trying to get close to the schoolhouse, hoping to stage a jail-break. But the roads were blocked and I had to head for the foothills. About four o'clock I pulled into a little stable where a dozen men were hiding. My eyes were shut almost before I lay down on the hay.

"I was awakened about six by the Italians laughing. They were amused at the stupidity of the Germans. It seems a patrol of 30 had just gone right by the house, neglecting to search it. One of the Italians opened the door slowly and poked his nose out. Suddenly there was a bang, and he jerked it back. It seems the stupid Germans had guessed we were there, and so had let one patrol march conspicuously by while another crawled close on their bellies. The Italians busted out and started running like hell, the Germans picking off two of them on the wing.

"I let the Italians run about 200 yards and then, figuring attention would be on them, slid softly out the door, my back flat against the wall, tiptoeing around to the corner. I was just backing around this when I felt something hard pressing against one rib. Glancing over my shoulder, I saw that one of those stupid Germans had a gun there. He ordered me to turn around and marched me down a creek bottom.

"While I was an instructor at Fort Benning, I taught officer parachute candidates the way to disarm a man who has a gun. You suddenly grab his pistol wrist, bend over, give just the right quick pull, and he goes rolling over your shoulder, dazed, onto the ground. I had explained glibly that it was sure to work in combat, each time wondering privately if it would really work. Well, it did. This German landed right on his shoulders with his neck twisted up—dead.

"There were some Germans on a knoll who had seen my captor and me go down the creek bank. If they didn't see someone come out soon, they might get suspicious. I had no hope of hiding, so I decided to brazen it out. I stuffed my fur mountain hat into my blouse. I wore Army trousers and British battle-dress. Of course, I had no insignia. Ruffling my yellow hair to make it look as German as possible, I walked up the other bank of the creek, paying no attention to the fellows on the knoll, who I knew were looking at me. I kept glancing right and left as though I was a member of a German search party. Walking within 20 yards of them in plain sight, I kept straight on to a house about 300 yards away, opened its door as if I was bil-leted there and walked in.

"Sitting by the fireplace were an old woman and two young girls spinning wool by hand. When I told them I was an Amer-ican captain looking for a place to hide, they went right on with their spinning as though American captains dropped in for breakfast every morning. They hard-boiled some eggs, gave me bread to stuff in my pocket and then a girl led me to a ravine where she thought I would be safe. There I crouched, in the ice and snow, until about 10 that night, when I headed for Cherbro's house to see what news the four girls with bikes had brought in. Learning that Delanie and Ciccone were both safe with the partisans, I messaged them to keep out of sight until the heat was off. Buchhardt, I learned, was being hidden in the house of a patriot in Sant' Antonio. Bennucci too was safe.

"I needed rest, but it was time to get back to work again. I remembered some caves near the village of Dusoi that would serve for a rendezvous. I sent a message to Buchhardt to meet me there. I also asked help from a Communist leader called Bruno. He commanded the Messini Brigade, which, though part of the Communist Nanette Division, had actually proved eager to work with me and even to fight Germans.

"I made the trip to Dusoi at night. When I got to the caves I arranged with nearby partisans to bring us food, and next morn-ing a partisan showed up with Buchhardt, who told me all that had happened since I boosted him up the waterfall. From a house where he was hiding he had watched while Major Schroe-der's troops hanged Victor in the Sant' Antonio square.

"When Bruno, with 300 fully armed and well-trained men,

arrived at my caves he put me in touch with an Italian secret radio operator to replace Silsby. This operator's battle name was Gi-gi. Now we were ready for business, and we moved into a new zone near Feltre, where there had been almost no partisan activity. It was an important area because the main road to Austria via the Brenner Pass ran through it.

"I radioed to our base the locations of the Germans' deposits of explosives around Feltre. They had three underground caches and two houses full—with which they intended to blow the bridges when they left the region. The Air Corps got my information and bombed every cache. I got a drop of new equipment for the recruits that were flocking to us, and sent for Delanie and Ciccone to train them. The equipment included road spikes, thermite pencils and emery dust. I gave this dust to partisans who would slip it into locomotive bearings at Bolzano and Innsbruck, where trains coming over the pass changed engines.

"Our work must have been good because on April 1 we got word that the Germans were moving in an entire division (at that time only about 5000 men) to run us down. We were tired of scampering over the hills, so we decided that we would move right into a town to hide while the Germans beat the bushes for us. While this German division roamed the Lower Alps, we got on with our work.

"Originally there had been in this zone four key bridges connecting Italy with the Reich, but our Air Corps had blown two up, leaving the Busche and Vidor bridges. Partisans then blew up the Vidor, and the Busche was now the Germans' last link over the Piave River. It was jammed with traffic. The Air Corps tried again and failed, so it was up to the partisans to knock out the Busche.

"We had used nearly all our explosives blowing the Vidor. However, we got 200 pounds of explosive from a brigade 20 kilometers away. Two days later the partisans blew the Busche bridge 100 yards into the Alpine sky. This forced the Germans to make a 60-kilometer detour for the rest of the war, and when their front started to crumble they piled up in there until the whole area was a vast bumper-to-bumper traffic jam.

"I established a command post just outside Feltre. It was a cave which we hollowed out in a creek bank. At night we had carried old parachute containers down from the hills. We opened them up and flattened them to serve as roofing. Over this we put a layer of sod and ferns. The entrance was a tiny wooden trapdoor with leather hinges, on top of which we had wired sod, watering it so that it would stay green. Around it we piled leaves to cover any crack. Here I lived with Buchhardt, Delanie, Ciccone and Gi-gi. At night we would go out to meet Bruno and the officers of his Messini Brigade. He now had 500 men engaged in sabotage. When there was nothing else to do they tossed time pencils and grenades into German barracks at night. It kept the Nazis in a constant turmoil, because they never knew when one of these explosions meant an attack. Now and then we did attack. The partisans got two or three German vehicles every night along the highways with booby traps or bazookas. The Germans feared to move by day because of our Air Corps, and our partisans were now making them almost as fearful after dark. After each strike the partisans would move 15 miles away or wait several days before striking again.

"By April 20 the Po offensive of our main army was going well. I realized that if the Germans retreated past our zone into the High Alps and Brenner Pass it might take months to dig them out. The best play would be to squeeze the retreating Germans between our main armies and the partisans. Bennucci and the Messini Brigade under Bruno, working south of the Alps, were operating smoothly and no longer needed my help, so I decided to get in touch with Ettore, commander of the partisans' courageous Val Cordevole Brigade, which was working in the High Alps, and strengthen it.

"To get into the High Alps we had to pass through three German roadblocks, and there was no way to travel overland because the mountains are as steep as cliffs; the roads are blasted out of their sides. Fortunately I had been in touch with a titled Italian woman who was working with us, a marchesa who owned much land in the region. A blonde in her early 30's, she wasn't beautiful but she had a schoolgirl figure. She also had plenty of guts. She was particularly useful because she was said to be the mistress of Dr. Schmidt, the German civilian commander of this zone; at any rate, she had the use of his car whenever she wanted it. Actually she was working closely with our Underground, helping them with money and supplies, and hiding American and British aviators who had been shot down, until they could be moved over the border.

"The marchesa arranged for a truck to pick up our party and take us as far as Cortina. At 3:30 in the early drizzly morning of April 24 we arrived at the marchesa's villa. The truck, a big wood-burning job, was parked in the enclosed courtyard. She gave us a fine ham-and-egg breakfast, with ersatz coffee, and after we'd had a last cigarette we headed for the truck. Its back end was piled high with large boxes about three feet square, all nailed together. In front, just behind the driver, was a tiny hole into which we could crawl. Then a box was nailed over that and a tarpaulin lashed over the whole. It was designed for only two, but Delanie, Ciccone, Gi-gi and I squeezed in, with full equipment.

"As we began grinding up the road we had our choice of three worries: (1) that the Germans would search the truck; (2) that some of our partisans might ambush us with a bazooka; and (3) that the American Air Corps might roar down to drill us with a 20-mm. cannon. Luckily it was a drizzly, foggy day, which eliminated the Air Corps.

"We pulled out a little after dawn. At the first three German roadblocks sentries would step out into the road and our driver would pull up. Our hearts would go up into our mouths as we heard the driver say that he had been sent to Belluno to get the month's cigarette ration for the Germans' road laborers but, finding no tobacco there, was returning with empty boxes. Had he said the boxes were full of tobacco, the sentries might have demanded some for themselves, and discovered us.

"When we passed the third roadblock we thought it was the last and were beginning to breathe easy when all of a sudden the truck slowed down and stopped again. The guards told the driver to take off the tarpaulin so that they could have a closer look. We lay as still as death. We could hear the creak of the ropes as the driver untied them, then the swish of the canvas as the tarpaulin was dragged off. The chill drizzle pattered down on our boxes. Then I heard them tell the driver the boxes would have to come off. Cramped in those boxes, we could not shoot, and since we had two radios we could hardly claim to be four innocent aviators.

"One German climbed up onto the boxes and pulled at the topmost one. Of course it didn't budge. Just then came a gust of wind and a more brisk pattering; the drizzle was turning into a rain. 'Oh, let him go on,' another German called impatiently. 'Let's get in out of the wet.' We could hear the sentry jump off the truck, and the crunching of the gravel as, with the other three, he walked over to their shelter house a few yards away.

"Half an hour later we were in Mareson, a tiny Italian village in an Alpine valley, sitting in the local café with Ettore and eating the good dinner he had ordered.

"As we ate, Ettore told us that his partisans now controlled all the territory between us and Mezzacanal, where there was a German garrison of 700. I decided to attack Mezzacanal next morning. Ettore's partisans were good men, and I could see that there was none of the intrigue that honeycombed the Communist brigades. That night I sent 20 of them, with automatic rifles, machine guns, grenades and a bazooka, to climb the mountain back of Mezzacanal and take positions overlooking the village. At dawn the next morning I rode toward Mezzacanal in a school bus with Ettore, Ciccone and 20 other partisans. My plan was that when the Germans came out of cover to attack us along the road, the partisans stationed on the cliff above would suddenly open fire on them.

"The people of Mareson didn't like the Germans, who had been on their necks through weary years of war—quartered in their houses, eating their food and taking their best men for the labor camps. So when they saw their partisans assembling, well armed and led by Americans, more than 100 old men and boys followed our bus. They had armed themselves with scythes, clubs, butcher knives, muzzle-loading muskets, sledge hammers, anything. I told Ettore to keep this motley crew at a safe distance behind, where none would get hurt. When we got about 500 yards from Mezzacanal, we deployed and opened fire. The Germans tried to leave from the far side of the town and the partisans began firing from the cliff. The garrison quickly surrendered. We distributed their weapons among the partisans.

"Then I had an idea. General Patton was now on the Austrian border and the Russians were in Vienna. We had the Brenner Pass blocked, and controlled the whole valley. So I issued passes to these Germans permitting the bearer to return to his home in Germany, and stamped them with my name, as a captain in

the U.S. Infantry and commander of the Val Cordevole Brigade. Then we set them free. What happened was what I expected. I learned later that they showed these passes to other Germans who were still fighting, and many of these promptly threw down their arms and hit the road for home.

"Our mop-up in that region sealed the route to the Brenner Pass. On April 28 I got word that retreating Germans were moving north toward the pass and were already at Feltre. Ettore blew a bridge north of town and had a work party chop down trees and move the logs nearby, so that when the Americans came and wanted a new bridge it could be quickly rebuilt.

"We placed ambushes along the road, and Ettore waited at the blown bridge with 10 men. When the Germans arrived to rebuild the bridge, Ettore's men opened fire. The Germans pulled back into Caprile, taking with them their 120 dead. From one of the wounded I found out that we held, trapped in this valley, 600 men of the 504th Panzer Battalion, 3000 Wehrmacht troops, and 300 SS troops under Major Schroeder.

"Looking down into Caprile from the rocks 600 yards above, we saw that the SS troops were dragging civilians from their houses and herding them into the church. Ettore and I now moved back into a tiny village in the valley. Pretty soon up the road came a German car flying a white flag of truce. In the car was the Caprile priest and with him a German sergeant who brought us a haughty ultimatum from Major Schroeder: if we did not permit all German military personnel to pass, every civilian in Caprile would be executed.

"Ettore replied that if any civilians were bothered in any way we would refuse the Germans any chance of surrender. At this the Caprile priest started crying and begged Ettore to spare the innocent civilians. But Ettore wouldn't budge—which took a lot of guts. I backed him up, and the sergeant went back. Soon Major Schroeder sent up a request for a conference. I knew he now realized we had him in a trap which he couldn't blast through or back out of.

"He arrived with a Captain Heim, a fine-looking soldier who was commander of the panzer battalion. I let Schroeder do the talking. He did a good deal of it, and repeated his threat about what he was going to do to the civilians. I told him what I would do to the Germans if he did.

"Then Heim spoke up. He talked straight, with no mention of murdering civilians. He said he would like nothing better than to give us a good fight, but he had almost no ammunition and couldn't see his men killed when they couldn't fight back. 'As far as my unit is concerned,' he said, 'we're placing ourselves in your hands.'

"Schroeder said that before he would consider surrender he must know whom he was surrendering to. I said I was Captain

Howard Chappell, of the OSS. He said he couldn't help remarking that I also looked very Prussian, being tall with blue eyes and yellow hair. Then he said he had often heard of my bravery and would be most happy to surrender to me personally because I was an officer and a Prussian and therefore a man of honor, and so would treat him and his seven SS officers exactly as he would have treated me had I been captured. I replied that this he could be extremely sure of. The next day Ciccone, Ettore, Gi-gi and I with one battalion of partisans moved north toward the Austrian border and captured a German garrison of 600. The Germans whom we had released at Mezzacanal had been through here, showing their 'passes' signed by me. This garrison had decided that they too wanted to go home.

"Just beyond here was Col Fasco, an Alpine village where there was a reserve pool of 3500 German soldiers. They were damned happy to surrender. All the telephone lines and radio channels connecting Italy with Berlin passed through Col Fasco, which we held. Now the entire road from the pre-Alps to the Austrian border was open and waiting for American troops.

"I borrowed a German car and drove all night toward Belluno. On May 3, I contacted the commanding officer of the 339th Infantry and told him the road from here to the Austrian border was held by partisans who were waiting for him; told him he would need chains for his trucks because of the deep snow; and gave him other helpful information. Then I went on into Feltre to contact the 85th Division.

"I hadn't had a haircut for five months and looked more like a partisan than a soldier. While waiting for the colonel in charge of G-2 (Army Intelligence), I picked up a copy of the *Stars and Stripes* and was catching up on what had happened in the world when suddenly someone said: 'What in hell are you doing in here, and who in hell are you?'

"It was a major general, so I got up and said: 'Captain Chappell, sir, of OSS.'

"'Are you a soldier? Stand at attention! Get out of this office.'

"I got out and was just about to head back to my mountains

when the G-2 colonel came in. He was very glad to get my report. Advance units were always glad to see us and get our fresh information, but sometimes the top commanders didn't want to admit that anyone else had helped them.

"I went on back into the Alps and turned over to OSS our 7500 prisoners, trucks, arms and supplies. Then, after giving our officers all I knew about the situation, I started off with Ettore and Sette on a round-up of war criminals.

"We didn't want to let any get away. For instance, we remembered the case of Steve Hall, an American boy who had been on a mission like ours near Cortina. Steve had gone alone into Cortina on skis to blow up a hydroelectric plant which supplied power for the railway. He was caught in a snowstorm, and witnesses told us that the next morning he was found unconscious near the church. The German police took him to jail. A man called Tell, who was a spy for the Germans, identified Steve as an American agent, and Steve was executed at Bolzano. We picked up Tell. He wrote out a statement admitting how he had wormed his way into Steve's confidence and then fooled him.

"It was nice to see Sergeant Farbrega again. He and Silsby had been sent together to the SS prison at Bolzano. When the war was almost over he had slid out of the prison and gone to Merano, where the SS top officials were holed up. He had gone to the SS barracks and said he was 'Captain' Farbrega of the U.S. Army and that, by his order, they were all restricted to barracks. He was a persuasive talker, and his bluff worked. When the 10th U.S. Division showed up, Farbrega turned the city over to them—by courtesy of one U.S. sergeant.

"Sette was in a hell of a position. Toward the end of the war the Gestapo was looking for him, finally convinced that he had been working for us. But many partisans who did not know the truth remembered that he had driven a car for the Germans, so they were after him too. I finally got him a job with our Counter Intelligence Corps, and he turned in many war criminals.

"And the marchesa? Well, the last I heard, an American infantry colonel whose headquarters was nearby was parking his jeep there regularly. Her apfelstrudel has a nice flaky crust."

The Nazi Counterfeit Plot

By Major George J. McNally, USA, with Frederic Sondern, Jr.

A few days after the surrender of Adolf Hitler's armies, an excited U.S. counter-intelligence officer in Austria called my office at Allied headquarters in Frankfurt. A German captain, he reported, had turned in a truck loaded with millions of dollars' worth of British bank notes. Huge amounts of currency, he added, were floating around in the Enns River; householders and Allied troops were busy fishing it out.

Startled and puzzled, I rushed to the place where the German captain and his truck had been taken. There, in 23 stout boxes about the size of coffins, were bundles and bundles of Bank of England notes. A quick tally of the hoard—aided by neatly written manifests tacked inside the cover of each case—showed that it totaled no less than 21 million pounds sterling!

It was impossible for me to determine, even under a powerful magnifying glass, whether the notes were genuine or not. I called my British colleagues in Frankfurt, and shortly afterward had a telephone call direct from the Bank of England. When I described the find, there was a long-drawn gasp at the other end of the wire. Soon a representative of the Bank arrived from London—a tall, angular and reserved gentleman named Reeves.

We took Reeves to the heavily guarded room where the treasure was deposited, and he began going from box to box, riffling the notes through his fingers. Finally he stopped and stared silently into space. Then for several seconds he cursed, slowly and methodically in a cultured English voice, but with vehemence. "Sorry," he said at last. "But the people who made this stuff have cost us so much."

From that moment Reeves, three detectives from Scotland

Yard and I collaborated in piecing together the fantastic story of Operation Bernhard.

First, I was told that during 1943 an alarming number of counterfeit English bank notes had been finding their way to London from Zürich, Lisbon, Stockholm and other neutral centers. They had begun to come in batches of £100,000 or more. It was clear to the Bank's experts that the notes were being manufactured by highly skilled craftsmen and distributed by a remarkably well-organized gang. Then a German spy was arrested in Edinburgh. He had been flown by seaplane to the Scottish coast and had come ashore in a rubber boat. The suitcase he carried was stuffed with the finest fake money the Bank of England had ever seen.

The Bank now realized that it was up against the German government itself, and that the very credit of Britain might well be at stake. For decades banks all over the world had been using Bank of England notes almost like gold; frightened Europeans and Asians had hoarded them against bad days. Now hundreds of thousands of pounds of fake British money were circulating outside of Britain. If doubt were cast on the integrity of these notes in neutral and Allied countries, particularly in the middle of a war, the result might prove extremely dangerous not only to Britain but to the Allied cause.

The whole financial world was jolted when the Bank announced that it was withdrawing from circulation all its bank notes of all denominations and would exchange them for five-pound notes of a new design. After a certain date all old notes would cease to be legal tender. To a confused Parliament, Britain's Chancellor of the Exchequer explained guardedly that widespread counterfeiting was one of the reasons for this action. He gave no more details, and the British press was discouraged from inquiring further. The facts were that in three years the Nazis had printed incalculable numbers of false English notes which were wrecking fortunes, snarling banks and industries, and costing the British Treasury millions of pounds.

With this background information, we began a search for the men and machinery behind the counterfeiting operation.

Finding the machinery was, by chance, not difficult. The German captain who had surrendered the boxes of bank notes told us he had received them from an SS officer whose truck had broken down near the village of Redl-Zipf. That was all the captain knew. We went to Redl-Zipf—and discovered one of the underground networks of storage corridors and workshops that honeycombed the Alpine redoubt where the Nazis had intended to make their last stand. There, in Gallery 16—a 200-foot-long tunnel stretching off a big shaft bored into the side of a mountain—we found bank-note presses and other machinery. But no plates, no paper, no records. "Now all we have to do, old boy," said Reeves, "is to find the chaps who ran this place."

Inquiries in Redl-Zipf revealed that all the men who had worked in the subterranean factory had been taken to the extermination camp at Ebensee, 40 miles away, just a few days before the German surrender. We got to Ebensee fast, but every one of our counterfeiters was gone. When the camp was liberated, the counterfeiters had simply walked out, each in his own direction. Fortunately, the camp records had been kept with typical German precision, even through the last mad days of the Reich. The names and birthplaces of this strange band were listed. Now began a search which lasted for months and took us to the four corners of the former Nazi empire.

One by one we rounded up more than 40 of the most important of the counterfeiters. From them we learned that a Czech named Oskar Skala—a political prisoner of the Nazis—had been chief bookkeeper of the operation. We found him, with the help of the Czechoslovakian police, peacefully selling beer in a little town near Pilsen. Skala was more than coöperative. A methodical man, he had kept in a tiny notebook a day-by-day description of the work of the forgers. The final pieces of the fantastic story of Operation Bernhard fell into place.

Early in the war SS Führer Heinrich Himmler had created an organization whose aim was to corrupt Great Britain's economy by counterfeiting her bank notes on a large scale. The project really hit its stride when Major Bernhard Krüger came in as executive director in 1942. A young, resourceful Nazi, Krüger soon learned that one of the difficulties had been the recruiting of the highly skilled, specialized personnel needed for a big counterfeiting plant. The experts at the Reichsbank and the Reich Printing Office—most of them strait-laced old Prussian civil servants—had rebelled at the idea of actually printing another nation's money, even in wartime. Krüger had a solution: a number of Germany's outstanding printing technicians were in concentration camps because of their racial origin; such men could be put to work—and at the same time be kept quiet.

Bernhard Krüger rounded up these technicians, promised them preferential treatment and had them transported to the Sachsenhausen concentration camp at Oranienburg, near Berlin. (Some were already imprisoned there.) In an isolated compound known as Block 19, surrounded by charged barbed-wire fences and picked guards from the notorious Deathshead Brigade sworn to absolute secrecy, Operation Bernhard got down to business. The last word in bank-note printing plants was set up. Plates were engraved with meticulous care. A German press manufacturer interrupted war production to supply the necessary precision machinery. A famous paper concern succeeded in reproducing the fine, light Bank of England paper with its elaborate watermarks. Experimental batches of the Bernhard product were sent to Gestapo representatives in German embassies and consulates in Turkey, Spain, Switzerland and Sweden with instructions to try them on the local banks. Most of the notes were accepted without question. Himmler was jubilant.

Now, as the notes came off the presses, they were meticulously inspected and graded. Grade One, the best, were distributed for purchases in neutral countries and as operation money for the more important of Himmler's spies and saboteurs abroad. Grade Two notes, which had slight imperfections but were still excellent fakes, were distributed to Gestapo units in occupied countries to buy information and subsidize collaborationists, who liked to have Bank of England notes on tap in case anything went wrong. Grade Three notes, still an extremely deceptive forgery, were accumulated and stored for small deals and miscellaneous needs that might arise.

One of the outstanding victims of Krüger's Grade One money was the now-famous "Cicero"—the Albanian spy who was butler and valet to the British Ambassador in Ankara during the war, and who became, he thought, the highest-paid spy in history when he received over $1,000,000 from German Intelligence for secrets he filched from the Ambassador's safe. (See "The Highest-Paid Spy in History," page 299, and photograph on page 332.) A more typical victim was a Swiss businessman who accepted in perfectly good faith British pounds worth a quarter of a million dollars from an irreproachable Turkish bank. The pounds were accepted in turn by a Swiss bank and eventually worked their way through several other neutral countries to Bank of England headquarters in Threadneedle Street. There Major Krüger's product was finally detected by an alert teller.

The discovery of the secret place where Mussolini was imprisoned after his arrest by the Italians in 1943 was made possible by large bribes. By the time SS Captain Otto Skorzeny had whisked Mussolini to temporary safety in Hitler's Reich, about £50,000 in counterfeit English bank notes had changed hands. (See "The Most Dangerous Man in Europe," page 468.)

Even as Operation Bernhard flourished, however, Major Krüger was worried. His plant was producing 400,000 notes a month and the total stipulated by Himmler would soon be reached. Whereupon the Major conspired with his foremen to slow down the presses and to condemn large quantities of first-class notes as faulty. "If we don't slow down," he said to his bookkeeper and principal lieutenant one day, "I will be sent to the front to fight and you will all be shot. That would be a great pity." It was fortunate for the Bank of England that he felt that way. On Krüger's orders, several hundred thousand Grade One notes which might have been circulated were secretly packed away in big wooden boxes.

To keep Operation Bernhard working at full capacity, Krüger embarked on another project which had been on his list for some time—the counterfeiting of American dollars. But his technicians found this a tougher job. The paper used in U.S. currency has never been successfully imitated, and the best paper mills in Germany, after exhaustive research, could turn out only a crude facsimile. Moreover, even the most skilled of Krüger's men found they could not produce the highly complicated engraved plates and colored inks which were needed.

Somewhere in Germany or in one of the occupied countries, Krüger reasoned, there must be at least one professional counterfeiter with experience in American notes who could break this impasse. The Gestapo and Himmler's other secret services began a search. In a German prison they found Solly Smolianoff, a first-class counterfeiter. Solly had never been to the United States, but he specialized in producing "American" notes of such outstanding quality that they had more than once come to the attention of the U.S. Secret Service. He had been jailed by several European countries for making them.

Solly found Block 19 a paradise. "Imagine," he said to his colleagues, "a counterfeiting plant *guarded* by the police!" By the end of 1944 he was ready with $50 and $100 bills that experts at the Reich Printing Office found eminently satisfactory. Operation Bernhard was ordered to tool up for production of these notes.

But now the tide of war was turning against the Reich. Berlin was being bombed more heavily every day, and Sachsenhausen was within the target area. Himmler wanted to shut down Operation Bernhard, but Krüger persuaded his chief to let him move the plant and men to one of the new underground factories in the redoubt area of the Austrian Alps. The transfer from Sachsenhausen took several months. It was April 1945 before Operation Bernhard was ready to set up its presses in Gallery 16 behind Redl-Zipf. By that time American troops were already closing in on the redoubt. Solly Smolianoff was never to use the plates he had so lovingly fabricated.

Orders came from Himmler himself: Every trace of Operation Bernhard was to be obliterated. All records were to be destroyed, fake currency and unprinted bank-note paper burned, plates and dies sunk in the deepest part of nearby Lake Toplitz. All 140 members of Operation Bernhard were to be taken to the Ebensee concentration camp. Master Counterfeiter Krüger disappeared and has never been heard of since, despite the concentrated efforts of half a dozen police forces to find him.

For three days the SS officers and the prisoners of Operation Bernhard stoked a big incinerator with records and inferior counterfeits. A squad sank the printing plates and many cases filled with counterfeit notes deep in Lake Toplitz. But these men could not bring themselves to destroy the finest of the fake notes, the hoard that Krüger had set aside to avoid the appearance of overproduction. As one of the counterfeiters told us later, "They were so beautiful." Coffin-sized boxes of them were loaded on trucks whose drivers were ordered to bury them in suitable places in the neighborhood from which they could be recovered at some future time.

One of the truckloads was that which was turned in to us by the German captain. Some simply disappeared. Others were dumped into the Enns River by frightened SS men who only wanted to get into civilian clothes and be on their way. In the turbulent Alpine stream, swelled by spring freshets, these boxes of Grade One notes were broken open by the rocks—and people from roundabout delightedly began fishing. (In July 1959 many of the counterfeit plates and cases of notes were recovered from the bottom of Lake Toplitz. See photograph on page 346.)

Our investigation at an end, we made a tally of Operation Bernhard's total production. It was startling. According to Oskar Skala's notebook and the corroborating evidence of other Krüger workers, the Major's plant turned out almost nine million Bank of England notes with a face value of approximately 140 million pounds sterling—then equivalent to $564,000,000! Six million dollars' worth went to Turkey and the Near East; $12,000,000 worth were distributed in France and the Low Countries; $30,000,000 worth paid German bills in Spain, Portugal, Switzerland and the Scandinavian countries. Another $250,000,000 worth escaped burning at Redl-Zipf and was either fished out of the Enns River by Austrians, Russians, Americans and British or cached by SS men for future use.

For a long while Krüger masterpieces which had been salvaged from a watery grave and not surrendered kept turning up

at British race tracks, in European black markets, even in New
York foreign-exchange houses.

New British five-pound notes—with a fine metallic thread
drawn through them by a secret process, and as counterfeit-
proof as any money can be—have now replaced the old currency.
But for the British, and for ourselves, Operation Bernhard was a
near thing. And it *could* happen again.

Adolf Hitler's Last Days

By Frederic Sondern, Jr.

Two books contain most of the details on which this account is based. The Last
Days of Hitler (*Macmillan*) *was written by Major H. R. Trevor-Roper, British
historian assigned to the case by the British Intelligence Bureau.* Ten Days to Die
(*Doubleday*) *is a compilation by Captain Michael A. Musmanno, USNR—Pennsyl-
vania jurist and a judge at the Nuremberg trials—of the findings of various Allied
intelligence agencies supplemented by exhaustive research of his own. Frederic
Sondern, Jr., was in Berlin soon after its fall and conferred with many of the intelligence officers investigating the facts.*

Three weeks after the collapse of Nazi Germany, Major Ivan
Nikitine, deputy chief of the Soviet Security Police, reported in Berlin that the Führer had neither shot himself in his
underground shelter nor been cremated nearby as generally believed—if, indeed, he had perished at all.

An immediate, exhaustive inquiry was ordered by General
Eisenhower's intelligence service in 1945. Special teams of
American, British and French experts gradually reconstructed
the details of Hitler's last days. The 28 people who had been
close to the Führer during the Battle of Berlin and had been captured by Western Allied forces were questioned and requestioned
and their stories checked and cross-checked. Mountains of documents were studied before the Allied investigation of the German
dictator's end was finally completed.

At approximately 3:30 on the afternoon of April 30, 1945, Adolf Hitler sat down beside his wife in the underground *Führerbunker*, put the barrel of a Walther automatic into his mouth and pulled the trigger, while Eva Hitler crunched a vial of cyanide between her teeth. At 10:30 that night what little remained of their bodies—which had been drenched repeatedly with gasoline and burned in the Chancellery garden—was buried by General Julius Rattenhuber and a detail of Elite Guardsmen. All night long an artillery barrage from the Russian lines churned up the whole area. Hitler's bones were scattered as his Thousand Year Reich had been.

Moscow did not want it that way, however. The Russian authorities did everything in their power to obstruct our investigation. Key witnesses captured by the Russians, including General Rattenhuber, disappeared. Our intelligence agents learned that a jawbone found by Russian investigators at the place of cremation was definitely identified as Hitler's by the two dental technicians who made his false teeth. The jawbone and the men were sent to Moscow and have not been heard of since.

Stalin himself set the official Russian attitude when he startled President Truman and Secretary of State Byrnes at the Potsdam Conference with the remark that he believed Hitler was still alive and hiding in Spain or Argentina. Stalin seemed determined to keep Hitler "alive." The record of those last terrible days in Berlin—when a crazed tyrant tried to pull his whole nation down with him—was not to Stalin's liking.

It was the Führer's birthday—April 20, 1945. In the *Fuhrerbunker*, 50 feet below the surface of the Chancellery garden, the chiefs of the German armed forces and the Nazi Party had gathered to pay their respects to the Supreme Warlord. Boots shone and decorations glittered, but most of the faces were haggard. The decimated German armies were falling back on every front. The Russians threatened Berlin; the Americans had crossed the Elbe and were racing to meet them.

Since his narrow escape 10 months before from the Generals' Plot and the briefcase-bomb attempt on his life, Hitler had sud-

denly become an old man, stooped and hunched, dragging one
foot and with a noticeable tremor in his left arm. But as his
courtiers murmured what birthday congratulations they could
muster, his voice was as incisive, his eyes as bright as ever.

In the conference that followed, the satraps could hardly believe their ears. When Field Marshal Wilhelm Keitel hesitatingly
tried to point out the gravity of the situation, Hitler impatiently
swept him aside. "Nonsense," he rasped. "The Russians will
meet their bloodiest defeat yet before the impregnable gates of
Berlin. And then we will roll the Allies back into the sea." The
mesmeric eyes swept over them, and no one moved.

Reichsmarschall Hermann Goering broke the spell for a few
moments. Germany would inevitably triumph, said the corpu-
lent master of the once mighty Luftwaffe, but it would be safer
for the Führer to direct his troops from the mountain fastness of
Berchtesgaden. Hitler glared. "What you are really recommend-
ing," he snapped, "is that *you* should leave for a safer place. You
may go, by all means." In stony silence Goering saluted with his
jeweled marshal's baton and took his leave; a few minutes later,
followed by a convoy of fast trucks loaded with treasure, his
armored Mercedes was streaking for Bavaria and, he thought,
safety.

Hitler had turned back to his maps and was explaining his
strategy. "We knew," one veteran general said later, "that most
of the divisions with which he was maneuvering were no longer
effective units. But, listening to him, most of us felt there might
still be a chance." Hitler had elaborate plans to throw the Russians back from Berlin. The counter-attack was to be led by one
of his favorite Elite Guard commanders, SS General Felix
Steiner. "Any officer who keeps a single man back from this operation," Hitler screamed, "will forfeit his life within five hours."

On the afternoon of April 22 the Führer announced to his
staff the first victory of the new campaign. Heinrich Himmler,
sycophantic leader of the SS, had reported by telephone that
Steiner's offensive was in full swing and that the Red troops
were falling back from Berlin. Then several messages were laid
in rapid succession in front of General Alfred Jodl, Chief of

Operations. For several minutes Jodl could not bring himself to speak. Then Hitler noticed his face. "Well? Well?" he demanded. "*Mein Führer*," said Jodl, "Steiner has *not* attacked. Marshal Zhukov's armor is reported in Berlin."

Hitler stared straight ahead, his face a slowly purpling mask. "The SS," he whispered. Then the whisper became a roar. "I have been betrayed by the SS! First the Army, then the Luftwaffe and now the SS. Traitors—all of you! Dogs of traitors!"

For three hours Hitler raged on. So devastating was the force of his unleashed personality that even the unemotional Generals Keitel and Jodl were "dashed to the wall," as one of them put it later. Finally Hitler staggered back to his chair. "The Third Reich has failed," he gasped hoarsely. "Nothing remains except for me to die. I shall remain here and wait for the end. Then I shall shoot myself. There's nothing left to fight with. Get Goering to negotiate with the Allies."

The Führer's words were reported to Goering, who by a Law of Succession promulgated by the Führer in 1941 had been established as Hitler's successor. The fat, pleasure-loving Marshal was positive he would be able to talk the Allies into reasonable surrender terms and, at the worst, be banished himself into a comfortable exile. He radioed:

> *Mein Führer*—In view of your decision, do you agree that
> I take over the total leadership of the Reich? If no reply from
> you is received by 10 tonight, I shall take it for granted.

Goering ordered his bodyguard increased to 1000 men, and to his staff he announced that he would fly to see General Eisenhower on the following day. But just as he was composing a message to the American Supreme Commander, a wire arrived:

> Goering—What you did calls for the death sentence. I shall
> not insist on proceedings if you voluntarily resign from
> your offices. Otherwise I shall take appropriate steps.
> Adolf Hitler

Goering was staring incredulously at this when the jackboots of an SS squad rang on the flagstones outside. The Herr Reichsmarschall was under arrest. Hitler had no intention of letting Goering succeed him.

Within an hour of his dramatic farewell in the *Führerbunker*, Hitler had begun to plan for the greatest funeral pyre in history. Calm and precise, he ordered General Wenck's 12th Army, then engaging the Americans, to move back to the capital. Meanwhile every man and boy in Berlin should be sent to the barricades to stem the Russian advance; shirkers would be hanged.

Hearing the order, one veteran Nazi stalwart, Gauleiter Wegener, in charge of all civil affairs for northern Germany, managed to get Hitler on the telephone. If the Führer, he pleaded, would only authorize surrender in the west to the Americans and British, the Russians could be held back until an armistice was arranged and much devastation could be avoided. "Devastation, Wegener," replied Hitler, "is just what I want. The better to illuminate my finish." The next day, April 25, the Russians had encircled Berlin. (See photograph on page 345.)

During the last seven days in the *Führerbunker* the group around the Führer grew small. Goebbels and his wife brought their six children—whom they later murdered before committing suicide themselves. Martin Bormann, Hitler's political right hand, elected to stay. Eva Braun, the Führer's mistress, refused to leave. In the two steel-and-concrete warrens adjoining Hitler's were 26 high officers and 30 secretaries and guards.

As the shells of the Russian guns came closer and began to shake the bunkers, "everybody gradually began to go mad." Liquor flowed like water while stiff Prussian generals took off their tunics and danced crazily with their stenographers. Hitler himself brooded over his maps and held conferences.

Finally, on April 28, a press dispatch from Stockholm was brought to the Führer. It reported that Heinrich Himmler—chief of the SS—was negotiating with Count Bernadotte for the Reich's surrender to the Allies. That was the last straw. "*Und jetzt der treue Heinrich!* [And now even the faithful Heinrich!]" Hitler shrieked. But the tantrum—his last—was short. Suddenly

he became calm and crisp. Himmler's betrayal shattered any further hope of resistance. This was the end.

The last two days in the *Führerbunker* were the strangest of all. Early on the morning of April 29, Hitler and Eva Braun were married in a short, simple ceremony while Russian shells crashed into the Chancellery almost over their heads and sent down a rain of plaster from the roof of the bunker. Then Hitler dictated to his secretary his "political last will and testament." It contains nothing he had not said many times before. Striking Goering and Himmler from the Nazi Party rolls, he appointed Admiral Karl Doenitz to succeed him as chief of state.

A digest of the news was brought to him as usual, and in it he read a detailed account of Mussolini's death before a partisan firing squad and the public exhibition of his and Clara Petacci's bodies, hung up by their feet, in a Milan square. Hitler had already given instructions that his and Eva's bodies should be destroyed after their suicide, but he now repeated his orders: "Completely destroyed, do you understand? Completely!"

At the regular staff conference that afternoon he quietly received the report of the Russian advance: the Chancellery would be attacked directly on May 1 at the latest. "Then we haven't much time," he said. "They mustn't take me alive under any circumstances."

Late that night an orderly summoned everyone to the main bunker. The Führer wished to say good-bye. When they were assembled, Hitler shook hands silently with each in turn. "His eyes were glazed," one witness recalled later. "He already seemed far away."

Afterward, back in the staff canteen, the storm broke. Someone seized a bottle and jumped up on a table. "Here's to the dead!" he yelled. Someone else started the phonograph. The dance, more and more uproarious, lasted well into the morning. Messages came from the *Führerbunker* ordering quiet, but no one paid any attention.

At three o'clock, April 30, Hitler had his lunch as usual. He was pale and quiet, but ate with apparent enjoyment. Then he and his wife went out to the main corridor, where Bormann,

Goebbels and the principal aides were waiting. They shook hands silently and returned to their suite. The door slammed and one of the Führer's bodyguard planted himself in front of it. A moment later a shot crashed. The Thousand Year Reich had come to an end.

Mystery Man of the A-Bomb

By John Gunther, author of Inside Europe, Inside Asia, *etc.*

One day in 1942 an American colonel representing our then top-secret atomic project walked into the New York office of a Belgian mine operator named Edgar Sengier and asked if Sengier could help America to get some uranium ore from the Belgian Congo. The request, the officer said, was vital to the Allied cause.

Monsieur Sengier listened politely and asked to see the colonel's credentials. When he was satisfied, he said that, yes, he would be able to deliver a sizable quantity of the precious ore. When did the colonel need it?

"We need it at once," the colonel said. "I realize that's impossible, of course."

"On the contrary," Sengier said. "The ore is here in New York. One thousand tons of it. I have been waiting for you."

Edgar Sengier was one of the most important unknown men of our time. Although he visited the United States 40 or 50 times, he came and went without notice from the press. This anonymity is remarkable because without Sengier there would have been no atomic bomb—at least not in the summer of 1945, when the Hiroshima and Nagasaki bombs ended the war against Japan. Not only did Sengier produce the deadly and essential uranium for those first atomic bombs, but for many years thereafter every atomic bomb made in the United States, every one we tested in Nevada or the South Pacific was made out of uranium from the mine his company operated in the Congo.

Edgar Sengier's story was not told for some years—for several reasons. First, Sengier's own self-effacement. In 1953, when I had dinner with him in Paris, he said, "If you are going to write about me, try to keep me out of it." He meant, of course, that I shouldn't stress his personal importance, or make him sound vain, which he wasn't. The second difficulty was security. Many details about Congo uranium were still top-secret.

I began hearing about Sengier when, in preparation for a book on Africa, I started to do research on the Congo. Upper Katanga, in the southeastern Congo, has uranium deposits and vast reserves of the richest copper ore on earth. Production of these and other minerals is dominated by the Union Minière du Haut-Katanga. And Sengier, as chairman of the executive committee of the Union Minière, was one of the most powerful men in the world.

Sengier was born in Belgium in 1879 and was educated to be an engineer. He was adventurous, tough, willing to take responsibility and extremely bright. When he was about 30 years old, he moved to Africa, and that continent played a great role in his life ever after. By 1939 he was president of the Union Minière.

At the museum in Elisabethville, the capital of Katanga, I saw a block of pitchblende—uranium ore—on display. As big as a pig, its color was black and gold, and it looked as if it were covered with a green scum. It came from Shinkolobwe, which is *the* mine in Katanga, and a sign said: "*Attention. Bloc radioactif!*" Photographers were warned not to get too close, or the film in their cameras would be spoiled.

Sengier had been producing pitchblende from the Shinkolobwe since 1921. But in those days no one thought the uranium contained in the ore had any value. All the interest then was in radium. In 1939, however, things began to happen. Sengier was approached in circumstances of the utmost secrecy and urgency by a British physicist who told him of the work German scien-

tists were doing in the field of atomic fission, and of the possibility that an atomic bomb might be made out of uranium. It
was of the most critical importance, he said, that no uranium
should get into enemy hands.

On his own responsibility, Sengier, fearing a Nazi invasion of
the Congo, arranged for the shipment of more than 1000 tons
of rich pitchblende ore to the United States. "I did this," he told
me, "without telling *anything* to *anybody*."

The ore reached America in 1940, and was stored in steel
drums in a New York warehouse. Between its arrival and its
eventual use by the Manhattan Project, however, some quaint
episodes occurred.

Sengier, in dead secrecy, announced to the proper American
authorities that the uranium was there. The State Department
was so impressed that it wanted to move the deadly stuff to Fort
Knox for safekeeping. But there was much delay, and well over
a year passed before the American government acted to take
advantage of Sengier's foresight. By this time those people who
had known had apparently forgotten where the ore actually was.

Then in 1942 the American colonel paid his historic call on
Sengier in his New York office. Within an hour the officer
walked out with a memorandum quickly drawn up on a piece of
yellow paper and signed by Sengier. The uranium essential to
the success of the atomic project was now the property of the
United States.

When Sengier visited the United States in 1946, General Leslie
R. Groves, in President Truman's presence, awarded him the
Medal for Merit. He was one of the few non-American civilians
to receive this esteemed honor, and naturally he was proud of it.
The reason for the bestowal was kept secret; the record was
impounded in the White House. The language of the citation is
purposely not specific. I have seen the text: it merely mentions
Edgar Sengier's "wartime services in the realm of raw materials."

Sengier was not much impressed by most honors, but of one
thing he was indeed proud. A new ore (composed of uranium,
vanadium and copper) was named sengierite. Sengier died in
France on July 27, 1963, at the age of 84.

The Silence of 600,000

By Thomas M. Johnson

A unique secret service guarded the development of the atom bomb. For nearly four years it protected the bomb from betrayal by talkative Americans or discovery by prying foreigners. In addition it spied out the Nazis' atomic research program.

In January 1942 Dr. James B. Conant told a Military Intelligence officer in strictest confidence of the vast experiment and its import. "But the Office of Scientific Research and Development is worried," he said. "Some of the workers may talk too much. Go out to Berkeley and check up."

Major (later Lieutenant Colonel) John Lansdale clothed himself in "civvies" and a plausible story. He began "research work" at the University of California, met and drew out several atomic scientists, penetrated a laboratory, visited the new cyclotron, heard of related work at Chicago. Then, donning uniform, he assembled the staff. "Suppose," he challenged, "I'd been a spy?"

"Do that everywhere," said Major General Leslie R. Groves, who was put in charge of the Project in September. "Make silence the rule of the Manhattan Project."

At Oak Ridge and at other places, tens of thousands of eager, talkative Americans were doing work that had to remain profoundly secret. Behind the motto "Protect the Project," Lansdale, assisted by Major William A. Consodine, launched history's greatest secrecy campaign. He formed an undercover corps of young men and women called "The Creeps." Its officers were mostly lawyers trained in security by the War Department; its agents came from the Army's Counter Intelligence Corps and Military Police. As a result of their work, there was not a single case of enemy-directed sabotage in our whole atom project.

They forbade mention of atoms, uranium or secret weapons. All Project workers, the Creeps included, had to use various codes, which were constantly changed. Atoms were "Tops"; the bomb was a "Boat." The Creeps investigated officers and stockholders of all corporations with which the Project dealt, including hundreds of contractors. For safety from spies and bombing planes, the Project's operations were scattered—at Oak Ridge in Tennessee; at Los Alamos in New Mexico; at Hanford in Washington, and elsewhere.

Every misplaced document was traced if it took a week; every carbon copy was listed. Each night every office was checked for loose papers, unlocked desks. Silence was dinned into the staff. President Roosevelt got frequent written reports, but Secretary of War Henry L. Stimson took them to the White House, watched him read them, then took them away again.

The 600,000 people who were employed on the Manhattan Project at one time or another all signed secrecy agreements. In nearly four years some 2000 loose talkers were reported. Military personnel when relieved for any reason were sent to posts safe from capture; civilians were fired very tactfully lest they get angry and talk.

Scientists were the most anxious problem. If the Germans knew where our prominent nuclear physicists were, they would deduce the rest. So the scientists received code names; Dr. Arthur H. Compton was A. H. Comas, Dr. Enrico Fermi was Henry Farmer. Each had a bodyguard. Most of the scientists were discreet, but one of them blurted some things out in a lecture. Another left a briefcase with important data on a train. Six agents worked all night and finally found it—intact.

Just before the war began, the Nazis had sent two top scientists here to find out what our atomic researchers were doing. After the Project was begun we intercepted messages, concealed in letters by the photographic micro-dot process (see "The Micro-Dot," page 175), from other spies who tried to contact our scientists.

Canada was the base for some spy raids on the secrets of atom-bomb production. There the British physicist Alan Nunn

May gave Russian intelligence agents uranium samples and partial reports on work at the Canadian Chalk River plant and our Chicago laboratories, which he visited three times. May wanted to come again, but the Creeps became suspicious and General Groves said "no." When arrested by British authorities, May pleaded guilty and was sentenced to 10 years in prison.

Dread that Hitler's "secret weapons" might include atom bombs hung over us ominously. Work on the Project was accelerated. Scientists of several nations were brought to the Western Hemisphere. Aided by British Intelligence, Niels Bohr, world-famous nuclear physicist, escaped from Denmark. For two years, as "Nicholas Baker," he worked with the Project.

Then word came that the Germans were speeding production at Europe's only considerable source of heavy water, the Norsk Hydro plant in Vemork, Norway. Norwegian commandos landed by air, wrecked portions of the works and destroyed a large amount of heavy water. The Germans tried to remove the remainder of the heavy water by ship—which Norwegian agents blew up. (See "Eleven Against the Nazi A-Bomb," page 291.)

In February 1944, Colonel Horace K. Calvert joined Major R. R. Furman in London and, with the British, began ferreting out information on the German atomic project, which the Germans too were trying to keep top-secret. First they checked on Germany's uranium supply. The Nazis had seized the large refining plant near Antwerp, but the Belgian Underground saw to it that uranium shipments went astray. A Czech agent reported the output of the mine at Joachimstal. All prewar dealers in uranium and thorium were listed, as well as metal refineries, power plants and any suspicious installation.

In their quest for Hitler's supposed atom-bomb laboratories the London intelligence group sought the whereabouts of the German physicists who alone were capable of doing such research. Airplane photographs indicated that the original laboratory at Dahlem, near Berlin, had been moved, and this information was confirmed by talkative German scientists. Secretly contacted, they said that their colleagues had left for parts unknown.

Then British Intelligence heard that a pro-Nazi Swiss scientist was helping work on a new explosive in a secret laboratory at Bisingen, in the Hohenzollern area of southern Germany. Next American censorship intercepted a letter to South America whose writer was working in "a research laboratory lettered D." The letter was postmarked Hechingen, three miles north of Bisingen. And near there, according to a report from a friendly Swiss scientist, was living Dr. Werner Heisenberg, perhaps Germany's top nuclear physicist. All Allied atomic scientists and many neutrals were asked which Nazi scientists would most probably be working there. Fifty men were listed, and presently the Creeps had descriptions, addresses and photographs of many—even a Linguaphone voice record of one. All intelligent prisoners from the vicinity were grilled, and all possible laboratory buildings were pinpointed.

In the spring of 1945 the Allies were sweeping over Germany. "Get to the Hohenzollern area first and fast," said Lansdale, by now a lieutenant colonel. "Snatch the scientists and their secrets before they can escape."

A group of nearly 100 handpicked soldiers, code-named "Alsos," was led by the dashing Colonel Boris T. Pash. They ran interference for a number of scientists, headed by Professor Samuel A. Goudsmit of Northwestern University. One of the first and most secret aims of the group was to find France's leading atomic scientist, Frédéric Joliot-Curie, son-in-law of Marie Curie and later France's High Commissioner for Atomic Energy. Because the Nazis had used Joliot's laboratory, Goudsmit believed he must know a lot about their work. Lest the Nazis kidnap Joliot as our forces approached, Colonel Pash and Colonel Calvert, with two CIC agents, accompanied the leading French tanks and fought their way into Paris. Joliot said that two German scientists had pre-empted his laboratory for work in nuclear physics. But they did not know how to make a bomb. So Alsos pressed on toward Germany, accompanying the troops which captured Strasburg. At the university there, scientists and GI's seized precious records. Indubitably the Hohenzollern area was the German atomic center.

Suddenly came the biggest scare since D-day: new aerial photographs showing slave-labor camps, power lines and a huge industrial site rising with incredible speed near the village of Bisingen. Then the Berlin radio announced that the Germans already had the atom bomb!

In a supreme effort to pierce the veil, scientists, sleuths and soldiers dashed toward Bisingen. There they encountered disappointment, but also immense relief: the big new plant was not designed to make atom bombs but to extract oil from shale. They pressed on to other installations. At Thalfingen, sitting at his desk in a large laboratory, was Otto Hahn, who had first smashed the uranium atom, and with him were a score of other scientists. The Nazis denied that they had ever tried to make an atom bomb. They said, too, that their papers had been destroyed. But one famous scientist greeted the Americans with "I've been expecting you," and handed them summaries of his work. Other valuable papers were fished from a cesspool where they had been concealed in an oil drum. Finally a few German scientists persuaded others to come clean. Then they revealed their laboratory supplies—small amounts of heavy water, hidden in an old mill; and of uranium oxide, buried in a field; and at last, in a big tunnel deep in the mountainside, their "pile."

It was a climax of irony. Their "uranium machine" or "pile" was a dud. It could not set up or maintain a chain reaction. The Germans could not produce plutonium and did not believe it feasible to separate U-235 from U-238. (We had found three ways to do it.) They had one cyclotron; we had more than 30. Germany's best atomic scientists had not emerged from the experimental stage.

Even after they were captured, they believed we were so far behind them that we would want to imitate their priceless work. The Creeps' secrecy campaign had succeeded.

The Secret
That Won the War

Condensed from the book No High Ground

By Fletcher Knebel and Charles W. Bailey II

The U.S.S. *Augusta* hurried westward across the Atlantic. It was near midnight and it was wartime—the date was August 5, 1945—but with Germany defeated, the war was half a world away and the heavy cruiser sparkled with lights.

In the wardroom the officers were sitting over a pot of coffee. They had just been given a glimpse of the future, and it had touched them all with excitement and wonder.

That evening they had entertained President Truman, who was traveling home with them from the conference with his British and Russian allies at Potsdam. Over dessert and coffee the talk had turned to that meeting. Lieutenant Commander Walter Berberich, the ship's doctor, raised a question they had all been wondering about. Had there been any commitments at Potsdam to bring Russia into the Pacific war and thus hasten Japan's fall?

The President responded with a statement that his listeners would never forget. No, he said, there had been no such deal made. And if the Russians had been difficult at Potsdam it did not matter, because the United States had a new weapon of such force and nature that we did not need the Russians—or any other nation. "It is so powerful," he said, "that one weapon is equal to 20,000 tons of TNT."

Truman told the *Augusta's* officers that the new weapon had been developed in total secrecy, that it had already been tested and that it could end the war. "It is the biggest gamble in history," he said. "Two billion dollars have been spent on it. We will have the final answer on its effectiveness within a very short time."

While President Truman ate Sunday dinner in the *Augusta's* wardroom on the Atlantic, it was already early the next morning in the Mariana Islands in the western Pacific. There U.S. Navy Seabees had been working since three a.m. as they had every morning, seven days a week, for over a month. They were the last link in a chain that was making the frantic effort to supply the U.S. 20th Air Force with high-explosive and incendiary bombs. Major General Curtis E. LeMay's B-29 bombers had unloaded 40,000 tons of bombs on Japanese cities in July; on the preceding Thursday, August 2, his pilots had celebrated the anniversary of the Army Air Force by dropping a single-day record total of 6632 tons.

That same Sunday, William H. Lawrence, a New York *Times* reporter, was on Guam. The previous week he had cabled his paper:

> There are a surprising number of people here as well as in the United States who think the Japanese may be forced into unconditional surrender without the necessity of even a token invasion. Existence of that sentiment here is the more important because lots of the people who talk that way wear stars and may therefore be presumed to be in a position to know what they are talking about.

Lawrence confessed in his dispatch that he did not share this view. He said he had wagered 10 dollars with "a one-star officer" who insisted that the war would be over within three months.

There was no such wagering going on among the men of the 13th U.S. Marines, one of the regiments of the Fifth Marine Division that was now restaging in Hawaii. Pulled out of Iwo Jima in March after fighting in that bloody engagement, the division had been getting ready for the next job: the assault landing on Kyushu, southernmost of the Japanese home islands. The prospect was one that prevented the men of the 13th from fully enjoying the attractions of Hawaii. Major William Miller, commanding the Third Battalion, had fought the Japanese at Guadalcanal and Cape Gloucester as well as on Iwo. He was engaged now in planning for an invasion in which overall initial casualties of 100,000 seemed to him a conservative estimate. In all, 750,000 men would be involved.

In a radish field outside Tokyo a crew of expert radiomen from the Japanese Navy kept a round-the-clock watch over a room jammed with 181 powerful radio receivers. Members of the Yamatoda Signal Corps, they were assigned to detect and record all radio signals emanating from U.S. transmitters. Now, early on the morning of August 6, the men working the night shift picked up a call sign they had first heard almost three weeks earlier. The monitors had located it on Tinian Island, and as it was heard daily during late July they had tagged it "New Task Company" for quick reference. The cryptographers in Tokyo had been unable to break the cipher, but the Japanese monitors had come to recognize it instantly, as trained radiomen will, by the individual touch of the American operator's hand on his Morse key.

Now the signal came out of the air again. To the Japanese, it was merely one more item to be logged and reported. They did not know that the "New Task Company" was the highly secret 509th Bomb Group, whose ultimate mission would be to end the war by dropping the first atomic bomb.

Three hundred miles to the east, one of the most powerful striking forces ever assembled steamed into the morning sun. Twenty-four hours earlier the U.S. Navy's Third Fleet had been lunging toward prearranged targets in southern Japan. Now it had been ordered to turn around and run out to sea—and its admirals were baffled and angry. Rear Admiral C.A.F. Sprague, commanding Carrier Division Two, summoned his combat intelligence officers to the flag cabin on the U.S.S. *Ticonderoga*. He waved an order at his aides. "This is a hell of a way to run a war. What's it all about? What do I have an intelligence staff for, anyway?"

The order, from Pacific Fleet headquarters, read:

> It is imperative that there be non-interference with operations of the 509th Bomb Group. It is accordingly directed that you send no planes over Kyushu or western Honshu until specifically authorized.

Sprague's officers had no answer for their chief. The discussion ended with all hands putting a dollar bill and a sealed guess, to be opened later, into a pool. Lieutenant Edwin P. Stevens of New York recalled a cocktail-party conversation in 1941 with a physicist friend who had told him how some scientists were seeking to release enormous amounts of energy by breaking the nuclei of atoms. Now Stevens scribbled something about "nuclear energy" on his slip of paper.

Another of the officers, Lieutenant James H. Rowe, Jr., had been an aide to F.D.R. in the White House before the war. His entry was a suggestion that some attempt to end the war by negotiation might be afoot and that the planned strike had been postponed for that reason.

Both Rowe and Stevens had, in a way, guessed right. But Rowe didn't win the pool. His timing was off. There had been attempts at negotiation, but on August 6, 1945, time had run out.

On June 18 the Supreme War Council of Japan agreed to propose, through neutral nations, that an effort be made to negotiate a peace. This could hardly be called a decision to surrender, but it was a beginning. (See "Hirohito's Struggle to Surrender," page 556.)

On that same day, in Washington, President Truman's inner council of war advisers also held a meeting, but with quite a different aim. At the end, the President put his stamp of approval on Olympic, the plan to invade the Japanese homeland. It was now scheduled for November.

War, however, was not the only item on Harry Truman's

agenda for June 18. In the United States as in Japan, the search for peace was under way even as both sides braced for final combat. That day Joseph C. Grew, Under Secretary of State, saw the President privately. He urged Truman to give Japan a chance to keep its Emperor if it capitulated, arguing that such an offer would greatly facilitate the surrender. Grew suggested that the President issue a statement calling for Japanese surrender, but holding out the possibility that the Emperor might be allowed to remain in power. (This proposal also had the support of Secretary of War Henry L. Stimson.) Truman told Grew that he liked the idea, but wanted to hold it up until he could talk to the allies at Potsdam. He asked Grew to put the matter on the Big Three agenda.

In Potsdam on July 24, Secretary Stimson conferred with Truman for 15 minutes. He had heard from James Byrnes, Secretary of State, that it had been decided not to mention the Emperor specifically in the ultimatum which had been approved by Truman and Churchill. The declaration would not go beyond a statement that the final form of government in Japan was to be left up to the Japanese people.

One day later, on July 25, in the most momentous decision he had to make as President, Harry S. Truman approved an order to use the atomic bomb if the Japanese should refuse the Potsdam ultimatum. That order was put into writing in Washington, then flown across the Pacific to Tinian Island.

On July 26 the United States and Britain, with China as a co-signer and Soviet Russia an approving kibitzer, issued the Potsdam Declaration.

There was instant concern in Japan, as Stimson and Grew had warned there would be. The ultimatum made no mention of the future status of the Emperor. The Supreme War Council and the Cabinet could not accept it as written. The Cabinet, after long discussion, decided not to answer but to disregard or *mokusatsu* (literally, "kill with silence") the ultimatum.

Truman received this advice shortly after he had been told by Stalin that the Japanese proposals for mediation were still considered by the Soviets as "too vague" for consideration. Stalin's attitude, combined with the report that Japan had decided to ignore the Potsdam ultimatum, left the President convinced that he now had no choice but to let the order he had started toward Tinian on July 25 stand as written. And on that tiny island events were already in motion which would sweep away all subtleties of diplomacy and politics in a single overwhelming blow.

The steps which led to these events had their beginning six years earlier.

In January 1939, American newspapers carried the news that German scientists had succeeded in splitting the atom. To the initiate it was obvious that Hitler might one day have a weapon of terrible proportions. Leo Szilard, a brilliant Hungarian who had fled German laboratories with the rise of Hitler, went with a fellow Hungarian physicist to see Albert Einstein in his Long Island summer home. Representing a group of scientists, the two hoped to persuade Einstein to warn President Roosevelt of atomic progress in Germany. Einstein was not abreast of the latest atomic developments, but his help was vital. He agreed to sign a letter to Roosevelt. The two Hungarians then enlisted the New York financier Alexander Sachs, who was an unofficial adviser to the President—a kind of lower-echelon Bernard Baruch—to deliver the letter in person.

F.D.R. was alone at breakfast in the second-floor study of the White House when Sachs called. "What bright idea do you have this morning?" Roosevelt asked cheerily.

"Just a story," Sachs replied. He told the President about one of Napoleon Bonaparte's missed opportunities. Hungering to conquer England, Napoleon was frustrated by the erratic Channel tides, which blocked an invasion by French sailing vessels. The young American inventor Robert Fulton proposed that France construct a fleet of steamboats, which could negotiate the Channel with ease. But Napoleon rudely brushed aside the idea as being visionary. How, asked Sachs, might the history of Europe have been changed if Napoleon had heeded Fulton? And in the world of 1939, who would first sponsor the atom scientists as they sought to pioneer a weapon of untold force?

As the President listened, the big Roosevelt grin creased his face. He summoned Brigadier General Edwin M. "Pa" Watson, who served as a secretary, and handed him the relevant data. "Pa," he said, "this requires action." The United States government had begun to take an interest in the atomic bomb.

For two years the action was sluggish (although Hitler meanwhile was conquering Europe, and Japan's armies were rolling into Indochina). Uncoördinated atomic research proceeded in a few American universities, but nuclear enthusiasts groaned at the lack of money and at the torpid reflexes of Washington officials. Not until the summer of 1941 was a "uranium section" formed in the National Research Committee in Washington, and it was the end of 1941 before real government muscle was put into it. Vannevar Bush, head of the Office of Scientific Research and Development, reported to President Roosevelt on progress at that time and got a pledge of more men and money for the effort. On December 6, Bush announced the new all-out drive to his colleagues. It was none too soon. The next day Japanese carrier planes bombed Pearl Harbor, and the United States declared war on the Axis.

What followed on the atomic-research front was an only-in-America miracle. A nation that had performed many industrial feats now undertook, in rigorous secrecy, the most prodigious scientific-industrial-military enterprise ever conceived by man. Years later many of those who played leading roles in it still could not quite believe that it really happened.

By the end of the summer of 1942 the Manhattan District Engineers, as the bomb's builders were designated, had been assigned AAA priority. Brigadier General Leslie R. Groves, a 46-year-old West Point engineer, took command of the operation that September and set out—without known tools, blueprints or materials—to transform an invisible compound of equations, theory and scientific faith into a practical military weapon.

The scale of Manhattan's operations was staggering. Since nobody knew which of three methods of separating U-235 was best, all three were initiated. All were costly and all developed two new problems for every solution. Although less than 100 pounds of fissionable material was produced for the three bombs ready by the summer of 1945, at its peak the project and its allied payrolls included well over half a million persons, enough for 30 divisions of infantry.

The Manhattan District became the melting pot of American science. Such home-grown geniuses of the new physics as J. Robert Oppenheimer mingled with physicists from England's atomic program, and with refugee scientists from Italy, Germany and Hungary. Ph.D.'s outnumbered the clerical help in some facilities, and Nobel Prize winners marched as privates in the ranks.

Within months of its establishment Manhattan achieved a historic triumph. On the afternoon of December 2, 1942, in a squash court under the football stands at the University of Chicago, its scientists produced man's first controlled chain reaction. Their apparatus was crude by current standards, but before darkness fell that day the physicists knew that the fission process they had created would someday be placed in a weapon of untold power.

Still, there were stubborn practical problems. The scientists calculated that one pound of U-235 (about the size of a golf ball) would release energy equivalent to about 9000 tons of TNT. But a single pound of this bomb material by itself was too small to sustain a chain reaction. There had to be a certain amount, the so-called "critical mass" (its quantity was as yet unknown), before an explosion could develop. And the scientists had to keep the components of this mass separated enough so that it would be uncritical until the exact moment for firing.

To solve these problems, the Manhattan Project built a bomb laboratory on an isolated mesa near Los Alamos, N.M. Oppenheimer was appointed scientific director. Security regulations at this plant and at the other installations were rigid. Few Americans had any inkling of the revolutionary weapon being developed in their midst. (See "The Silence of 600,000," page 524.)

Meanwhile General Groves was already nursing along another project in another desert. To ensure that the as-yet-nonexistent A-bomb could actually be delivered to enemy targets, 1500 officers and men were gathered into the singular 509th Composite Group, the only complete "do-it-yourself" unit in the Air Force. The 509th was given everything it needed for combat and survival—transport, ordnance, food, maintenance and airplanes. And its men were all hand-picked.

For the top job, General Henry H. "Hap" Arnold, chief of the Army Air Force, selected Colonel Paul W. Tibbets, Jr. A handsome 29-year-old flier, Tibbets had been a crack bomber pilot in European combat, and had flown first Mark Clark and then Eisenhower from England to Gibraltar when we invaded North Africa. (See photograph on page 348.)

Within an hour of receiving his assignment, Tibbets felt as though he had been set down on another planet. He was instructed in the mysteries of the split atom, told what we hoped from it militarily, and learned that if an A-bomb was ever produced, he himself might pilot the plane that dropped the first one. He was also to take over the task of organizing the flying nucleus of the 509th Group, and was to pick out a training field to his liking. When Tibbets set out in a B-29 to find one, his first stop was at Wendover, Utah. He looked no further. Wendover was a barren expanse of desert 125 miles from Salt Lake City.

The 509th was different from the outset. Tibbets enjoined the top officers to secrecy without informing them what it was they weren't supposed to reveal. Flight operations were unlike anything ever seen by airmen. Bombing practice was constant from 30,000 feet, and each plane always dropped only one 10,000-pound bomb. Relentless emphasis was placed on visual bombing. This puzzled veteran bombardiers, since clear days for visual bombing had been rare in the air war over Europe—and would be even rarer over Japan.

The reasons were plain to those initiated in Manhattan secrets. The practice with single bombs simulated the eventual atomic flight when only one precious bomb, worth hundreds of millions of dollars, would be in the bomb bay. On that occasion we simply could not afford to miss the target; and bombing by radar could not be trusted.

After dropping their dummy bombs, the pilots practiced a

most unorthodox maneuver. In order to be clear of the blast and to avoid the ensuing shock waves, scientists calculated that any plane dropping the atomic bomb should be at least eight miles away when it exploded, 43 seconds later. Hence the pilots made sharp, 158-degree turns and nosed their planes down to gain speed. To make the planes themselves as light as possible, they were stripped of all armament except for the .50-caliber machine guns in the tail. This was particularly baffling to airmen not in on the secret.

In Manhattan District the frantic effort to create an A-bomb never once flagged. By December 30, 1944, Groves felt able to announce his timetable. "The first bomb should be ready about August 1, 1945," he wrote in a memorandum to the Chief of Staff, General George C. Marshall. Since this would be too late to use the bomb against Germany, where the Nazi regime was already tottering toward collapse, Groves suggested that the Pacific naval command be alerted; the 509th would need a base from which it could reach Japan. General Marshall, Stimson and Roosevelt gave their approval.

The island of Tinian in the American-held Marianas was selected for basing the 509th. A level limestone platform, about six miles wide in the middle and 13 miles long, the island made an ideal anchored aircraft carrier, and its very smallness adapted it to secrecy.

On April 5 the War Department approved the code name "Centerboard" for the mission of delivering the atomic bomb on Japan. And late in April, Tibbets' men, who now had 15 stripped-down B-29's, began moving overseas.

Almost at once the 509th became the island curiosity. Tokyo Rose, punctual if not fully enlightened, greeted its arrival by radio from Japan, but that was the last "official" news the other B-29 crews had of this strange outfit. The 509th's own military police promptly strung barbed wire around certain areas and set up machine guns to guard them. Even a general had to show a pass to get in.

But it was chiefly the 509th's flying that raised eyebrows among other B-29 crews. Never did Tibbets and his men participate in the mass raids—or share the sight of empty bunks afterward. Instead they flew solo missions, occasionally bombing a Japanese-held island or making the round trip of almost 3000 miles to Japanese cities just to drop one bomb each—or so the rumor ran in Wing headquarters.

General Groves' timetable for the completed A-bomb—August 1—proved to be marvelously exact. The place chosen for testing it was an arid expanse of land in New Mexico, 50 miles from Alamogordo; the time was 5:30 a.m., July 16. On that date the atomic age opened with a flash that lighted the skies 250 miles away and brightened Ground Zero with the dazzle of many suns. A giant sphere of fire, laced with hues of deep purple and orange, spread out for a mile. The earth shook. A blast of hot air rolled out in a wave. The 100-foot tower on which the bomb rested was vaporized. At observer posts 10 miles out, the roar of the instant chain reaction came many seconds later. A column of white smoke shot straight up, then flowered into a mushroom that finally climbed to 40,000 feet. All over the Southwest, inhabitants marked the clap of thunder and the strange way the sun seemed to rise and then go right back down again. Miles away a blind woman cried out that she had seen a light.

A press release, which had been prepared in advance and gave a fake explanation for the unearthly eruption, was handed to newspapermen in Albuquerque:

> An ammunition magazine exploded early today in a remote area of the Alamogordo Air Base reservation, producing a brilliant flash and blast which were reported to have been observed as far away as Gallup, 235 miles northwest.

The scientists were awestruck at their triumph. "The test was successful beyond our most optimistic hopes," General Groves wrote in a confidential memorandum which was delivered to Secretary Stimson at Potsdam. The bomb had generated energy estimated to equal 20,000 tons of TNT, as predicted.

A few days after the bomb test General Carl Spaatz was

recalled to Washington from Europe. In connection with his reassignment to command the Strategic Air Force in the Pacific, he was given verbal orders which he adamantly refused to accept. "Listen, Tom," he said to General Thomas T. Handy, who was acting chief of staff while General Marshall was away at Potsdam. "If I'm going to kill thousands of people, I'm not going to do it on verbal orders. I want a piece of paper." Although it violated the normal Manhattan District procedure (the less in writing, the less chance of breaking security), eventually Spaatz got his paper.

The decision to drop atomic bombs on Japan was made with great reluctance after months of soul-searching. From the start some scientists had hoped that the Manhattan research would prove futile, and when the A-bomb was nevertheless produced many of them wrote impassioned memoranda and got up petitions asking that it not be used.

Among war leaders Admiral William D. Leahy made no effort to mask his repugnance toward the bomb, and Rear Admiral Lewis L. Strauss and General Hap Arnold both expressed strong reservations about using it. General Dwight Eisenhower, briefed on the subject at Potsdam, hoped the bomb would not have to be used against Japan. But most military chieftains believed the new bomb presented no ethical questions not found in TNT or the fire bomb. For mass bombardment of civilians had become commonplace in World War II. (On the night of March 9, for example, 16 square miles of Tokyo had been set ablaze by incendiaries, and 78,000 people killed.)

An Interim Committee, appointed by President Truman, recommended that the bomb be dropped on Japan as soon as possible, without specific warning. To make the maximum imprint, it was determined to explode the atomic weapon over a city hitherto relatively untouched by bombing. There were few such cities left in Japan by now, and the list submitted for consideration contained only four names: Kyoto, Kokura, Niigata and Hiroshima—Nagasaki was added at the last moment. Eventually the list of primary target cities was narrowed to one. On August 2 a top-secret field order was issued at Guam, stating that the bomb was to be dropped on August 6. Primary target: *Hiroshima urban industrial area.*

Hiroshima was known throughout Japan as a place where exceptionally beautiful willow trees grew. This big port and manufacturing city, now marked for death, had in three and a half years of war felt the concussion of only 12 enemy bombs. Nevertheless, the city's people knew very well that the war was going badly. Down by the docks, from which almost every Nipponese soldier who went to the southwestern Pacific fighting area had sailed, a deathlike quiet hung over the big embarkation facilities. The Gaisenkan, "Hall of Triumphal Return," where troops had listened to final instructions and exhortations, was now quiet and empty. Where the city in earlier years had bulged with as many as 100,000 troops en route to the front, it now held only one division, and that was preparing for defense, not attack. Including support troops, there were about 24,000 soldiers in Hiroshima. The once busy harbor was almost dead. American planes had dropped so many mines into the waters of the Inland Sea that few ships came to Hiroshima any more.

August 6, 1945, was little different in Hiroshima from previous Mondays in this year of shortages, defeats, evacuations and forced labor. Women in almost every house were cooking breakfast over the little charcoal burners that served Japanese homes as combination stoves and heaters. Busy with morning routines of one kind or another, most people in the city paid little attention to the air-raid alert that sounded at nine minutes past seven o'clock. Those who looked up at the faint drone of engines found, if their eyes were sharp, a single B-29, flying very high. Probably it was a weather plane of the kind that often flew over in the morning. It crossed the city twice and then, at 7:25, flew out to sea. The warning system sounded the all-clear at 7:31.

The single B-29 *was* a weather plane. Its name was *Straight Flush.* The order which sent it over Hiroshima was designated as Special Bombing Mission No. 13. Seven of Tibbets' 15 B-29's had been assigned to this mission.

On August 4 the seven crews were summoned to the briefing

hut, and Navy Captain William Parsons, who was to arm the
A-bomb, showed movies of the atomic test at Alamogordo.
After viewing its chilling and awful majesty, every man there
knew why pilots had practiced steep breakaway turns at high
altitude. Parsons also warned pilots not to fly through the mushroom cloud because of the danger of radioactivity. He stated
frankly that no one could be sure what would happen.

The next day, August 5, was a Sunday, hot with a glaring sun.
At the 509th's bomb-assembly hut, physicists, ordnance men,
MP's, security agents and Air Corps brass gathered to peer
respectfully at the A-bomb as it swung from its chain hoist.

About 14 feet long and five feet in diameter, the bomb
weighed just under 10,000 pounds. The fissionable core was
far less than one half of one percent of this weight, and was
tucked away in the interior, as Oppenheimer once remarked,
"like a small diamond in an enormous wad of cotton." A proximity fuse would be set for 1850 feet. When the falling projectile
reached this altitude the fuse would detonate an explosive
charge which would shoot a small chunk of U-235 forward at a
speed of 5000 feet per second until it collided with a larger
chunk of U-235, a cup-shaped piece in the nose. At that instant
the atomic explosion would occur.

Two special couriers had brought that vital, cup-shaped target to Tinian in a lead cylinder about the size of a potato-chip
can. Their orders had been explicit: under no circumstances were
they to save lives before the U-235. If the ship sank—it was the
heavy cruiser *Indianapolis*—the U-235 was to have the first
motor launch or life raft. From San Francisco the cruiser had
raced for Tinian, pausing only a few hours at Pearl Harbor to
refuel, and had delivered the U-235 to the island on July 26.
(Four days later the ill-starred *Indianapolis* was torpedoed and
sunk.) Three smaller chunks of U-235 had also been shipped to
Tinian, by air, each on a separate plane, and each accompanied
by a Manhattan security agent.

Around midnight the chaplain of the 509th said a brief prayer
for the mission. Then the seven crews had breakfast, and at
1:37 a.m. the three weather planes took off for Hiroshima,

Kokura and Nagasaki, respectively. (If Hiroshima was fogged over, the other two cities were alternate targets.)

A little over an hour later—the time was 2:45 a.m., August 6—Tibbets' heavily loaded plane, the *Enola Gay* (named for his mother), rolled down the coral runway and, with only yards to spare, left the ground. It was followed at two-minute intervals by two other B-29's—one to measure blast and radiation, one to take photographs. A fourth B-29, which would stand by to transfer the bomb at Iwo Jima and carry on in case the *Enola Gay* developed trouble, had left earlier. Special Bombing Mission No. 13 was now on the way.

As it climbed above the Pacific with a sharp upward thrust, the *Enola Gay* shuddered with the strain of the lift. The crew breathed easier when Tibbets had gained sufficient altitude to swing left and seek his compass heading for Iwo, 622 miles to the north. At 4000 feet Tibbets throttled back to cruising speed. Parsons knocked out a cold pipe, lowered himself into the forward bomb bay and began completing the final assembly. The entire job took only about 25 minutes.

Aside from its revolutionary nuclear character, the weapon, now fully armed and ready to go, was a maze of electronic ingenuity. When it was dropped, a series of intricate timers would shut off for the first 15 seconds, so that the device could not possibly detonate during that interval. Another cluster of instruments prevented the bomb from exploding above 10,000 feet. After 15 seconds of fall, barometric gauges would alert the radio proximity fuses, set to trigger the explosion at 1850 feet. There were four of these fuses, at least two of which had to agree on the exact altitude before detonation could occur. All these devices had to operate within the estimated 43 seconds from the moment of bomb release to the instant of explosion.

To ensure against mechanical failure, a "black box" aboard the plane monitored the bomb's electrical circuits. It was checked every half-hour during the flight, and every instrument on its panel had to read correctly or the bomb would have to be brought back to Tinian undropped.

At 4:55, well after daylight, the *Enola Gay* rendezvoused over

Iwo Jima with the two following B-29's, which were to accompany her. Then in wide V formation, maintaining strict radio silence, the three B-29's headed northwest toward the Japanese island of Shikoku.

Presently Tibbets called all hands over the intercom. From here on in, he said, every man must be at his station. And when they reached the coast of Japan, all intercom conversation would be recorded. "This is for history," said Tibbets. "So watch your language. We're carrying the first atomic bomb." It was the first time most of the crew had heard the phrase.

At 7:09, far ahead of them, the weather plane *Straight Flush* approached the outskirts of Hiroshima. A solid undercast covered Japan as far as the eye could see. Minutes later, however, a view of the entire city opened up. At the point where the *Enola Gay* was scheduled to release its cargo, the city was so clear below that the crew could see patches of green grass. A 10-mile hole in an otherwise solid cloud bank marked Hiroshima as though fate had driven a spike into the city's heart.

At 7:25 the *Straight Flush* radioed its report, which ended, "Advice: Bomb primary." When Tibbets had decoded the message, he turned to his navigator, Captain Theodore J. Van Kirk, standing at his elbow. "It's Hiroshima," he said.

At 7:50 the *Enola Gay* passed over the edge of Shikoku Island. Crew members pulled on their flak suits. The monitoring console showed all of the bomb's electrical circuits in perfect order, with no evidence of Japanese jamming.

By 8:09 the outlines of Hiroshima were in view through an opening in the clouds. "We are about to start the bomb run," Tibbets announced on the intercom. "When you hear the tone signal, pull on your goggles until after the flash." All hands had specially manufactured goggles in which quinine crystals would admit only one color, purple, through the lenses.

As the *Enola Gay* flew west at 31,600 feet, Hiroshima lay open and bare beneath the plane. Through the bombsight it unrolled in a pattern familiar to bombardier Major Tom Ferebee from target photographs. The aiming point, the center of a main bridge over the Ota River's widest branch, moved to the cross hairs. "I've got it," Ferebee said, and started the automatic synchronization for the final minute of the bomb run. Forty-five seconds later he turned on the radio tone signal which meant that in 15 seconds the bomb would drop.

At 8:15 plus 17 seconds the bomb-bay doors sprang open and the aircraft lurched up, suddenly 10,000 pounds lighter. Tibbets nosed the plane over to the right in a 60-degree bank and tight turn of 158 degrees. The fuselage screamed with the violence of the maneuver.

Hastily instructing Bob Caron, the tail gunner, to tell everyone what he saw, Tibbets began measuring the 43 seconds mentally. Each moment now seemed endless.

"See anything yet?" Tibbets asked Caron after about 35 seconds had elapsed.

"No, sir."

First Lieutenant Morris R. Jeppson, in charge of the console which had been monitoring the bomb's circuits, had started his own count and was now nearing the end: 40 . . . 41 . . . 42 . . . Jeppson stopped the count. The thought flashed through his brain, "It's a dud."

At that instant the world went purple in a flash before Bob Caron's eyes. His eyelids shut involuntarily behind his goggles. I must be blinded, he thought. Even when he had looked directly at the sun through the goggles a moment earlier it had shown only faintly. He was too stunned at first to report through the intercom.

Caron had been looking at an explosion which, in a slice of time too small for any stopwatch to measure, had become a ball of fire 1800 feet across, with a temperature at its center of 100 million degrees. Hiroshima was already a missing city.

The sounding of the all-clear signal in Hiroshima at 7:31 a.m. on August 6 made little change in the tempo of the city. Most people had been too busy, or too lazy, to pay much attention to the alert. The departure of the single, high-flying B-29—the weather plane—caused no more stir than its arrival over the city 22 minutes earlier.

At 8:15 the few people in Hiroshima who caught sight of a new small formation of planes noticed that three parachutes blossomed from one of them. These had been dropped from the blast- and radiation-measuring plane; they supported instruments to broadcast such measurements. Seeing the parachutes, some people cheered, thinking the enemy planes must be in trouble and the crews were starting to bail out.

For three quarters of a minute there was nothing but the parachutes in the clear sky over the city. Then suddenly, without a sound, there was no sky left over Hiroshima.

For those who survived to recall it, the first instant of the atomic explosion over Hiroshima was pure light, blinding, intense, but of awesome beauty and variety. One witness described a flash that turned from white to pink and then to blue as it rose and blossomed. Others seemed to see "five or six bright colors." Some saw merely "flashes of gold" in a white light that reminded them—this was perhaps the most common description—of a huge photographic flash bulb exploding over the city. The sole impression was visual. If there was any sound, no one remembered hearing it.

Thousands did not see anything either. They were simply incinerated where they stood by the radiant heat that turned central Hiroshima into a gigantic oven. Thousands of others survived for perhaps a second or two, only to be shredded by the scattered window glass that flew before the blast waves, or crushed underneath walls, beams, bricks or other solid objects that stood in the way of the explosion.

Several factors combined to produce more devastation than the nuclear experts had predicted. First, the precision of the drop. For Major Ferebee's aim was nearly perfect. Despite the fact that it was released from a fast-moving aircraft over three miles to the east and nearly six miles in the air, the bomb was detonated only a little more than 200 yards from the designated aiming point.

Then, the time of the explosion. All over Hiroshima, thousands of charcoal braziers were full of hot coals from the breakfast cooking. Almost every stove, knocked over by the massive

blast waves, became a torch to fire the wood-and-paper houses. Oppenheimer had assumed that most people would be in air-raid shelters and had estimated 20,000 casualties. But there had been no specific alert—small formations of planes had flown over the city many times without dropping bombs—and most people were on their way to work. Thus there were more than 70,000 casualties.

The initial flash spawned a succession of calamities. First came heat. It lasted only an instant but was so intense that it melted roof tiles, fused the quartz crystals in granite blocks, charred the exposed sides of telephone poles for almost two miles and destroyed nearby humans so thoroughly that nothing remained except the outline of their shadows, burned into asphalt pavements or stone walls.

Ten miles from the city, the mayor of Kabe distinctly felt the heat on his face as he stood in his garden. At two and a half miles from Ground Zero the heat still burned skin. At a mile and a half, a printed page exposed to the heat rays had the black letters burned completely out of the white paper. Hundreds of women had the darker parts of their clothing burned out while lighter shades remained unscorched, leaving the skin underneath etched in precise detail with the flower patterns of their kimonos.

After the heat came the blast, sweeping outward from the fireball with the force of a 500-mile-an-hour wind. Only objects which offered a minimum of surface resistance—handrails on bridges, pipes, utility poles—withstood its force. The walls of a few office buildings which had been especially constructed to resist earthquakes remained standing. But they enclosed only rubble. The blast broke water mains everywhere, so that Hiroshima's surviving firemen—two thirds of them were immediate casualties—were helpless to cope with the thousands of fires that started within seconds. Between them, blast and fire wrecked every single building within an area of almost five square miles.

After heat, blast and fire the people of Hiroshima had further ordeals to face. A few minutes after the explosion a strange rain began to fall. The raindrops were as big as marbles—and they

were black. This frightening phenomenon resulted from vapor-
ization of moisture in the fireball and condensation in the cloud
that spouted up from it. There was not enough of this "black
rain" to put out the fires, but enough to heighten the panic of
people already unnerved by what had hit them.

After the rain came a wind, the great "fire wind" which blew
back in toward the center of the catastrophe, increasing in force
as the air over Hiroshima grew hotter because of the fires. The
wind blew so hard that it uprooted huge trees in the parks
where survivors were collecting. It whipped up high waves on
the rivers and drowned many who had gone into the water to
escape from the heat and flames.

Tibbets had been warned that a shock wave would probably
hit the plane about a minute after the bomb exploded. In anticipation of this, he pointed the nose upward to gain altitude and
lose speed—a tactic which aerodynamics experts calculated
would lessen the impact.

From the rear turret, Bob Caron presently saw a shimmering
line rushing toward the plane. It resembled a heat wave as seen
far down an asphalt highway, but it extended in a long curve
like a ripple from a rock tossed in a pond. It was visible because
the heavy compression of air was followed by a vacuum in which
vapor condensed instantaneously, forming a belt of speeding
mist. The shock wave raced at the plane at a speed of 12 miles a
minute. Although its probable force had been stressed in briefings, the actual violence of it astounded the crew.

"Flak!" Tibbets yelled involuntarily as it struck. Parsons experienced a similar reaction. It felt as though a large anti-
aircraft shell had burst 20 feet from the plane.

"Here comes another one," Caron warned on the intercom
from his rear vantage point.

A reflection of the blast from the ground, this second shock
wave hit them; then the peril was over. In formation with the
two accompanying planes, the *Enola Gay* now flew south along
the outskirts of Hiroshima, and for the first time the crew observed what they had wrought.

Dust boiled up from the entire city and long, swirling gray shafts rushed toward the center. A column of white smoke, incredibly tidy in form, stood straight up. At the base it was flecked with red and orange, and at the top it spilled into an almost perfect mushroom. The stem of the strange cloud-flower reminded one man of an enormous grave marker. Within minutes the cloud mushroom pushed upward almost four miles.

Conflicting emotions jostled the minds of the airmen over the ruined city. Some were elated that the bomb had worked, and hoped it would end the war. Some were torn between pride and dismay. Some simply could not relate what they saw to reality. Captain Robert A. Lewis, Tibbets' co-pilot, was one of the first to speak. "My God," he said, "what have we done?"

Tibbets ordered an uncoded radio message sent, notifying Tinian that the *Enola Gay* had bombed its primary target visually with good results; no fighters, no flak. Then, as they settled down to the long flight back to Tinian, the report was elaborated in code: "Clear-cut, successful in all respects. Visible effect greater than Trinity [the New Mexico test]."

When the *Enola Gay* returned she had barely taxied to her hardstand before 200 officers and enlisted men crowded under her wings. The greeting delegation included General "Tooey" Spaatz, new Strategic Air Force boss; General Nathan F. Twining, new chief of the Marianas Air Force; Brigadier General John Davies, 313th Wing Commander—indeed, more generals and admirals than most of the plane's crew had ever seen.

"Attention to orders!" barked General Davies.

Spaatz stepped forward and pinned the Distinguished Service Cross on the breast of Tibbets' dirty flight overalls. Tibbets, his eyes red-rimmed from lack of sleep, and hours overdue for a shave, was caught off guard. He hastily palmed his pipe in his left hand and tucked the stem under his sleeve. Spaatz shook Tibbets' hand and the crowd milled around again. Every man of the *Enola Gay* was the center of a group of eager interviewers.

The entire 509th was now given a hot-dog roast and beer party. But the *Enola Gay* crew were subjected to an intensive official interrogation that lasted for two hours. When they arrived for the party, the last hot dog and can of beer had been consumed. Later, however, every airman who had participated in the mission was decorated.

A moment after 8:16 a.m. the Tokyo control operator of the Japanese Broadcasting Corporation noticed that his telephone line to the radio station in Hiroshima had gone dead. He tried to re-establish his connection, but found that he could not get a call through to the city. Twenty minutes later the men in the railroad signal center in Tokyo realized that the main-line telegraph had stopped working. The break seemed to be just north of Hiroshima. Reports began to come in from stations near Hiroshima that there had been some kind of explosion in the city. Railroad signalmen forwarded the messages to Army General Headquarters. It was almost 10 o'clock when Ryugen Hosokawa, managing editor of the Tokyo newspaper *Asahi*, received a telephone call at his home. It was the office, reporting that Hiroshima had "almost completely collapsed" as the result of bombing by enemy planes.

At about the same time Major Tosaku Hirano, a staff officer of the Second Army Corps, was in General Headquarters in Tokyo. He had come up from Hiroshima a week earlier to report on the status of military supplies in the port city, and had been scheduled to fly back on Sunday, But he had put off his departure and thus was still in the capital. Now his telephone rang. It was a call from Central Headquarters in Osaka, an installation under the control of the Second Army Corps in Hiroshima, reporting that its communications to Hiroshima and points west had failed.

Tokyo GHQ tried several times to raise the Hiroshima communications center, but could not get through. There was no explanation. The succession of reports from the radio network, from the railroad signal center, from *Asahi's* newsroom and from Osaka indicated that something serious had happened, but no one could find out what it was. Then, shortly after one p.m., General Headquarters finally heard from the Second Army Corps. The message was short but stunning: "Hiroshima has been annihilated by one bomb, and fires are spreading." This flash came from the Army shipping depot on the Hiroshima waterfront, which was outside the blast area.

Reports continued to trickle in. By the middle of the afternoon the Army knew that only three enemy planes had been over Hiroshima when the bomb exploded. It had been told that two of these did not drop any bombs. In mid-afternoon the managing editors of the five big Tokyo newspapers were called to the office of the government Information and Intelligence Agency. An Army press officer addressed the group.

> We believe that the bomb dropped on Hiroshima is different from an ordinary one. We intend to make some announcement when proper information has been obtained. Until then, run the story in an obscure place in your papers and as one no different from the report of an ordinary air raid.

In other words, the lid was on. The Army already had a strong suspicion that the Hiroshima bomb might be an atomic weapon. (Japanese naval intelligence had reported U.S. work on the bomb in late 1944, noting the interest of the American government in buying up all available uranium ore.) But the Army, anxious to keep the war going so that it could fight a showdown hand-to-hand battle with the Americans on Japanese soil, was determined to withhold the news from the Japanese people as long as it could.

The truth about Hiroshima was soon to be revealed, however. In Saitama prefecture outside Tokyo, Domei, the quasi-governmental news agency, operated a big monitoring station where nearly 50 workers, many of them Nisei girls born in the United States, listened to American broadcasts. About one a.m. on August 7 (noon on the 6th in Washington, D.C.) Hideo Kinoshita, chief of the monitoring room, was awakened by the Japanese youth who had charge of the operation that night. The boy reported that U.S. stations were all broadcasting a statement by President Truman describing the weapon that had been dropped on Hiroshima as "an atomic bomb."

Kinoshita listened to the account. Then he quickly called his own superior, Saiji Hasegawa. Hasegawa had no idea what an atomic bomb was, but he hustled to his office. When he saw the text transcripts that were beginning to come through from the Saitama monitors, he called Hisatsune Sakomizu, chief secretary of the Cabinet.

Sakomizu quickly called Prime Minister Kantaro Suzuki, with whom he had been working in the effort to arrange a peace settlement. They knew immediately, he said later,

> . . . that if the announcement were true, no country could carry on a war. Without the atomic bomb it would be impossible for any country to defend itself against a nation which had the weapon. The chance had come to end the war. It was not necessary to blame the military side, the manufacturing people or anyone else—just the atomic bomb. It was a good excuse.

The Army, however, was unwilling to accept this attitude. The generals, sitting in an emergency Cabinet meeting on August 7, argued that the bomb was not atomic but was merely a huge conventional projectile. They flatly refused Foreign Minister Shigenori Togo's proposal to take up for immediate consideration the possibility of surrender on the terms of the Potsdam ultimatum, and insisted on keeping the Truman atomic statement from the Japanese people until the Army could conduct an investigation on the ground at Hiroshima.

The military had already started such a check. Major Hirano, the staff officer from the Hiroshima headquarters whose desire to spend a couple of extra nights in Tokyo had saved his life, called Yoshio Nishina, the nation's ranking nuclear scientist. He told Nishina of the Truman claims and asked him to ride down to Hiroshima in a liaison plane to investigate the matter. Nishina agreed to make the trip.

It was almost seven in the evening when Hirano's little plane came down over Hiroshima. It was still light, however, so he got the full picture with shocking suddenness:

Since I am a soldier, my eye had been inured to the effects of bombing, by that time. But this was a different sight. *There were no roads in the wastes that spread below our eyes:* that was my first impression. In the case of a normal air raid, roads were still visible after it was over. But in Hiroshima everything was flattened and all roads were covered with debris.

When Hirano stepped from his plane, the first person he saw was an Air Force officer who came out on the runway to meet the team from Tokyo. His face was marked by a sharp dividing line right down the middle. One side was smooth and unhurt. The other, the one that had been toward the explosion, was burned, blistered, blackened. The investigators picked their way through the city to the wreckage of Second Army Corps headquarters. Nobody was there. They finally found what was left of the headquarters—a few officers holed up in a hillside cave. Long before they began their formal investigation the next morning, the men from Tokyo knew the truth. Hirano, in fact, had known it the moment he caught sight of what was left of Hiroshima from his circling plane, just as Bob Caron had known it for the first time at 8:16 a.m. the day before, when he looked back from the *Enola Gay.*

In Washington it was agreed that news of the atomic strike should be released to the general public at once. Correspondents immediately went to work on what they recognized as one of the greatest stories of all time. As official bulletins about the bomb were released, the news startled the entire world. For most, the information was impossible to comprehend, yet almost everyone sensed that it was of tremendous importance. The first official communiqué came from the White House. After describing the nature and power of the weapon, the dispatch continued:

It was to spare the Japanese people from utter destruction that the ultimatum of July 26 was issued at Potsdam. Their leaders promptly rejected that ultimatum. If they do not now accept our terms, they may expect a rain of ruin from the air, the like of which has never been seen.

To speed the empire's surrender, Washington decided to launch an intensive propaganda campaign, dropping 16 million leaflets on 47 Japanese cities. They also moved up a scheduled second atomic strike from August 11 to August 9, reasoning that a swift one-two sequence would convince Japanese leaders that Hiroshima was not some freak of nature.

The second atomic-bomb flight was jinxed from the start and, in the end, almost nothing about it went right. The bomb was plutonium, the type which had been exploded in New Mexico. (The Hiroshima bomb had been uranium, a type hitherto untested.) The weapon was flown by Major Charles W. Sweeney in a plane not his own. The primary target, Kokura, was so closed in that three passes over the city failed to disclose the smallest hole. When Sweeney flew on to Nagasaki, the alternate target, it too was hidden by cloud. Commander F. L. Ashworth, the weaponeer aboard the plane, ordered a radar drop if necessary, taking it upon himself to countermand Washington's orders because of a shortage of fuel. The entire bomb run was made by radar, and although the bombardier found a hole at the last minute, he missed the aiming point by three miles. Even so, the devastation was enormous.

On the following day the Japanese Cabinet agreed to send a message through Switzerland accepting the terms of the Potsdam ultimatum, with the "understanding" that the Emperor would remain in power. Except for the formalities, the war was over.

Hirohito's Struggle to Surrender

By Colonel Bonner Fellers, USA, Retired

Bonner Fellers, a brigadier general on the staff of General of the Army MacArthur, was in charge of psychological warfare against Japan up until VJ-day. He then served as Secretary General to the Allied Council for seven months. Investigating the results of his psychological campaign, he interrogated members of the Japanese Cabinet and other highly placed Japanese.

In the fall of 1945, I stood in the doorway of the impressive American Embassy in Tokyo as a black limousine pulled to the curb. Out stepped a nervous, bespectacled Japanese, dressed in a prewar cutaway and high buttoned shoes. As my hand snapped down from a rigid salute, he edged close enough to seize it and shake it firmly. We exchanged greetings and walked side by side into the Embassy. Thus, as military secretary to General of the Army MacArthur, I officially met Hirohito, Emperor of Japan. Subsequently from him and from his Cabinet I began to learn the well-nigh incredible facts behind Japan's surrender.

These facts show indisputably that the U.S.S.R. repeatedly smothered Japanese overtures for peace with the Allies for six months before Japan's surrender. The U.S.S.R. was determined to obtain a dominant position in the Orient, both territorial and political, and therefore planned to enter the war at a time most favorable to Russia's interest.

The Emperor's personal decision to surrender and his first attempt to obtain Russian mediation trace back to February 14, 1945, after General MacArthur's forces entered Manila, nearly six months before the first atomic bomb was dropped on Japan. He and Prince Fumimaro Konoye—thrice premier of Japan and relatively pacifistic—met at the palace for a conference. Pacing the floor and obviously shaken, Hirohito declared bluntly that he believed defeat to be unavoidable but that the militarists wanted to fight on. They argued that the Allied demands for unconditional surrender could only mean the abolition of the Emperor system.

Konoye informed Hirohito that he did not believe America would continue fighting merely to destroy the Emperor's dynasty. Hirohito assented, but said that with the militarists controlling all means of communication it would be impossible to deal directly with the United States. The Emperor particularly wanted to know if Konoye would assist him in surrender negotiations. Konoye readily agreed. Immediately Hirohito began to press his militarists with extraordinary vigor. The Emperor pointed out that they had lied consistently about the war's progress, even informing troops that the Army had landed on the American west coast and claiming to have sunk more battleships than the United States possessed.

In April 1945, tough, grizzly, 77-year-old Kantaro Suzuki—a moderate who had been shot and left for dead in the uprising of the so-called "young militarists" in 1936—was appointed prime minister. This was regarded by many as a signal to the Allies that Japan desired peace. Suzuki and the Emperor had been lifelong friends, so that for the first time since the war started Hirohito felt he had a leader in whom he could confide. In secret conferences Hirohito told Suzuki that he did not trust his Imperial Headquarters and could not understand why they blindly continued a hopeless war. Further loss of life, the Emperor declared, was criminal.

But, to Hirohito's and Suzuki's amazement, no offer to negotiate came from the Allies. As each day passed, Hirohito's determination to end the war grew stronger. In a single B-29 attack on Tokyo, 185,000 casualties had been inflicted; American leaflets, picked up by the Emperor himself on moody walks through the palace grounds, promised more such attacks. Yet the militarists continued to argue that when invasion came they could win at the beaches.

Nonetheless, ex-Premier Koki Hirota was told to open unofficial peace conversations through the Russian Embassy in Tokyo. The militarists reluctantly agreed to this, in the hope that Russian mediation would prevent a Soviet attack in Manchuria. But Jacob Malik, Soviet Ambassador in Tokyo, proved strangely cool to Hirota's talk of peace. Hirota tried to make deals concerning territory and raw materials.

As the Emperor and Suzuki worked secretly to develop an acceptable surrender formula, bombs were steadily destroying every major city. The Emperor told his household that he proposed to stop the war, no matter what happened to him personally. Finally, on June 18, after a bitter fight, the Supreme Council tentatively agreed to approach Moscow directly in an effort to attain peace. Even then the members of the Supreme Council could not bring themselves actually to start negotiations. To the worn, harassed Hirohito, this delay was the last straw.

On June 22, Hirohito had Japanese radio stations broadcast a statement which, though phrased with Oriental obliqueness, unmistakably meant that Hirohito intended to assume personal leadership of Japan, above and beyond the Japanese Diet or control by the Army and Navy.

Meanwhile the Emperor learned that the U.S.S.R. was cold toward the peace and, even though not at war with Japan, would discuss no proposal other than what amounted to unconditional surrender.

Because the rigid military grip on all communication facilities barred direct contact with the United States, Hirohito on July 7 ordered Suzuki to request Russia's permission to send the Emperor's own personal emissary to Moscow. The Emperor had already selected Prince Konoye for this mission and given him carte blanche to obtain peace at any price, even unconditional surrender to the Allies—whereupon the Emperor would publicly approve the decision before the militarists even knew about it.

But this plan, too, failed. A radio message was dispatched to Moscow on July 10 requesting the Soviet government to receive Konoye, but days dragged by without a reply. Stalin and Molotov left Moscow for Potsdam in enigmatic silence four days after the message had been received. On July 22, Moscow finally asked to be "enlightened more clearly on the objectives of the Konoye mission." The Emperor replied that Japan sought Russian mediation for peace, but no answer at all came to this second message.

On July 26, the Potsdam Declaration was issued. To the Emperor and liberal Japanese it appeared to be an acceptable basis for surrender, but the Supreme Council was not satisfied. Then the atomic bombs exploded on August 6 and 9, and Russia declared war on Japan. On August 9, the Supreme Council had voted to accept the Potsdam terms with four reservations—that the dynasty survive, that Japan not be occupied, that she direct disarmament and evacuation of her own troops, and that she herself handle persons responsible for the war.

Hirohito felt positive that these terms would not even stop the Allied bombings. Therefore he ordered the Supreme Council to reconvene shortly before midnight in his temporary palace—a small cottage built over one of the deepest air-raid shelters in Japan.

Here, in gutted Tokyo, lit only by the smoldering fires which burned throughout the city day and night, there began the most portentous debate in Japan's history. The midsummer night was hot and humid; mosquitoes from the stagnant palace moat buzzed viciously around the conference table as Japan's perspiring leaders seated themselves, shaken and trembling. Present were the Emperor, the six members of the Supreme Council and Baron Kiichiro Hiranuma, president of the Privy Council.

One after another, the three chief militarists of the Council—War Minister Korechika Anami, Army Chief of Staff General Yoshijiro Umezu, and Navy Chief of Staff Admiral Soemu Toyoda—spoke against capitulation. Gone was their usual taciturnity and stoical calm. All wept. Surrender was unthinkable. Fight on! Frenzied, their voices shrilled as they begged for delay. Peremptorily, aged Prime Minister Suzuki, his head trembling with emotion and exhaustion, demanded a vote. With two bullets in his body from the assassination attempt by military extremists nearly 10 years before, he knew the murderous fanaticism of the militarists could easily result in a *coup d'état* and the death of all who opposed them. Yet Suzuki was implacable. One by one, members cast their votes.

The three militarists remained unalterably opposed to surrender except on condition that they disarm their own troops and Japan remain unoccupied. Only four of the seven—Suzuki, Foreign Minister Shigenori Togo, Navy Minister Mitsumasa Yonai and Baron Hiranuma—voted for surrender, the sole condition being that the Emperor's dynasty remain intact.

By rigid custom, never before broken, the Council's decision must be unanimous. And now the Emperor, who had remained quiet, spoke. Calmly yet coldly, he pointed out that from the start of the war the plans of the military had been far removed from the facts. "Considering the true state of affairs," he went on, "it is useless to continue the war at the cost of lives and property. I have been listening to those who oppose ending the war. But I have not changed my opinion; I trust the Allies and their terms. I want to accept the terms as they are." He paused; then, in a voice of command—the first command a Supreme Council had ever heard from a Japanese Emperor: "I wish all of you to agree with me on this point."

The meeting had been going on now for hours, and it was nearly three a.m. Tears streaming, members of the Council bowed their heads as Hirohito finished speaking. The silence was broken by War Minister Anami. Falling to his knees, he crawled toward Hirohito. Contemptuously, the Emperor turned his back. Anami's voice rose to a scream: "Please, we have a plan, you must not surrender!" Approaching closer, still on his knees, he reached for the Emperor's coat, but Hirohito disdainfully turned away. Waiting a moment, the Emperor said again, "I wish all of you to agree with me," and left the room.

At dawn the Council members left, complying with the Emperor's demand by dispatching a cablegram to Sweden and

Switzerland for transmission to the United States, Great Britain, China and Russia. It accepted the Potsdam Declaration unconditionally if the continuance of the Imperial Household and rights of sovereignty be confirmed. But the battle with the militarists—temporarily overcome by awe of the Emperor—had not ended. Three days later the Allies replied that the "ultimate Japanese Government must be established by the freely expressed will of the Japanese people." The Supreme Council disputed angrily, the War Minister and chiefs of staff of the Army and Navy again demanding that the war go on, arguing that the Allied reply meant abolition of the Emperor system. Meanwhile, American planes were dropping copies of the Potsdam Declaration and Japan's answer throughout the nation.

Marquis Koichi Kido, Keeper of the Privy Seal and one of the Emperor's confidants, carried a leaflet direct to Hirohito. Both feared that the Army—mostly deployed along the sea coasts and thus largely unaware of the terrific destruction in the cities—might revolt when they learned Japan had agreed to surrender. Fanatic officers might even persuade their men that the Emperor's acceptance of such terms was faked, and urge them to fight on. But the Emperor knew that the people were sick of bombing, that they had long known the true war picture from air-dropped leaflets and would welcome surrender. To prevent murderous disorder, therefore, an Imperial Rescript to end the war must be broadcast immediately.

On the morning of August 14 the Emperor summoned the Supreme Council. When the two chiefs of staff and the War Minister violently opposed surrender, the Emperor eyed them menacingly. "My decision to accept the Potsdam Declaration was not made lightly," he declared. "It has undergone no change at all. Unless the war is terminated at this juncture, not only will Japan's national polity be destroyed but the Japanese people will be ruined. In the future, Japan will be entirely separated from the means to wage war and thus will enjoy true eternal peace. As I want to make myself understood by the people, prepare a draft of an Imperial Rescript. I require"—here again he looked menacingly at the militarists—"that all present agree."

By evening the Rescript was ready. At 11 p.m. the Emperor finished recording it and a messenger stood ready to take it to Radio Tokyo's studio for broadcast to the nation. But at this moment nearly 1000 dissident soldiers infiltrated the palace grounds. Before they could reach the cottage the recording was locked in Hirohito's safe.

Six different times the rebel troops invaded the cottage, seeking the recording and Marquis Kido, whom they were determined to kill for the part they believed he had played in the surrender. Kido hid in a secret underground passage, with the Emperor hidden in another part of the cottage, also fearing assassination. Meanwhile, other troops burned Suzuki's residence to the ground. At four a.m. War Minister Anami, overwhelmed because of the attempted *coup d'état* and his opposition to the Emperor, committed suicide. Shortly after eight a.m., General Shizuichi Tanaka of the Eastern Defense Command arrived and persuaded the soldiers to disperse. Two of their officers shot themselves. Then General Tanaka went to his room and shot himself. By evening the Imperial Rescript had been broadcast and the nation had heard their own Emperor's voice tell them of Japan's final capitulation.

As titular leader of Japan, of course, the Emperor shared technically the war guilt of his leaders. Yet that did not lessen the high drama of a figurehead Emperor who dared face down his own fanatic militarists, usurp their power and by sheer strength of will compel them to surrender.

Now It Can Be Told

By Thomas M. Johnson

The flood of "now-it-can-be-told" stories about wartime secret-service exploits gives the impression that our secret war was a processional from victory unto victory. The truth is that, while we had our brilliant triumphs, we had many defeats and failures—often unnecessarily—that cost us heavily in time, money and lives.

Both our successes and our failures taught the same lesson. The spectacular results of good intelligence work showed how valuable it was. Our failures, most of which occurred early in the war, showed how costly were unpreparedness and improvisation.

It was shocking how little we knew when the fury of Pearl Harbor burst upon us. Wartime Under Secretary Dean Acheson admitted that the State Department technique of gathering information differed little in essentials from that of Revolutionary War days. Naval Intelligence unerringly selected wrong estimates of the Japanese carriers' whereabouts: it believed them to be in home waters. Of our several services gathering information—State, War, Navy and others—none was doing a good job. None knew what to expect of the others, and they seldom worked together.

Instructions from Washington to Naval Intelligence officers on how to improve their work were found after Pearl Harbor in a safe—still undistributed. One diplomat protested: "Change my code! Why, that code's *good!* I've been using it 20 years!" The State Department took days to decode messages and distribute them to 127 different offices. There was no message center. A Joint Intelligence Board, authorized three months before Pearl Harbor, got going three days after the fatal morning—about the time we decoded some Japanese messages, intercepted six days earlier, that would have revealed the enemy's plans.

Although war in the Pacific had long threatened, about all we knew of some Japanese-held islands was their latitude and longitude. The State Department, thinking such activity might irritate a "friendly power," had hampered the Navy's efforts to investigate them before Pearl Harbor. Afterward, Naval Intelligence frantically questioned anyone—beachcomber, pearl diver, whaler, missionary—who had ever seen a Japanese island, no matter how long ago.

We massed ships and troops against Kiska after the Japanese had sneaked away. On Guadalcanal our Marines had to depend on captured Japanese maps. Although the Japanese had rehearsed jungle warfare for years and learned many tricks, we knew neither that fact nor the tricks.

In Africa we suffered our first defeat on land partly because when Rangers captured an enemy order concerning Rommel's counter-attack through Faid Pass an important headquarters had no one who could translate it. We were keeping our carefully trained intelligence experts too far in the rear. It was a costly lesson. Immediately operatives were flown to Africa from Camp Ritchie, Md., and thereafter all U.S. combat intelligence worked close to the front—with excellent results.

We knew almost nothing about the enemy's vulnerable bombing targets either in Europe or in Asia. Seventy percent of the Japanese aircraft engines were made in two plants which no American had ever seen. Air Intelligence said the German electric system could not be crippled by bombing power plants, so we did not try. Later we knew it could and should have been done.

Our parsimony with regard to gathering intelligence now seems incredible. One "Far Eastern Intelligence Section"— covering Japan, China, Southeast Asia and Siberia—consisted of one officer and one woman clerk. An intelligence officer who gave $500 for diagrams of a hostile power's airfields was rebuked for extravagance. Washington made a military attaché in Berlin pay from his own pocket for a code cable warning that Hitler would march into Prague.

State, War and Navy gathered intelligence largely the cheap way—through openly accredited diplomatic and consular representatives and occasional patriotic volunteers. But, in general, our attachés saw and heard what their hosts let them. Some ambassadors forbade attachés to travel, or seek information in libraries, lest they appear to be spying.

We gratefully accepted the work of volunteers, but it was fitful and unaccountable. One amateur spy reported a new Japanese submarine with a 16-inch gun that later proved to be a crane; others reported seeing more Japanese warships than the Japanese actually had.

After Pearl Harbor the British and French made their intelligence information available to us, and we replaced improvisation with scientific intelligence work of our own. We set scholars, scientists and analysts to work, as well as ordinary men with common sense who gathered information in obvious ways. Topographical and weather data on the Aleutians came from the Library of Congress. A picture in a German magazine first told us of a new 40-mm. anti-aircraft gun. German newspaper photographs of a plane standing before a factory indicated where that type of aircraft was made. A Nazi guidebook photograph of an *Autobahn* tunnel suggested an underground factory, and an aerial photograph confirmed it.

Intelligence tried everything, however laborious. By checking freight-rate reports and railroad carloadings and bills of lading, researchers were able to locate German oil refineries for bombing. Tokyo city directories giving business addresses of metallurgists and chemists, matched with aerial photographs, revealed camouflaged war plants. Through statistical studies, obituaries of German officers in local German newspapers gave away the strength of the whole German Army.

A German prisoner helped solve the mystery of one of the submarine's trickiest defenses, the *Pillenwerfer*, which shot chemical pills into the water astern the U-boat. The pills made bubbles which gave off a noise that agitated our ships' listening devices. While we depth-charged the bubbles, the submarine would escape.

This fooled us until April 1942, when a depth-charge explosion brought bright-red bubbles to the surface. Intelligence officers gathered and analyzed samples. Presently they captured the commander of another submarine. The intelligence officer remarked casually to the German, "The bubble didn't work this time."

The German started.

"Oh, we know all about that." The American gave details—inspired guesswork—which so impressed the German that he told all. Experiments showed a difference between bubble sound and submarine sound—and we trained our sub-hunters to spot that difference.

A German general, captured early in 1943 in Tunisia and expertly "drawn out," boasted of having seen the first V-2 rocket experiments. Shortly afterward an aerial photograph caught the keen eye of Flight Officer Constance Babington-Smith, expert photo-interpreter for British-American Air Intelligence. She spotted a white mark, T-shaped, on a tiny ramp near big earthworks and other mysterious installations at Peenemünde. Peenemünde was bombed, and 735 people—including a great many scientists and technical men working there—were killed. German research on many new weapons was retarded six months. Some believe Britain was saved and the war won by that six-month delay. (See "The Secret at Peenemünde," page 273.)

In the Pacific some 4000 Japanese-Americans risked capture and torture in front-line intelligence work that yielded two million reports, orders, maps and diaries taken from killed or captured Japanese and from Japanese installations. One sheet of carbon, closely scrutinized, revealed a ship movement, a regimental strength-table and anti-malaria treatments; a sketch showed how troop transports were camouflaged.

In all our European invasion landings the first waves were accompanied by intelligence officers who, quickly as enemy headquarters were captured, cracked safes and rushed back valuable papers. Thus was found a chart of minefields off Sicily. Cherbourg was captured more quickly and cheaply because American secret agents seized a plan of its defenses. This one achievement justified the Army's special training of its intelligence personnel.

Painstakingly our researchers developed scientific aids to intelligence. Outstanding progress was made in radio and radar, in the system of interception and decoding of enemy messages, in weather forecasting. We developed the tri-metrogon angle-camera which, with cameo-clear detail, photographed terrain at the angle from which the flier viewed it, thereby increasing accuracy in bombing and reconnaissance. Many large areas were mapped completely for the first time.

The enormous value of spies who could drop behind enemy lines by parachute and report quickly by short-wave radio was recognized. The Office of Strategic Services was formed not only to train spies but also to perform other kinds of intelligence work and to fight and sabotage behind the lines. OSS accomplishments were sometimes spectacular, often substantial, not infrequently both. (See "Jungle of Hidden Friends," page 263, and "The Great Ambush," page 485.) To Underground movements in 16 countries OSS dropped 27,000 tons of weapons and supplies and thousands of agents. Other agents rescued more than 5000 American airmen. OSS casualties totaled about 100, not exorbitant for success in the most extensive covert operations in American history.

Scarcely less extraordinary was "Saco" (pronounced "Socko"), the Sino-American Coöperative Organization of guerrillas and radio operators of both nations that covered the Chinese coast and most of the interior. Its director, General Tai-li, chief of Chiang Kai-shek's secret service, also conducted, with American help, a school where Chinese women were taught how to ingratiate themselves with Japanese officials and generals to get information from them.

Among Saco agents were American Navy and Marine radio operators who, disguised as Chinese and protected by Chinese guerrillas, raided and reported on Japanese dispositions and destroyed hundreds of depots, bridges and locomotives. But Saco's greatest contributions were radio reports on the weather and the movements of Japanese ships—important in the blockade that helped strangle Japan.

We built, finally, the biggest and best intelligence service we had ever had. It saved us and our Allies from defeat. Never again would we allow our diplomats to face foreign diplomats who were better informed than they, or permit our generals and admirals to face sudden attack by nations whose intentions and capabilities we misunderstood. Americans, an alert people always, now had more reason than ever for wanting to know what was going on in the world.

A strong intelligence service means a more secure nation.

INDEX

Page numbers in italics refer to photographs.